Database Machines

Database Machines

Fourth International Workshop
Grand Bahama Island, March 1985

Edited by
D.J. DeWitt and H. Boral

With 142 Illustrations and 35 Tables

Springer-Verlag
New York Berlin Heidelberg Tokyo

D.J. DeWitt
Computer Sciences Department
University of Wisconsin
Madison, WI 53706
U.S.A.

H. Boral
Microelectronics and Computer Technology Corporation
Austin, TX 78759
U.S.A.

(C.R.) Computer Classification: H.2, H.2.6

Library of Congress Cataloging in Publication Data
Main entry under title:
Database machines.
Proceedings of the Fourth International Workshop on Database Machines.
1. Data base management—Congresses. 2. Electronic digital computers—Congresses. I. DeWitt, D.J. (David J.) II. Boral, H. (Haran) III. International Workshop on Database Machines (4th : 1985 : Grand Bahama Island)
QA76.9.D3D316 1985 005.74'028 85-14792

Printed and bound by Braun-Brumfield, Ann Arbor, Michigan.
Printed in the United States of America.

9 8 7 6 5 4 3 2 1

ISBN 0-387-96200-X Springer-Verlag New York Berlin Heidelberg Tokyo
ISBN 3-540-96200-X Springer-Verlag Berlin Heidelberg New York Tokyo

PREFACE

This volume contains the papers presented at the Fourth International Workshop on Database Machines. The papers cover a wide spectrum of topics including descriptions of database machine implementations, analysis of algorithms and database machine components, architectures for knowledge management, recovery and concurrency control issues, and solutions to the I/O bottleneck problem. As at the previous workshops in Florence, San Diego, and Munich, a diverse collection of countries, universities, research labs, and database machine vendors were represented by the authors and conference attendees. Our thanks go to the authors for writing excellent papers and for their efforts in meeting deadlines, to the VLDB Endowment for its cooperation, and to MCC for all its support. Finally, as usual, it is our secretaries that really deserve the credit for making the workshop a success. We wish to thank Cerise Blair of MCC for taking care of all the arrangements for the workshop and Sheryl Pomraning of the University of Wisconsin for her help in preparing this proceedings.

Haran Boral
David J. DeWitt

March 1985

Table of Contents

Mass Storage Systems

Non-French Filters

Associative Processing in Standard and Deductive Databases

K. Hahne, P. Pilgram, D. Schuett, H. Schweppe, G. Wolf
Corporate Laboratories for Information Technology
Siemens AG, Munich, West Germany

Abstract

Progress in computer technology, microprocessors and storage chip design in particular, has had a major impact on computer architecture. Until now, research in database machine architecture focussed on search accelerators attached to slow background storage devices, and on multiprocessor configurations exploiting the parallelism inherent in database tasks.

The use of a quasi-associative device of large capacity, the Hybrid Associative Store (HAS), in standard and non-standard database applications including the inference subsystem of a deductive database management system is discussed. The HAS has been under development at the research laboratories of Siemens AG since 1983.

1. Introduction

Progress in computer technology, microprocessors and storage chip design in particular, has had a major impact on computer architecture. Until now, research in database machine architecture focussed on search accelerators attached to slow background storage devices, and on multiprocessor configurations exploiting the parallelism inherent in database tasks.

System performance has remained an important issue even in new applications like text, image and speech processing, and in the enhancement of databases by deduction facilities. Technological progress, VLSI in particular, opens up new solutions in all these areas.

"Logic on the chip" is one of the most promising directions: processing power can be integrated into memory chips, thus permitting high-performance implementations of parallel and of associative algorithms. In spite of their associative characteristics, achieved by tightly coupling (simple) processors and memory, such devices are obviously different from, though much more cost effective than, proper associative memory. We will call the former device quasi-associative.

In this paper we are going to discuss the use of devices supporting quasi-associative processing in standard and non-standard DB applications.

We base our discussions on the Hybrid Associative Store (HAS), a quasi-associative device still built with off-memory processors. It has been under development at the research laboratories of Siemens AG since 1983 [Wolf85].

Finally, we discuss the application of HAS in the inference subsystem of a deductive database management system.

2. The Hybrid Associative Store (HAS), Principle of Operation.

This chapter will focus on the HAS philosophy, mentioning hardware details only in passing. - Fig. 2.1 shows the general layout of a computer system with HAS.

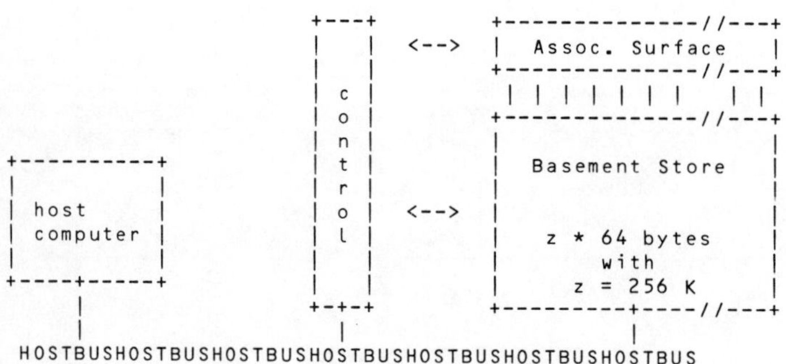

Fig. 2.1: computer system with HAS

HAS is a combination - a "hybrid" - of:

- A very large memory, the "Basement Store", organised as a 2-dimensional array with 64 columns and some large number of lines (e.g. 256000). Each HAS memory cell is of single-byte size. Text strings are usually written "top to bottom" into memory.

- 64 processor elements (PE), i.e. simple computing units. All PEs run synchronously and, at any single moment, they refer all to the same line of memory (called a "byte slice"). Due to this synchronous operation, HAS can perform certain byte array operations (e.g. certain searches) at an extremely high throughput. Every PE is directly linked to its respective memory column; an entire line of memory can thus be dealt with in one blow. In detail, every PE consists of an ALU-and-test unit (together with two registers A and B), a masking register M, and a bank of registers C; all are in some way connected to the memory bus (fig. 2.2). The ensemble of the PEs is called the "Associative Surface".

- A central control unit; it initiates each and every action in the PEs (i.e. it sends a succession of commands to the PEs). It can also access computation results of the PEs, and its further proceeding can be influenced by such findings. - The control unit contains among others a microprogram control unit and an address unit for the Basement Store.

HAS requires a host computer for its operation. The host computer looks after input and output, loads data into HAS, retrieves results back from it, and issues computation requests to it. Typically, HAS would be attached directly to the host bus: the HAS store would function as the host's main memory, or at least part of it, and the HAS control unit would behave like a DMA I/O device (with command and status registers, and with a provision for mutual interrupts).

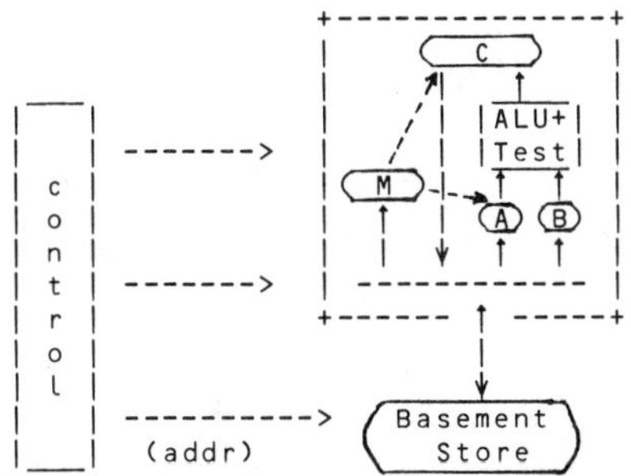

Fig. 2.2: one vertical slice of HAS

HAS is clearly a SIMD machine (array processor), and is as such ideal for the uniform processing of large volumes of data. A certain degree of flexibility is obtained by means of the masking register M.

The HAS concept can be summarised:

- The HAS hardware divides up into two main components, the Basement Store and the Associative Surface. Due to the modular design, the Basement Store can always be upgraded to the latest type of memory chips. Moreover, these chips can be bought off-the-shelf, thus greatly reducing its cost of manufacture.

- The Basement Store consists of dynamic RAM chips, i.e. the present standard technology. The Associative Surface, on the other hand, is built in a high performance technology (version 1: ECL, version 2: VLSI with pipelined command execution) which matches the speeds of Basement and Surface: the Surface can go through an entire cycle of computation while the Basement goes through one memory cycle. The memory chips are thus used at their maximum read/write rate.

The Associative Surface is the most decisive part of HAS: most of the processing takes place here, and most of the innovative ideas are also to be found here. Fig. 2.2 shows a highly simplified diagram of a single PE with its integration into HAS. On the left we see the control unit; it supervises all parts of HAS. The Basement Store BS (more precisely: its column relating to "this" PE) is shown at the bottom. Essentially, all data flow from BS to the ALU, its result flows on into a C register from where it can return into BS:

BS -> ALU -> C -> BS

The ALU-and-test unit can also perform the usual tests (equality, less, greater, overflow etc). The masking register M serves to inhibit the changing of any register.

The PEs are tailored for some particular algorithms (byte array operations, especially search and sorting), while many other algorithms may harmonise rather poorly with HAS. Searching a given string out of 64 candidate strings is probably the most "natural" HAS operation.

In the control unit, a microprogram determines the order in which to carry out the various actions (placing values in registers, setting switches, triggering computations). HAS is thus able to perform, upon one host instruction, even the most complex algorithms. An entire search command, for example, could be one such instruction. One should differentiate between instructions which can be concluded in a single Basement memory cycle, and those requiring more time. Among the former are:

- search for the occurrence of a given character,
- comparing the entire byte slice with a given character.

Instructions of the latter kind are necessary as soon as we need to handle more than 64 bytes. Such applications would be:

- comparing arbitrary strings,
- searching sets of strings,
- minimum, maximum, sorting, similarity,
- weighed search,
- join operation.

In cases where sorting is of prime importance, a significant speed-up can be achieved by a simple hardware extension (see [Wolf85]).

3. Standard Database Applications

The SIMD architecture makes HAS a powerful tool for set operations in database applications. In particular, operations known from the relational model such as selection, projection, and join can be performed efficiently through the parallelism offered by the 64 PEs.

3.1 Basic Database Operations

Let us assume that all relations to be processed have already been loaded into HAS. Each relation consists of one or more segments, a segment being a section of store one tuple deep and 64 bytes wide (see also fig. 3.1).

We introduce a simplified subset of HAS instructions with the intention of demonstrating how basic database operations can be processed on HAS. The six instructions are not claimed to describe HAS exhaustively and precisely.

(1) Uniform load b(i) into A
loads one byte from address i into the A registers of all PEs.

(2) Vector load sl(j) into B
loads one byte slice from BS line j into the corresponding registers B of the PEs. In contrast to (1), all B-registers contain in general different values after loading.

(3) Vector load A into B
loads, in each PE, the contents of register A into register B.

(4) Vector test for equality A and B
compares the contents of registers A and B of each PE. In case of equality, the corresponding result is set to one. The instruction delivers a vector as result.

(5) Vector store test result into C(k)
stores the result vector of a preceding instruction (4) into address k of the C register bank of the PE.

(6) Rotate A by one
Transfers the contents of each A register to the A register of its cyclic neighbour PE. In reality, this transfer is not achieved directly but via a bus connecting all PEs.

We shall now demonstrate, in terms of these six instructions, how the selection, projection, and join operation on a segment can be accelerated by the use of the parallelism offered by HAS.

The selection operation on a segment in HAS can be processed in the following way:

```
for  i = 0  to  (length-1)
   do
     uniform load  b(i+i0) into A
     vector  load sl(i+j0) into B
     vector  test for equality A and B
     vector  store test result in C(i+k0)
   od
```

We assume that the search argument and the segment have been loaded into Parameter Store (addresses i0 to i0+length-1) and Basement Store (addresses j0 to j0+length-1) respectively (fig. 3.1). Here, the uniform load instruction loads byte b(i+i0) of the search argument into all A registers. The vector load instruction moves the bytes of byte slice sl(i+j0) from BS to the corresponding B registers. After a test for equality has been performed in parallel for all PEs, the result vector is stored into address i+k0 of the C register bank. By "vertically" ANDing all (n=length) result vectors, the tuples equal to the search argument can be located.

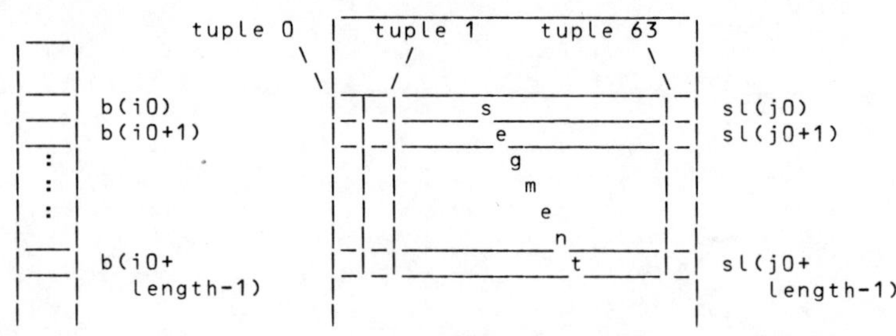

Fig. 3.1: layout of search argument and segment

The projection operation consists, in the first step, in cutting off domains. The second step, i.e. detecting duplicates among the tuples of the cut segment, can be accomplished by HAS in the following way:

```
for  i = 0  to  (length-1)
   do
      vector  load sl(i+i0) into A
      vector  load A into B
      for  j = 0  to  31
         do
           rotate A by one
           vector test for equality A and B
           vector store test result in C((j+k0)*(i+1))
         od
   od
```

The same byte slice sl(i+i0) is loaded into both PE registers. The byte slice residing in the A registers is rotated. After each step of rotation a test for equality is performed, and the result is stored in the C register bank. The stored results of the comparisons can be used to finally identify and eliminate all duplicates.

A join operation on 2 segments of different relations can be performed by HAS in the following way:

```
for  i = 0  to  (length-1)
   do
     vector  load sl(i+i0) into A
     vector  load sl(i+j0) into B
     for  j = 0  to  63
        do
          vector test for equality A and B
          vector store test result in C((j+k0)*(i+1))
          rotate A by one
        od
   od
```

The byte slices sl(i+i0) and sl(j+j0) from the first and second relation are respectively loaded into the registers A and B. Byte slice sl(i+i0) is stepwise rotated in registers A; after each step of rotation, a test for equality is performed. The result is kept in the C register bank for later evaluation.

3.2 Operations on the Application Level

As in most database machine concepts, the overall performance of HAS depends strongly on the load profile of the particular application.

Although a Basement Store capacity of some 16 Mbytes is envisaged for HAS, many applications require a much larger working set. This gives rise to the problem of fast mass data transfer between primary and secondary store, a problem not unknown from, but nevertheless unsolved in, typical database machine architectures (various solutions are discussed in [BoDe83]). Taking into consideration data rates of available mass stores, no device exists at present which can cope with the HAS data rate of about 80 Mbytes/sec. For the time being, we focus on applications which require only little external loading.

The parallelism provided by the SIMD architecture of HAS is well suited to support low-level set operations. Since strong synchronism is established between processor elements of the Associative Surface, only little communication is necessary during these operations. Parallelism on higher levels, however, cannot be easily achieved with this type of architecture.

Nowadays, many applications require on a low level single-record operations, thus prohibiting parallelism. It is not clear how often this results merely from the original database design where a discourse world was modelled for a database management system without set operations. A redesign of the original application by means of a conceptual model may in those cases lead to a structure more suitable for this type of database machine architecture.

3.3 Performance Considerations

The internal search speed attainable with HAS is only limited by the cycle time of memory chips. Nowadays, even memory chips of large capacity have cycle times of 500 ns or less. Since whole byte slices of 64 bytes are accessed and processed in parallel, search data rates of 128 Mbytes can be achieved.

4. Associative Processing in Deductive Databases

4.1 Deductive Databases and Prolog

Databases can be augmented by deduction rules serving to infer information not explicitly stored in the database. Although such "deductive databases" (DDB) can in principle be implemented in any language, we will in this section study a Prolog-like implementation. Our discussion will thus deal not only with DDBs but with the efficient implementation of the internal database of Prolog and logic programs in general.

We do not intend to explore the problems entailed in interfacing a Prolog system to a database residing on background store. This problem, though important, will be investigated separately. We will concentrate on the non-evaluational approach [Chan78], and assume that all relevant data have been brought from the disk-based database into the Prolog runtime environment beforehand. Since the standard depth-first execution strategy tends to be very inefficient, parallel execution of logic programs is being explored intensely by others [UmTa83].

Associative devices like HAS are ideally suited for synchronous operations on sets of data with regular structures. AND-parallelism in the evaluation of subgoals, on the other hand, requires independently running operations, which would be hard to implement on HAS; multiprocessor architectures are better suited for this purpose.

However, two important performance issues of Prolog implementations are amenable to associative processing (e.g. by a coprocessor of a DB machine): unification and OR-parallel execution of facts (i.e. a unit clause, a clause without body). Both problems are strongly interrelated. Unsuccessful unification of facts poses a major performance problem as has been shown in a measurement study of a Prolog system [Bull84]. The ratio of successful to unsuccessful unifications was reported to be roughly 1:6 in a DB-oriented program. We therefore concentrate subsequently on the enhancement of unification.

4.2 Implementation of Facts and Rules using the HAS

Due to the flexible loading mechanism of the HAS Basement Store, rules and facts can easily be stored either horizontally or vertically (fig. 4.1).

We assume functor and variable names as well as constants to be encoded into fixed length format. First, we will only deal with facts.

If facts are stored horizontally they occupy one or more 64-byte memory slices. Suppose, the clause

```
P(X,Y) :- Q(Z,X), R(Z,Y).                                (*)
```

is to be evaluated and X has already been bound to the constant a. Let Q and R be facts. Many unsuccessful unifications are usually attempted on Q. Their number cannot be decreased by using HAS, but the execution time will be vastly reduced: for example, if we take a fact Q(<const>, <const>) and call it f,

```
f   :=  Q(<const>, <const>)
j   :=  number of bytes required to represent f in HAS
k   :=  entier( (j+63)/64 )
```

only k memory cycles are needed to match Q(Z,a) against f.

```
+------------------+      +---------------------+
| Assoc. Surface   |      |   Assoc. Surface    |
+-------------//---+      +----------------//---+
  | | | | | | |    |        |   |   |   |     |
+-------------//---+      +---+---+---+-----//---+
|  rule / fact 0   |      | r | r | r | r ... r |
+------------------+      | / | / | / | / ... / |
|  rule / fact 1   |      | f | f | f | f ... f |
+------------------+      |   |   |   |   ... 6 |
|     r / f    2   |      | 0 | 1 | 2 | 3 ... 3 |
|        .         |      +---+---+---+---------+
|        .         |      | r | r | r | r ...   |
|        .         |      | / | / | / | / ...   |
|        .         |      | f | f | f | f ...   |
|                  |      |   |   |   |   ...   |
+------------------+      | 6 | 6 | 6 | 6 ...   |
                          | 4 | 5 | 6 | 8 ...   |
   a)                     +---+---+---+---------+
                          |     ...             |
                          +---+---+---+---------+
                          | r | r | r | r ...   |
                          | / | / | / | / ...   |
                          | f | f | f | f ...   |
                          |   |   |   |   ...   |
                          | n |   |   |   ...   |
                          | * |   |   |   ...   |
                          | 6 |   |   |   ...   |
                          | 4 |   |   |   ...   |
                      b)  +---+-+-+-+-+-+-------+
```

Fig. 4.1: rules/facts stored a) horizontally or
b) vertically in HAS

Furthermore, the set of all solutions for Q(Z,a) is generated in one blow, in contrast to the standard depth-first evaluation of Prolog. Unification of the above type is obviously only a special case: it corresponds directly to the selection operation of DB processing. It is implemented as an associative (horizontal) search, using the masking facility of HAS for the variable parts of the "query". Coming back to (*), we need to determine now those Y-values which correspond to one of the Z-values obtained in the previous step. However, this requires merely to join {b : Q(b,a)} with the facts given by R. The join operation has already been discussed in chapter 3.

If we store the facts vertically in the HAS memory, 64 facts can be unified with a goal statement in parallel. The goal is compared character by character with the clauses. Variable parts of the goal are masked, and replaced by constants, if the match succeeds. It should be remembered that we deal with a simple form of unification where a constant / constant check is carried out. This method (fig. 4.2) is very similar to searching among conventional relations.

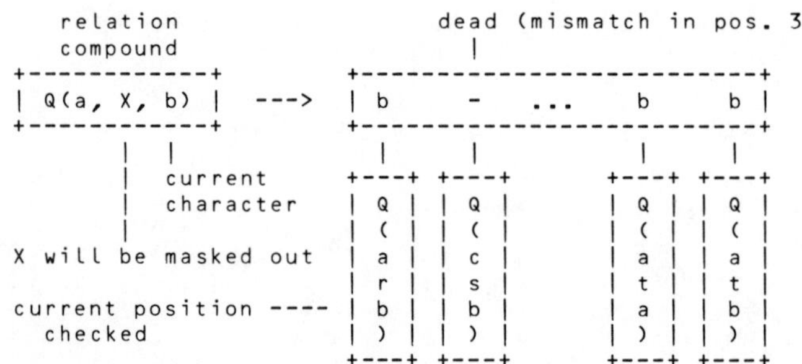

Fig. 4.2: parallel matching in HAS

All solutions to Q(...,X,...) are generated (OR-parallelism) just as in the case of the horizontally arranged clauses. Performance is primarily determined by the memory cycle time. Supposing each fact was stored in 200 bytes, and a 500 microsec RAM was used, it would take 1 msec to unify 640 facts (plus the time to read the variable bindings).

The situation gets more complicated when dealing with rules instead of simple facts. Rule bodies may be conjunctions of any number of predicates. If the defining clauses for Q have such bodies, synchronous reduction of a subgoal Q will work only as long as the bodies are conjunctions of the same predicates, e.g.:

```
Q(a,X) :- P(X,a,b).
Q(X,a) :- P(X,Y,a).
```

However, an associative device like HAS can be of advantage if the clauses are laid out in HAS memory in a special way. Let us symbolise each instance of a predicate in the set of rules and facts by an index <i,j> where i is the clause identifier and j is the position within clause i (<i,0> thus being the head of clause i). Facts and clauses (with any number of subgoals) can be uniformly represented in HAS memory through sequences of such an index put together with functor and arguments. The following example illustrates the method:

Prolog Program (including "database"):

```
line                              (In Prolog, atomic constants are
  1      D(h).                     denoted by lower case letters.)
  2      M(m,e).
  3      M(m,w).
  4      M(h,X) :- M(X,w).
  5      S(X,Y) :- D(X), M(X,Y).
  6      S(h,g).
         |          |      |
         0          1      2   (depth level)
```

HAS representation:

HAS column no.	0	1	2	3	4	5	6	7	8	... 63
prog. line \ > index	1	2	3	4	5	6	4	5	5	
depth level /	0	0	0	0	0	0	1	1	2	
functor	D	M	M	M	S	S	M	D	M	
argument 1	h	m	m	h	X	h	X	X	X	
argument 2	-	e	w	X	Y	g	w	-	Y	
:										
:										

In order to solve the goal ?-S(h,X) the following steps are performed:

(1) Search all columns starting with <*,0> and unify them with the subgoal (* means "don't care").

Result: rules <5,0> and <6,0>
(OR-parallel execution of subgoals).

(2) Search all columns starting with <5,1> or <6,1>, in order to find the first subgoals of the clauses found in step (1).

Result: No column has the index <6,1>, so that we find:
a) rule <6,0> is a fact.
Another success (a match) is:
b) column 7 contains predicate <5,1>.

(3) Bind variables.

a) X in the initial goal is substituted for g from fact <6,0>; g is thus the first element of the result set.
b) X in <5,0> and <5,1> is bound to the h (from initial subgoal).

The following steps are similar to those from above: first the subgoal <5,1> D(h) is solved, then <5,2> M(h,Y), with the final result m being substituted for Y.

The five inferences, four of which are performed sequentially in the standard depth-first manner of Prolog, need 4*length(predicate) memory cycles. Using the figures from above, execution takes 400 microsec.

There are, however, some problems with general inferences on quasi-associative systems like HAS. The first one is inherent in unification and binding of variables in general: the bindings have to be performed by the processing elements, and this will slow down the PEs considerably. The second problem: there is only little scope for parallelism when processing disjunctive rules (as opposed to facts). For example:

```
Q(X,Y) :- P(X), R(Y).        and
Q(X,Y) :- P(X), S(Y,Z).
```

may be processed in parallel for their first subgoals since they happen to be identical. But parallel operation is not possible when solving R and S.

However, the situation is different in an environment with many processors, each occupied with a different subproblem. Subgoals and results are passed as messages between these processors. Such a system ("The Bagle") has been proposed by E. Shapiro [Shap83] as an architecture for a parallel inference system. There, each of the processors has a private associative memory where all rules and facts are stored. A HAS-like memory system would serve this purpose very well.

5. Conclusion

It has been demonstrated in this paper that quasi-associative devices can be successfully employed for certain database management tasks. However, only tasks of a "regular" nature permit their potential parallelism to be exploited. This limits the applicability of such devices in some important cases. The same holds for Prolog-based deductive databases. In a Logic Programming environment, system performance is determined by the rapid execution of operations like unification and variable binding, and any associative device for such an environment needs therefore to be more flexible than, say, hardwired high performance search processors. The concept of quasi-associative processing by tightly coupling conventional RAM and simple processors is thus a significant contribution to "new generation" computer architecture.

Bibliography

[Chan78] Chang C.: "Deduce 2: Further Investigations of Deduction in Relational Databases", in: Gallaire H., Minker J. (eds.): "Logic and Databases", Plenum Press, 1978.

[BoDe83] Boral H., DeWitt D.J.: "Database Machines: An Idea whose Time has Passed? A Critique of the Future of Database Machines" in: Leilich H.-O. and Missikoff M. (eds.): "Database Machines", Springer-Verlag, Berlin 1983.

[UmTa83] Umeyama S., Tamara K.: "A Parallel Execution Model of Logic Programs", Proc. Int. Conf. on Comp. Architecture, Stockholm 1983.

[Bull84] Bull Research Center: "Report on Prolog II Interpreter Measurements", Apr 1984

[Shap83] Shapiro E.: "The Bagle", lecture at ICOT, October 1983.

[Wolf85] Wolf G.: "The Hybrid Associative Store", (in German) to appear in: "Siemens Forschungs- und Entwicklungsberichte", Siemens AG, Munich 1985.

The Design and Implementation of Relational Database Machine Delta

Takeo Kakuta, Nobuyoshi Miyazaki, Shigeki Shibayama, Haruo Yokota, Kunio Murakami

ICOT Research Center

Institute for New Generation Computer Technology

Tokyo, Japan

ABSTRACT

Delta is a relational database machine under development at ICOT. It has specially designed hardware components to perform relational database operations and a large semiconductor memory to be used as disk cache area. The machine will be used in an experimental local area network environment along with Personal Sequential Inference Machines which are also being developed at ICOT. This paper describes design decisions concerning Delta's architecture and processing algorithms, as well as its overall functions. Delta is expected to be operational with a data storage capacity of 20 GB by March, 1985.

1. Introduction

Japan's Fifth Generation Computer Systems (FGCS) research and development aim to build a prototype of a knowledge information processing system capable of efficiently performing knowledge-based problem solving and inference. Toward this end, a ten-year period has been assigned to the FGCS project, and this period has been divided into three stages.

The knowledge base machine and parallel inference machine are the most important hardware components of the FGCS. In the FGCS prototype to be completed as the final product of the project, the two machines will be integrated through a close link. In the initial stage, however, research and development are proceeding separately for each machine, since the initial stage mainly aims to conduct research and development of individual component technologies to establish the basic technology for the hardware, called the knowledge base subsystem and inference subsystem to be built in the intermediate stage.

In the initial three-year stage, a relational database machine is being developed in order to research and develop the basic techniques necessary for developing a knowledge base machine in the intermediate stage of the project and for investigating a prototype database machine capable of parallel relational and knowledge operations [Murakami83].

Development of the ICOT relational database machine (called Delta) has two purposes. One is to create an experimental environment in which various knowledge base functions and their implementation can be investigated. The other is to connect the machine via a local area network (LAN) [Taguchi84] with the personal sequential inference machine (called PSI) being developed separately [YokotaM83]. PSI is a software development tool that makes use of a logic programming language, Kernel Language Version-0 (KL0) [Chikayama83].

This paper gives an overview of the architecture, functions, processing algorithms, and the implementation of Delta. Details of its architecture, query processing flow, and implementation have been reported elsewhere [Shibayama84a,b],[Sakai84]. Various database machines (DBM) has been reported and implemented [IEEE79],[Bancilhon82],[Schweppe82],[Hsiao83]. Some are software oriented and others are hardware oriented. Hardware oriented database machines are designed to improve the performance of database operations. Delta is a hardware oriented database machine that adopts set-oriented internal operations and specialized hardware to realize these operations. It is one of the first hardware oriented DBMs implemented to store and manipulate large scale databases.

In chapter 2, some fundamental design decisions concerning the architecture are discussed. Functions that are made available to host computers and database administrators are described in chapter 3. Processing algorithms and methods for several basic operations are discussed in chapter 4, and implementation considerations are presented in chapter 5. Performance estimation is described in chapter 6.

2. Architecture

2.1 Fundamental Design Decisions

We have to solve two key problems in the design of a high performance DBM:

(1) Fast relational operations

(2) Efficient access to database storage.

Most DBMs so far proposed adopt parallel processing or specialized hardware to solve the first problem. Our solution is to perform all relational operations on sorted sets and to use a specialized preprocessing hardware to sort data. It is well known that join, a very time-consuming operation, can be executed extremely fast if both operand relations are sorted by their join attributes. Basic set operations are also processed quickly if operand relations are sorted. Thus, relational operations can be performed efficiently if we can sort relations fast enough. The best software algorithms can sort N items in $O(N \log N)$ time, but there are several algorithms to sort them in $O(N)$ time using specialized hardware. We designed a relational database engine (RDBE) based on a pipelined merge-sort algorithm [Todd78] [Sakai84]. Because most RDBE operations can be done in $O(N)$ time, its processing can be synchronized with the data transfer between itself and the memory subsystem. This is called data-stream processing and can be regarded as an extension of "on-the-fly" processing. Delta has four RDBEs, which can be used in parallel or independently.

There are several methods we may use to solve the access problem:

(a) Parallel I/O devices to reduce access time

(b) Use of search filters attached to storage devices to reduce the amount of data to be processed by the upper layers

(c) Large cache (buffer) memory to reduce access time

(d) Clustering and indexing techniques to reduce the amount of data to be processed.

Delta adopts a combination of (c) and (d), because they provide more flexibility, and a large low-cost memory is available. This decision may seem somewhat conservative, because several devices that incorporate methods (a) or (b) have already been proposed and implemented. However, because the usefulness and feasibility of these devices remains unproved, we believe our method is more realistic, given the relatively short time allotted to RDBM development.

2.2 Internal Schema

Conventional database management systems (DBMSs) store a relation as a file in which a tuple is treated as a record and an attribute as a field. To rapidly obtain tuples satisfying specific criteria, indexing and hashing techniques are applied. These methods are more useful if the number of attributes frequently used in the criteria is kept small. A DBMS has to scan the entire relation if an indexed or hashed attribute cannot be used as an access path for a given query.

We expect Delta to have an unconventional access characteristics, because a logic programming language is used as PSI's language, and because the system is used for knowledge information processing. Access to the database stored in Delta is predicted on the following characteristics, based on the usage of Prolog programs:

(1) Relatively few attributes in typical relations

(2) Uniform distribution of attributes used in conditions

(3) Relatively uniform frequency of access to tuples.

Delta adopts an attribute-based schema to efficiently process these kinds of requests. Instead of storing all the attributes of a tuple together, it splits a relation into a collection of attributes and stores all occurrences of each attribute together. A TID (tuple identifier) is stored along with an attribute value to identify the tuple to which it belongs. To reduce the amount of data to be processed by the RDBE, a two-level indexing method is used, as shown in Figure 1 [Shibayama84a]. The merits of Delta's attribute-based schema are as follows:

(1) Attributes that are not necessary for a given request need not be read from the secondary storage to work buffer area.

(2) Attributes are treated uniformly.

(3) Unnecessary attributes need not be transferred between RDBE and the memory subsystem.

There are several disadvantages as well.

(1) Transformation between tuple format and attribute-based format is necessary

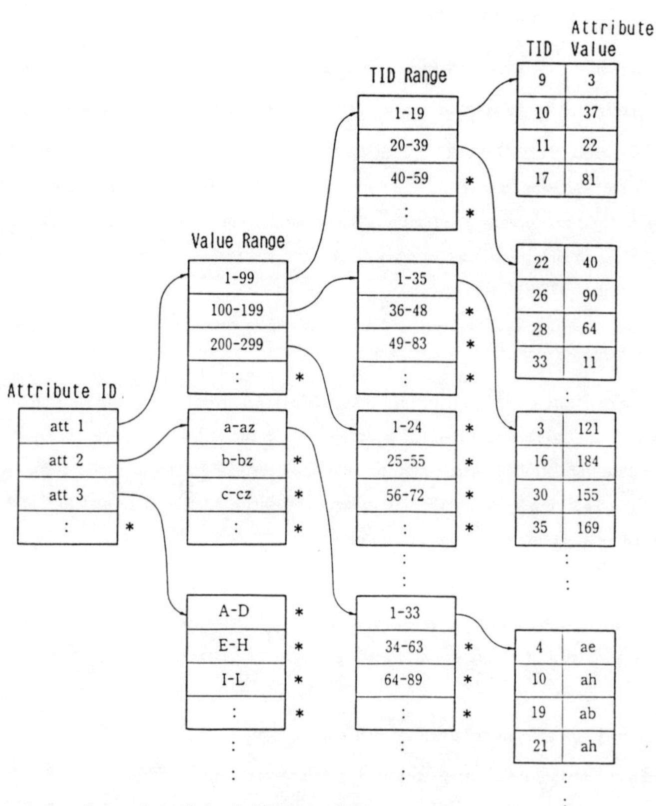

Figure 1. Internal Schema of Delta

(2) Tuple identifiers occupy additional storage space.

To prepare tuples for output (called tuple reconstruction) is a formidable task for conventional DBMSs because it is an operation similar to join. Delta can make effective use of the attribute-based schema because it can efficiently reconstruct tuples using the RDBE. The characteristics of the attribute-based schema are briefly analysed in [Miyazaki83].

2.3 Architecture of Delta

The Delta architecture was designed based on functional decomposition. Delta principally consists of three kinds of units: RDBEs, a Hierarchical Memory (HM), and a Control Processor (CP). A front-end processor (Interface Processor: IP) is used to connect Delta to the outside world. One more unit, a Maintenance Processor (MP), is included mainly for system supervising, as described later. Thus, Delta consists of five kinds of functional units, as shown in Figure 2. A logical request specifying the operation of an individual unit by another unit is called a subcommand.

RDBE performs basic data-manipulation operations such as selection, join, and sort. RDBE subcommands resemble relational algebra operators, except that their operands are usually attributes instead of relations. Operands of RDBE subcommands are called streams which are usually arrays of the form <TID, attribute-value, optional fields>, or sometimes arrays of combined attributes. Most subcommands are of the form [output-stream := OPERATION (input-stream1, input-stream2, options)], where input-stream2 does not appear for one operand operation, such as selection (restriction). Input-streams are read from HM and the output-stream is written back to HM. Examples of operations are "join", "restrict", "sort", "unique", and "union". There are four RDBEs which can be used in parallel or independently.

HM is a hierarchically structured memory subsystem, which serves as Delta's system work area as well as secondary storage. Physically, it has two layers. The upper layer is a large semiconductor memory, called the database memory unit (DMU). The lower layer consists of large-capacity moving-head disk units (MHDs). Logically, HM has three layers because the DMU is divided into two areas: a buffer area and a cache area. The buffer area is used as a system work area, which stores streams (for RDBE) and sets of

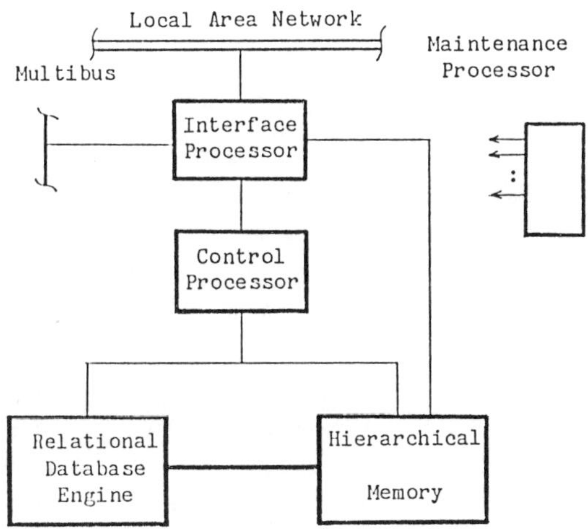

Figure 2. Delta Functional Architecture

tuples. The cache area serves as a large disk cache to reduce access to the disks. It adopts the write-after strategy to reduce access further. HM has a battery back-up system to protect database against power failures.

HM provides the other units with a high-level interface for access to buffers and data. For instance, buffer-IDs are used instead of memory addresses for buffer access. Moreover, other units can specify the conditions of the permanent data (an attribute) to be read into a buffer from secondary storage (or cache area). HM maintains and manages the two-level attribute indices mentioned previously and uses them to find pages which contain data satisfying the given conditions. Thus, HM performs a kind of pre-screening of data to be used by other units. It also provides a low-level physical addressing interface for the storage area that contains the system directory. A Shadow-page mechanism [Lorie77] and logs are also supported in HM to be used for transaction roll-back and data recovery.

Most database functions can be performed by a combination of RDBE and HM functions. Therefore, the main functions of the CP are to compile requests from the host into sequences of RDBE and HM subcommands, and to control their execution. The CP uses a system directory stored in HM to bind names to internal IDs. Other functions are as follows:

(1) Transaction scheduling and concurrency control

(2) Resource management

(3) Transaction commitment control and data recovery

(4) Management of dictionary and system directory.

3. Functions

Delta acts as a database server to a number of PSIs (Personal Sequential Inference Machines) in a local network (LAN) [YokotaM83] [Taguchi84]. A LAN may be a little slower than other interfaces, but it is currently the best available method of connecting a number of hosts to Delta. A faster direct interface is also available for experimentation with PSI. These experiments include interfacing the PSI logic programming language with Delta [YokotaH84]. Figure 3 shows the environment in which Delta will be used. It has been suggested that we incorporate as many database management and on-line I/O functions as possible in a special-purpose back-end computer to free the front-end general-purpose computer from database management chores [Hsiao80]. This might be true for a database backend that served a few host computers. However, Delta could prove to be a system bottle-neck if we assign it all the DBMS functions, because it will have to serve several dozen high performance PSIs. Therefore, some high-level functions are not implemented in Delta; some of them will be incorporated in PSI's software.

Delta functions can be classified into three groups:

(1) Database access functions

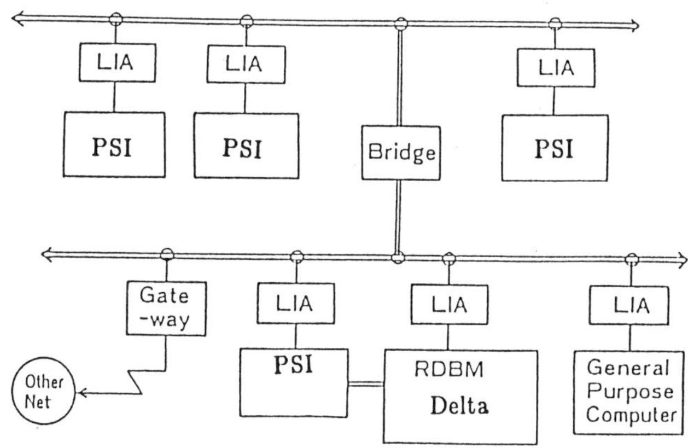

Figure 3. Total System Environment

(2) Database (access) controls

(3) System supervising.

3.1 Database Access Functions

Delta is based on the relational model and provides "relationally complete" but not "fully relational" DBMS functions according to Codd's definition [Codd82]. The relational model was selected, for (1) its compatibility with logic programming languages, (2) greater freedom in the design of internal schemas and processing algorithms made possible by its higher level of abstraction, and (3) fewer interactions with the host enabled by the set-based interface. The Delta access language is based on relational algebra; requests expressed in user-level query languages are compiled into the Delta access language by the host. Relational algebra has the expressive power equivalent to the relational calculus, and is easier to compile into internal operations. Moreover, adding special operators such as "sort" and "set comparison" is easy in a language based on relational algebra. The Delta access language uses attribute-numbers instead of attribute-names because it is designed for use with logic programming language as the host language. Another difference between the Delta access language and relational algebra is that it allows complex conditions to be specified in conjunctive normal form in the selection operator in order to reduce the number of operators. A list of the primitives called Delta commands that are available in the Delta access language has been provided in [Shibayama84a].

Delta provides the following access functions:

(1) Relationally complete access to relations

(2) Aggregate functions

(3) Data definition and updating

(4) Arithmetic operations for updating and in retrieval conditions

(5) Special operators, such as "sort" and "set comparison"

(6) Support of null values.

On the other hand, the following functions are not supported in the current system:

(a) Views

(b) Predefined requests

(c) Least-fixed-point operations.

Views are not included to reduce the load on Delta. Predefined requests are not supported because the anticipated frequency of repetitive requests does not seem to justify implementation of this function. Least-fixed-point operation are very desirable in a logic programming environment because they reduce the number of interactions required; we may later include this function in Delta [YokotaH84].

3.2 Database Controls

Delta supports the following database (access) control functions:

(1) Support of the (atomic) transaction concept

(2) Transaction concurrency control

(3) Data recovery

(4) Data dictionary

(5) Special functions for database administrators (DBAs).

The transaction concept is essential to every DBM and DBMS. The host can direct Delta to commit or abort a transaction at any time during its progress. Although a host may issue multiple update requests in a transaction, the result is treated as if the transaction were a single (atomic) operation.

Because Delta has to serve many PSIs simultaneously, it should be able to process concurrent transactions. Delta automatically locks and unlocks necessary relations so as to preserve their consistency. The granularity of locks is a relation, although finer granularity may be necessary for high throughput. It is fairly difficult to design concurrency control algorithm using finer granularity for DBMs such as Delta that have a functionally distributed architecture and set-oriented basic operations, because finer granularity must also be supported by recovery algorithm. A combination of deferred update and short-term locking methods is applied to the data dictionary so as to improve performance of transactions that involve dictionary update.

Data recovery is another function essential to every DBM and DBMS in case of system or media failure. Delta rolls-back all transactions in progress after a major failure. All transactions committed, or in the process of being committed, are preserved. Moreover, back-up dumps and magnetic tape logs can be used to restore database, if roll-back processing fails due to destruction of magnetic disk contents. In this case, roll-back processing is performed after restore processing.

The data dictionary consists of schema information for database relations. It is defined as a set of special relations whose consistency with user-defined relations is preserved by Delta so that hosts can look them up just as they can normal relations. A host may access the dictionary each time it accesses a relation to determine its schema. It may temporarily preserve the current contents of the dictionary in order to reduce interactions with Delta and improve overall performance. Thus, there could be schema information for the same relation in both the host and Delta, and we have to make sure this information is consistent. Beside the concurrency control mentioned above, Delta attaches a kind of time-stamp to schema information to indicate the latest update; this time-stamp is checked each time a host accesses a relation.

There are several special functions available for the convenience of database administrators. The bulk loading and unloading facility using magnetic tapes is useful for exchanging data with other systems or efficiently inputting large amounts of data. This facility can also be used to restructure the database so as to improve performance. Other examples of functions are the commands for storage management.

Delta does not currently have some functions that may be found in other systems:

(a) Security management

(b) Integrity control

(c) Support for the database schema design.

It was decided to incorporate security management in hosts because this function should be unified with the security functions of PSI's operating system, although it can be implemented easily on either side of the system. However, part of this function may be supported by Delta when the overall strategy for system security management is decided upon.

The other two functions were excluded from Delta, since there exist no fully-developed matured methods of implementing them. Some ICOT researchers are studying integrity control mechanisms for logic programming environment, and their methods will be applied to the PSI software that provides the interface to Delta.

3.3 System Supervising

In conventional computer systems, the system supervising functions are provided by the operating system rather than by the DBMS. If a DBM is a back-end, tightly-coupled with its host, some of the system supervising functions may be incorporated in the host's operating system. However, these functions must be provided in DBM if it is an independent database server such as Delta. Delta's system supervising functions include the following functions:

(1) System console (Operator or DBA interface)

(2) Control of system status

(3) Status report to host upon request

(4) Modifying parameters (size of the buffer area, etc.)

(5) Maintenance of log tapes, etc.

(6) Failure detection and system reconfiguration (disconnecting faulty equipment, etc.)

(7) Diagnosing faulty equipment

(8) Collection of statistical data for evaluation.

Most of these functions were designed and implemented especially for Delta, although a few made use of existing facilities.

Functions for registering users and maintaining their records are not supported, because Delta does not support security by itself. An accounting function is probably necessary for some DBMs; Delta does not need one because it is to be used in a closed research environment.

4. Basic Processing Algorithms

Delta processing algorithms are described in this chapter. The sequence of request processing is as follows. IP receives a request from a host and passes it to the CP. The CP compiles the request into a sequence of internal operations. A compiled request consists mainly of RDBE and HM subcommands. Then, CP controls the execution of the compiled request by RDBE and HM. The path between IP and HM is used to transfer tuples to and from host; the CP does not process them directly.

4.1 Retrieval

Processing algorithms are best explained by some examples. For readability, host requests are written in an SQL-like syntax instead of in the Delta access language. Some trivial operations are omitted.

Example 1: simple selection

Request: Select A,B
from R
where B> "10" and B<= "20"

Compiled request: (modified for readability)

1: HM: Templ := R.B where (range ["10"<, <="20"])

2: HM: allocate Temp2

3: RDBE: Temp2 := restrict (Templ, range ["10"<,<="20"])

4: HM: allocate Temp3

5: RDBE: Temp3 := sort-by-tid (Temp2)

6: HM: Temp4 := R.A where (tid in Temp3)

7: HM: allocate Temp5

8: RDBE: Temp5 := restrict (Temp4, equal-tid [Temp3])

/* this performs tid-join */

9: HM: allocate Temp6

10: RDBE: Temp6 := sort-by-tid (Temp5)

11: HM: allocate Temp7

12: HM: Temp7 := transpose-to-tuple (Temp6, Temp3)

/* result in Temp7 */

13: HM: release Templ, Temp2, ..., Temp6

Data transfers between RDBE and HM are directed by RDBE. For instance, RDBE issues two HM subcommands, start-stream-in (Templ) and start-stream-out (Temp2), when it executes step 3. These subcommands do not appear in the compiled sequence, because they are automatically issued by RDBE and CP is not involved.

In step 1, HM gets items of attribute B that may satisfy the condition "10"<B<="20" using clustering indices. Then, RDBE extracts only those items that actually satisfy the condition (step 3). Next, HM gets those items of attribute A that may correspond to the same tuples as the result of the previous operations (step 6), and RDBE extracts the exact items (step 8). This operation is called a tid-join because it resembles to a join. At this stage, the result is obtained, but it is still split between two buffers although both are sorted by tids. Thus, the final step is conversion to the tuple format.

In this example, steps 2, 4, 7, 9, 11 simply involve just the buffer allocation. Different buffers are used for different data for simplicity in this example, but buffers may be reused in actual operations. If they are reused, some allocation steps shown here are not necessary. All buffers except the buffer containing the result are released at or before the last step. Allocation and release of buffers are not shown in the other examples because they are trivial operations.

Steps 5 and 10 prepare for the subsequent steps by sorting data. They may be skipped if the result of previous operation does not exceed a specific limit (64KB or 4K items), because they are already sorted in previous steps or can be automatically sorted at the next steps in such cases.

In Delta operations, projections do not usually appear explicitly in internal operations. There may be more than two attributes in relation R, but the internal operation is the same as above. Thus, those attributes which are not output and are not conditions are not accessed in Delta.

Example 2: semi-join

Request: select A, B, C

from R

```
        where C in
              (select C
               from S
               where D = "d")
Compiled request:
  1: HM: Templ := S.D where (equal "d")
  2: RDBE: Temp2 := restrict (Templ, equal ["d"])
  3: HM: Temp3 := S.C where (tid in Temp2)
  4: RDBE: Temp4 := restrict (Temp3, equal-tid [Temp2])
  5: HM: Temp5 := R.C where (equal Temp4)
  6: RDBE: Temp6 := restrict (Temp5, equal [Temp4])
               /* this performs semi-join */
  7: HM: Temp7 := R.A where (tid in Temp6)
  8: HM: Temp8 := R.B where (tid in Temp6)
  9: RDBE: Temp9 := restrict (Temp7, equal-tid [Temp6])
 10: RDBE: Temp10 := restrict (Temp8, equal-tid [Temp6])
 11: HM: Templl := transpose-to-tuple (Temp9, Temp10, Temp6)
```

In this example, several trivial operations (allocate, release, and sort) are not shown. The semi-join can be performed by RDBE as a restriction, with the condition being given in a stream. Note that semi-join and tid-join are done by almost identical operations in Delta.

Example 3: join

```
 Request: select R.A, R.B, S.C
          from R, S
          where R.A = S.A and S.D = "d"
 Compiled request:
   1: HM: Templ := S.D where (equal "d")
   2: RDBE: Temp2 := restrict (Templ, equal "d")
   3: HM: Temp3 := S.A where (tid in Temp2)
   4: RDBE: Temp4 := restrict (Temp3, equal-tid [Temp>2])
   5: HM: Temp5 := R.A where (equal Temp4)
   6: RDBE: Temp6 := join (Temp4, Temp5, equal)
   7: RDBE: Temp7 := join (Temp5, Temp6, equal-tid)
              /* tid-join for result relation */
   8: HM: Temp8 := R.B where (tid in Temp6)
   9: HM: Temp9 := S.C where (tid in Temp6)
  10: RDBE: Temp10 := join (Temp8, Temp6, equal-tid)
  11: RDBE: Templl := join (Temp9, Temp6, equal-tid)
```

12: HM: Temp12 := transpose-to-tuple (Temp7, Temp10, Temp11)

The result of the join (step 6) is an array of triplets (new-tid, R's-tid, S's-tid) and does not include the values of R.A or S.A because of hardware limitations. Thus, [new-tid, R.A] := join ([R's-tid, R.A], [new-tid, R's-tid, S's-tid], equal R's-tid) must be done at step 7. Steps 10 and 11 are tid-joins, but are a little different from examples 1 and 2, because new tids are attached.

4.2 Updating

There are three kinds of update operations in Delta: insert, delete and update. An update is basically performed by a combination of delete and insert of necessary attributes. The example below shows the basic of update operations.

Example 4: Updating

Request: update R

set A = A + "a"

where B = "b"

Compiled request:

1: HM: Temp1 := R.B where (equal "b")

2: RDBE: Temp2 := restrict (Temp1, equal "b")

3: HM: Temp3 := R.A where (tid in Temp2)

4: RDBE: Temp4 := restrict (Temp3, Temp2, equal-tid)

5: RDBE: Temp5 := add (Temp4, "a")

6: RDBE: Temp6 := delete (Temp3, Temp2, equal-tid)

/* Temp6 := Temp3 - Temp2 */

7: HM: R.A := update pages corresponding to Temp3 by Temp6

/* R.A := R.A - Temp2 */

8: HM: R.A := insert (R.A, Temp5)

Selection of the qualified tuples is performed from step 1 to step 4. Calculation of new values is done in step 5 by RDBE. Actual updating takes place after these preparations. In steps 6 and 7, old value items of attribute A are deleted from the database. New value items are inserted in step 8.

When items are deleted from an attribute table, they are actually erased from the (indexed) pages of the table. In this case, indices remain unchanged because pages are not deleted even if they become empty. On the other hand, new items are inserted into the overflow pages. Thus, newly inserted items are not indexed and are read as possible candidates for whatever conditions are specified for subsequent retrievals. Indices must be restructured if the retrieval performance is degraded by these update operations. This restructuring is called reclustering; it is performed automatically by special system transactions whenever a specific trigger condition is satisfied.

5. Implementation

Delta consists of an RDBM Supervisory and Processing (RSP) subsystem, which takes charge of overall control, monitor and operation processing, and a Hierarchical Memory (HM) subsystem, which is responsible for storage, retrieval, and updating of relation data. Each functional unit identified in chapter 3 is being implemented by a separate piece of hardware, as shown in Figure 4. Delta is s loosely-coupled, functionally-distributed multiprocessor. The RSP and the HM are connected through a total of 11 channel interfaces. Figure 5 shows the specifications for the Delta systems.

5.1 RSP Subsystem Configuration

The RSP subsystem consists of the CP (Control Processor), IP (Interface Processor), MP (Maintenance Processor), and RE (Relational Database Engine), each of which consists of hardware and software.

5.1.1 RSP Hardware Configuration

Each unit basically consists of a 16-bit processor with a main memory size either 512 KB or 1 MB. The RE is provided with dedicated hardware for sorting and merging, and the CP is provided with a 30 MB semiconductor disk storage for increasing memory capacity. CP's control program temporarily stores the directory and other tables in the semiconductor disk storage. The MP is connected to the Delta system status monitoring display, the desk console, and the MTU for collecting RSP log information. Each RSP unit is connected to the others via three IEEE 488 buses. Each CP, IP, and MP unit is provided with one HM adapter (HMA), which serves as interface hardware for the HM. The RE is provided with an HMA for input and another for output.

(1) Relational database engine

The RE comprises of a sorter and a merger, which performs relational operations for pre-sorted results. Although various kinds of sorting algorithms have been studied [Knuth73], a two-way merge-sort algorithm has been adopted for the sort, a major component of the RE.

(a) Two-way merge-sort algorithm

This algorithm rearranges input record values in either ascending or descending order. An array of input records is regarded as a collection of sorted arrays, each of which has a length of 1. Sorted arrays are merged in pairs so that the length of each sorted array is doubled at each sort stage. When this operation is carried out in the pipeline processing configuration, the use of the $\log_2 n$-stage sorter enables a sort output with a cycle time of $2n + (\log_2 n) - 1$ [Todd78] (n=number of records).

(b) Configuration of the RE

The RE consists of an IN module, a sorter consisting of 12-stage sorting cells, a merger, two

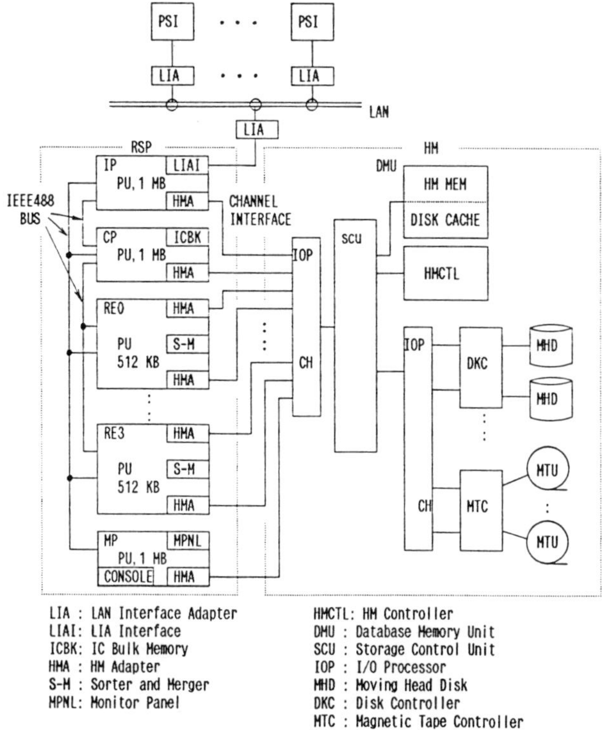

Figure 4. Delta Hardware Configuration

	Configuration of May, 1984	Final configuration
(1) RSP subsystem		
Control Processor	1	1
Relational DB Engine	1	4
Interface Processor	1	1
Maintenance Processor	1	1
(2) HM subsystem		
HM Controller	1	1
DB Memory Unit	16 MB	128 MB
Moving Head Disk	2.5 GB ×2units	2.5 GB ×8units
Magnetic Tape Unit	2	4

Figure 5. Delta System Specifications

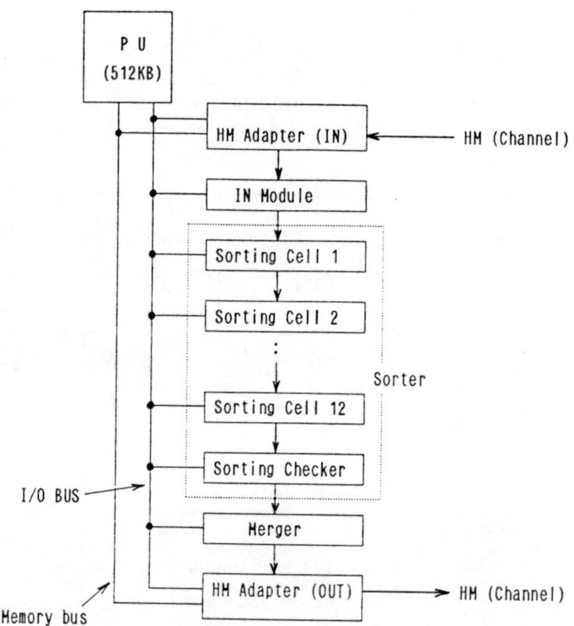

Figure 6. RE Configuration

HMAs, and the processor and RE control programs, which controls the above units. Figure 6 shows the configuration of the RE.

RE operations, based on relational algebra, sort item groups consisting of attribute values and TIDs while transferring them as a stream, perform relational operations from the head of sort output, and output combinations of items based on the results of the operation [Sakai84].

The IN module transforms input stream data item into an internal format suitable for the sorter and merger: field ordering, which replaces the head of each item to be sorted, and data type transformation. The sorting cell is made of two FIFO buffers, a comparator, and a multiplexer for merging. Each FIFO buffer has a capacity of 16 bytes at the first stage and 32K bytes at the twelfth stage.

The merger consists of an operation section, and an output control section. The operation section comprises of a comparator and two 64 KB memories having FIFO function, and performs relational algebra operations by comparing two sorted stream data. The output control section comprises of two 16 KB buffers, two field-ordering, field-selection and data-type transformation circuits, a selector and an output sequence controller. This section performs field reordering and selecting of an output data item, and adding a new TID to it, and then transferring output data items to the HM via an HMA.

5.1.2 RSP Software Configuration

Some pieces of software, such as the operating system and the IEEE 488 bus driver, are common to IP, CP, and MP. The IEEE 488 bus driver is used for intra-RSP subsystem communications and also used for the physical level interface with the LAN Interface Adapter (LIA). The following is a list of software functions assigned to the RSP units.

(1) IP

(a) LAN interface control

(b) Delta command and data extraction from packet-typed data

(c) Parallel reception of command tree

A command tree consists of one or more Delta commands, and is the unit in which any sequence of meaningful processing is carried out. This software identifies and controls a command tree for each transaction in the received packet data array.

(d) Data format conversion

When data is input from the host, it is provided each tuple with a tuple identifier (TID). The TID is removed when data is sent to the host.

(e) Data transfer with the HM

After the CP completes an instruction execution that reserves a buffer for data transfer between the IP and the HM, the IP performs data transfer with the HM.

(2) CP

(a) Transaction management

The CP is responsible for transaction execution management, Delta command analysis, generation and execution of HM, RE and IP subcommands, and Delta resource management.

(b) Dictionary/directory management

Dictionary is used for the host user reference and directory is used for the Delta command analysis, subcommand generation and concurrency control. Dictionary includes two meta relations, "Relations" relation and "Attributes" relations, but directory does not include the unnecessary part of dictionary information. Dictionary is stored in HM based on attribute-based schema, but directory is stored in HM in special data structures for the efficiency in look-up. The semiconductor disk storage in the CP stores the directory for repeated use. If necessary, the CP obtains directory pages from the HM by directory-access subcommands.

(c) Concurrency control

Concurrency is controlled by locking the relations based on the two-phase locking method. Relations to be locked during a transaction can be explicitly locked using a start-transaction command, or they can be automatically locked before command-tree execution. All the relations are unlocked at the end of a transaction whether it is a normal or an abnormal termination.

(d) Recovery management

When an abort-transaction command is received from the host during command-tree execution or hardware failure in Delta and media failure are detected, relations are restored in a status before the transaction has been started.

(3) RE

(a) RE control

The RE software analyses subcommands from the CP, controls the sequential operations of RE hardware and controls I/O data transfer with the HM.

(b) Relational operation support

The RE software performs arithmetic operations that cannot be processed by the merger hardware.

(4) MP

(a) Delta system status monitoring, and system configuration control

(b) Delta system start-up and shut-down

(c) Database loading and unloading

(d) Operator command and message management

(e) Statistical information collection

5.2 HM Subsystem Configuration

The HM subsystem consists of HM hardware and software designed to efficiently manage the storing of large amount of data to and the retrieving of data from storage area, as instructed by the RSP subsystem.

5.2.1 HM Hardware Configuration

In the final configuration, the HM hardware comprises of a non-volatile high speed Database Memory Unit (DMU) having a memory capacity of 128 MB, magnetic disk units having a maximum capacity of 20 GB, disk controllers, a 32-bit processor (named HM controller, HMCTL), which controls HM execution, and magnetic tape subsystem for system logging and database loading and unloading.

5.2.2 HM Software Configuration

HM software functions are listed below.

(1) HM subcommand processing

The following processing is performed by HM subcommands specified by the RSP.

(a) Attribute definition and operation

This processing generates and deletes attribute definitions, transposes tuples to attributes, and vice versa.

(b) Update processing

This processing inserts, deletes, and updates attributes.

(c) Clustering operation

Clustering tables are generated and updated in accordance with the value of attributes and TIDs by HM subcommands instructed from the CP.

(d) Data transfer management

Stream data transfers between the HM and the RE, and packed data between the HM and the IP or CP

(e) RSP buffer management

RSP buffer inside the HM is reserved and released by HM subcommands.

(2) Memory and MHD space management

The data transfer of attributes and directory information is performed between secondary storage and the DMU, and memory resource is managed for storing such information.

(3) Data recovery processing

Data recovery of attributes information is performed by recovery subcommands from the CP.

Delta can be classified as a hardware-oriented DBM because it incorporates a new piece of hardware in its kernel, and its processing algorithms for primitive relational operations are totally different from those of conventional DBMSs. However, some basic operations and additional functions are implemented in software. We expect to learn more about which functions to implement in hardware by evaluating Delta in actual operation.

6. A Delta Performance Estimation

We now consider an example selection query in SQL form for a Delta performance estimation:

SELECT $a_1, a_2, \ldots, a_n$

FROM A

WHERE a_i IN [value list]

where A is a relation composed of 10 attributes, having 10000 tuples. The a_1,a_2, and so on are the attributes among the 10 attributes. We assume 10 Bytes for each attribute here.

The execution time characteristic for selectivity according to an estimation is shown in Figure 7. This figure assumes a high hit ratio of disk cache in DMU. For certain range of selectivity, there are different

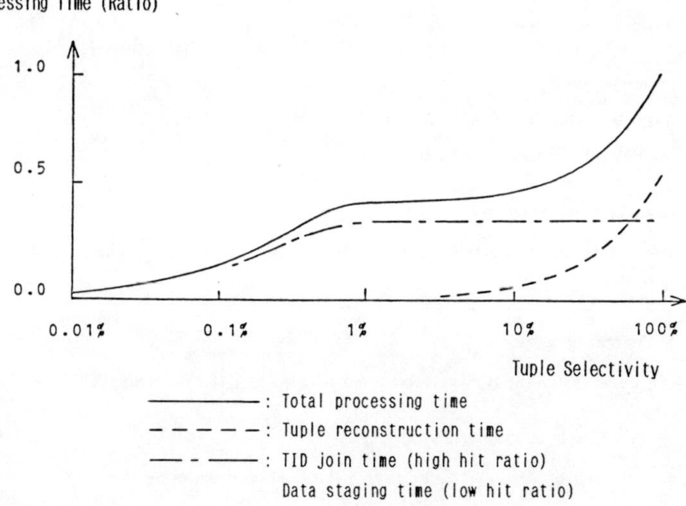

Figure 7. Estimated Delta Performance Characteristics

dominating factors. For the selectivity range between 0.01 % and 1 %, the dominating factor is the increasing TID join time. Buffer preparation in DMU is not so time-consuming, because the intra-buffer data transfer in DMU is fairly fast compared with TID joins. For selectivity factors between 1 % and 10 %, the estimation curve shows a plateau. In this area , the processing time is dominated by the full TID joining. All contents of the attributes should be scanned for TID join in this area. For the selectivity range between 10 % and 100 %, along with the TID join in this time which forms the plateau, tuple reconstruction time becomes influential. The effect of tuple reconstruction rapidly becomes great.

This result, though still not sufficiently quantative, indicates that the incorporation of a large capacity DMU is effective for a high performance database machine. The effort to increase the hit ratio by the wise replacement algorithm is the key to effectively utilize the DMU.

Delta incorporates statistical data collection functions for the evaluation of its usage and performance. The performance measurement and evaluation of Delta in logic programming environments are planned to be performed using these functions and the results will be reported later.

7. Conclusions

We have presented an overview of relational database machine Delta. Part of its hardware, along with 5 GB of storage, was installed at ICOT in April 1984, and has been used to debug and test the control software. The design of most of the control software has been finished and it is currently being tested. The remaining hardware was installed in December 1984, and we expect Delta to be fully operational by March 1985.

The functions described here and the performance of the machine will be tested in ICOT. Our goal is not just to build a good database machine, but to pave the way for future knowledge base machines. We hope these tests will prove our most crucial decision correct: that developing an RDBM is the first logical step toward a true knowledge base machine.

ACKNOWLEDGEMENTS

The authors express their appreciation to the Toshiba and Hitachi researchers and engineers who have participated in the development of Delta.

REFERENCES

[Bancilhon82] F. Bancilhon et al., VERSO: A Relational Back-End Data Base Machine, Proc. of Int'l Workshop on Database Machines, Aug. 1982.

[Chikayama83] Takashi Chikayama et al., Fifth Generation Kernel Language, Proc. of the Logic Programming Conference'83, Mar. 1983, Tokyo Japan.

[Codd82] E. F. Codd, Relational Database: A Practical Foundation for Productivity, Comm. of ACM, Feb. 1982.

[Hsiao80] David K. Hsiao, Data Base Computers, in (ed.) M.C. Yovits, Advances in Computers, Vol. 19, Academic Press 1980.

[Hsiao83] David K. Hsiao (ed.), Proc. of Int'l Workshop on Database Machines, Aug. 1982, and also revised version : Advanced Database Machine Architecture, Prentice-Hall, 1983.

[IEEE79] Special Issue on Database Machines, IEEE Transactions of Computers, Vol. c-28, June 1979.

[Knuth73] D. E. Knuth et al., Sorting and searching, The Art of Computer Programming, vol.3, Addison-Wesley Publishing Co., 1973.

[Lorie77] Raymond A. Lorie, Physical Integrity in a Large Segmented Database, ACM TODS, 2-1, Mar. 1977.

[Miyazaki83] Nobuyoshi Miyazaki, et al., On Data Storage Schemes for Database Machines, Proc. of 29th National Conf. of Information Processing Society of Japan, Oct. 1983 (short paper in Japanese), English version available as ICOT TM-0021 (English).

[Murakami83] Kunio Murakami, et al., A Relational Data Base Machine: First Step to Knowledge Base Machine, Proc. of 10th Symposium on Computer Architecture, Stockholm, Sweden, June 1983.

[Sakai84] Hiroshi Sakai, et al., Design and Implementation of the Relational Database Engine, Proc. of Int'l Conf. on Fifth Generation Computer Systems 1984, Nov. 1984, Tokyo Japan.

[Schweppe82] H. Schweppe et al., RDBM - A Dedicated Multiprocessor System for Data Base Management, Proc. of Int'l Workshop on Database Machines, Aug. 1982.

[Shibayama84a] Shigeki Shibayama, et al, A Relational Database Machine with Large Semiconductor Disk and Hardware Relational Algebra Processor, New Generation Computing, Vol.2, No. 2, June 1984, Ohmsha, Ltd. and Springer-Verlag.

[Shibayama84b] Shigeki Shibayama, et al., Query Processing Flow on RDBM Delta's Functionally-Distributed Architecture, Proc. of Int'l Conf. on Fifth Generation Computer Systems 1984, Nov. 1984, Tokyo, Japan.

[Taguchi84] Akihito Taguchi, et al., INI: Internal Network in ICOT and its Future, Proc. of ICCC, Australia, Oct. 1984.

[Todd78] S. Todd, Algorithm and Hardware for a Merge Sort Using Multiple Processor, IBM J. of Research and Development, Vol.22, No.5, Sep. 1978.

[YokotaH84] Haruo Yokota, et al., An Enhanced Inference Mechanism for Generating Relational Algebra Queries, Proc. of 3rd ACM Symposium on Principles of Database Systems, Apr. 1984, Waterloo, Canada.

[YokotaM83] Minoru Yokota, et al., The Design and Implementation of a Personal Sequential Inference Machine: PSI, New Generation Computing, Vol. 1, No. 2, 1983, Ohmsha, Ltd. and Springer-Verlag.

THE EQUI-JOIN OPERATION ON A MULTIPROCESSOR DATABASE MACHINE: ALGORITHMS AND THE EVALUATION OF THEIR PERFORMANCE

Ghassan Z. Qadah
EECS Department
Northwestern University
Evanston, IL 60201/ USA

ABSTRACT

The equi-join operation is one of the most important operations of the relational data model. It participates in all queries which reference more than one relation. In this paper, a large set of parallel algorithms for implementing the equi-join operation on a multiprocessor database machine called MIRDM (MIchigan Relational Database Machine), is presented. An outline of a study for the performance of the proposed algorithms in carrying out the equi-join operation on MIRDM, is also presented. The main objective of this study is twofold: the determination of the overall best performing equi-join algorithm and the investigation of the effectiveness (from the equi-join operation point of view) of performing some tuning to the architecture of MIRDM. This study shows, among others, that for a given MIRDM configuration; the overall best performing equi-join algorithm is not unique and different algorithms score the best performance depending on the characteristics of the data participating in the equi-join operation.

1. Introduction

During the past decade, several conventional relational database systems have been designed [1,2]. These systems are large complex software systems running on a conventional general-purpose von Neumann computer. The low reliability of these systems, their poor performance in supporting a large class of database operations and the advancement in the processor-memory technology inspired a new approach to support relational databases. This approach replaces the general-purpose von Neumann computer with a dedicated machine, the database machine (DBM), tailored for data processing environment and, in most cases, utilizing parallel processing to support some or all of the functions of the database system. The new approach claims to overcome the drawbacks of the conventional one.

Many database machines have been designed and some of these designs have also been implemented [3,4,5,6,7,8,9,10,21]. Most of these designs organize the DBM as a backend machine to one or more general purpose computer(s), called the Host(s). While the host is responsible for interfacing the users to the DBM, the DBM itself is responsible for the database access and control. An important class of DBMs is the multiprocessor machines. In this class, a DBM is organized as a set of microprocessors intercommunicating through a shared memory [7,8], an interconnection network [11] or both [12]. These DBMs use the shared memory or a separate interconnection structure to interface the system disks, where the database is stored, to the set of microprocessors.

One of the most important operations of the relational systems and probably the most important limiting factor to their performance is the Θ-join (or simply join) operation. The join [13] of a source relation S and a target relation T on attributes A from S, and B from T, is the result relation R, obtained by concatenating each tuple $s \in S$ and each tuple $t \in T$ whenever $s[A] \ \Theta \ t[B]$ is true. "Θ"is one of the operators $=$, $<$, $\leq$, $\geq$, $>$, $\neq$. The join operation is generally needed in formulating queries which reference more than one relation. The most frequently used type of the join operation is the equi-join, where Θ is the operator $=$.

Several parallel algorithms have been proposed to implement the equi-join operation on the various multiprocessor DBMs [7,11,14,15]. Each of these algorithms has been developed around one of the following basic techniques, namely:

1. Broadcasting
2. Sorting
3. Hashing
4. Filtering

Dewitt, et al. [7] propose the use of braodcasting as the basis for a parallel equi-join algorithm. The algorithm assumes that both of the relations S and T are stored in page units on the system disk. The algorithm, the parallel nested-loops algorithm, starts by having each of the processors read a different page from relation S. Next, all the pages of relation T are broadcast, one at a time, to all the processors. Upon receiving a page of T, each processor joins its page of S and the incoming page of T using the nested-loops[1] algorithm [7]. The previous steps are repeated until all the pages of S are joined. The parallel nested-loops algorithm has been extended in [15] to allow a number of pages from relation S to be read into a processor before the broadcast of pages from relation T

---

[1] Using this algorithm, a processor joins the tuples in the S page and the T page by comparing the join attribute value of every tuple in the former page with that of all the tuples in the T page. Throughout this process, the tuples with matching join attribute values are joined.

would begin. This extention improves the speed of the parallel nested-loops algorithm by reducing the number of times the relation T has to be broadcast to the processors during the execution of such algorithm.

Bitton, et al. [14,16] propose the use of sorting as a basis for a parallel equi-join algorithm. The algorithm, the Sort-Merge-Join algorithm, proceeds in two steps. First, the processors are used to sort both relations S and T on the join attribute, using a parallel version of the uniprocessor two-way merge-sort algorithm (described in [17], pp. 247). Second, one processor is used to merge the two sorted relations. During this step, the tuples from the two relations with equal join attribute values are joined. An extention to the Sort-Merge-Join algorithm has been presented in [15]. This extention involves the use of the parallel version of the uniprocessor P-way Merge-Sort algorithm, where P > 2, to perform the sorting in the first step of the Sort-Merge-Join algorithm.

Goodman [11] propose the use of hashing as a basis for a parallel equi-join algorithm. This algorithm assumes that the tuples of both relations S and T are initially distributed among all the processors in a uniform fashion. The algorithm begins with each processor applying the same hashing function to the join attribute of its own tuples. The hashing function uses the join attribute value of a tuple to compute a processor number. The tuple is then sent to the processor having such number. During the second phase of the algorithm, each processor joins the tuples it receives as a result of the first phase.

Babb [5] propose the use of the filtering concept as a basis for a uniprocessor equi-join algorithm. This algorithm begins by intializing two boolean-array's in the uniprocessor memory. The boolean-array's are vectors of bits with the same length. Next, the uniprocessor reads all the tuples of relation S. As one tuple is read, the uniprocessor computes a hashing function on its join attribute value. The result of this computation is an index. The bit in boolean-array BA-S which correspond to this index is set to 1. The previous steps are repeated to set the bits of BA-T according to the join attribute value of every tuple in relation T. The boolean-array's BA-S and BA-T are then bitwise "ANDed" to produce one combined boolean-array. During the second phase of this algorithm, all the tuples of both relations S and T are read into the uniprocessor. As one tuple is read in, the hashing function of the first phase is used to compute an index based on the tuple's join attribute value. The bit of the combined boolean-array which correspond to this index is then checked. The tuple is retained for further processing in phase 3 only if the bit has the value 1. During the third phase of this algorithm, all the tuples from relations S and T which survive the filtering process of phase two, are joined using a uniprocessor equi-join algorithm. Goodman [5] extended this algorithm to the multiprocessor environment.

In this paper, the broadcasting, sorting, hashing and filtering techniques, presented above, are extended and used individually as well as in combinations to develop new sets of parallel algorithms to carry out the equi-join operation on a multiprocessor database machine called MIRDM (MIchigan Relational Database Machine) [12,18]. An outline of a study for the performance of the new algorithms is also presented. The outcome of this study suggests that, for a given MIRDM configuration, the best performing parallel equi-join algorithm is not unique, and different algorithms score the best performance based on, among others, the characteristics of the two relations participating in the operation. It also shows that the best performing parallel algorithms are those which combine more than one of the above techniques to execute the equi-join algorithm.

In summary, section 2 presents an overview of the hardware organization of MIRDM. Section 3 presents a set of parallel algorithms for implementing the equi-join operation on MIRDM. A scheme for classifying these algorithms is also introduced. The scheme consists of two levels. At the first level, it groups the equi-join algorithms, into four categories. At the second level, the algorithms within each of these categories are classified according to three attributes. These attributes characterize the way the data participating in the equi-join operation, is distributed among the different hardware units of MIRDM for processing.

Section 4 presents a comprehensive probabilistic average-value framework for modeling the execution, by MIRDM, of the parallel algorithms proposed for the equi-join operation. Because of space limitation, we omit the presentation of the models developed within such framework for the proposed algorithms. The interested reader is refered to [18] for a complete presentation of these models.

In Section 5, the models developed for the execution of the various equi-join algorithms [18] are used to study and determine the overall best performing ones. The evaluation process is carried out in two steps. In the first step, the best performing algorithm within the individual equi-join algorithmic categories is determined.

In the second step, the overall best performing algorithm(s) is then determined. Section 5 presents also an investigation of the effectiveness of performing some tuning to the architecture of MIRDM.

Finally, Section 6 presents some concluding remarks.

2. The Organization of MIRDM

MIRDM [12], shown in Figure 2.1, consists of four main components, namely, the master back-end controller (MBC), the processing clusters subsystem (PCS), the mass storage subsystem (MSS) and the interconnection network subsystem (INS). The MBC, implemented as a powerful mini/micro computer, interfaces the Host(s) computer(s) to MIRDM, schedules and monitors the query execution, manages and controls the different components of MIRDM and stores and maintains part of the system's dictionary and directory.

The MSS is organized as a two level memory, namely, the mass memory (MM) and the parallel buffer (PB). The MM is organized as a set of moving-head-disks controlled and managed by the mass storage controller (MSC). Each disk is provided with the capability of reading(writing) from(to) more than one track in parallel. Tracks which can be read(written), in parallel, from(to) one disk, form what is called the minimum access unit (MACU). The MACU is the smallest accessible unit of data as well as the unit of data transfer between the MM, the PB and the PCS. The MACU is expected to be a cylinder of a moving-head-disk. The MM stores two types of data, namely, the database and the major portion of its directory [12]. The database, a set of time-varying relations, is partitioned into a set of units, each having the size of one MACU. Only the tuples from one relation can reside in the same unit. The tuples of an MACU are laid out on the corresponding moving-head-disk tracks in a "bit serial-word serial" fashion.

The parallel buffer (PB) is organized as a set of blocks, each having the size of one MACU. A block is further partitioned into a set of subblocks. Each subblock can buffer one track of a moving-head-disk. The PB can be implemented using the semiconductor random access memory technology.

The processing cluster subsystem (PCS) is organized as a multiple "single instruction stream-multiple data stream" system. The PCS consists of a set of processing clusters (PCs) which share a common buffer, the parallel buffer. A PC, shown in Figure 2.2, has a "single instruction stream-multiple data stream (SIMD)" organization.

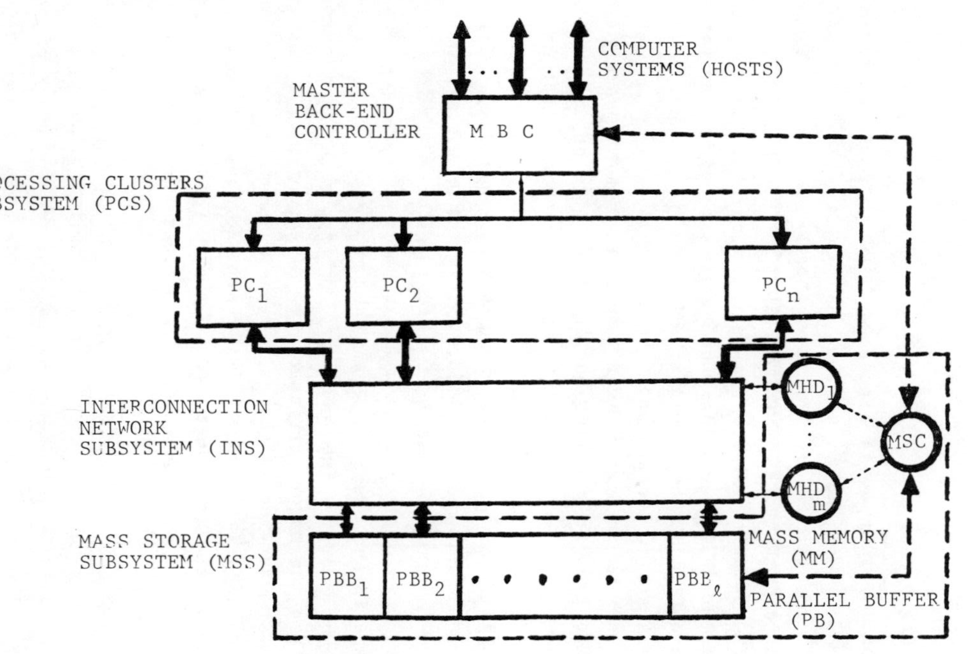

FIGURE 2.1 THE ORGANIZATION OF MIRDM

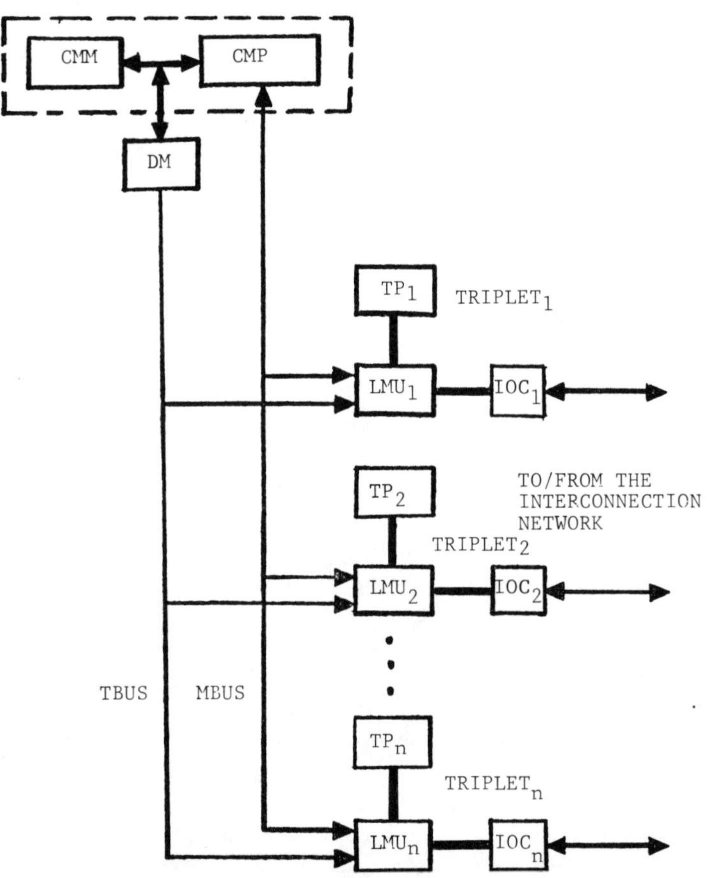

FIGURE 2.2 THE PROCESSING CLUSTER ORGANIZATION

A PC consists of a set of triplets, each of the form:

<I/O controller (IOC), triplet processor (TP), local memory unit (LMU)>.

The number of triplets within one PC is equal to the number of subblocks within one block of the PB. The set of triplets within a PC is controlled and managed by the cluster master processor (CMP). The CMP accesses its triplets through a broadcast bus, the master bus (MBUS). The MBUS permits the CMP to write the same data to all LMUs of its triplets, simultaneously.

Within a PC, the data is moved between triplets via a bus, the triplet bus (TBUS), contolled by a high speed DMA controller, the datamover (DM). The TBUS is provided with both point-to-point and broadcast capabilities.

The LMU of a triplet has a relatively large capacity (multiple the size of a moving-head-disk track) and is implemented using the semiconductor random access memory (RAM) technology. An IOC and a TP of a triplet are implemented as a high-speed DMA controller and an off-the-shelf microprocessor, respectively.

The Interconnection Network Subsystem (INS) interconnects the moving-head-disks of the MM, the Parallel buffer blocks and the processing clusters, together (refer to Figure 2.1). The INS is provided with two capabilities, namely, enabling any number of PCs to read from the same PB block and enabling any number of PCs or moving-head-disks to read(write) from(to) different blocks of the PB, simultaneously. In other words, the network possesses the broadcasting capability (from a PB block to a set of the PCs) and the crossbar interconnection capability (between the PCs, the PB blocks and the MM moving-head-disks).

The INS consists of a set of bidirectional buses, each associated with one subblock. Only one triplet in each PC as well as one head of each moving-head-disk is connected to the same bus (subblock). The bus is provided with broadcast capability which permits the corresponding subblock to broadcast its content to all the triplets attached to the bus. The MSC (refer to Figure 2.1) is responsible for preventing more than one PCs or disks or PCs and disks to write to the same parallel buffer block, simultaneously.

3. Performing the Equi-Join Operation on MIRDM

In MIRDM, one or more PCs are used to perform the equi-join operation. In general, the number of PCs assigned to perform such an operation is a decision of the master back-end controller (MBC). This decision is based on many factors, such as the size of the input relations, the nature of the join attribute, the number of available PCs and the priority class to which the query of the operation belongs.

The flexibility and generality of MIRDM architecture permits the implementation of a large set of parallel algorithms for the equi-join operation. These algorithms can be grouped into four categories, namely, the "basic," "target relation partial filtering (TPF)," the "source-target relations partial filtering (STPF)" and the "source-target relations complete filtering (STCF)." In the following subsections, the algorithms within the different equi-join categories are presented.

3.1 The Basic Equi-Join Algorithms

In general, the execution of a "basic" equi-join algorithm by MIRDM can be decomposed into a number of phases. A typical phase is carried out by one PC and involves the joining of some source and target tuples. The different phases of a basic algorithm can be carried out serially by one PC or in parallel by a number of PCs.

The "basic" algorithmic category is comprised of twelve different algorithms. Each of these algorithms can be viewed as a result of a series of decisions, and the decision space forms a four level tree (Figure 3.1). The individual basic algorithms correspond to the leaves of this tree. The root of the tree is the decision representing the choice of a method to assign tuples from the source and target relations to phases. This decision is called the "global tuple distribution" decision. Below the root are the decisions representing the choice of a method to distribute the phase assignment from the source and target tuples among the triplets of one PC for joining, and the method of performing the join of one target tuple with the set of source tuples within one triplet of a PC. These decisions are called, the "local tuple distribution" and the "intra-triplet join processing," respectively.

Two methods exist for assigning tuples from the source and target relations to phases. These two methods are:

(a) The Global Broadcast Method

In this method, a different set of NT minimum access units (MACUs) from the source relation and all the MACUs of the target relation are assigned to every phase (therefore, the number of phases

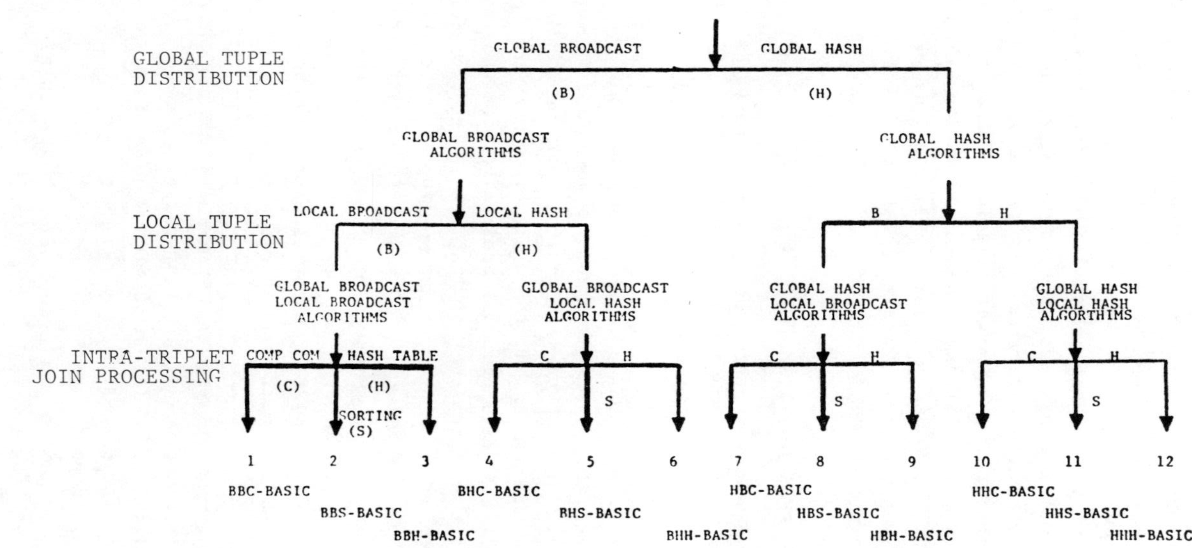

FIGURE 3.1 THE BASIC EQUI-JOIN ALGORITHMS

in one algorithm of the "global broadcast" basic algorithmic group is equal to that of the MACUs which store the source relation divided by NT). That is, a PC carrying out a typical phase needs to read, from the PB and process NT source MACUs and all the target MACUs. Usually, a number of phases are executed in parallel by an equal number of PCs. The PB then takes advantage of the crossbar capability of the INS to deliver the different sets of source MACUs to the participating PCs, in parallel. It also takes advantage of the broadcasting capability of the INS to broadcast the target MACUs, one MACU at a time, to the participating PCs. When the set of participating PCs are done with processing one target MACU against their source ones, another target MACU is broadcast to be processed next. This is done because the PC's local memory units have limited buffering capabilities.

(b) The Global Hash Method

In this method, a hashing function partitions the domain that underlies the join attribute of both the source and target relations into disjoint subsets (global buckets) such that the expected number of tuples from the source relation per subset would fit in the local memory units (LMUs) of a typical PC. The set of source and target tuples which hash to one global bucket constitutes the tuples which are assigned to one phase for joining (that is, the number of phases in one algorithm of the "global hash" basic algorithmic group is equal to that of the global buckets). Selecting the tuples of phase i of a global hash algorithm requires a PC to read from the PB into its LMUs all the source and target MACUs, one MACU at a time. As one MACU is read into the LMUs of the PC, the corresponding triplet processors, in parallel, compute a hashing function over the join attribute value of every tuple of the MAUC. A tuple is collected if the hashing function computation results in the value i. Usually, a number of phases are executed in parallel by different PCs. The PB then takes advantage of the broadcast capabilities of the INS to deliver a source or target MACU to all the participating PCs, simultaneously.

The tuples read(collected) by a particular PC during the initial execution of one phase of a basic algorithm can be distributed among the PC's triplets for joining using one of two methods, namely:

(a) The Local Broadcast Method

In this method, the source tuples read(collected) by each triplet of a PC during the initial execution of a phase are left in the triplets' LMUs. However, the target tuples of that phase, temporarily buffered in the LMUs of the PC (and the mass storage subsystem in the case of the global broadcast algorithms) is broadcast, one tuple at a time, by the cluster's data mover (DM) to all the triplets of the PC. Then, the triplets, in parallel, join the broadcast tuples with their share of the source ones.

(b) The Local Hash Method

In this method, the source and target tuples of a phase are hashed based on their join attribute values to the triplets of the PC which execute that phase. The hashing function, statistically independent of the global one in the case of global hash algorithms, is computed by the triplets themselves for every tuple of that phase. The data mover moves the hashed tuples to their destination triplets for joining.

Three methods are available to a triplet for joining one locally broadcast(hashed) target tuple with the triplet's assignment from the source tuples of one phase. These methods are:

(a) The Complete Comparison Method

In this method, the join attribute value of the target tuple is compared to that of every source tuple in the triplet. The target tuple is concatenated with a copy of every source tuple having the same join attribute value.

(b) Sorting the Source Tuples Method

In this method, the source tuples assigned to a triplet are first sorted based on their join attribute values. The joining is performed by using the binary search method [17] to locate those source tuples whose join attribute values are the same as that of the target one. The concatination of copies from the matching source tuples (if any) and the target tuple is then followed.

In a triplet, the sorting of the source tuples is implemented by actually sorting a table of pointers through which the source tuples are referenced. The storage allocated for the source tuples within the LMU of a triplet is divided into two areas, namely, the primary and the secondary ones. The latter area stores the source tuples in linked list structures[2]. The headers of the linked lists are stored, in the primary area, in a sorted fashion based on the join attribute values of the corresponding source tuples. This implementation avoids the high cost of tuples' movement which could result from the actual sorting of the source tuples.

---

[2] A linked list stores only the source tuples which have the same join attribute value.

(c) The Hash Table Method

In this method, the source tuples assigned to a triplet are first hashed, based on their join attribute values, to a hash table using a suitable hashing function. The join is then performed by hashing the target tuple, based on its join attribute value and using the same hashing function, to the hash table. A scan of the join attribute value of all the source tuples within a bucket of the hash table is needed to locate those source tuples whose join attribute values are the same as that of the target one.

The hash table of a triplet is implemented as two storage areas, namely, the primary and the secondary areas. The latter area stores the source tuples which hash to the same bucket in a linked list structure. The headers of the linked lists are stored in the primary area.

The different basic equi-join algorithms is named using the preceeding scheme. An algorithm name can be thought of as the ordered quadruple $\langle nam_1, nam_2, nam_3, basic \rangle$ where nam_1, nam_2, nam_3 are the results of the three decisions taken by the named algorithm and the word "basic" indicates that the algorithm belongs to the basic algorithmic category. For example, algorithm number 1 of Figure 3.1 is called the "global broadcast-local broadcast-complete comparison-basic" equi-join algorithm. For simplicity, this name is abbreviated to "BBC-BASIC". Figure 3.1 contains the abbreviated names of all the equi-join algorithms within the basic category.

From the PC point of view, the execution of one phase of a basic equi-join algorithm involves six subphases. During the first subphase, a set of source tuples (the tuples of NT source MACUs for the global broadcast algorithms, or the tuples of the source relation which hash to a global bucket for the global hash algorithms) are read(collected) by the PC triplets. During the second subphase, the CMP in cooperation with the cluster triplets and the data mover (do nothing with)/(hash to the cluster triplets) those tuples of the source relation which were selected during the first subphase. During the third subphase, every triplet, within the PC, (do nothing with)/sort/(store in a hash table) those source tuples it receives during the second subphase. The PC executes the first, second and third subphases in a pipeline fashion with the tuple as the unit of the pipeline. That is, as soon as the tuple is read(collected) in the first subphase it triggers the execution of the second subphase which in turn triggers the execution of the third one. When all the tuples of source relation, read(collected) in the first subphase are processed through the second and the third ones, then the execution of the fourth subphase is started.

During the fourth subphase, a set of target tuples (all the tuples within the target relation for the global broadcast algorithms or the target tuples which hash to a global bucket for the global hash algorithms) are read(collected) by the PC triplets. During the fifth subphase, the cluster master processor, in cooperation with the cluster triplets and the data mover broadcast(hash to the cluster triplets) those target tuples which are selected during the fourth subphase. During the sixth subphase, every triplet, within the PC, joins its share from the source and target tuples. Just as in the first three subphases, the PC executes the fourth, the fifth and the sixth subphases in a pipeline fashion. That is, as soon as a target tuple is read(collected) in the fourth subphase by a triplet, it triggers the execution of the fifth subphase (broadcast/hash the target tuple to the PC's triplets), which, in turn, triggers the execution of the sixth subphase [joining the broadcast/hashed target tuple with the source tuples of the triplet(s)].

3.2 The Other Equi-Join Algorithmic Categories

The algorithms within the TPF, STPF and STCF equi-join algorithmic categories can be obtained from those of the basic ones by slightly modifying their execution. The modification involves the use of one or more "boolean-arrays" to speed up the the execution of the basic equi-join algorithms. In the following, the TPF, STPF and the STCF algorithmic categories are presented.

3.2.1 The TPF Equi-Join Algorithms

The algorithmic category TPF is comprised of twelve different algorithms. Each algorithm is an extension of a basic one and has the same number of phases. Furthermore, a typical phase of a TPF algorithm has the same number of subphases as that of the corresponding basic algorithm.

Processing the source and target tuples of one phase of a TPF algorithm is similar to that of the corresponding basic algorithm except that it includes the use of one boolean-array, BA-S. The boolean-array of a suitable number of bits is initialized (at the begining of each phase), maintained and updated by the CMP. The boolean-array and a hashing function are used to encode the join attribute values of the set of source tuples which belong to one phase (say phase i) of a TPF algorithm. The join attribute value of a source tuple read(collected) by a PC's triplet during the execution of the first subphase of phase i is hashed, based on the tuple's join attribute value, to the boolean-array. The hashing function is computed by the triplet itself during the execution of the second subphase. The triplet then passes the result of the hashing function to its CMP, which, in turn, sets the corresponding bit in the boolean-array to "1."

After setting the boolean-array of the PC according to the source tuples of phase i, a typical target tuple of the same phase is processed during the fifth subphase by checking its join attribute value against the encoded set of the source tuples' join attribute values. This is done by transforming, using the hashing function of the second subphase, the join attribute value of the target tuple into an index to the boolean-array. The triplet which performs the transformation forwards the resulting index to its CMP, which, in turn, checks the corresponding bit in the boolean-array. If the bit is set, then the target tuple is procesed through the rest of the fifth and the six subphases; otherwise, the target tuple is ignored.

With a small modification, the naming convention adopted for the basic algorithms can be used to name the various TPF equi-join algorithms. The word "basic" in the name of a basic algorithm must be replaced by the word "TPF" to give the name of the corresponding TPF algorithm. Adopting this naming convention, the TPF algorithm which corresponds to the basic algorithm number 1 of Figure 3.1, for example, is to have the name "global broadcast-local broadcast-complete comparison-TPF." For simplicity, this name is abbreviated to "BBC-TPF".

3.2.2 The STPF Equi-Join Algorithms

The algorithmic category STPF is comprised of six different algorithms. Each algorithm within this category is an extension of one of the "global hash" basic equi-join algorithms. Processing the source and target tuples using a typical STPF equi-join algorithm is similar to that of the corresponding "global hash" basic one except that the number of phases (global buckets) in the STPF algorithm is larger than that of the corresponding basic one. In addition, the processing of one phase of the STPF algorithm includes the use of two boolean-array's. The number of phases in a STPF algorithm is selected such that the number of the source and target tuples (rather than the source tuples only as in the "global hash" basic algorithms case) which hash to the same phase (global bucket) can be stored in the LMUs of a PC.

A hashing function and the two boolean-arrays, BA-S and BA-T, are used to encode the sets of join attribute values of both the source and target tuples which belong to one phase of a STPF algorithm, respectively. The boolean-arrays are initialized (at the begining of each phase), maintained and updated by the CMP. The hashing function computations are performed by the triplets of the PC which execute the STPF phase.

From the PC point of view, the execution of the ith phase of a STPF equi-join algorithm involves six subphases. During the first subphase, the triplets of the PC collect the target tuples which hash to phase i. In addition, the PC's triplets compute a hashing function for the join attribute value of every collected tuple. The result of the hashing funcion computation for a collected tuple is stored together with that tuple in the LMU and a copy of this result is then forwarded to the CMP which sets the boolean-array BA-T, accordingly. When all the target tuples which belong to phase i have been collected, processed through the first subphase and stored, then the exectuion of the second subphase is triggered.

During the second subphase, the PC's triplets collect the tuples of the source relation which hash to phase i. In addition, the join attribute value of every collected source tuple is encoded using the boolean-array BA-S and the hashing function of the first subphase. Also, the collected source tuples are checked against the boolean-array BA-T. When a bit, in BA-S, is set due to a source tuple, the same bit in BA-T is checked. If the bit in BA-T is set, then the source tuple is retained for further processing; otherwise it is discarded. During the third subphase the source tuples which survive the checking process of the second subphase are left in the triplets (local broadcast STPF algorithms) or distributed among the PC triplets according to a hashing function (local hash STPF algorithms). During the fourth subphase, the source tuples within a triplet, received during the second phase, are stored in a random/sorted/hash table form. The PC's triplets execute the second, the third and the fourth subphases in a pipeline fashion with the tuple as the unit of the pipeline. When all the surviving source tuples of phase i are processed through the second, third and fourth subphases, then the fifth subphase is started.

During the fifth subphase, the join attribute value of every target tuple collected during the first subphase is checked against the encoded set of the source tuples' join attribute values. The index stored together with a typical target tuple is used by the CMP to check the boolean-array BA-S. If the corresponding bit, in BA-S, is not set, then, the target tuple is discarded. If the bit is set, then the tuple is (broadcast to)/(hashed to one of) the PC's triplets, for further processing. During the sixth subphase, every triplet join the target tuples which survive the BA-S checking with the source tuples received during the fifth subphase. Notice that the PC executes the fifth and the sixth subphases in a pipeline fashion with the tuple as the unit of the pipeline.

With a little modification, the naming convention adopted for the "global hash" basic algorithms can be used to name the various STPF equi-join algorithms. The word "basic" in the name of a "global hash" basic equi-join algorithm must be replaced by the word "STPF" to give the name of the corresponding STPF algorithm.

3.2.3 The STCF Equi-Join Algorithms

The algorithmic category STCF is comprised of twelve different algorithms. An STCF algorithm is comprised of two major phases, namely, the global filtering phase and the join phase. The objective of the global phase is to filter out many tuples from the source and target relations which are not needed for constructing the final result of the equi-join operation. The global filtering phase is followed by the join phase where one of the basic equi-join algorithms is used to join the source and target tuples which survive the filtering process of the "global filtering phase."

The global filtering phase common to all the STCF algorithms is carried out by one PC. This phase can be divided into three subphases. During the first subphase, the PC reads all the MACUs that store the relation with the smaller cardinality (call it the source relation), one MACU at a time, from the MSS into the PC's LMUs. As one MAUC unit is read, the PC's triplet processors, in parallel, encode the join attribute value of every tuple in the MACU. The encoding scheme involves a hashing function and the boolean-array BA-S initialized (only once for an equi-join operation), maintained and updated by the CMP. During the second subphase, the PC reads all the MACUs which store the target relation, one MACU at a time, from the MSS into the PC's LMUs. The PC's triplet processors encode the tuples' join attribute values. The encoding scheme involves the hashing function of the first subphase and the boolean-array BA-T, initialized, maintained and updated by the CMP. During this subphase, the tuples of the target relation are checked against the BA-S. The set of all the target tuples which survive this checking process (we refer to this set by the name "ftarget") are then stored in the mass storage subsystem (MSS), in MACU units.

During the third subphase, the tuples of the source relation are read again from the MSS and checked against BA-T. The set of all source tuples which survive this checking process (we refer to this set by the name "fsource") are then stored in the MSS, in MACU units.

During the join phase, one or more PCs are assigned to execute the physical join of the tuples of relations fsource and ftarget. The physical joining is carried out using one of the basic equi-join algorithms.

From the above presentation, it is easy to conclude that every algorithm in the STCF category is an extension of one of the algorithms in the basic category. Therefore, the same naming convention adopted for the basic algorithms can be used to name the STCF algorithms. However, in naming the STCF algorithms, an algorithm name needs to include the word "STCF" instead of the word "basic."

3.3 The Equi-Join Algorithms Memory Requirements

In order to support the equi-join algorithms, the LMU of a typical triplet must, at least, have three buffers. The first buffer stores the triplet's assignment from the source tuples (and the target tuples when executing a STPF algorithm) of one phase. This buffer is called the tuple buffer (BUFT). The second buffer stores the source or target tuples while being read from the parallel buffer. This buffer is called the input buffer (BUFI). The third buffer stores those tuples of the output relation waiting to be written into the parallel buffer. This buffer is called the output buffer (BUFO). BUFI and BUFO must have the capacity of a track of the system disk. An additional buffer with capacity equal to that of BUFI(BUFO) is needed if the tuple I/O is to be overlaped with the triplet's other activities.

To support the "global broadcast" equi-join algorithms, BUFT must have the capacity of NT tracks of the system disk. On the other hand, the "global hash" equi-join algorithms must have enough capacity to store the triplet's share from those tuples of the source relation (and the target relation when executing the STPF algorithms) which hash to a global bucket. Some small extra memory is needed, in each LMU, to support the algorithms' data structures (if any) and the communication between the CMP and its triplets.

The TPF, STPF and STCF equi-join algorithms require an additional storage space, in the CMP memory, to support the boolean-array(s).

4. Modeling the Proposed Equi-Join Algorithms

One of the most important objectives of this research is to study the performance of the proposed algorithms in carrying out the equi-join operation on MIRDM and to study the effectiveness of carrying out some tuning to the architecture of MIRDM. In this study, one of the most important measures to be used in evaluating the performance of an equi-join algorithm, is the algorithm's total execution time (TTIME). Within the context of MIRDM, the TTIME of an equi-join algorithm is the total time required to execute the algorithm on MIRDM assuming no overlapping between the activities of MIRDM different hardware units. There are two exceptions to the previous assumption, namely the activities of the different triplets are overlapped with each other, and the activities of moving (broadcasting) tuples over the TBUS of a PC completely overlap the activities performed by the cluster master processor [updating and checking the boolean array(s)]. To compute TTIME for the different equi-join algorithms, we have developed in [18] a set of analytical average-value probabilistic models, called the equi-join execution models. Each of them models the execution of an equi-join algorithm by MIRDM and allows the computation of the corresponding TTIME as a function of a large number of parameters, the model input parameters. In developing the equi-join execution models, the following basic assumptions have been made, namely:

1. The hardware of MIRDM consists of only MBC, one PC, one PB block and one moving-head-disk.
2. The MACU is a cylinder of the moving-head-disk. The disk is modified for parallel readout(write in) from(to) all the tracks of one cylinder.
3. A tuple of the source or target relation is equally likely to carry, in its join attribute, any value from the attribute's underlying domain.
4. All the hash functions, which are used by an equi-join algorithm, are ideal and statistically independent of one another. A hash function is ideal if it is equally likely to map a value

from its domain to any value in its range.

The set of input parameters of all the equi-join execution models can be grouped into three categories, namely, the data parameters, the hardware parameters and the hardware-algorithms parameters. These sets of parameters characterize the two relations participating in the equi-join operation, the hardware of MIRDM and the interaction between MIRDM hardware and the equi-join algorithms. The parameters within the data, hardware-algorithms and hardware categories together with their meanings and the values(s) which some of these parameters assume throughout our performance studies, are presented in Tables 4.1, 4.2 and 4.3, respectively. The assignment of value(s) to the individual input parameters is discussed in the next section.

The equations which relate the input parameters of every execution model to the model's output parameter TTIME have been derived and presented in [18]. The space limitation imposed on this paper as well as the fact that these derivations occupy many pages [3] prevents us from presenting them in this paper. However, the interested reader should refer to the previously mentioned reference.

Four computer programs, one for the execution models of every algorithmic category, have been written. These programs implement the equations developed for each equi-join execution model and are used next as a vehicle to carry out our performance studies.

5. Performance Studies

5.1 The Determination of the Best Performing Equi-Join Algorithm

In this section, the algorithm with the best performance in executing the equi-join operation on MIRDM, is determined. Throughout this process, the hardware input parameters of all models are kept constant at some assigned values; however, the rest of the input parameters are varied to study their effect on the choice of the best performing algorithm. The measure's TTIME and the number of hashing functions are used to evaluate the performance of the different equi-join algorithms. In general, the best performing algorithm among a set containing others over a range of a parameter value, is

[3] Although, the scheme used to present the proposed equi-join algorithms in Section 3 helped us in cutting down on the number of equations which had to be derived, nevertheless, modeling 42 different algorithms takes a lot of derivations.

Table 4.1 The Data Parameters

Name	Meaning	Value(s)
NTy	the cardinality of the relation y, where y ε{ S,T }	10^3-10^5 tuples
LTy	the tuple length of relation y, where y ε{ S,T }	100 bytes
LJ	the join attribute length	10 bytes
ND	the cardinality of the domain underlying the join attribute	---

Table 4.2 The Hardware-Algorithm Parameters

Name	Meaning	Value(s)
NBP	the number of buckets in a hash table of a triplet	---
NBIT	the number of bits in a boolean-array	---

Table 4.3 The Hardware Parameters

Name	Meaning	Value(s)
NP	the number of triplets within one PC (or the number of tracks within one cylinder of the moving-head disk)	15
NT	the ratio of BUFT Capacity and that of a disk track (positive integer)	1
MACUC	the capacity of an MACU	$.71 \times 10^{+6}$ bytes
TCD	time to directly compare the join attribute value of a source tuple with that of a target one	.02 ms
TH	time to calculate a hashing function with the tuple's join attribute value as the input argument	.102 ms
TEP	time to swap two pointers within the LMU of a triplet	.007 ms
Ty	time to move a tuple of relation y across the TBUS, where $y \in \{ S,T \}$	.1 ms
TDAC	the average access time of the system disk	16 ms
TSK	time for the moving-head disk to seek one track	3 ms
TDT	time to transfer an MACU between the system disk and the parallel buffer block	16.7 ms
TBT	time to transfer an MACU between the parallel buffer block and the triplets	16.7 ms

the one with the smallest values of TTIME over that range. However, if more than one equi-join algorithms have close TTIME values over that range, then, the best performing algorithm is the one with the minimum number of hash functions. The last criterion is adopted to compensate for the fact that in this study, the average behavior of the hash fuctions are considered and not their worst-case ones; moreover, to compensate for the fact that the overhead involved in handling the overflow phenomena associated with hashing functions are not considered either.

The values assigned to the hardware parameters (refer to Table 4.3) have been choosen to reflect the current state of art in hardware technology. The values of those hardware parameters that characterize the moving-head-disk (NP, MACUC, TDAC, TSK and TDT) are those of an IBM 3380 [19] moving-head-disk. The disk is assumed to be modified for parallel read(write) from(to) a whole cylinder. It is also assumed that this modification does not affect the disk transfer rate. The time to read(write) one track of the disk is taken as the value to read(write) the whole cylinder (TDT). It is also assumed that NT has the value of one and TBT has the same value as that of TDT.

In calculating the values of the hardware parameters that characterize the triplet (TC, TH, TMS, TMT, TMO and TEP), it is assumed that a triplet processor is an Intel 8086/1 microprocessor [20]. In general, a triplet parameter represents an operation carried out by the corresponding microprocessor. To calculate the value of such parameter, a procedure is written in the 8086 assembly language, which carries out the corresponding operation [18]. The execution times, obtained from the Intel 8086 microprocessor user's manual [20], for the instructions in the procedure are added up to obtain the value of the corresponding parameter.

The values of the parameters that characterize the TBUS (TS and TT) are calculated assuming that the TBUS has an effective bandwidth of 1 Mbytes. This is reasonable since such bus is within the current technology limits.

To reduce the number of variable[4] input parameters, we have assumed that both NTS and NTT have the same values. ND is to change indirectly by changing the ratio (NTS/ND). In [18], it is shown that throughout the ranges of NTS and [NTS/ND], one can assign values to the parameters NBP and NBIT using the following formulas:

---

[4] That is, variable with respect to this performance study.

$$NBP = \begin{cases} \text{Min}\left[\dfrac{NDD_{BP}}{4},\ \left\lceil FNBP \cdot \dfrac{NTS}{NMS \cdot NP}\right\rceil\right] & \text{for the global broadcast algorithms.} \\ \text{Min}\left[\dfrac{NDD_{BP}}{4},\ \left\lceil FNBP \cdot \dfrac{NTS}{NGB \cdot NP}\right\rceil\right] & \text{for the global hash algorithms.} \end{cases}$$

and

$$NBIT = \begin{cases} \text{Min}\left[\dfrac{NDD_{BI}}{4},\ FNBIT \cdot [NTS + NTT]\right] & \text{for all algorithms with one boolean-array.} \\ \text{Min}\left[\dfrac{NDD_{BI}}{4},\ FNBIT \cdot [NTS + NTT]/2\right] & \text{for all algorithms with two boolean-arrays.} \end{cases}$$

where NDD_{BP} and NDD_{BI} are functions of ND (together with some other input parameters). FNBP is the ratio of the number of buckets in a triplet's hash table and the triplet's expected number of source tuples per one phase of a basic equi-join algorithm and FNBIT is the ratio of the number of bits in the boolean-array(s) and the number of tuples in both the source and target relations, respectively. Both FNBP and FNBIT are related to the amount of storage allocated to a hash table and to the boolean-array(s), respectively.

The process of determining the best performing equi-join algorithm proceeds in two steps. In the first step, the performance of the algorithms within each category are analyzed and studied, under the variable input parameters, using the corresponding execution models. As a result of this step, the best performing algorithm within each category is selected. In the second step, the best performing algorithms within the algorithmic categories are compared together and the overall best performing one is determined.

The set of computer programs developed to implement the equi-join models are run for NTS(=NTT) ϵ $\{10^3-10^5\}$, NTS/ND ϵ $\{1, .1, .01\}$ and for many values of the parameters FNBP and FNBIT. The behavior of the TTIME for the algorithms within each equi-join algorithmic category is plotted against the parameter NTS(=NTT) for different values of the parameters NTS/ND, FNBP and FNBIT, in [18]. Based on these figures some interesting conclusions have been reached. First, beyond the value of 1, increasing the value of FNPB produces almost null improvement in TTIME of those equi-join algorithms that use the hash table technique at the triplet level. Second, at small values of NTS/ND (.1 - .01), the TTIME for the algorithms in the TPF, STPF and STCF categories decreases exponentially with increasing the value of the parameter FNBIT. However, as FNBIT increases beyond the value of 10, the relative improvement in TTIME decreases rapidly to zero. When the values of NTS/ND is relatively large ($\geq$ 1), the performance measure TTIME for the algorithms in the TPF, STPF and STCF categories, becomes independent of FNBIT. Third, is the fact that "which equi-join algorithm is the best performing one within its individual category" is a function of the parameters NTS/ND, NTS, FNBT and FNBIT.[5]

It is important to note that the parameter NTS/ND is directly related to the join probability between the tuples of the source and target relations. The source(target) join probability is defined as the probability that a tuple from the source(target) relation joins with at least one tuple from the target(source) relation. In this study, the source and target join probabilities have the same values.

Figures 5.1 through 5.3 display the performance measure TTIME of the best performing algorithms within each equi-join category, versus the parameter NTS(=NTT). The three figures correspond to the values 1, .1 and .01 of the parameter [NTS/ND]. In all of these figures, the parameters FNBP and FNBIT are fixed at the values of 1 and 10, respectively. Refering to Figures 5.1 through 5.3, one can make the following observations:

1. For large values of the parameter NTS/ND ($\sim$1), the algorithm HBS-basic is the overall best performing (see Figure 5.1). Any other algorithm is either having an inferior performance (HBS-STCF) or equal performance but requiring more overhead and storage (HBS-TPF and HBS-STPF).
2. For moderate values of the parameter NTS/ND ($\sim$ .1), the overall best performing algorithm is the BBS-TPF algorithm (see Figure 5.2). Any other algorithm is having either an inferior performance (HBS-basic, HBS-STPF when joining relations with large cardinalities and the HBS-STCF when joining relations with small cardinalities) or little performance advantage that does not justify the extra overhead these algorithms incur (HBS-STCF when joining relations with small cardinalities and HBS-STCF when joining relations with large cardinalities).
3. For small values of the parameter NTS/ND ($\sim$.01), the overall best performing equi-join algorithm is a function of the number

---

[5] The best performing algorithm within the basic category is a function of only the first three parameters.

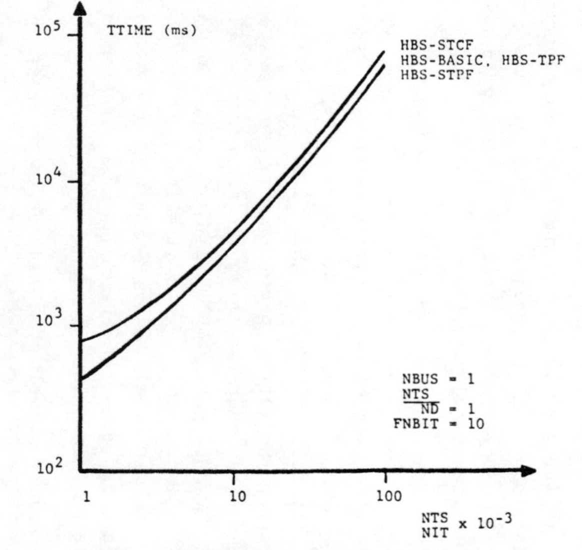

FIGURE 5.1 THE BEST PERFORMING EQUI-JOIN ALGORITHM WITHIN EACH ALGORITHMIC CATEGORY

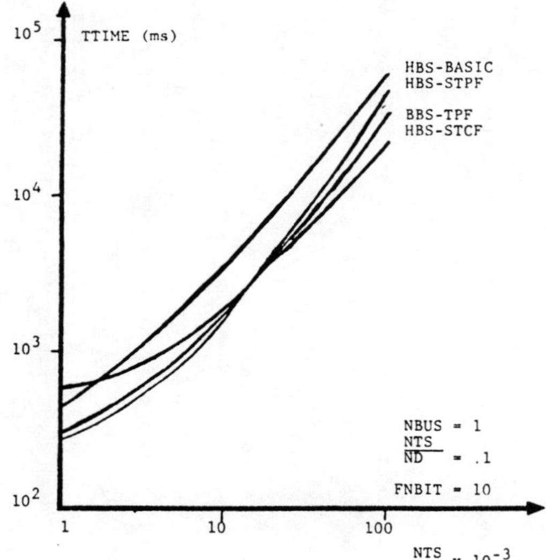

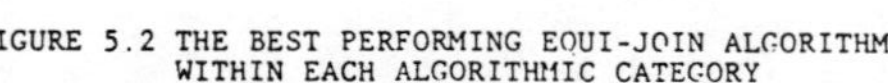
FIGURE 5.2 THE BEST PERFORMING EQUI-JOIN ALGORITHM WITHIN EACH ALGORITHMIC CATEGORY

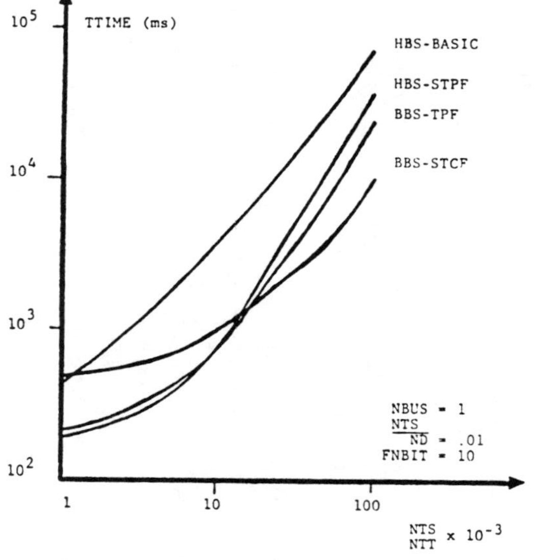

FIGURE 5.3 THE BEST PERFORMING EQUI-JOIN ALGORITHMS WITHIN EACH ALGORITHMIC CATEGORY

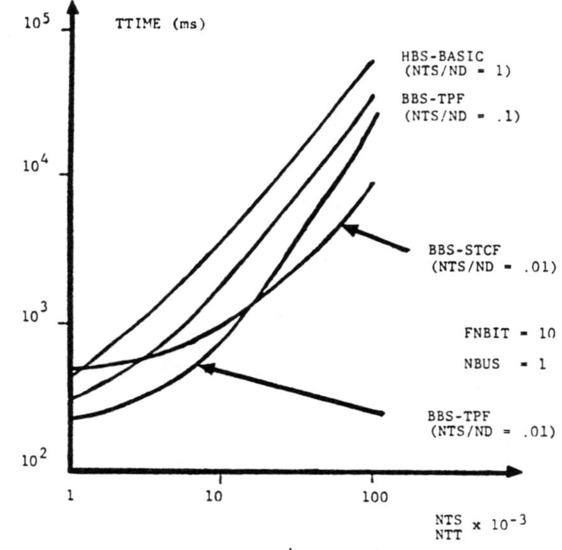

FIGURE 5.4 THE SELECTED EQUI-JOIN ALGORITHMS

of tuples participating in the operation (see Figure 5.3). For relations with small cardinalities [NTS(=NTT) < 15000 tuples], the overall best performing algorithm is BBS-TPF. On the other hand, the overall best performing algorithm for relations with large cardinalities (>15000 tuples) is BBS-STCF.

Based on the above observations, one can conclude that "which equi-join algorithm is the overall best performing one" is not unique. Each one of the algorithms HBS-basic, BBS-TPF and BBS-STCF score the best performance over different ranges of the parameters NTS and NTS/ND [refer to Figure 5.4]. The latter parameters characterize the relations which participate in the equi-join operation. By providing MIRDM with a simple optimizer to estimate the values of NTS and NTS/ND, the optimal algorithm to perform a given equi-join can be choosen and, thus the operation can be performed in the most cost-effective way.

Another important conclusion is the fact that both the "global hash" and the "boolean-array" techniques can individually be used to speed up the execution of the equi-join operation. However, the combination of both techniques to speed up the equi-join execution is not good since not much gain in speed up would result over that of the proper use of one of them.

5.2 The Effectiveness of Some Tuning to the Architecture of MIRDM

Recall that a processing cluster in MIRDM is organized as a set of triplets which intercommunicate, indirectly, over a single bus, the TBUS. During the modeling process of the various equi-join algorithms, it was felt that the adoption of this bus as the only path between the triplets, will not allow some equi-join algorithms to capture their full performance potential. These algorithms are those which use the local hash method to distribute the tuples of both the source and target relations among the triplets of a PC for processing. In general, this class of algorithms can benefit from a multipath communication structure among the triplets of the cluster that executes them.

In this section, the effectiveness of providing the triplets of the processing cluster in MIRDM with a multipath intercommunication structure is investigated. In particular, the addition of more buses, each similar in architecture, bandwidth and function to TBUS, is evaluated.

The addition of one or more buses to the PC does not affect the performance measure TTIME of those equi-join algorithms that use the local broadcast method. On the other hand, it affects the performance of those equi-join algorithms that use the local hash method. TTIME for the latter algorithms can be calculated using a slightly modified version of the corresponding models already developed for the one-bus organization. The modification to these models involves updating the equations which compute TTB, the time needed to communicate tuples between the triplets during the execution of an equi-join algorithm, to take into account the new multiple bus organization of PC. That is, the TTB of a "local hash" algorithm must be divided by NBUS, the number of TBUS'S in the new organization.

The TTIME for each one of the "local hash" equi-join algorithms has been computed using the corresponding modified execution model. These computations have been done, for NTS(=NTT) ϵ $\{10^3-10^5\}$, [NTS/ND] ϵ {1, .1, .01} and the values of 1 and 10 for the parameters FNBP and FNBIT, respectively. The values of the hardware parameters are kept as those presented in Table 4.3. In order to obtain an upper bound on the performance improvement, the parameter NBUS is assigned its highest value (NP). The plots of the TTIME versus NTS for the various "local hash" algorithms and for the different settings of the other parameters, revealed that the best performing algorithm within this group is also NTS and [NTS/ND] dependent. For NTS/ND $\sim$ .1, the best performing algorithm is BHS-TPF and for NTS/ND $\sim$ 1, the BHS-Basic is the best performing one. For NTS/ND $\sim$ .01, the best performing algorithm is a composite one. For relations with small cardinalities, the BHS-TPF algorithm is the best performing one. On the other hand, the best performing algorithm for relations with large cardinalities is the BHS-STCF.

In Figure 5.5, the performance parameter TTIME of the best performing equi-join algorithms is plotted for the case when NBUS=1. The same figure displays the TTIME of the "local hash" best performing algorithms for the case when NBUS=NP(=15). By referring to Figure 5.5, the following observations can be made.

1. For large values of the parameter NTS/ND ($\sim$1), or in the absence of a boolean-array, the adoption of the multiple bus organization together with the BHS-Basic algorithm improves substantially the performance of the equi-join over that executed on a single bus organization. However, this improvement becomes insignificant when joining relations with large cardinalities.
2. For moderate to small values of the parameter NTS/ND (< .1) the

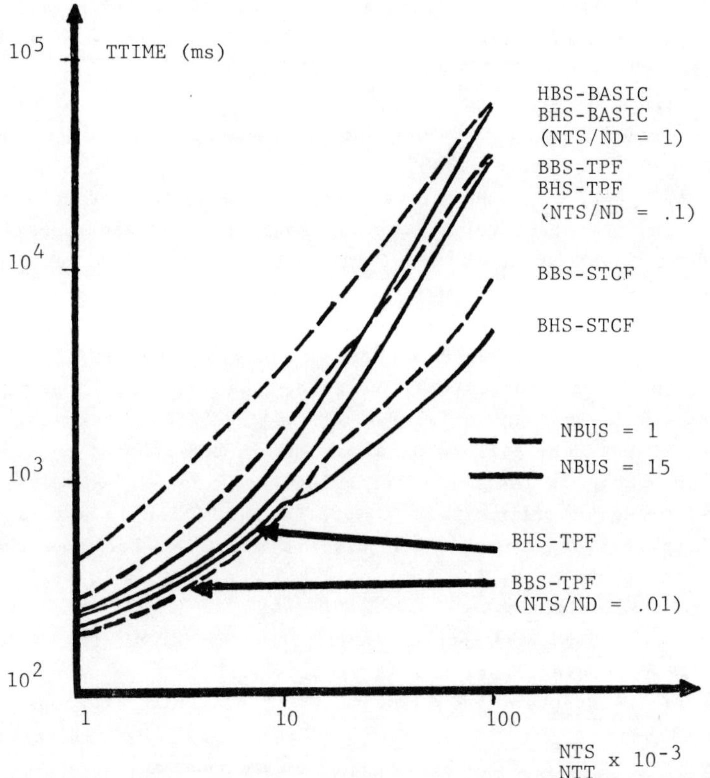

FIGURE 5.5 THE COMPARISON BETWEEN THE BEST PERFORMING ALGORITHMS ON THE TWO ARCHITECTURES

adoption of the multiple bus organization and the best performing local hash algorithm, results in slight improvement in the equi-join performance or none at all.

The above observations, coupled with the fact that most equi-join operations tend to have small values for the parameter NTS/ND (small number of tuples respond to the join operation) suggest that the single bus organization is more cost-effective in executing the equi-join operation, especially in the very large database environment.

6. Conclusion

The equi-join operation is one of the most important operations of the relational database systems. In this paper, a large set of parallel algorithms for implementing this operation on a multiprocessor relational database machine, called MIRDM, is presented. A probablistic average-value framework for modeling the proposed algorithms as well as MIRDM hardware organization, is also presented. A study for the performance of the proposed algorithms in carrying out the equi-join operation on MIRDM, is outlined. This study reveals that the best performing equi-join algorithm is not unique, and different algorithms score the best performance depending on the characteristics of the data participating in the equi-join operation.

References

[1] D. D. Chamberlin, A. M. Gilbert, and R. A. Yost, "A History of System-R and SQL/Data system," in _7th International Conference on Very Large Data Bases_, Cannes, France, Sept. 1981.

[2] M. Stonebreaker, E. Wong, and P. Kreps, "The Design and Implementation of INGRES," _ACM Trans. on Database Systems_, 1,3, Sept. 1976.

[3] E. A. Ozkarahan, S. A. Schuster and K. C. Smith," _RAP-An Associative Processor for Database Management_," AFIPS Proceedings, Vol. 45, 1975, pp. 379-387.

[4] J. Banerjee, D. Hsiao and K. Kannan, "DBC-A Database Computer for Very Large Databases," _IEEE Transaction on Computers_, Vol. C-28, No. 6, June 1979, pp. 414-429.

[5] E. Babb, "Implementing a Relational Database by Means of Specilized Hardware," _ACM Trans. on Database Systems_, Vol. 4, No. 1 (March 1979), pp. 1-29.

[6] G. J. Liposki, "Architectural Feature of CASSM: A Context Segment Sequential Memory," Proceedings of the Fifth Annual Symp. on Computer Architecture, Palo Alto, CA, April 1978, pp. 31-38.

[7] D. J. Dewitt, "DIRECT - A Multiprocessor Organization for Supporting Relational Database Management Systems," IEEE Trans. on Computers, Vol. C-28, No. 6, June 1979, pp. 395-408.

[8] G. Gardrain, "An Introduction to SABRE: A Multi-Microprocessor Database Machine," 6th Workshop on Computer Architecture for Non-Numeric Processing, Hyeres, France, June 1981.

[9] D. K. Hsiao and M. J. Menon, "Design and Analysis of a Multi-Backend Database System for Performance Improvements, Functionality Expantion and Capacity Growth (Part I and II)," Technical Reports, OSU-CISRC-TR- 81-81-7 and OSU-CISRC-TR-81-8, The Ohio State University, Columbus, Ohio, 1981.

[10] R. Epstein and P. Hawthorn, "Design Decisions for the Intelligent Database Machine," Proceedings of NCC4, AFIPS, 1980, pp. 237-241.

[11] J. R. Goodman, "An Investigation of Multiprocessor Structures and Algorithms for Database Management," Memo No. UCB/ERLM81 (May 1981), Electronic Research Lab., College of Engineering, Univ. of California/ Berkeley.

[12] G. Z. Qadah and K. B. Irani, "A Database Machine for Very Large Relational Databases," Proceedings of the International Conference on Parallel Processing, August 23-26, 1983, pp. 307-314.

[13] E. F. Codd, "A Relational Model of Data for Large Shared Databanks," Comm. ACM, Vol. 13, No. 1, June 1970, pp. 377-387.

[14] D. Bitton, et al., "Parallel Algorithms for the Execution of Relational Database Operations," ACM Trans. on Database Systems, Vol. 8, No. 3, September 1983, pp. 324-353.

[15] P. Valduriez and G. Gardarin, "Join and Semijoin Algorithms for a Microprocessor Database Machine," ACM Trans. on Database Systems, Vol. 9, No. 1, March 1984, pp. 133-161.

[16] D. B. Friedland, "Design, Analysis, and Implementation of Parallel External Sorting Algorithms," Computer Science Technical Report #464, University of Wisconsin-Madison, January 1982.

[17] D. E. Knuth, The Art of Computer Programming, Vol 3: Sorting and Searching," Addison-Wesley, Reading, Mass., 1973.

[18] G. Z. Qadah, "A Relational Databases Machine: Analysis and Design," Ph.D. Thesis, 1983. The Electrical and Computer Engineering Department, the University of Michigan, Ann Arbor.

[19] IBM Corporation, "IBM 3380 DIRECT Access Storage Description and User's Guide," IBM Document GA26-1664-0, File No. 51370-07, 1980.

[20] Intel Corporation, "iupx86, 88 User's Manual," July 1981.

[21] H. Schweppe, H. Zeidler, W. Hell, H. Leilich, G. Stiege and W. Teich, "RDBM--A Dedicated Multiprocessor System for Database Management," Advanced Database Architecture, Prentice-Hall, 1983, pp. 36-86.

A TECHNIQUE FOR ANALYZING QUERY EXECUTION IN A MULTIPROCESSOR DATABASE MACHINE

F. CESARINI
Dipartimento di Sistemi e Informatica
v. S.Marta, 3 - 50139 Firenze (Italy)

F. PIPPOLINI
IAMI - CNR
viale Morgagni, 67/a - 50134 Firenze (Italy)

G. SODA
Dipartimento di Sistemi e Informatica
v. S. Marta, 3 - 50139 Firenze (Italy)

ABSTRACT

In this paper a methodology for representing and evaluating the execution of relational queries by a multiprocessor data base machine (DBM) is presented. The starting points are the parallel algorithms implementing the relational operators in the DBM in question and the query to be executed. A structure, called query execution graph, is obtained by the analysis of this information. A query execution graph is the detailed description of the operations the DBM must carry out in order to execute the query. A procedure for computing the execution cost of the query is given. This procedure operates on the query execution graph and also takes into account the strategy used to allocate processors to the subqueries which can be executed in parallel.

1. INTRODUCTION

During the past years several Data Base Machines (DBM) have been proposed. They have mainly been designed to answer complex relational queries better than conventional Data Base Systems do. They refer to multiprocessor architectures designed to execute requests in parallel.

In order to evaluate the performance of a DBM design, the analysis of query execution can be performed by following a number of approaches.

Simulation /BOD81, CDS83, SSS83/ and queueing analysis /STV83/ seem to be very attractive since they allow us to model many aspects of the machine in detail, including parallelism capability, and to represent congestion phenomena explicitly. On the other hand, simulation is intrinsically very expensive because of the number of experiments to be performed and the duration of the single runs; queueing analysis requires adapting the reality to solvable models and it can involve considerable effort and the necessity of forming many simplifying assumptions.

Other approaches /OSS77, DEH81, SHZ84/ make a sort of deterministic analysis of query execution in order to establish formulas which give the value of the selected performance index as function of the processed data and of the DBM hardware characteristics. Such an approach is less expensive than the above ones but presents some limits, mainly because situations which are typically dynamic are expressed by means of fixed parameters, for example the presence of specific data in a cache memory is usually globally expressed by a constant cache hit ratio. Moreover, congestion phenomena can not be adequately represented. In spite of these limits, we can obtain significant results which allow us to compare different architectures or execution algorithms. This is especially useful in making preliminary analysis. The significance of the results naturally depends on an accurate and systematically carried on analysis.

From this point of view, recent papers /BBD83, VAG84/ about the analysis and comparison of different algorithms for executing relational operations on a specific DBM architecture are particularly interesting. They examine the execution of parallel algorithms in a multiprocessor cache system.

The analysis of an algorithm is performed by following a static approach, i.e., its execution is decomposed a priori into a sequence of steps and each step is associated with a cost which represents its execution time. The sum of these costs is the index used for evaluating the performance of the algorithm and it is called execution cost. When a step is composed of n parallel equal operations, the cost associated with the step is the execution time of a single operation, c, if the number p of processors devoted to the step execution allows the parallel execution of all the operations, i.e., if $p>=n$; otherwise the cost is $(n/p)c$. We can note that this kind of analysis considers one relational operation at a time and the number of processors available for its execution is maintained constant from the first to the last step.

In this paper we want to extend the above approach to evaluating the execution cost of relational query trees, i.e., of relational queries whose execution is represented by trees, where the nodes are the relational operations to be executed to answer the query and the tree structure gives their execution order.

A query tree represents explicitly the possibility of executing different relational operations in parallel. Therefore, it introduces a further level of parallelism with respect to the above mentioned analysis. In this context, the distribution of the available processors to parallel relational operations is a crucial point, since it substantially affects the performance of the query execution. Processor allocation must take into account both their parallelism or precedence relationship in the query tree, and the nature of the algorithms themselves, especially their degree of parallelism and the amount of work required for their execution.

We propose to represent the execution of query trees by means of directed graphs which allow us to define these concepts formally on the basis of the graph structure and the costs associated with the nodes. Therefore, parameters useful for formulating processor allocation criteria can be derived from the analysis of the graph.

The execution cost of a graph is also defined. If the graph represents a single relational operation, the definition of the execution cost coincides with the approach used in the previous analysis. Otherwise, it extends this approach to more complex situations.

In section 2 we propose a technique for representing parallel algorithms. The way the DBM executes a given query is described in section 3. The description results from combining information given by both the parallel algorithms and the query itself. We call "query execution graph" the structure we represent it with. Section 4 contains some definitions, properties and operations regarding query execution graphs. We define the cost of query execution graphs in section 5. The cost is defined by considering a processor partition criterion, i.e., a criterion used for assigning the available processors to the subqueries which can be executed in parallel. Three examples of processor partition criteria are given in section 6. In section 7 we give an example in which we apply our proposed strategy to a given query.

2. HARDWARE AND SOFTWARE CAPABILITY OF THE DBM

When the performance of a DBM has to be evaluated, two different types of parameters must be considered: the workload parameters (WLPs) and the DBM parameters (DBMPs). WLPs are concerned with the description of both the data and transactions to be considered in performance evaluation process. DBMPs refer to the description of the hardware and software capabilities of the DBM. As far as the DBM architecture is concerned, we deal with the MultiProcessor-Cache System (MPCS) described in /BBD83/. We outline its main aspects in the following subsection. In the other subsection we propose a methodology for representing the parallel algorithms used by the DBM.

2.1 MULTIPROCESSOR ORGANIZATION

The MPCS we refer to is shown in figure 1 and it consists of the following:

(1) a set of general-purpose processors;

(2) a number of mass storage devices;

(3) an interconnection device connecting the processors to the mass storage devices via a high-speed cache.

The processors operate independently and are responsible for executing relational operations. One processor acts as a controller which coordinates the activities of the other processors. The processors form a MIMD machine.

The memory hierarchy is divided into three levels. The disk devices are at the bottom level; the disk cache is in the middle; the internal memories of all the processors are at the top. The page is the unit of data transfer occurring between all levels of the hierarchy. The top two levels of the memory hierarchy are connected via an interconnection device having the following two properties:

- the contents of a page can be broadcasted to any number of processors;

- several processors can read or write different pages in the cache memory simultaneously.

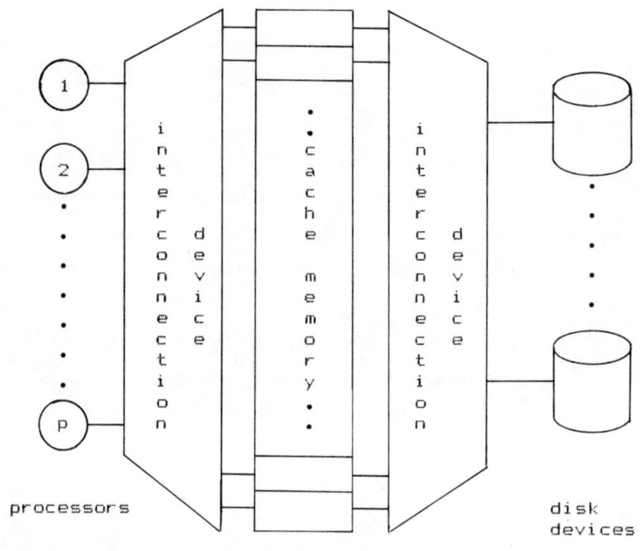

Figure 1

The hardware architecture of the MPCS is described by a set of parameters concerning all aspects of the computation (processing, communication and I/O costs) and by a set of parameters describing the actual configuration of the system (such as number of processors).

As far as the physical organization of data is concerned, relations are represented as flat files and no indices are used as tools for implementing complex relational queries. A set of appropriate parameters must be used for describing the characteristics of the data.

2.2 PARALLEL ALGORITHMS REPRESENTATION

When a DBM has been designed, the physical organization of data is defined and a set of data primitives (such as, sending a message and sorting or reading a page) referring to data organization is defined by using the basic DBM operations. For example, this approach is used in /BBD83, VAG84/.

We assume that any data primitive is constituted by elementary operations carried out by a single processor (e.g., transferring a page from the cache to a processor memory, comparing two attributes, etc.). The cost of each data primitive is defined as a function of the parameters which characterize the DBM hardware. This cost must take into account all the aspects of the computation, including processing, communication and I/O.

The parallel algorithms for relational data base operations are defined by using some of the data primitives in an appropriate order. The data primitives to be executed in parallel must also be indicated.

The number of times each data primitive will be executed cannot be known when the algorithm is defined. It can depend on the quantity of data operated on by the algorithm or on the number of available processors. For example, reading a relation of n pages requires n executions of the "read a page" data primitive. n is a parameter whose actual value can be known only when the algorithm is executed on an actual data base relation.

We suggest describing a parallel algorithm as a <u>definition pseudo graph</u> (DPG).

A formal definition of DPGs can be found in appendix B. Here we want to point out that a DPG is the description of the parametric definition of an algorithm. An example of DPG is in figure 2.

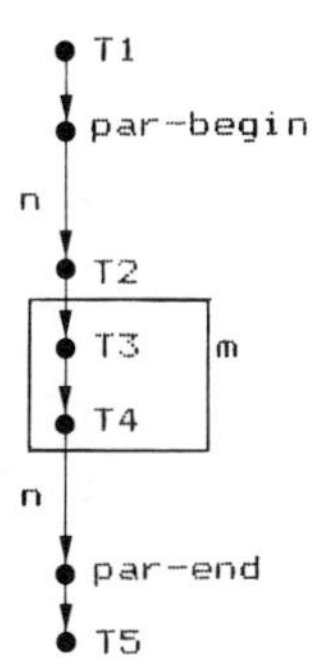

Figure 2

An arc from Ti to Tj means that Tj must be executed after executing Ti. The box containing T3 and T4 means that sequence T3, T4 must be executed m times. The nodes par-begin and par-end denote the beginning and the end of a parallell execution. The parameter n means that n parallel executions of the path between T1 and T5 must be executed after T1 and before T5.

We note that m and n are parameters. Their actual value will be determined when the algorithm is executed. In this way, a DPG describes the structure of the algorithm and which data primitives have to be executed. A DPG depends on the amount of data to be processed only in a parametric way.

When we consider the execution of a relational operator on some given data by a given DBM configuration, the definition pseudograph must be transformed into an <u>execution graph</u> (EG). An EG is obtained from a DPG by considering the present values of the parameters appearing in DPG. Hence an EG describes which and how many data primitives really have to be carried out. In this way, only well-defined execution graphs are referred to during the performance evaluation process.

We can cite as an example the DPGs of parallel algorithms for Join, Select and Project in appendix C. The algorithms are derived from /BBD83/. The data primitives considered when defining the parallel algorithms can be found in appendix A.

3. QUERY EXECUTION GRAPHS

The representation of relational queries as trees and the procedure transforming query trees into query execution graphs are outlined. This procedure takes execution graphs defined by the query itself into account.

3.1 QUERY TREES

In the approach we propose, relational queries are represented as query trees (see figure 3). The nodes describe the relational operators to be performed for answering the query; the leaves describe the relations that the relational operators must operate on. The tree structure describes the execution order of the relational operators. The numbers associated with the relations are their sizes in pages. The numbers associated with the operators are the sizes of the resulting relations.

For example, the query shown in figure 3 requires the execution of a select operation on a file of 500 pages; the result is a 50-page relation which is then joined with relation A, constituted by 100 pages. The Join operator produces a 5-page relation to be projected so as to obtain the final result constituted by 3 pages.

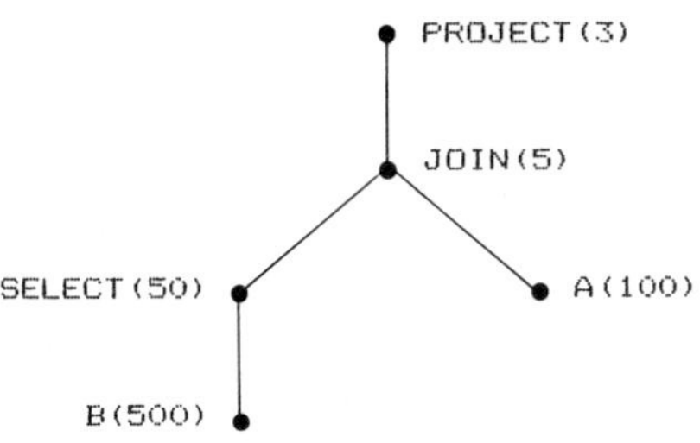

Figure 3

We consider Select-Join-Project queries in the way that we suppose that only one project operation is performed on the result obtained by the application of select and join operations.

3.2 THE TRANSFORMATION PROCEDURE

During the performance evaluation process we propose to refer to a _query execution graph_. A query execution graph is obtained from a query tree by means of the t-procedure.

We remark that we start from queries represented as trees. Optimization criteria may be taken into consideration only if they maintain a tree representation of the query /ULL80/.

t-procedure

1) Define the execution graphs of the relational operators involved in the query tree Q. This means defining the present values of the parameters appearing in the definition graphs by using the information about the quantity of data to be processed by the relational operators.

2) Delete the leaves from Q so as to obtain a new tree Q′ where the leaves are relational operators.

3) Connect the root of Q′ with a special node called _query stop_ and a special node called _query start_ with all the leaves of Q′.

4) Substitute the relational operators in Q′ with the corresponding execution graphs.

The nodes in a query execution graph are a complete description of which and how many data primitives have to be executed for evaluating the given query. The arcs give the information about the execution order of the data primitives and about where it is possible to use MIMD parallelism. In particular, the query start node points out the possibility of evaluating the query by starting out from the parallel execution of several relational operators.

4. PROPERTIES OF QUERY EXECUTION GRAPHS

Let B be the set of DBM data primitives. A relational query is processed by executing a number of data primitives following certain precedence relationships. In other words, the primitives executed during query processing are partially ordered. Furthermore, we assume that a "start" operation is executed at the beginning and a "stop" operation is executed to complete the query. For this reason, we represent the execution of a relational query Q by means of a directed acyclic graph, with a source and sink node, called _query execution graph_.

Let T={T1, T2, ..., Tn} be the set of the nodes of the graph. The nodes Ti belong to set B and an arc from Ti to Tj means that Tj must be processed only after processing Ti. We say that Ti (Tj) is an _immediate predecessor_ (_immediate successor_) of Tj (Ti). We note that if there are m arcs from Ti to Tj ... Tj+m-1, these m data primitives can be executed by m processors in parallel.

We say that Th (Tk) is a _predecessor_ (successor) of Tk (Th) if T1, T2,...Tm exist such that T1=Th, Tm=Tk and Ti is an immediate predecessor of Ti+1, i=1...m-1. For each Ti, we call _Pred(Ti)_ the set of all the predecessors of Ti, and we call _Succ(Ti)_ the set of all the successors of Ti.

Nodes Ti and Tj are _independent_ if neither Ti precedes Tj nor Tj precedes Ti. The _width_ of a graph G, w(G), is the maximum size of any set {T1,...Tm} where Ti is independent from Tj for i,j=1...m, where i is not equal to j.

Given graph G, a _closed subgraph_ S is a subgraph of G, with source a(S) and sink b(S), constituted by all, and only all, the nodes which are both predecessors of b(S) and successors of a(S). We call H(S) the set of all the possible paths from a(S) to b(S).

A path from Th to Tk is unique if each node in the path (except Th and Tk) has only one immediate predecessor and only one immediate successor. A graph G with source a(G) and sink b(G) is irreducible if all the paths from a(G) to b(G) are unique.

A node Ti is a separator node if set T-{Ti} can be partitioned into two subsets, T′ and T" (possibly empty), so that T′=Pred(Ti) and T"=Succ(Ti).

Let us now define two operations on a graph G.

v-split(G). Let a(G) and b(G) be the source and sink nodes of G. Let T1...Tm be the immediate predecessors of b(G). If m >= 2 and the sets {Pred(Ti)-a(G)}, i=1...m, are mutually disjoint, the graph G is v-splitable. If G is v-splitable, the result of the v-split operation is constituted by m closed subgraphs G1...Gm, so that a(G) is the source of all of them and Ti is the sink of Gi.

h-split(G). Let T1...Tk be the separator nodes of graph G, where Ti precedes Ti+1, i=1...k-1. If k >= 3, then graph G is h-splitable. If G is h-splitable, the result of the h-split operation is constituted by the closed subgraphs G1...Gk-1, where Gi is the subgraph with source a(Gi)=Ti and sink b(Gi)=Ti+1.

A graph G is separable if all closed subgraphs with more than three nodes are v-splitable or h-splitable.

Let us consider the graph in figure 4 for illustrating these definitions.

T1 and T12 are the source and sink nodes, respectively. T2 is an immediate predecessor of T8 and T8 is an immediate successor of T2. T2 and T4 are independent nodes. The width of the graph is 4, i.e. the size of the set {T2, T4, T5, T6}. The subgraph consisting of the nodes T1, T2, T3, T4, T5, T6, T7 and T8 is closed but it is not irreducible. The subgraph with source T3 and sink T7 and the subgraph with source T8 and sink T12 are closed and irreducible. T1, T8 and T12 are separator nodes and the graph is h-splitable. Two closed subgraphs result from the h-split operation; namely the closed subgraph with source T1 and sink T8 and the closed subgraph with source T8 and sink T12. The subgraph with source T1 and sink T8 is v-splitable. The result of the v-split operation is constituted by the subgraph with source T1 and sink T2 and the subgraph with source T1 and sink T7. Since also the subgraph with source T3 and sink T7 and the subgraph with source T8 and sink T12 are v-splitable the graph is separable.

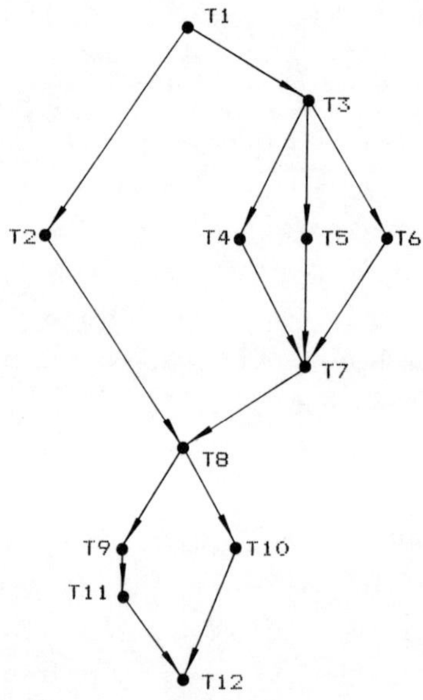

Figure 4

We note that, when the execution graphs for relational operators are irreducible, the query execution graph G obtained by applying the t-procedure to a query tree Q is separable.

The execution graphs of the algorithms we use are irreducible.

5. EXECUTION COST OF SEPARABLE GRAPHS

Let the cost c(Ti) be associated with each node Ti of the graph G. Without losing any degree of generality, we can assume c(Ti)>=1. The cost of a path h from Ti to Tj is the sum of the costs associated with the nodes in the path.

The cost c(G,p) of executing a irreducible graph G with source a(G) and sink b(G) by p processors is :

c(G,p)=(w(G)/p) x max c(h) , for h belonging to H(G), if w(G)>p;

c(G,p)=max c(h) , for h belonging to H(G), if w(G)<=p.

From now on, we refer to the concept of <u>p-processor-partition criterion</u>. This is a rule used for assigning subsets of available processors to the parallel execution of given subgraphs. We note that the number of processors assigned to the execution of a subgraph is assumed to be constant during its entire execution. This approach is consistent with the assumption of executing an irreducible graph by means of a constant number of processors.

The cost C(G,p) of executing a graph G by p processors is given by the following procedure:

<u>C-procedure</u>

If G is irreducible then C(G,p)=c(G,p);

if G is h-splitable then

C(G,p) = c(a(G)) + SUM(C(Gi,p) - c(a(Gi)))

where Gi are the graphs obtained by applying the h-split operation to G;

if G is v-splitable then

C(G,p) = c(b(G)) + max C(Gi,pi)

where Gi are the graphs obtained by applying the v-split operation on G, and pi are the constants obtained by applying a p-processor-partition criterion.

6. PROCESSOR PARTITION CRITERIA

We propose three heuristic allocation criteria in order to show how the concepts of parallelism and work amount can be both expressed by some precise characteristics of the query execution graphs and used in formulating the criteria.

Let G be v-splitable and G1...Gm be the graphs resulting from the v-split of G.

Let p be the number of processors to be used for executing G.

<u>Criterion A</u>

Let p1...pm values such that

SUM pi=p and pi=k x w(Gi)

where k is constant; now we give a procedure for evaluating w(G) when G is separable.

w-procedure

If G is irreducible then

w(G) is the number of immediate successors of a(G);

if G is h-splitable then

w(G)=max w(Gi)

where Gi are the graphs obtained by applying h-split on G;

if G is v-splitable then

w(G)=SUM w(Gi)

where Gi are the graphs obtained by applying v-split on G.

Criterion B

Let p1...pm values such that

SUM pi=p and pi=k x e(Gi)

where k is constant and e(G) is given by the following procedure.

e-procedure

If G is irreducible then

e(G)=c(a(G))+c(b(G))+w(G) x max(c(h)-c(a(G))-c(b(G)))

for h belonging to H(G);

if G is h-splitable then

e(G)=max e(Gi)

where Gi are the graphs obtained by applying h-split on G;

if G is v-splitable then

e(G)=c(a(G))+c(b(G))+SUM(e(Gi)-c(a(Gi)))

where Gi are the graphs obtained by applying v-split on G.

Criterion C

Let p1...pm values such that

SUM pi=p and pi=k x q(Gi)

where k is constant and q(Gi) is given by the following procedure.

q-procedure

If G is irreducibile, then

q(G)=c(a(G))+c(b(G))+w(G) x max(c(h)-c(a(G)-c(b(G)))

for h belonging to H(G);

If G is h-splitable then

q(G)=c(a(G))+SUM(q(Gi)-c(a(Gi)))

where Gi are the graphs obtained by applying h-split on G;

If G is v-splitable then

q(G)=c(a(G))+c(b(G))+SUM(q(Gi)-c(a(Gi))).

Criterion A is based on considering the maximum degree of parallelism in the execution of the Gi subgraphs. The number of processors varies according to the request of parallelism.

Criterion B is based on considering the maximum request of parallel computations by the Gi subgraphs. In other words, both the number of possible parallel operations and their cost are taken into consideration.

Criterion C is based on considering the total amount of computation requested by the Gi subgraphs.

The computational complexities of mentioned criteria are linear in the number of irreducible subgraphs. Each irreducible subgraph is taken into consideration only once during the execution of the procedures. The computations on an irreducible subgraph are linear in the number of nodes in the subgraph.

7. AN EXAMPLE

Let us now consider the query tree in figure 5 as a basis for an example of the approach we propose.

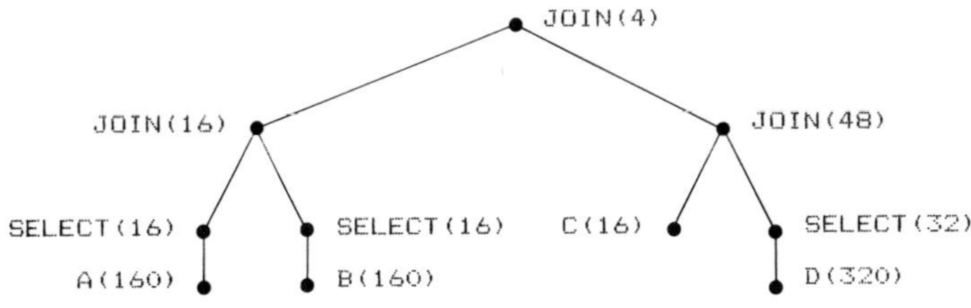

Figure 5

The query execution graph resulting from the application of the t-procedure is illustrated in figure 6 where, for the sake of simplicity, the execution graphs of relational operators are represented in a synthetic way. They can be derived by the definition graphs found in appendix B.

The present widths of the subgraphs are the following: w(S1)=160, w(S2)=160, w(S3)=320, w(J1)=32, w(J2)=16, w(J3)=48.

If we have mc(G) = max c(h) for h belonging to H(G), then

mc(S1)=57.71 msec mc(S2)=57.71 msec mc(S3)=57.71 msec

mc(J1)=2029 msec mc(J2)=1910.2 msec mc(J3)=1692.4 msec

Each mc(G) corresponds to the cost of executing a path in the execution graph G of a relational operator. They are obtained by using the costs reported in appendix A.

Let us now apply the cost evaluation algorithm to the QEG in figure 6.

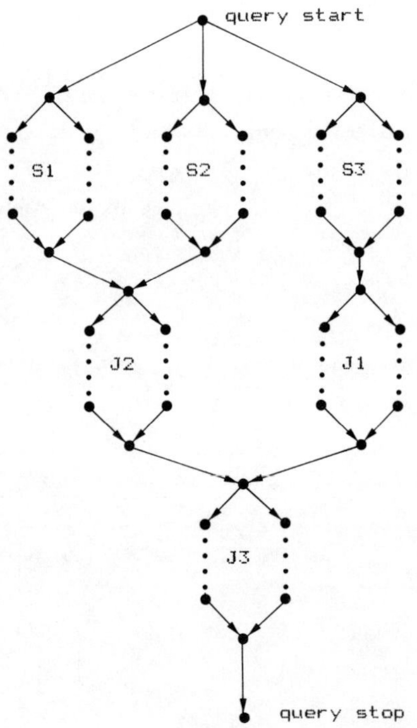

Figure 6

First of all the h-split operation is applied so as to obtain the three subgraphs of figure 7.

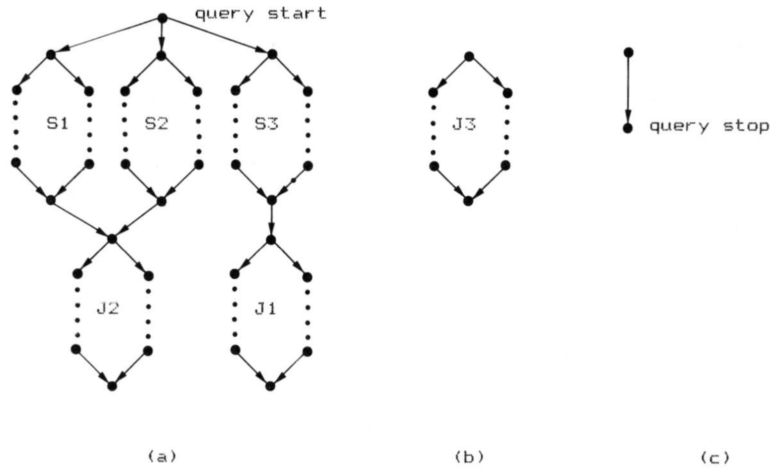

Figure 7

The (b) and (c) subgraphs are irreducible. Hence the v-split operation is applied to (a) subgraph and the subgraphs of figure 8 are obtained.

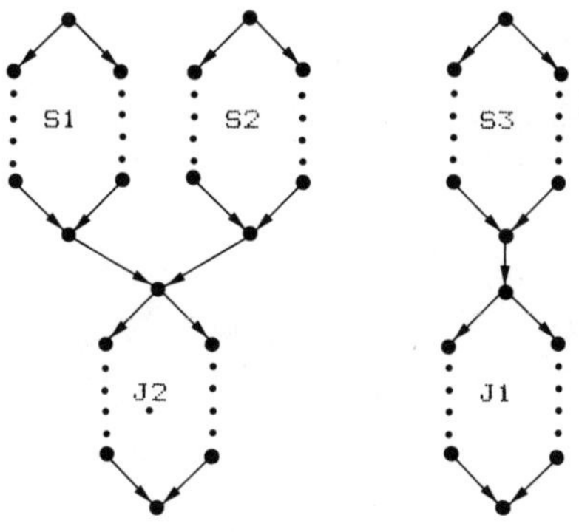

Figure 8

It is possible to proceed in a similar way until all possible irreducible subgraphs are obtained.

The corresponding cost function is:

C(G,p)=max(max(C(S1,pS1);C(S2,pS2))+C(J2,pJ2);C(J1,pJ1)+C(S3,pS3))+
C(J3,pJ3)

where pJ3=p; pS3=pJ1; pS1+pS2=pJ2; pS1+pS2+pJ1=p.

It can be noted that the costs of the query start, query stop, select start, select stop, join start and join stop nodes are considered negligible with respect to the costs of the data primitive nodes.

As far as the processor partition criteria are concerned, we have the following results:

criterion A	criterion B	criterion C
pS1+pS2=pJ2=0.5p	pS1+pS2=pJ2=0.32p	pS1+pS2=pJ2=0.37p
pJ1=pS3=0.5p	pJ1=pS3=0.68p	pJ1=pS3=0.63p
pS1=0.25p	pS1=0.16p	pS1=0.185p
pS2=0.25p	pS2=0.16p	pS2=0.185p
pJ3=p	pJ3=p	pJ3=p

where p is the total number of processors.

The costs, in seconds, of the query execution by 16, 32, 48, 64 processors are shown in table 1. The costs in Appendix A are associated with the data primitives when computing the costs in table 1.

p	16	32	48	64
criterion A	15.5	7.75	5.17	4.30
criterion B	14.65	7.32	4.88	4.49
criterion C	13.35	6.68	4.64	4.38
criterion S	13.35	7.63	6.40	6.20

Table 1

The query execution costs obtained by means of another processor allocation criterion S are reported in table 1. It consists in evaluating the relational operators which appear in the query one at a time. All the processors are assigned to carry out one operator in parallel. In the case of criterion S, the costs are sensitive only to intra-relational operator parallelism.

Criterion A is always the worst one, but the case p=64 where it becomes the best.

Criterion C is always better than all the other criteria, but the case p=64 where it is slightly worse than criterion A.

Criterion S is our datum-criterion. We can see that it works worse as the number of processors increases, and it is better than some other criteria only for low numbers of processors.

When the total number of processors is less than the widths of all the relational operators in the query, the processors are always busy even if one relational operator at a time is executed. It means that inter-relational operator parallelism does not give any benefit with respect to intra-relational operator parallelism.

Presently we are investigating the relationships between the criteria and the particular graph structure we have examined; the goal is to obtain some general rules for determining the most appropriate criterion for a given query.

8. CONCLUSIONS

This paper deals with a strategy for evaluating parallel execution of complex relational queries by a multiprocessor DBM. The approach we use is sensitive both to the parallel algorithms designed for the DBM and the processor allocation strategy used during the query execution. As far as parallel algorithms are concerned, they have been widely and profoundly analyzed one at a time. Our main efforts have been devoted to obtaining a suitable way of representing algorithm execution when several relational operators are executed in parallel to answer a given query. The way the DBM does this is represented by a query execution graph. The nodes in the query execution graph represent the data primitives of the DBM. When a cost is given for each data primitive, we give a procedure for computing the execution cost of the query. It is possible to use this cost in order to compare the performance of different algorithms for relational operators when the parallel evaluation of subparts of given queries is being investigated. Another goal could be to compare different processor allocation strategies.

In the present paper the analysis of query execution assumes static processor allocation criteria, i.e., the subset of processors assigned to the execution of a query subtree cannot migrate from the subtree to another one until its execution is completed. In spite of their limits, static criteria remain appropriate when their induced overhead is compared with that of more sophisticated dynamic criteria. Now we want to investigate if the proposed technique can be used when taking other kinds of processor allocation criteria into account. In particular we want to remove the above constraint by means of allowing the processors to migrate from a subtree to another one.

APPENDIX A - DATA PRIMITIVES

The data primitives we refer to in the DPGs of relational operators are listed in this appendix. A cost is associated with each data primitive. It is obtained by evaluating a function according to appropriate parameters. The parameters are related to the functional characteristics of the hardware configuration actually taken into consideration. The costs are computed by means of the formulae and the parameter values given in /BBD83/. We refer to these costs when evaluating the execution cost of a given query (section 7).

Read request - A read request moves a page into a processor memory from the cache, fetching it from mass storage if necessary. The cost is: Cr = 50.2 msec.

Write request - A write request moves a page from a processor memory to the cache, if a free page frame is available, or otherwise to the mass storage. The cost is: Cw = 64.2 msec.

Merge - The tuples of two sorted pages are merged. The cost is: Cm = 51.2 msec.

Scan - The tuples of a page are scanned in order to select the tuples matching a given predicate. The cost is: Cs = 1.1 msec.

Sort - The tuples of a page are sorted. The cost is: Cso = 173.4 msec.

APPENDIX B - SYNTAX AND SEMANTICS OF DEFINITION PSEUDO GRAPHS

Now we are going to define the syntax and the semantics of definition pseudo-graphs (DPG) of relational operators.

SYNTAX

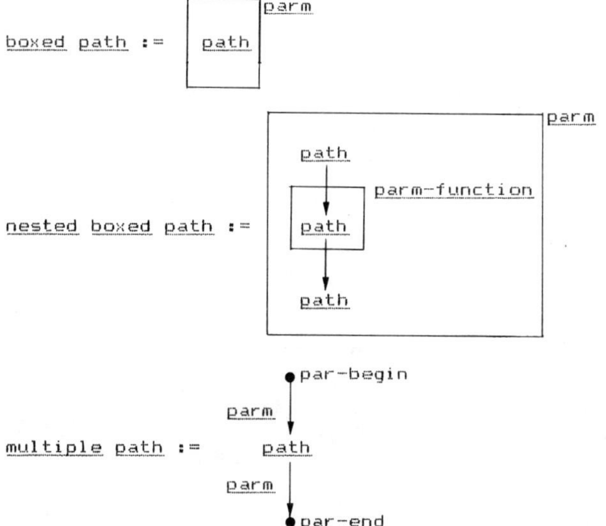

parm := all the parameters taken into consideration

parm-function := all the possible functions defined on the parameters

data primitive := all the data primitives taken into consideration

SEMANTICS

The main element of any DPG is a path included between a start node and a stop node.

A path is a concatenation of several different constituting elements. Each of them is basically defined on data primitives associated with nodes.

A multiple path means that parm parallel paths must be considered between the two utmost nodes denoting the beginning and the end of the parallel execution (the two parms must be equal).

A boxed path means that the path must be repeated, in a sequential way, parm times.

A nested boxed path means that parm different paths must be concatenated; the i-th path is obtained by repeating the path in the inner box ki times between the two paths described in the outer box. Each ki is obtained by applying the parm function to the values 1,2,...,parm.

APPENDIX C - DEFINITION PSEUDOGRAPHS

The definition pseudographs of the Join, Select and Project operations are reported in this Appendix. The pseudographs represent the algorithms described in /BBD83/.

Join operation

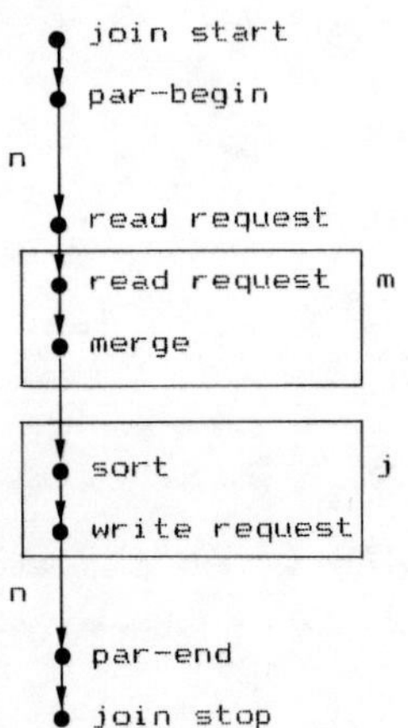

We refer to the parallel nested-loops Join algorithm. Let n and m be the sizes, in pages, of the relation R and R′ to be joined; we assume n >= m. j is the join selectivity factor and indicates the average number of pages produced by the join of a single page of R with a single page of R′.

Select operation

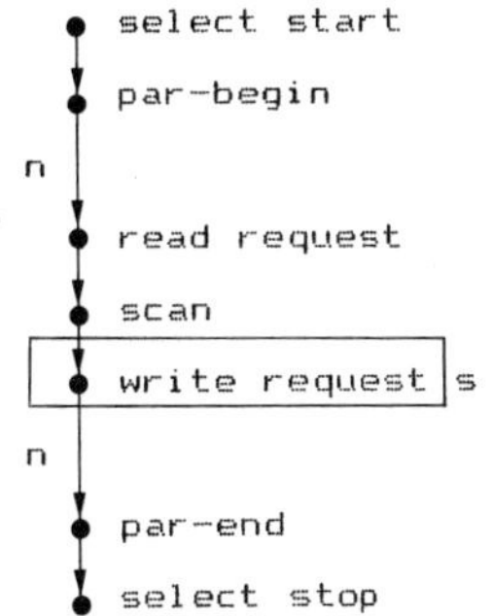

n is the size, in pages, of the relation R to be selected. All the pages in R are scanned to obtain the tuples which satisfy the selection predicate. s is the select selectivity factor.

Project operation

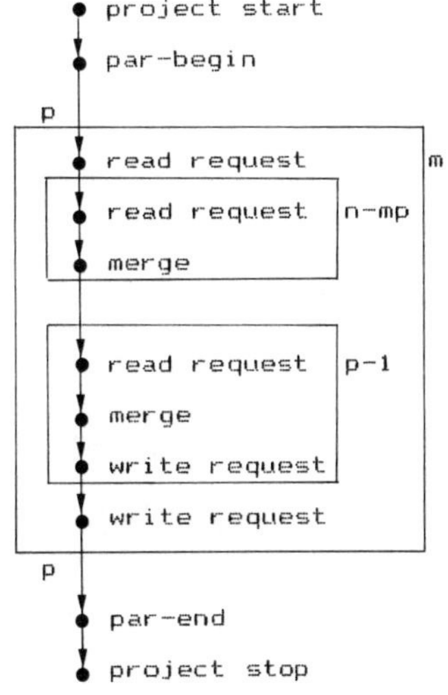

Let p be the number of processors used to perform the project operation. n is the number of pages to be projected. m = n/p is the number of distinct phases involved in executing the algorithm.

REFERENCES

/BBD83/ D. Bitton, H. Boral, D.J. DeWitt and W.K. Wilkinson: Parallel Algorithms for the Execution of Relational Database Operations, ACM TODS, Vol. 8, n.3, Sept. 1983.

/BOD81/ H. Boral, D.J. DeWitt: Processor Allocation Strategies for Multiprocessor Data Base Machine, ACM TODS, Vol. 6, n.2, June 1981.

/CDS83/ F. Cesarini, D. De Luca and G. Soda: An Assessment of the Query-Processing Capability of DBMAC, in "Advanced Database Machine Architecture", D.K. Hsiao Ed., Prentice-Hall, 1983.

/DEH81/ D.J. DeWitt, P.B. Hawthorn: A Performance Evaluation of Data Base Machine Architectures, Proc. 7th Int. Conf. on VLDB, Cannes, 1981.

/OSS77/ E.A. Ozkarahan, S.A. Schuster and K.C. Sevcik: Performance Evaluation of a Relational Associative Processor, ACM TODS, Vol.2, n.2, June 1977.

/SHZ84/ R.K. Shultz, R.J. Zingg: Response Time Analysis of Multiprocessor Computers for Database Support, ACM TODS, Vol. 9, n.1, March 1984.

/SSS83/ G. Schiffner, P. Scheuermann, S. Seehusen, H. Weber: On a Specification and Performance Evaluation Model for Multicomputer Database Machines, Proc. of 3rd Int. Workshop on Database Machines, Munich, Sept. 1983.

/STV83/ S. Salza, M. Terranova and P. Velardi: Performance Modeling of the DBMAC Architecture, Proc. of 3rd Int. Workshop on Database Machines, Munich, Sept. 1983.

/ULL80/ J.D. Ullman: Principles of Database Systems, Computer Science Press, Maryland, 1980.

/VAG84/ P. Valduriez, G. Gardarin: Join and Semijoin Algorithms for a Multiprocessor Database Machine, ACM TODS, vol. 9, n.1, March 1984.

PERFORMANCE EVALUATION OF A DATABASE SYSTEM IN MULTIPLE BACKEND CONFIGURATIONS

Steven A. Demurjian and David K. Hsiao
Department of Computer Science
Naval Postgraduate School
Monterey, CA 93943

Douglas S. Kerr
Dept. of Computer and Info. Science
The Ohio State University
Columbus, OH 43210

Jai Menon
IBM San Jose Research Lab
San Jose, CA 95193

Paula R. Strawser
IBM T. J. Watson Research Center
Yorktown Heights, NY 10598

Robert C. Tekampe
Marine Corps Development and
Education Command
Quanico, VA 22134

Robert J. Watson
Headquarters, Marine Corps
Washington, D. C. 20380

Joel Trimble
Office of Naval Research
Arlington, VA 22217

ABSTRACT

The aim of this performance evaluation is twofold: (1) to devise benchmarking strategies for and apply benchmarking methodologies to the measurement of a prototyped database system in multiple backend configurations, and (2) to verify the performance claims as projected or predicted by the designer and implementor of the multi-backend database system known as MBDS.

Despite the limitation of the backend hardware, the benchmarking experiments have proceeded well, producing startling results and good insights. By collecting macroscopic data such as the response time of the request, the external performance measurements of MBDS have been conducted. By collecting microscopic data such as the time entering and leaving a system process, the internal performance measurements of MBDS have been carried out. Methodologies for construction test databases, directories, and requests have been devised and utilized. The performance evaluation studies verify that (a) when the database remains the same the response time of a request can be reduced to nearly half, if the number of backends and their disks is doubled; (b) when the response set of a request doubles, the response time of the query remains nearly constant, if the number of backends and their disks is doubled. These were the performance claims of MBDS as predicted by its designer and implementor. It should be noted that these results are preliminary and focused on retrievals as we are moving MBDS to more modern backend hardware, with a larger number of backends (, say, ten), and for more intensive and exhaustive testing.

1. INTRODUCTION

The multi-backend database system (MBDS) is a database system designed specifically for capacity growth and performance enhancement. MBDS consists of two or more minicomputers and their dedicated disk systems. One of the minicomputers serves as a controller to broadcast the requests to and receive the results from the other minicomputers, which are configured in a parallel manner and are termed as backends. All the backend minicomputers are identical, and run identical software. The database is evenly distributed across the disk drives of each backend by way of a cluster-based data placement algorithm unknown to the user. User access to the MBDS is accomplished either via a host computer, which in turn communicates with the MBDS controller, or with the MBDS controller directly. Communication between the controller and backends is accomplished using a broadcast bus. An overview of the system architecture is given in Figure 1.

There are two basic performance claims of the multi-backend database system, which have been projected in the original design goals [Hsia81a, Hsia81b]. The first claim states that if the database size remains constant, then the response time of requests processed by the system is inversely proportional to the multiplicity of backends. This claim implies that by increasing the number of backends in the system and by replicating the system software on the new backends, MBDS can achieve a reciprocal decrease in the response time for the same requests. The second claim states that the response time of requests is invariant when the response set and the multiplicity of backends increases in the same proportion. This claim implies that when the database size grows, the response set for the same requests will

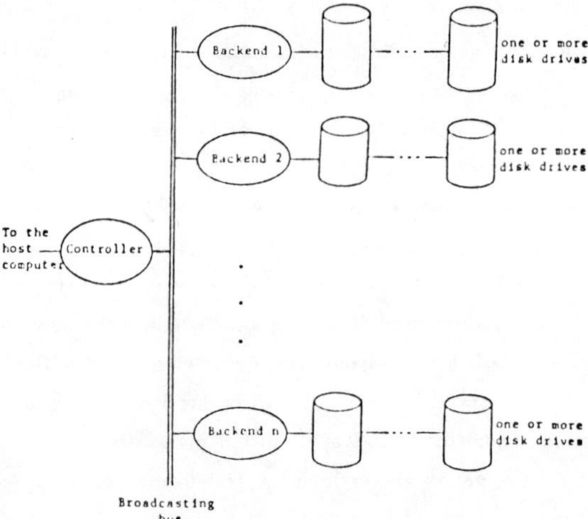

Figure 1. The Multi-Backend Database System

grow. By increasing the number of backends accordingly, MBDS can maintain a constant response time.

In this paper we provide a preliminary evaluation of the validity of the MBDS performance claims. The main focus of this paper is on the external performance measurement of MBDS. The external performance measurement evaluates a system by collecting the response times of requests. External performance measurement is a macroscopic evaluation of the system. Ingres, Oracle, and the Britton-Lee IDM/500, have all been evaluated using external performance measurement techniques [Bitt83, Stra84, Schi84]. We also seek to provide some insight into the internal performance of MBDS. Internal performance measurement provides a microscopic view of a system, by collecting the times of the work distributed and performed by the system components.

The remainder of this paper is organized as follows. In Section 2 we provide a brief overview of the multi-backend database system. In Section 3 we discuss the general testing strategy that was used to evaluate the system. In Section 4 we examine the evaluation results. Finally, in Section 5 we conclude this paper and summarize the results.

2. THE MULTI-BACKEND DATABASE SYSTEM (MBDS)

The current hardware configuration of MBDS consists of a VAX-11/780 (VMS OS) running as the controller and two PDP-11/44s (RSX-11M OS) running as backends. Intercomputer communication is supported by three parallel communication links (PCL-11Bs), which is a time-divisioned-multiplexed bus. The implementation efforts are documented in [Kerr82, He82, Boyn83a, Demu84]. MBDS is a message-oriented system (see [Boyn83b]). In a message-oriented system, each process corresponds to one system function. These processes, then, communicate among themselves by passing messages. User requests are passed between processes as messages. The message paths between processes are fixed for the system. The MBDS processes are created at the start-up time and exist throughout the entire running time of the system.

In the rest of this section we begin by discussing the data model of MBDS, the attribute-based data model. Then, we present a brief review of the attribute-based data language (ABDL) of MBDS by focusing on the retrieve request only. Next, we discuss the directory structure used in the system, since it plays an integral role in the specification of the test database (see Section 3). Lastly, we overview the execution of a RETRIEVE request, to provide a general overview of the structure and the operation of MBDS.

2.1. The Attribute-Based Data Model

In the attribute-based data model, data is modeled with the constructs: database, file, record, attribute-value pair, directory keyword, directory, record body, keyword predicate, and query. Informally, a *database* consists of a collection of files. Each *file* contains a group of records which are characterized by a unique set of directory keywords. A *record* is composed of two parts. The first part is a collection of *attribute-value pairs* or *keywords*. An attribute-value pair is a member of the Cartesian product of the attribute name and the value domain of the attribute. As an example, <POPULATION, 25000> is an attribute-value pair having 25000 as the value for the population attribute. A record contains at most one attribute-value pair for each attribute defined in the database. Certain attribute-value pairs of a record (or a file) are called the *directory keywords* of the record (file), because either the attribute-value pairs or their attribute-value ranges are kept in a *directory* for addressing the record (file). Those attribute-value pairs which are not kept in the directory for addressing the record (file) are called non-directory keywords. The rest of the record is textual information, which is referred to as the *record body*. An example of a record is shown below.

(<FILE, Census>, <CITY, Monterey>, <POPULATION, 25000>,
{ Temperate climate })

The angle brackets, <,>, enclose an attribute-value pair, i.e., keyword. The curly brackets, {,}, include the record body. The first attribute-value pair of all records of a file is the same. In particular, the attribute is FILE and the value is the file name. A record is enclosed in the parenthesis. For example, the above sample record is from the Census file.

The database is accessed by indexing on directory keywords using *keyword predicates*. A keyword predicate is a tuple consisting of an attribute, a relational operator (=, !=, >, <, ⩾, ⩽), and an attribute value, e.g., POPULATION ⩾ 20000 is a keyword predicate. More specifically, it is a greater-than-or-equal-to predicate. Combining keyword predicates in disjunctive normal form characterizes a *query* of the database. The query

(FILE = Census and CITY = Monterey) or
(FILE = Census and CITY = San Jose)

will be satisfied by all records of the Census file with the CITY of either Monterey or San Jose. For clarity, we also employ parentheses for bracketing predicates in a query.

2.2. The Attribute-Based Data Language

MBDS is designed to perform the primary database operations, INSERT, DELETE, UPDATE, and RETRIEVE. Additionally, an aggregate operation (i.e., AVG, COUNT, SUM, MIN, or MAX) may be applied when using the RETRIEVE operation. Users access MBDS through the host computer or the controller by issuing a request. A *request* is a primary operation along with a qualification. A *qualification* is used to specify the information of the database that is to be performed by the primary operation. A user may wish to treat two or more requests as a *transaction*. In this situation, MBDS executes the requests of the transaction without permuting them, i.e., if T is a transaction containing the requests R1 R2, then MBDS executes the request R1 before the request R2. Finally, we define the term *traffic-unit* to represent either a single request or a transaction in execution.

Now, let us examine the retrieve request, the main focus of our study in this paper. An example of a retrieve request would be:

RETRIEVE ((FILE = Census) and (POPULATION > 10000)) (CITY)

which retrieves the names of all those cities in the Census file whose population is greater than 10000. Notice that the *qualification* component of a retrieve request consists of two parts: the *query* which specifies records of the database to be retrieved and the *target list* which specifies the attribute-value(s) to be returned to the user. Aggregate operators may be applied to attributes listed in the target list. In this example, there is the query of two predicates ((FILE = Census) and (POPULATION > 10000)) and the target list (CITY).

2.3. The Directory Tables

To manage the database (often referred to as user data), MBDS uses directory data. Directory data in MBDS corresponds to attributes, descriptors, and clusters. An attribute is used to represent a category of the user data; e.g., POPULATION is an attribute that corresponds to actual populations stored in the database. A *descriptor* is used to describe a range of values that an attribute can have; e.g, (10001 < POPULATION < 15000) is a possible descriptor for the attribute POPULATION. The descriptors that are defined for an attribute, e.g., population ranges, are mutually exclusive. Now the notion of a *cluster* can be defined. A cluster is a group of records such that every record in the cluster satisfies the same set of descriptors. For example, all records with POPULATION between 10001 and 15000 may form one cluster whose descriptor is the one given above. In this case, the cluster satisfies the set of a single descriptor. In reality, a cluster tends to satisfy a set of multiple descriptors.

Directory information is stored in three tables: the Attribute Table (AT), the Descriptor-to-Descriptor-Id Table (DDIT) and the Cluster-Definition Table (CDT), examples of which are given in Figure 2. The *Attribute Table* maps directory attributes to the descriptors defined on them. A sample AT is depicted in Figure 2a. The *Descriptor-to-Descriptor-Id Table* maps each descriptor to a unique descriptor id. A sample DDIT is given in Figure 2b. The *Cluster-Definition Table* maps descriptor-id sets to cluster ids. Each entry consists of the unique cluster id, the set of descriptor ids whose descriptors define the cluster, and the addresses of the records in the clusters. A sample CDT is shown in Figure 2c Thus, to access the user data, we must first access directory data via the AT, DDIT, and CDT.

In designing the test database, one of the key concepts is the choice of the directory attributes in order to determine the necessary descriptors and therefore clusters. Thus, we provide a brief introduction to the three classifications of descriptors. A *type-A* descriptor is a

Attribute	Ptr
POPULATION	•
CITY	•
FILE	•

Figure 2a. An Attribute Table (AT)

$0 \leqslant$ POPULATION $\leqslant$ 50000	D11
$50001 \leqslant$ POPULATION $\leqslant$ 100000	D12
$100001 \leqslant$ POPULATION $\leqslant$ 250000	D13
$250001 \leqslant$ POPULATION $\leqslant$ 500000	D14
CITY = Cumberland	D21
CITY = Columbus	D22
FILE = Employee	D31
FILE = Census	D32

Dij: Descriptor j for attribute i.

Figure 2b. A Descriptor-to-Descriptor-Id Table (DDIT)

Id	Desc-Id Set	Addr
C1	{D11,D21,D31}	A1,A2
C2	{D14,D22,D32}	A3

Figure 2c. A Cluster-Definition Table (CDT)

Figure 2. The Directory Tables

conjunction of a less-than-or-equal-to predicate and a greater-than-or-equal-to predicate, such that the same attribute appears in both predicates. For example, ((POPULATION $\geqslant$ 10000) and (POPULATION $\leqslant$ 15000)) is a type-A descriptor. A *type-B* descriptor consists of only an equality predicate. (FILE = Census) is an example of a type-B descriptor. Finally, a *type-C* descriptor consists of the name of an *attribute*. The type-C attribute defines a set of type-C sub-descriptors. *Type-C sub-descriptors* are equality predicates defined over all unique attribute values which exist in the database. For example, the type-C attribute CITY forms the type-C sub-descriptors (CITY=Cumberland) and (CITY=Columbus), where "Cumberland" and "Columbus" are the only unique database values for the CITY.

2.4. The Execution of a Retrieve Request

In this section, we describe the sequence of actions for a retrieve request as it moves through MBDS. The sequence of actions will be described in terms of the messages passed between the MBDS processes. The MBDS controller processes are Request Preparation (REQP), Insert Information Generation (IIG), and Post Processing (PP). The MBDS backend processes are Directory Management (DM), Record Processing (RECP) and Concurrency Control (CC). For completeness, we describe the actions which require data aggregation.

First the retrieve request comes to REQP from the host computer or the controller itself. REQP sends out three messages. The first two messages are sent to PP: the number of requests in the transaction and the aggregate operator of the request. The third message is broadcasted by REQP to DM in all of the backends. The message is the parsed transaction, i.e., the traffic unit. DM sends the type-C attributes needed by the request to CC. Since type-C attributes may create new type-C sub-descriptors, the type-C attributes must be locked by CC. Once an attribute is locked and descriptor search can be performed, CC signals DM. DM will then perform Descriptor Search on (m/n) predicates, where m is the number of predicates specified in the query, and n is the number of backends. DM then signals CC to release the lock on that attribute. DM will broadcast the descriptor ids for the request to the other backends. DM now sends the descriptor-id groups for the retrieve request to CC. A *descriptor-id group* is a collection of descriptor ids which define a set of clusters needed by the request. Descriptor-id groups are locked by CC, since a descriptor-id group may define a new cluster. Once the descriptor-id groups are locked and Cluster Search can be performed, CC signals DM. DM will then perform Cluster Search and signal CC to release the locks on the descriptor-id groups. Next, DM will send the cluster ids for the retrieval to CC. CC locks cluster-ids, since a new address may be generated for an existing cluster. Once the cluster ids are locked, and the request can proceed with Address Generation and the rest of the request execution, CC signals DM. DM will then perform Address Generation and send the retrieve request and the addresses to RECP. Once the retrieval has executed properly, RECP will tell CC that the request is done and the locks on the cluster ids can now be released. The retrieval results are aggregated by each backend and forwarded to PP. PP completes the aggregation after it has received the partial results from every backend. When PP is done, the final results will be sent to the user.

3. THE BENCHMARK STRATEGY

In this section we analyze the basic benchmark strategy for the preliminary performance evaluation of the multi-backend database system. The benchmark strategy focuses on collecting macroscopic and microscopic measurements on the systems performance.

Macroscopic measurements correspond to the external performance measurement of the system, which collects the response time of requests that are processed by the system. Internal performance measurement involves the detailed measurement of the working processes of the system. In particular, we are measuring the time taken to process a particular message in MBDS. Each MBDS process has a group of functions, called message-handlers, that control and oversee the processing of a message. The time spent in a particular message-handler is collected in internal performance measurement.

To adequately conduct both the internal and external performance measurement of the system, software was developed to collect timing information and data. The performance software was bracketed in conditional compilation statements to facilitate an easy transition between a testing system and a running system. We constructed two software bases of the MBDS. The first consisted of the MBDS code and only the testing software required for external performance measurement. The second had the testing software for both the internal and external performance measurement software compiled in. We hope to use the difference in timings collected from the two bases to calculate the overhead incurred by the addition of internal performance measurement software.

The rest of this section is organized as follows. First, we give a high-level description of the test database organization and system configurations used in the performance evaluation. Next, we present a detailed discussion of the test database organization. Third, we examine the request set used to collect the timings. Finally, we review the relevant tests that are to be conducted, and the measurement statistics that are collected and calculated.

3.1. The Test Database Organization and Testing Configurations

To properly evaluate a database system, various record sizes need to be used. The sizes are chosen based on the size of the unit of disk management. In MBDS, this is the block. MBDS processes information from the secondary memory using a 4Kbyte block. Given a blocksize of 4Kbytes, it was recommended to construct the database with record sizes of 200 bytes, 400 bytes, 1000 bytes, and 2000 bytes [Stra84]. This gives a range of 2 to 20 records per block. Since we are engaged in only the first test of MBDS, we limited the scope of the testing to a database with a 200 byte record size.

In addition the virtual and physical memory limitations of each backend restricted the database size to a maximum of 1000 records per backend. This limitation, coupled with the two software versions of the system and the need to verify the two performance claims, led us to the specification of five different system configurations for the MBDS performance measurements. Table 1 displays the configurations.

Tests A.E, B.E, and C.E are conducted without internal performance software in place. Test A.E configures MBDS with one backend and one thousand records in the test database.

TEST	No. of Backends	Records/Backend	Database Size
A.E	1	1000	200K bytes
B.E	2	500	200K bytes
C.E	2	1000	400K bytes
A.I	1	1000	200K bytes
B.I	2	500	200K bytes

Table 1. The Measurement Configurations

Test B.E configures MBDS with two backends and one thousand records split evenly between the backends. The transition from Test A.E to Test B.E is used to verify the first performance claim (see Section 1). Test C.E also configures MBDS with two backends, but, the size of the database is doubled to two thousand records. The transition from Test A.E to Test C.E is used to verify the second performance claim (see Section 1). Test A.I and B.I are conducted with internal performance software in place. Test A.I configures MBDS with one backend and one thousand records in the test database. Test B.I configures MBDS with two backends and one thousand records split evenly between the backends. The transitions from A.E to A.I and from B.E to B.I are used to determine the overhead incurred by the addition of internal performance measurement software. Overall, using these five configurations, the verification of the MBDS performance and capacity claims is simplified and the performance measurement methodology of computing the internal measurement overhead is facilitated.

3.2. The Detailed Test Database Organization

We have chosen the test record size to be 200 bytes. The 200-byte record minimizes the primary memory required to store the record template. In actuality, a record of 198 bytes is used. The record consists of 33 attributes, each requiring 6 bytes of storage. The record template is used to specify the attributes, both the directory and the non-directory attributes, of the record. Of the 33 attributes listed (see Figure 3), INTE1 and INTE2 are directory attributes. MULTI and STR00 to STR29 are non-directory attributes.

The descriptor types and the descriptor ranges for the two directory attributes, INTE1 and INTE2, must also be defined. The values for INTE1 are classified by using five type-A descriptors, each of which represents a range of 200, i.e., the ranges would be [1,200], [201,400], ..., [801,1000], where [a,b] is used to represent the type-A descriptor range. The values for INTE2 are also classified by using type-A descriptors. The first twenty-three ranges for INTE2 cover 40 values, with the last range covering 80 values, i.e., the type-A descriptor ranges would be [1,40], [41,80], ..., [881,920], [921,1000]. The INTE2 descriptor ranges are not uniform.

Attribute Name	Attribute Type
INTE1	integer
INTE2	integer
MULTI	string
STR00	string
STR01	string
.	.
.	.
.	.
STR29	string

Figure 3. The Record Template

Next, we examine the records which are generated and stored in the test database. INTE1 and INTE2 have identical value, i.e., numbers, being the next sequential number after the previous record, starting at 1. Therefore, the one thousandth record would have the (INTE1, INTE2) pair set to 1000. The MULTI attribute, which is of the type of character string, is set to One for a database of only 1000 records. The intent of this attribute is to increase the number of records per cluster in the database. This is done by setting MULTI to Two, Three, etc., for each (INTE1, INTE2) pair in the database. Therefore, to double the size of the database, every (INTE1, INTE2) pair will have an associated MULTI attribute with values of One and Two. The remaining attributes, STR00 to STR29, are set to Xxxxx as fillers for the rest of the record body. Figure 4 depicts the general layout of the file for 1000 records where MULTI is set to One.

The cross-product of INTE1 ranges and INTE2 ranges has resulted in the specification of 24 descriptor groups for the INTE1 and INTE2 attributes. Coupled with the record template, they generate a test database that contains 24 clusters. The first 23 clusters contain 40 records each. The last cluster contains 80 records. To maintain consistency in the retrieval requests (discussed in the next section), we avoid any requests that access the last 80 records in the test database using the INTE2 attribute.

INTE1	INTE2	MULTI	STR00	STR01	...	STR29
1	1	One	Xxxxx	Xxxxx	...	Xxxxx
2	2	One	Xxxxx	Xxxxx	...	Xxxxx
.	.	.	.	.	.	.
.	.	.	.	.	.	.
.	.	.	.	.	.	.
1000	1000	One	Xxxxx	Xxxxx	...	Xxxxx

Figure 4. The Generated Records

3.3. The Request Set

The request set used for our performance measurement is given in Figure 5. The retrievals are a mix of single or double predicate requests. Since the majority of the work done on a database is to retrieve data, we limit our first measurements to only retrieve requests. In every request, 1/2 of the target attribute values for each record is returned. The first request is for only two records from two separate clusters. The second request retrieves 1/4 of the database. Seven of the 24 clusters must be examined. All records in each of the first six clusters are retrieved. Only 1/4 of the seventh cluster, defined by the INTE2 range from 241 to 280, is retrieved. In the third request, 1/2 of the database is retrieved. Thirteen of the 24 clusters must be examined. All records in each of the first twelve clusters are returned. Only 1/2 of the thirteenth cluster, defined by the INTE2 range from 481 to 520, is retrieved. The system searches only for records having values in the INTE2 range from 481 to 500 in this cluster.

The entire database is examined in the fourth request. The fifth request retrieves 2/5 of the database. The query is divided into two predicates, to obtain all records from the first five clusters, and the last four clusters. The sixth request is a retrieval of 4/5 of the database. Again the query is divided into two predicates, to obtain all records from the first 10 clusters, and the last nine clusters.

The seventh and eighth requests are similar in intent. The seventh request examines 10 clusters, requiring only 1 record to be retrieved from the 6th cluster and needing all records from the first five clusters. The eighth request examines 15 clusters, requiring only 1 record to be retrieved from the 11th cluster and needing all records from the first ten clusters. The ninth and final request is similar to the fifth request. But unlike the fifth request, ten additional clusters must be examined. Only two of the records with INTE1 values of 201 and 801, are retrieved from the ten additional clusters. All records in the remaining nine clusters,

Request Number	Retrieval Request
1	(INTE1 = 10) or (INTE1 = 230)
2	(INTE2 $\leqslant$ 250)
3	(INTE2 $\leqslant$ 500)
4	(INTE1 $\leqslant$ 1000)
5	(INTE1 $\leqslant$ 200) or (INTE1 $\geqslant$ 801)
6	(INTE1 $\leqslant$ 400) or (INTE1 $\geqslant$ 601)
7	(INTE1 $\leqslant$ 201)
8	(INTE1 $\leqslant$ 401)
9	(INTE1 $\leqslant$ 201) or (INTE1 $\geqslant$ 800)

Figure 5. The Retrieval Requests

like the fifth request, are also obtained by this retrieval. Table 2, a presentation of the number of clusters examined versus the percent of the database retrieved, is a synopsis of the previous discussion in tabular form.

3.4. The Measurement Strategy, Statistics and Limitations

The basic measurement statistics used in the performance evaluation of MBDS is the response time of request(s) that are processed by the database system. The *response time* of a request is the time between the initial issuance of the request by the user and the final receipt of the entire request set for the request. The response times are collected for the request set (see Figure 5) for each of the five configurations (see Table 1). Each request is sent a total of ten times per database configuration. The response time of each request is recorded. We determine that ten repetitions of each request produce an acceptable standard deviation. Upon completion of the ten repetitions for a request, we calculate the mean and the standard deviation of the ten response times. There are two main statistics that we calculate to evaluate the MBDS performance claims, the response-time improvement and the response-time reduction.

The *response-time improvement* is defined to be the percentage improvement in the response time of a request, when the request is executed in n backends as opposed to one backend and the number of records in the database remains the same. Equation 1 provides the formula used to calculate the response-time improvement for a particular request, where Configuration B represents n backends and Configuration A represents one backend. The response-time improvement is calculated for the configuration pairs (A.E, B.E) and (A.I, B.I), respectively. The configuration pair (A.E, B.E) is evaluated for the retrieve requests (1)

Request Number	Number of Clusters Examined	Volume of Database Retrieved
1	10	2(4) records
2	7	25%
3	13	50%
4	24	100%
5	9	40%
6	19	80%
7	10	20% + 1(2) record
8	15	40% + 1(2) record
9	19	40% + 2(4) records

Table 2. The Number of Clusters Examined and the Percent of the Database Retrieved

through (9) (see Tables 5 and 6). The pair (A.I, B.I) is evaluated only for the retrieve requests (1) through (6). Overall, the difference in the collected times of the two configurations, i.e., (A.I - A.E), and (B.I - B.E), respectively, should provide us with a measure of the overhead incurred when internal performance measurement software is present in the system.

$$\begin{matrix}\textit{The}\\ \textit{Response-Time}\\ \textit{Improvement}\end{matrix} = 100\% * \left[1 - \left(\frac{\begin{matrix}\textit{The Response}\\ \textit{Time of}\\ \textit{Configuration } B\end{matrix}}{\begin{matrix}\textit{The Response}\\ \textit{Time of}\\ \textit{Configuration } A\end{matrix}} \right) \right]$$

Equation 1. The Response-Time-Improvement Calculation

The *response-time reduction* is defined to be the reduction in response time of a request, when the request is executed in n backends containing nx number of records as opposed to one backend with x number of records. Equation 2 provides the formula used to calculate the the response-time reduction for a particular retrieval request, where configuration A represents one backend with x records and configuration C represents n backends, each with x records. The response-time reduction is calculated for the configuration pair (A.E, C.E), for the retrieve requests (1) through (9).

$$\begin{matrix}\textit{The}\\ \textit{Response-Time}\\ \textit{Reduction}\end{matrix} = 100\% * \left[\left(\frac{\begin{matrix}\textit{The Response}\\ \textit{Time of}\\ \textit{Configuration } C\end{matrix}}{\begin{matrix}\textit{The Response}\\ \textit{Time of}\\ \textit{Configuration } A\end{matrix}} \right) - 1 \right]$$

Equation 2. The Response-Time-Reduction Calculation

The internal processing times of the message-handling routines which are used to process a retrieval request are also timed. Retrieval (1) and Retrieval (2) are selected to conduct internal timing. These requests are selected since they retrieve the smallest portion of the test database and the processing time for each request is minimal. Each message-handling routine is timed independently of all others and each routine must process multiple requests so that an accurate average may be computed for the time required to process that request type. Sixteen message-handling routines are required to process a retrieve request. If we send twenty requests to each routine, a total of 320 requests must be processed by MBDS. Based on these figures, the time required to conduct the internal performance measurement of a retrieval that has a response time of twenty seconds will be approximately 107 minutes. This figure does not include the administrative time required to process the internal measurement data. For this reason, we limited the internal performance measurement requests to requests

(1) and (2).

Additionally, we also limited the number of repetitions per message handler to twenty. This is done to reduce the processing time per message handler. However, this decision reduces the accuracy of the internal performance measurement, from ten-thousands to hundredths of a second. Thus, the internal performance measurement times provide only a rough estimate of the time required to handle the respective messages. There are additional limitations. The last two versions of MBDS differ in the implementation of the directory tables, i.e., the AT, the DDIT, and the CDT (see Figure 2 again). The newest version of the system, called Version F, implements the directory tables on the secondary storage. The previous version, called Version E, stored the directory tables in the primary memory. The major roadblock that we have encountered in the performance measurement of MBDS has been the hardware limitations of the backend processors (PDP-11/44). With only 64K of virtual memory per process and a total of 256K physical memory, we found that we could not provide enough virtual space to MBDS for an extensive test of the system on a larger database. These restrictions have forced us to benchmark the primary-memory-based directory management version of the system. By excluding the directory table management routines which handle the secondary-memory-based directory tables, we free up considerable virtual space for benchmarking software and database buffers. The two versions of MBDS are nevertheless equivalent in functionality.

4. THE BENCHMARKING RESULTS

In this section, we present the results obtained from the performance measurement of MBDS. We also review the results of external performance measurement, overhead incurred by internal performance measurement software and internal performance measurement. One final note, the units of measurement presented in the tables of this section are expressed in seconds.

4.1. The External Performance Measurement Results

Table 3 provides the results of the external performance measurement of MBDS without the internal performance measurement software. There are three parts to Table 3. Each part contains the mean and the standard deviation of the response times for requests (1) through (9), which are outlined in Section 3.3. The three parts of Table 3 represent three different configurations of the MBDS hardware and the database capacity. The first part has configured MBDS with one backend and the database with 1000 records on its disk. The second part has configured MBDS with two backends, with the database of 1000 records, split evenly between the disks of the backends. The third part has configured MBDS with two backends and with a database doubled to 2000 records, where the disk of each backend has 1000 records. In Table 3 we notice one data anomaly, the standard deviation for request (9)

Request Number	One Backend 1K Records (A.E)		Two Backends 1K Records (B.E)		Two Backends 2K Records (C.E)	
	mean	stdev	mean	stdev	mean	stdev
1	3.208	0.0189	2.051	0.0324	3.352	0.0282
2	13.691	0.0255	7.511	0.0339	14.243	0.0185
3	26.492	0.0244	14.164	0.0269	26.737	0.0405
4	52.005	0.0539	26.586	0.0294	52.173	0.0338
5	21.449	0.0336	11.309	0.0375	21.550	0.0237
6	42.235	0.0326	21.622	0.0424	42.287	0.0400
7	12.285	0.0408	6.642	0.0289	12.347	0.0371
8	22.532	0.0296	11.764	0.0300	22.583	0.0110
9	23.913	0.1115	12.624	0.0350	24.169	0.0181

Table 3. The Response Time Without Internal Performance Evaluation Software

in the one-backend-with-1000-records configuration. Since we did not conduct an internal performance measurement on this request, we are not sure what causes this skewed standard deviation, and hence will not attempt to offer an explanation of this anomaly.

Given the data presented in Table 3, we can now attempt to verify or disprove the two MBDS performance claims. We begin by calculating the response-time improvement for the nine requests. In Table 4 we present the response-time improvement for the data given in Table 3. Notice that the response-time improvement is lowest for request (1), which represents a retrieval of two records of the database. On the other hand, the response-time

Request Number	Response-Time Improvement (A.E,B.E)
1	36.07
2	45.14
3	46.53
4	48.94
5	47.27
6	48.81
7	45.93
8	47.79
9	47.21
No Internal-Measurement Software	

Table 4. The Response-Time Improvement Between Configurations A.E and B.E.

improvement of request (4), which retrieves all of the database information is highest, approaching the upper bound of fifty percent. In general, we find that the response-time improvement increases as the number of records retrieved increases. This seems to support a hypothesis that even if the database is larger, the response-time improvement will remain at a relatively high (between 40 an 50 percent) level.

Next, we calculate the response-time reduction for each of the nine request. In Table 5 we present the response-time reductions for the data given in Table 3. Notice that the response-time reduction is worst for request (1), which represents a retrieval of two records of the database. On the other hand, the response-time reductions for the requests which access larger portions of the database, requests (4) and (6), have better response-time reductions. In general, we found that the response-time reduction decreases as the number of records retrieved increases, i.e., the response time remains virtually constant. Again we seem to have evidence to support the hypothesis that, as the size of the response set increases for the same request, the response-time reduction will decrease to a relatively low (0.1% or less) level.

Table 6 provides the results of external performance measurement of MBDS with internal performance measurement software in place. There are two parts to Table 6. Each part contains the mean and the standard deviation of the response-times for the requests (1) through (6). The two parts of Table 6 represent two different configurations of the MBDS hardware and the database capacity. Part one has configured MBDS with one backend and with the database of 1000 records. Part two has configured MBDS with two backends, with the database of 1000 records, split evenly between the disks of the backends. We did not

Request Number	Response-Time Reduction (A.E,C.E)
1	4.49
2	4.03
3	0.92
4	0.32
5	0.47
6	0.12
7	0.50
8	0.23
9	1.07
No Internal-Measurement Software	

Table 5. The Response-Time Reduction Between Configurations A.E and C.E

Request Number	One Backend 1K Records (A.I)		Two Backends 1K Records (B.I)	
	mean	stdev	mean	stdev
1	3.205	0.0436	2.219	0.0474
2	13.418	0.0172	7.401	0.0277
3	25.903	0.0119	13.854	0.0361
4	50.750	0.0374	26.402	0.0596
5	20.972	0.0271	11.244	0.0528
6	41.262	0.0331	21.517	0.0575

Table 6. The Response Time (in seconds) With Internal Performance Measurement Software

measure the response times with two thousand records distributed over two backends. We felt that no additional information would be gained by conducting the measurements.

4.2. The Internal Performance Measurement Overhead

An interesting anomaly is discovered when we compare the response times of the external and internal performance measurement tests, i.e., parts one and two of Tables 3 and 6 for requests (1) through (6). We had anticipated that the addition of internal performance measurement software would add an overhead to the response time of requests. In the transition from A.E to A.I and from B.E to B.I we expected there to be in an increase in the response times for the common requests. We actually found a general improvement, from 0.1% to 5%, in the response times of the requests when the internal performance measurement software is part of the MBDS code. What could have caused the anomaly? One hypothesis is that this is due to the manner in which MBDS is implemented on the backends. Currently, there is not sufficient virtual memory per process available on each backend. The result is that disk overlays are used to organize the code for each process in MBDS. The additional internal performance measurement code may cause the operating system to overlay differently, thereby benefiting the overall performance of MBDS. We still believe that there is an overhead induced by the internal measurement code and Table 7 provides evidence by demonstrating that the response-time improvement achieved by adding a backend is inferior to the corresponding figures in Table 4.

4.3. The Internal Performance Measurement Results

Table 8 provides the results of the internal performance measurement of MBDS for a retrieval request. The times measured for each message-handling routine are given for both request (1) and (2). The message-handling routines are listed with the MBDS process which contains the routine. Although the results are given to four decimal places, we only trust the

Request Number	Response Time Improvement (A.I,B.I)
1	30.76
2	44.84
3	46.52
4	47.98
5	46.39
6	47.85
Evaluation Software	

Table 7. The Response Time Improvement Between Configurations A.I and B.I.

accuracy to the second decimal place (see Section 3.4). Basically, what can we observe about the collected message-handling times? We see that the controller processes, i.e., Request Preparation and Post Processing, spend very little time in processing the retrieval request. This is a major design goal of MBDS and is necessary to prevent a bottleneck at the controller when the number of backends increases substantially. It appears that this goal is met successfully. We also observe that the results obtained from Concurrency Control are consistent and of short duration. This is expected since there is only one request in the system at a time and no access contention can occur. These tables should then be considered as containing the best-case times. The majority of work done in the backend is at Record Processing. Observing the process timings in Record Processing, we see that, for both requests, the addition of an extra backend reduces the record processing time by nearly half.

5. CONCLUSIONS AND FUTURE WORK

We have shown that the two basic performance claims of the multi-backend database system are valid. While these results are preliminary, they are encouraging. Overall, the response-time improvement ranged from 36.07 percent to 48.94 percent, when the number of backends and their disks is doubled for the same database. The low end of the scale represented a request which involved the actual retrieval of only two records. The high end represents a request which has to access all of the database information. The response-time reductions were also impressive, ranging from a 4.49 percent change to a 0.12 change. In other words, when we double the number of backends and their disks, the response time of a request is nearly invariant despite the fact that the response set for the request is doubled. Another crucial discovery that we made was that the results were consistent and reproducible. The tests were conducted at least twice for most of the request set, with the testing done on different days by different people. The resulting data was consistent and reproducible. The data presented in this paper represents the last set of tests for the request

MBDS Process	Message Handling Routine	Request Number	One Backend 1K Records	Two Backends 1K Records
Request Preparation	Record Count To Post Proc	1	0.0005	0.0015
		2	0.0000	0.0000
	Parse Traffic Unit	1	0.0200	0.0190
		2	0.0180	0.0185
	Broadcast Results	1	0.0025	0.0025
		2	0.0065	0.0030
Post Processing	Collect Results	1	0.0465	0.0250
		2	0.0890	0.0813
Directory Management	Parsed Traffic Unit	1	0.0699	0.0450
		2	0.0925	0.0491
	Did Sets Locked	1	0.0516	0.0510
		2	0.0566	0.0566
	Cid Sets Locked	1	0.0533	0.0349
		2	0.0450	0.0433
	Descriptor Ids	1	na	0.0391
		2	na	0.0558
Concurrency Control	Cids for Traffic Unit	1	0.0424	0.0433
		2	0.0425	0.0433
	Did Sets Traffic Unit	1	0.0566	0.0408
		2	0.0508	0.0516
	Did Sets Released	1	0.0025	0.0016
		2	0.0008	0.0008
Record Processing	Entire Process	1	2.6462	1.3775
		2	12.7100	6.5716
	Request with Disk Address	1	0.0466	0.0433
		2	0.0433	0.0383
	Old Request	1	0.0130	0.0148
		2	0.0131	0.0168
	PIO Read	1	0.0844	0.0865
		2	0.8593	0.8863
	Disk Input/Output	1	0.0799	0.0741
		2	0.0783	0.0725

Table 8. Message Handling Routine Processing Times for a Retrieval Request

set.

The next logical step in the performance of the multi-backend database system is to extend the testing to include the other request types, update, insert and delete. Additionally, there are still some more tests to run on the retrieval request. We should also investigate the effect of the directory structure on performance. In particular, we should try to determine how much of an effect the descriptor definitions for a directory attribute have on the performance data. Finally, we should conduct some tests on the secondary-memory version of the directory tables to evaluate just how much an effect this version will have on the performance data.

Because MBDS is intended for microprocessor-based backends, winchester-type disks and an Ethernet-like broadcast bus, we will not continue our benchmark work on the present VAX-PDPs configuration. Instead, we plan to download MBDS to either MicroVaxs or Sun Workstations. With either choice, we can utilize a broadcast bus, which was not available when the project began. We may also eliminate all the physical and virtual memory problems. In the new environment we can perhaps obtain a more accurate measurement of the internal performance measurement software overhead, conduct a more thorough benchmarking of MBDS, and study various benchmarking strategies.

ACKNOWLEDGEMENTS

The work reported herein is supported by Contract N00014-84-WR-24058 from the Office of Naval Research and conducted at the Laboratory for Database Systems Research, Department of Computer Science, Naval Postgraduate School, Monterey, CA 93943.

REFERENCES

[Bitt83] Bitton, D., DeWitt, D. and Turbytil, C., "Benchmarking Database Systems: A Systematic Approach," *Proceedings on Very Large Data Bases,* 1983.

[Boyn83a] Boyne, R., et al., "A Message-Oriented Implementation of a Multi-Backend Database System (MDBS)," in *Database Machines,* Leillick and Missikoff (eds), Springer-Verlag, 1983.

[Boyn83b] Boyne, R., et al., "The Implementation of a Multi-Backend Database System (MDBS): Part III - The Message-Oriented Version with Concurrency Control and Secondary-Memory-Based Directory Management," Technical Report, NPS-52-83-003, Naval Postgraduate School, Monterey, California, March 1983.

[Demu84] Demurjian, S. A., et al., "The Implementation of a Multi-Backend Database System (MDBS): Part IV - The Revised Concurrency Control and Directory Management Processes and the Revised Definitions of Inter-Process and Inter-Computer Messages" Technical Report, NPS-52-84-005, Naval Postgraduate School, Monterey, California, March 1984.

[He82] He, X., et al., "The Implementation of a Multi-Backend Database System (MDBS): Part II - The First Prototype MDBS and the Software Engineering Experience," Technical Report, NPS-52-82-008, Naval Postgraduate School, Monterey, California, July 1982.

[Hsia81a] Hsiao, D.K. and Menon, M.J., "Design and Analysis of a Multi-Backend Database System for Performance Improvement, Functionality Expansion and Capacity Growth (Part I)," Technical Report, OSU-CISRC-TR-81-7, The Ohio State University, Columbus, Ohio, July 1981.

[Hsia81b] Hsiao, D.K. and Menon, M.J., "Design and Analysis of a Multi-Backend Database System for performance Improvement, Functionality Expansion and Capacity

Growth (Part II)," Technical Report, OSU-CISRC-TR-81-8, The Ohio State University, Columbus, Ohio, August 1981.

[Kerr82] Kerr, D.S., et al., "The Implementation of a Multi-Backend Database System (MDBS): Part I - Software Engineering Strategies and Efforts Towards a Prototype MDBS," Technical Report, OSU-CISRC-TR-82-1, The Ohio State University, Columbus, Ohio, January 1982.

[Schi84] Schill, J., "Comparative DBMS Performance Test Report," Naval Ocean System Center, San Diego, CA, August 1984.

[Stra84] Strawser, P. R., "A Methodology for Benchmarking Relational Database Machines," Ph. D. Dissertation, The Ohio State University, 1984.

HARDWARE VERSUS SOFTWARE DATA FILTERING :

THE VERSO EXPERIENCE

S. Gamerman
LRI, Université de Paris XI, 91405 Orsay, France

M. **Scholl**
INRIA, 78153 Le Chesnay, France

Abstract

In several relational systems such as VERSO, elementary processing of relational operations (filtering) is relegated to a processing unit close to the mass storage device.

The work presented below addresses the problem of choosing among two competitive approaches for implementing filtering :

(i) the database machine approach : filtering is implemented by means of a dedicated hardware,

(ii) the software approach consists in writing code to be run on a regular "off-the-shelf" microprocessor.

Both approaches have been experimented in the VERSO system. The objective of this paper is to compare the Selection/Projection response times provided by both the hardware filter and the software filter.

(*) This research was partially supported by a grant N° 84077 from the French Association pour le développement de l'Informatique.

1. - INTRODUCTION

This work relates to relational Database Management Systems (DBMS) improvement. Because of these systems complexity, any improvement should not only lie on current technology advances but requires also questionning whether architecture is well adapted to the application.

The belief that architecture should be designed according to the DBMS application specificity and functionnalities gave birth to the Database Machine (DBM) approach : over the past ten years, several prototypes were designed and a few commercial products were announced whose main characteristics was the implementation of the data access function by means of dedicated hardware [1,2,3,4,5].

Concurrently, technology has significantly evolved : current microcomputer architectures allow DBMS implementation with a performance that should increase with time.

Based on the experience gained into realizing two prototypes of a relational DBMS called VERSO, one following the DBM approach, the other one being a software system [6], the work presented below addresses the problem of choosing among these two competitive approaches for implementing a performant relational DBMS.

The VERSO DBM was designed with the two following objectives in mind :

1) to justify the approach consisting in relegating some tasks to a dedicated hardware close to the mass storage device : under the conventional assumption that DBMS are I/O bound (the data access function is the one to be optimized), in the VERSO DBM a hardware filter performs unary relational operations as well as binary relational operations under some restrictions ;

2) to check that an automaton-like device for the hardware filter is well adapted to the requests as well as to the structure of the files to be processed : the VERSO filter uses a programmable finite state automaton (FSA) mechanism [7].

In these respects the current VERSO architecture is as follows : a SM 90 microcomputer architecture was chosen with the following characteristics :

- a SM bus is shared by, (i) a processing unit (PU), (ii) a Filter, (iii) common RAM memory, (iv) an external interface.

- the PU utilizes a Motorola 68000 processor (8MHz) and is in charge of high level DBMS functions (query decomposition, access path, transaction management and concurrency control) as well as of the filter's control through the SM bus.

- the Filter (7 european boards) is connected to mass storage as well as to the SM bus and is in charge of data transfers and data filtering.

Concurrently, another approach was experimented the hardware filter was replaced by a standard disk exchange module utilizing an Intel 8086 processor and a 128 K-byte RAM memory. The FSA filtering mechanism was implemented by software on this Module.

The goal of this paper is to compare the expected performance of both hardware and software filters for the relational selection/projection operation.

Section 2 describes the hardware filter, studies which are the best algorithms for implementing the unary operations and gives under some assumptions the expected response time for a Selection/Projection request.

Basically, an important parameter is the relative speed r of the filtering mechanism itself with respect to the frequency and the speed of the data transfers between Disk and RAM memory. With the hardware filter, whatever the query is, it takes approximately 400 ns (cycle time) to scan one character of the source file, to analyze it and to eventually write this character onto a target buffer. Filtering a character is then twice faster as reading/writing it from/to disk (SMD interface with a 10 Mbits/s rate).

Section 3 describes the software filter architecture. In order to study the response time performance with such a filter, the relative speed r of the filtering mechanism must be estimated. If the same algorithm as for the hardware filter were utilized, the performance would be disastrous.

The modifications to the filtering mechanism are described. In spite of these modifications, the software filter is of course still significantly slower than the hardware filter. In order to evaluate the filter speed several design parameters have first to be estimated. Among them the expected cycle time is the most important : while with the hardware filter, the source file is thoroughly scanned one character at a time, only the fields of interest are scanned one byte at a time with the software filter, the other fields being skipped. This feature allows the filter speed to be significantly increased.

Both filters are compared in Section 4 in terms of response time performance. Of course software filtering response time is higher than hardware filtering response time but much less than what was expected from the examination of the ratio between the hardware filtering speed and the software one.

2. - HARDWARE FILTERING RESPONSE TIME

We first describe the Filter's architecture (Fig. 1). The reader is reported to [6,7] which thoroughly describe the filtering mechanism and the architecture of the VERSO DBM.

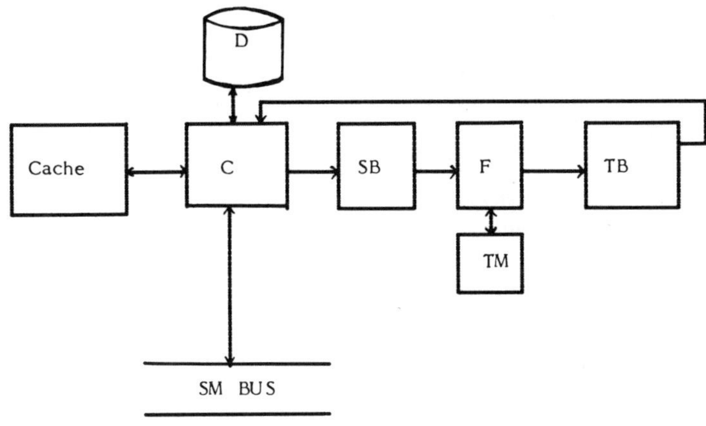

Figure 1 : VERSO HARDWARE Filter Architecture

2.1. - Filter's architecture

The hardware filter includes the following components :

1. - A controller C realized from AMD microprocessors is microprogrammed and is in charge of Disk I/0, transferring data between the Cache, the Disk D, the buffers SB, TB and the filter's memory TM ;

2. - An 512 K-byte extension memory, unproperly called CACHE ;

3. - Two 32 K-byte RAM memories : the Source Buffer (SB) and the Target Buffer (TB) ;

4. - A 256 K-byte RAM memory, called TM ;

5. - A moving head disk D with SMD interface ;

6. - The Filter F itself realized from AMD processors. Given a query and a file structure there exists a FSA for filtering the file [7]. The filter F is a dedicated machine whose code (representing the FSA) is loaded into memory TM before filtering.
SB is loaded with data to be filtered from D or Cache or from the mainframe memory through the SM bus. The filter F sequentially scans data in SB and places the result into TB. Unloading of the target relation consists in transferring TB's contents into Cache, D or the mainframe memory. SB (and TB) can be decomposed into two logical 16 K-byte buffers.

Before describing the filtering algorithms, several definitions, notations and assumptions are necessary.

2.2. - The Model

We are interested in evaluating the response time to a selection/projection operation.

Basically, once the filter's memory has been loaded, the filter is given a list of M blocks of the Source Relation to be scanned. The result of filtering is a list of R blocks including the target relation.

Let p be the selectivity factor defined as the ratio between the sizes of the target relation and the source relation :

$$p = R/M$$

We choose the following rather pessimistic assumption in order to obtain a lower bound on the filter's performance : we assume the sizes M and R are large and that both the Source Relation and the target one are stored on Disk. Blocks are of size one disk track.

We furthermore assume the M Source blocks are contiguous on Disk for simplicity. This is a rather optimistic assumption since it depends on the placement algorithm as well as on the access path(*).

The reader is referred to [8] which utilizes a more realistic assumption on the placement of the M blocks on disk.

(*) If the source relation consists in M' contiguous blocks, a non Dense Index delivers to the filter a list of $M \leq M'$ disk tracks which are not necessarily on the same Disk cylinder.

Let T denote the filter's response time (in seconds). T includes the time necessary for loading from disk the M Source blocks, the time for filtering them and the time necessary for unloading the R result blocks onto disk.

Let τ denote the average filter's cycle time, i.e. the time necessary for the filter to read one source character, analyse it and eventually write it onto the target buffer.

Note that one important characteristics of the finite-state-Automaton filtering mechanism is that the filtering time is independent of the query complexity and of the file structure as well. The actual filtering time is proportional to the size of the Source Relation.

With the architecture described above, τ=400ns. Because of the pipelined structure of the filter τ is less than the sum of the times necessary for accessing the buffers SB and TB (150ns) plus the analysis time.

If we denote by T_F, the time necessary for filtering one 16 K-byte block, we have :

$$T_F = 16 \text{ K} \times \tau = 6{,}4 \text{ ms}$$

Since the access time to the Cache memory is of the order of δ=400ns and the time for accessing the buffers SB and TB is very small (of the order of 150ns), the time T_C necessary for transferring one block from TB to Cache is :

$$T_C = 16 \text{ K} \times \delta = 6{,}4 \text{ ms}$$

Let T_D, t_s and t_ℓ respectively denote the time required for transferring one block between disk and RAM memory (Cache, SB or TB), the seek time and the latency time.

With the current SMD interface which transfers data at a 10 Mbits/s rate, the time for transferring one byte is of the order of 2δ=800ns and then we have :

$$T_D = 16 \text{ K} \times 2\delta = 12{,}8 \text{ ms}$$

We suppose the seek time, i.e. the expected time for moving the disk head between any two cylinders is :

$$t_s = 25 \text{ ms}$$

The latency time i.e. the time it takes the head to reach the beginning of the track(*) once it has been moved from one cylinder to another is taken as :

$$t_\ell = \frac{T_D}{2} = 6{,}4 \text{ ms}$$

Finally let r denote the relative filtering speed defined as the ratio between the time for filtering one block and the time for transferring one block between RAM memory and disk :

$$r = T_F/T_D$$

In the case of the architecture described above, r=1/2 : the filter is twice as fast as the disk transfer.

2.3. - Hardware filtering algorithms and response time

The general filtering algorithm works as follows :

i) the M blocks of the Source Relation are successively loaded from Disk into SB.

ii) the filter scans SB one byte at a time and places the result into TB.

iii) once the target buffer (TB) is full it is unloaded onto Cache.

iv) Once Cache is full it is unloaded onto Disk.

Even though the target relation is too large to be stored into Cache, the transit through the Cache gives a better response time than writing directly the target relation from TB onto Disk. This will be justified below.

The synchronization between loading, filtering and unloading (steps (i), (ii), (iii)) has now to be specified.

For this we need more information about the connection between the controller C and the filter F through the Source Buffer (SB).

Basically there exists two types of connection between 2 processors sharing the same memory :

(*) Recall blocks are of size one disk track.

<u>**a) with flip-flop buffers,**</u> the two processors access separate banks of memory : If SB is divided into two flip-flop buffers of size 16 K-byte, F may scan data in one buffer while C is loading the other one ;

<u>**b) Concurrent access on the same memory :**</u> the two processors share a single memory bank through a bus multiplexed in time. Depending on the hardware implementation and the processors speed, one processor is more or less slowed down when it accesses memory concurrently to the other one. Two strategies may then be applied :

(i) <u>**Sequential Loading/Filtering**</u> C loads data in SB and stops. Then F filters SB's contents and stops. Then loading resumes, etc...

(ii) <u>**Concurrent Loading/Filtering :**</u> while C is loading one block of data into SB, F can concurrently scan data from SB.

The impact of the relative speed r and of the type of connection between the controller C, the filter F and the buffer SB are thoroughly studied in [8] for the type of architecture described above and in each case an 'optimal' algorithm is given.

We describe below two variants which correspond to the actual VERSO implementation. In this implementation, there exists a concurrent access between C and F to SB such that :

i) the filter is only slightly slowed down when accessing SB concurrently to C.

ii) after a few bytes have been transferred from disk into SB, filtering can start (on the <u>same</u> block of data)

iii) an hardware mechanism stops the filter if it goes ahead the controller C.

Then the VERSO type of connection belongs to the above b) class (concurrent access).

2.3.1. - <u>Concurrent Loading/Filtering</u>

Since the filter is much faster than disk transfer, filtering is always performed concurrently to disk transfer. Filtering time is "hidden" behind transfer time.

Then the response time is the sum of

1) the loading time of the Source Relation into SB
2) the time for unloading TB into Cache for all target blocks
3) the time for unloading the Cache onto Disk.

Then we have :

$$T = M \times T_D + pMT_C + pMT_D + 2\left\lceil \frac{pM}{S} \right\rceil (t_s + t_\ell) \qquad (1)$$

The three first terms respectively account for the loading into SB of the M source blocks, the unloading of the R=pM target blocks from TB into Cache and the final unloading of the target relation from Cache onto Disk.

Let S be the number of blocks that can be stored into Cache. Then each time Cache is full (this happens $\left\lceil \frac{pM}{S} \right\rceil$ times), one has to move the disk arm from the current source cylinder to the current target cylinder and then wait a latency time before actually transferring the Cache contents onto Disk. When this transfer is over one has to switch back to Source relation before resuming loading. Then each time Cache is full, a time equal to $2(t_s+t_\ell)$ is lost.

A few remarks are noteworthy :

1) Blocks are of size one disk track. Then since the M source blocks are supposed to be contiguous there is neither seek nor latency between 2 successive blocks loadings (we assume the switching time between two adjacent cylinders is negligible).

2) Without special hardware to support concurrent memory access, one would use a pool of two buffers : SB would be divided into two logical buffers, one for loading, one for filtering :
First, the filter has to wait until one buffer is loaded. Then while C is loading the second block, F is filtering the first one. Since F is faster(*) than disk transfer, it still has to wait until the second block has been loaded. The loading continues into the first buffer, while F filters the second buffer's contents.

Then the response time is only slightly larger than T (equation 1) : one has to add T_F which accounts for the filtering of the last block.

Therefore, one may question whether a complicate mechanism such as that of the Verso architecture is useful.

(*) even though it is slowed down because of concurrent access

3) Finally note that a flip-flop buffers mechanism which differs from the previous one by the fact that there is a real parallelism between loading and filtering (C and F access separate memory banks) would not provide a better performance :

Whatever mechanism we use loading is performed through a DMA at the disk speed. In the case a flip-flop buffers mechanism is used, filtering is accelerated. But this is of no interest in one I/0 bound application.

The response time is still $T + T_D$.

2.3.2. - Sequential Loading/Filtering

One may wonder whether the parallelism between loading and filtering as studied in the previous section actually provides a significant improvement on response time. This section studies the following algorithm :

1) First load SB until it is full ;
2) Filter SB's contents until either TB is full (then unload TB and resume filtering) or SB has been completely scanned.
3) Then resume loading, etc...

Therefore, the filter always waits until SB has been loaded before filtering data.

Then the response time is the sum of

(i) the loading time,
(ii) the M blocks filtering time,
(iii) the Mp blocks unloading time,
(iv) the Cache to Disk unloading time
(v) the seek + latency times (each time Cache is unloaded).

Then we have :

$$T' = T + MT_F \qquad (2)$$

where T is given by equation (1).

The loss in performance is depicted in Figure 2 where T and T' (equations (1) and (2)), normalized with respect to T_D are plotted versus M for p = .5 and S = 32

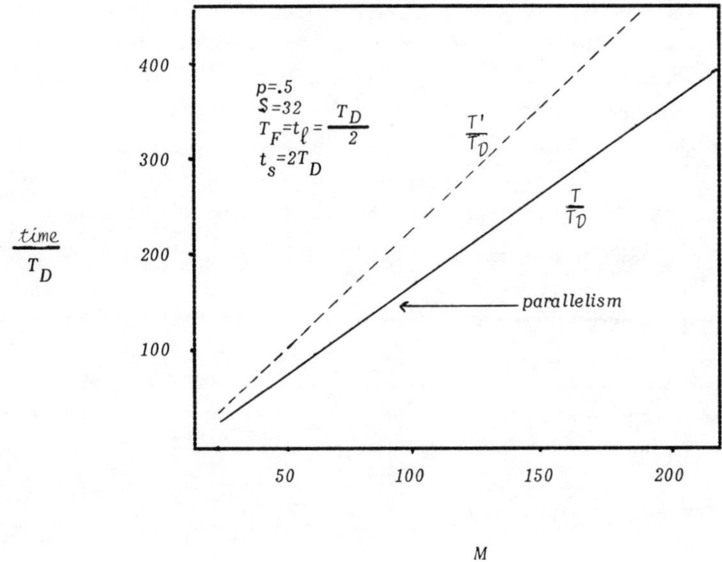

Figure 2. Impact of parallelism on response time

2.4. - Cache Impact on Response Time

Cache is useful for storing target relations even though these are too large to completely lie into Cache.

Indeed, recall the previous algorithms include two unloading steps :

(i) each time the target buffer is full, it is emptied into Cache

(ii) each time Cache is full, it is unloaded onto Disk.

Then one may argue that since in these algorithms, Cache is anyway emptied onto Disk, one could save step (i) by directly emptying the target buffer TB.

However, one must take into account the switching time between the loading process and the unloading one : each time TB is unloaded, one should move the disk arm and wait on the average half a rotation. Once TB has been emptied, then one should switch once more to the Source Relation to be loaded. Switching lasts approximately 3 to 5 times unloading a block from TB to Cache. This switching time is saved with the above algorithms, since switching happens only when Cache is full.

Another way to minimize switching time would have been to design a Target Buffer TB whose size is that of Cache. Then anyway we run into the problem of retransferring from TB into the Source Buffer intermediate results that have to be filtered again (indeed temporary relations, if they are short enough are stored in RAM memory). Furthermore the expected cycle time τ is sensitive to the RAM memory size : significantly increasing TB would increase the filtering time.

Figure 3 shows how the response time T decreases as the Cache Size S increases. Clearly over S=32 blocks (512Kbytes), increasing S does not provide a significant improvement on T. Indeed, recall (Equ. 1), the part of the response time spent in moving the head and in latency is linear in $\frac{1}{S}$.

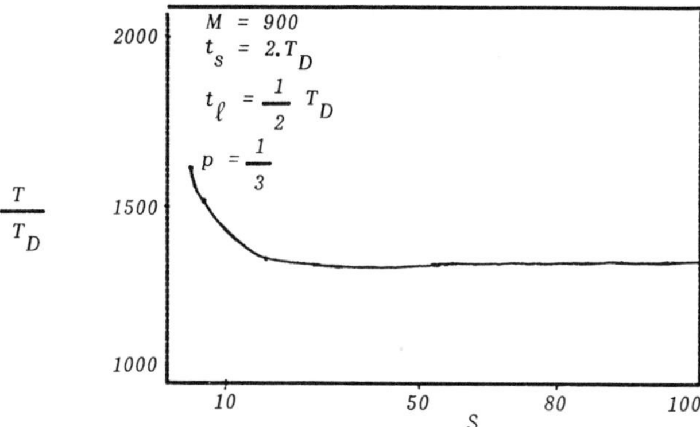

Figure 3. Impact of the Cache Size on the response time

3. - SOFTWARE FILTERING

We study in this section software filtering as an alternative to the hardware filter described above. The latter is replaced by a software program implemented on a regular disk exchange module (EM) connected between a moving head disk and the SM bus.

The EM architecture is first presented. The purpose of this section is to evaluate the filtering response time with this architecture for the selection/projection operation. For this a general filtering algorithm is discussed which differs from the algorithms presented in the previous section by several respects :

1) First, the expected cycle time τ, i.e. the expected time it takes to read one source character, process it and eventually write it onto the target buffer is not anymore independent of the query and the source file as for hardware filtering. Furthermore it depends on the software code as well as on the processor speed. The latter speed varies with time : It depends on whether the processor is sharing or not the RAM memory with the DMA in charge of disk accesses.

   This issue is discussed below and an estimate for the expected cycle time is given. This allows us to evaluate the relative filtering speed r i.e. the ratio between the cycle time and the time necessary for transferring one byte between Disk and RAM. The latter time depends only on the Disk interface characteristics.

2) Second, the hardware filter has several RAM memories, namely a CACHE, source and target buffers and the filter's memory. With the EM, intermediate results, source data, target result, and sofware code share the same unique RAM local memory (LM). The number of source and target buffers is not anymore limited as for the hardware filter (at most two source and target buffers). The filtering algorithm is based on the pipelining of three processes :

   (i) loading the source file into one among n_s source buffers,

   (ii) filtering a loaded source buffer, the result being stored in one among n_t target buffers,

   (iii) unloading one target buffer onto Disk (We have no Cache anymore).

   We then have two pools of buffers, the 'optimal' sizes of which are estimated.

Once the filtering speed and the number of buffers have been specified, the selection/projection response time can be evaluated.

3.1. - EM architecture

The exchange module includes the following components sharing a 16 bits local bus [fig. 4]

(i) an 80186 processor in charge of filtering and loading, unloading blocks (8MHz clock),

(ii) an EPROM memory where a system kernel is stored including a real time monitor and tasks for disk transfers and the dialogue with the PU (recall the PU is in charge of high level DBMS functions),

(iii) a DMA sharing with the 80186 processor, the local bus and the local memory (LM),

(iv) a 512 K-byte dynamic RAM memory LM where we store the filtering code, and the two pools of source and target buffers. LM is shared between the DMA and the 80186 processor on the one hand (local access) and the PU on the other hand (global access).

The disk transfer rate is of 10 Mbits/second (SMD interface). Therefore the time for transferring one byte between the disk and the LM memory is 800 ns.

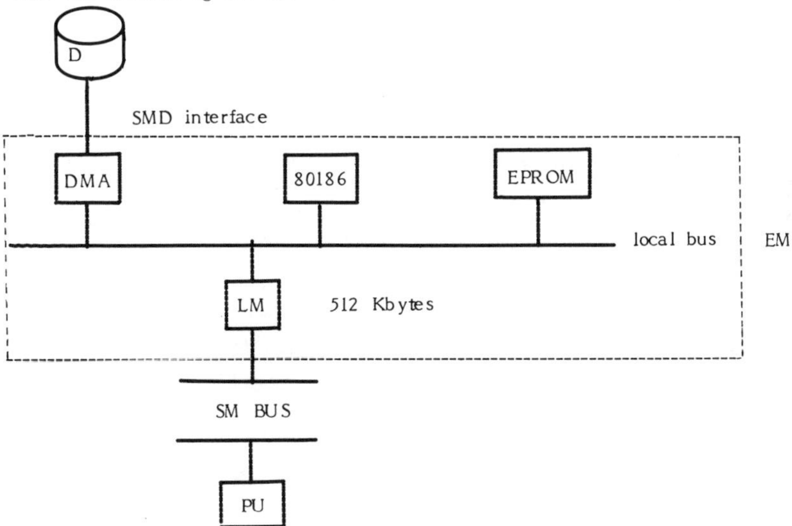

Figure 4. EM architecture

Even when the DMA is transferring data and thus accessing LM, the 80186 processor can still work and access LM, although it is slowed down.

Let c be the expected instruction execution time when the DMA is quiet and $c(1+\gamma)$ the expected execution time when the DMA is transferring data. It was shown in [9] that during a cycle time lasting 1600 ns, the 80186 processor is stopped 270 ns. Therefore $\gamma = .17$.

γ is called the 'slowing' rate.

3.2. - Cycle time and filtering speed

As for hardware filtering, the source data is sequentially scanned. However while, with the hardware filter, data is scanned one byte at a time, it may happen that the software filter skips some attributes values in the Source Relation. An attribute value has the following representation :

<tag><length><value>

where <tag> is an internal attribute name, <length> is the number of bytes of the attribute value and <value> is a string of characters.(*) Then given a Selection/Projection query and a file to be filtered, there exists three types of attributes in the file :

(i) attributes to be projected : these are the attributes whose values are to be written into the target buffer if the selection condition is satisfied.

(ii) attributes to be compared : the values of these attributes are compared to values specified in the selection condition. These attributes are eventually projected.

(iii) attributes to be skipped : attributes which are neither to be projected nor to be compared are skipped. If their number and their relative size in a file are large, then filtering time may be drastically diminished. Indeed, let BAR be the buffer address register where we store the address of the next character to be read in the source buffer. Processing such attributes is reduced to incrementing BAR with the attribute length.

(*) In hardware filtering, attributes are represented as follows : <tag><value> ; where ';' is an end tag.

Recall τ denotes the expected cycle time, i.e. the average number of μs it takes to process one byte of the source file. We have

$$\tau = \theta \quad t_c \tag{3}$$

where θ is the expected number of processor clocks for processing one byte and where a clock lasts (8MHz processor) :

$$t_c = .125\mu s \tag{4}$$

Recall the relative filtering speed, denoted by r is the ratio between the expected cycle time and the time τ_D required for transfering one byte between Disk and the memory LM :

$$r = \frac{\tau}{\tau_D} \tag{5}$$

where $\tau_D = 2\delta = 800\text{ns}$ (6)

From equations (3) to (6) we have :

$$r = \frac{\theta}{6.4} \tag{7}$$

θ depends on (i) the query, (ii) the file, (iii) the implementation of the filtering mechanism (number of 80186 instructions), (iv) number of clocks per instruction.

We use below the following estimation of θ [9].

$$\theta = 22$$

Then from equation (7) :

$$r = 3.4$$

This estimation is rather optimistic. In section 4 we study the robustness of the results with respect to r.

Such an estimation relies on the following assumptions :

(i) all attributes have the same length of 10 characters,

(ii) the ratio ρ between the number of attributes to be either projected or compared and the total number of attributes of the relation being filtered is : $\rho = .4$

(iii) the algorithm is generated in INTEL 80186 assembly language.

In conclusion, while hardware filtering is I/0 bound (since τ=400ns and r=1/2) i.e. the filter is twice as fast as the disk transfer, software filtering is CPU bound : the filter is significantly slower than disk transfer : with the above estimation the software filter is 7 times slower than the hardware filter.

3.3. - Selection/Projection Algorithm

Filtering is implemented on the EM, in a fairly straightforward manner, by means of three processes sharing as resources the two buffer's pools as well as two FIFO's [Fig. 5] and synchronized by means of events through the real time monitor.

These three processes are :

(i) The loader

This process is given the sequence of disk blocks addresses of the Source relation. For each block to be loaded, it asks for a source buffer. Once the block is loaded into a buffer, the buffer address is entered in FIFO F1 (Fig. 5).

(ii) The Filter

It asks for (i) a block to be filtered (in FIFO F1) and (ii) a free Target buffer (to place the filtering result). It then starts filtering and stops when either the target buffer is full, or the source block has been completely scanned.

In the former case, the target buffer address is entered into FIFO F2, and another target buffer is allocated.

In the latter case, the source buffer is liberated (its address is added to the source buffer pool), and another source block to be filtered is obtained by popping FIFO 1.

(iii) The Unloader

It unloads the target buffer whose address is poped from FIFO 2 (by writing its contents onto disk, or by asking the PU to read its contents). Once the target buffer has been unloaded it is liberated.

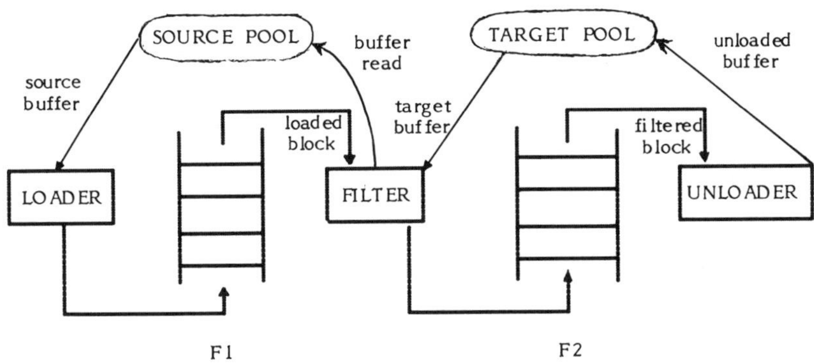

Figure 5. Filtering Processes Sharing

3.4. - Size of the Pools

We intuitively show below that the EM architecture described above in which the filter is much slower than the disk transfer (r=3.4), two buffers pools are sufficient for the Source as well as for the target.

Let us look first at the source case. The loader loads 2 buffers. Then two cases arise. Either the filter has filtered the first block (Fig. 6a). Then the loader can load a new block into the first buffer ;

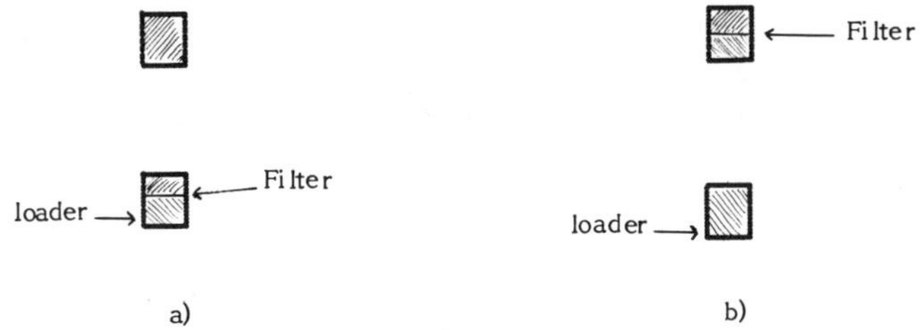

Figure 6. Loading

or the filter has not filtered yet the first block (Fig. 6b) : The loader waits until the first block has been filtered to resume loading.

Once one target block is full, the unloader can start unloading. Meanwhile filtering continues on the second target block.

While one block is filtered, since filtering is slow, one always has time enough for (i) loading one block, (ii) moving the disk head, (iii) unloading one target block onto disk.

Therefore, except the initial loading of the first block and the final unloading of the last target block, the loading/unloading time is "hidden" behind the filtering time, and 2 source buffers and 2 target buffers are sufficient.

Of course when filtering happens concurrently with either loading or unloading, filtering is slowed down by a factor of γ=.17.

If the filter were faster the above results are not anymore true. It is shown in [9] that 2 source buffers are still sufficient but the larger the number of target buffers is the better the response time is.

3.5. - Response time

Let T denote the Selection/Projection expected response time for a Relation of size M blocks.
We have :

$$T = MT_F + 2T_D \qquad (9)$$

where T_F is the expected time necessary for filtering one block and T_D accounts for the block loading/or unloading time. Since filtering is much slower than disk transfer, loading/unloading is performed concurrently to filtering for all blocks except the initial loading of the first block and the unloading of the last block.

The block filtering time T_F is given by the following equation :

$$T_F = T_D \left[r + \frac{\gamma}{\gamma+1}(1+p)\right] \qquad (10)$$

where p denotes the selectivity factor, i.e. p is the ratio between the number of filtered blocks and the number M of blocks of the source relation ; r is the relative filtering speed and γ is the 'slowing' rate.

Equation (10) is justified as follows : during $M(1+p)T_D$ seconds the DMA is active loading the source relation and unloading the target relation. Meanwhile the filter is active filtering M $\times$ a blocks but it is slowed down by a factor of γ : the time to filter a block when the DMA is active is equal to $r(1+\gamma)T_D$. During the remaining time, the DMA is quiet and M(1-a) blocks are filtered at an actual filtering speed equal to r. Then this remaining time lasts $M(1-a)r\ T_D$.

Therefore we have

$$MT_F = Mar(1+\gamma)\ T_D + M(1-a)r\ T_D$$
$$Mar\ (1+\gamma)\ T_D = M(1+p)\ T_D$$

From this, we get Equation (10).

Recall Equation (10) is true under the assumption that once a target block is full, we always have time enough - when filtering the next block in sequence - for unloading a target block and loading another block to be filtered. Since the relative filtering speed r is equal to 3.4 (Equation 8), this is a very reasonable assumption.

4. - DISCUSSION

In this section, we compare the selection/projection response time performance (Equations 9 and 10) provided by the software filter to the performance of the hardware filter. For the latter architecture, we choose the algorithm which provides the best performance, namely that strategy in which the controller and the Filter concurrently access the source buffer (Equation 1).

In Figure 7, the expected response time normalized with respect to the block transfer time T/T_D is plotted versus the selectivity factor p for both architectures.

Two sizes are choosen for the Source relation : (i) M=96 blocks (=1.5 M-byte), (ii) M=16 blocks (250K-byte). A 512 K-byte Cache size is choosen (S=32 blocks).

The first result to be noted from the examination of Figure 7 is that software filtering is slower than hardware filtering but even for extremely large relations (M=96) and very selective queries (p=.1), the response time is only three times larger with software filtering than with hardware filtering. Note however that even for reasonable size relations (M=16 blocks) if the target relation size is large ($p > .5$) the software filter is almost as fast as the hardware filter.

Besides, it is interesting to note the response time dependency on the target relation size (Mp).

Software filtering is CPU bound : loading/unloading time is "hidden" behind filtering time. The latter time is proportional to the Source relation size and does not depend on the result size.

On the contrary, hardware filtering is I/0 bound : filtering time is 'hidden' behind transfer time. The unloading time of course is proportional to the target relation size.

In summary, the software filter's performance as predicted by Figure 7 turns out to be quite good. However such a result strongly lies on the estimation of the software filtering speed r (Equation 8), since in the case of software filtering, response time is very sensitive to r. One may question whether such an estimation is optimistic and see how the performance behaves with increasing values of r.

In Figure 8 we plot the ratio between the software filter's response time T_S and the hardware filter's one T_H versus the software filter's speed r for two values of p. We keep the same parameters values as in Figure 7 and M is choosen equal to 16 blocks.

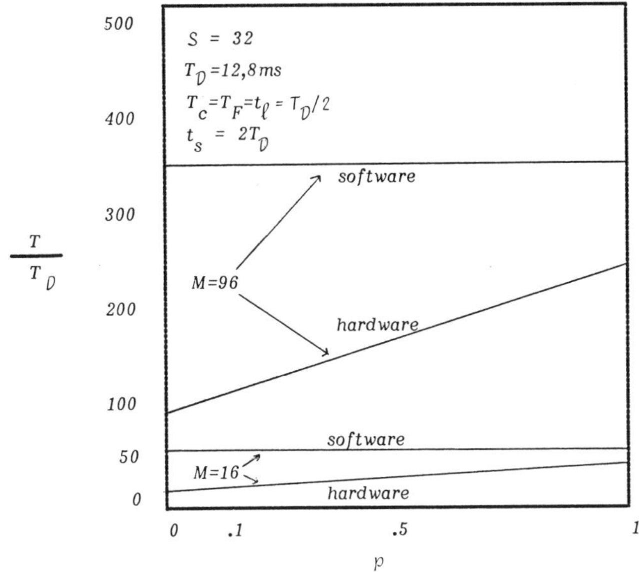

Figure 7. Expected Response time vs Selectivity factor (Hardware and Software filters)

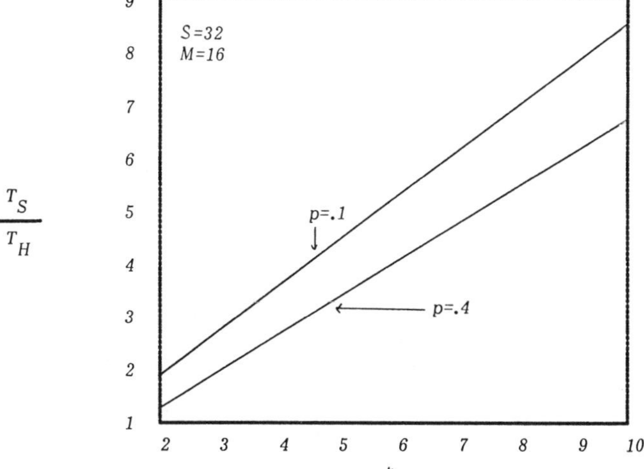

Figure 8. Influence of the software filter's speed on the response time

Clearly in the worst case, where the result is short (e.g. with M=16 blocks and p=.1 the target relation lies into less than 2 blocks), software filtering is almost r times slower than hardware filtering.

Finally it is worth noting that the above performance study and comparison between hardware and software filtering lay on the worst case assumption that relations are large. How robust the above results are when the relation number of blocks M is small should be studied in more details. (In particular when M < S, the target relation is not necessarily written onto Disk).

5. - CONCLUSION

Two architectures for data filtering have been experimented in the design of the VERSO relational system.

The first architecture uses a dedicated hardware filter, while in the second one, filtering is implemented by means of software run on a standard processor.

The goal of this paper was to help the designer in his choice of the best among these two approaches.

We restricted our attention to the response time performance expected for the selection/projection operation performed on large relations.

The major conclusion of this study, is that - although inferior to the performance expected with hardware filtering - the performance provided by software filtering is reasonably good. In particular we have shown under some assumptions that software filtering should not be more than three times slower than hardware filtering.

At first glance, this result seems surprising since the hardware filter's cycle time is 400ns while it takes a large number of instructions in software filtering to do the same job as dedicated hardware does in a single cycle, and the software basic instruction time is of the order of $1\mu s$.

As a matter of fact, the hardware filter's power is badly utilized. Indeed, the filter is idle more than half of the time : If we denote by U_F the filter's utilization, i.e. the ratio of the actual filtering time over the total response time, one may show [8] that U_F ranges from .18 to .50 depending on the size of the result. Then the filter is too fast and a speed of half the current speed would have been sufficient. The filter's utilization is still worse for binary operations such as Join [8].

Other very powerful features of the VERSO hardware filter turn out to be badly utilized. We have already questionned the choice of a complicate concurrent access mechanism for the Source Buffer. One may also mention the parallelism between Cache ⟷ Disk transfers and filtering which the architecture permits and which is not useful for the DBMS application.

Finally, there is no evaluation methodology available yet which allows the designer to decide which - among filtering and the high level DBMS functions execution - is the system's bootleneck.

In summary, with respect to the VERSO experience, hardware filtering performance is deceiving compared to the system's complexity, while software filtering can be designed easily and rapidly and provides an acceptable performance although inferior to that of hardware filtering.

These conclusions should be confirmed by the study of binary operations such as join and by real life measures.

REFERENCES

[1] Dewitt, D.J. : DIRECT - A Multiprocessor organization for supporting Relational Database Management Systems, IEEE Transaction on Computers, Vol. 28, n° 6, 1979.

[2] Schweppe, H. et al. : RDBM - A Dedicated Multiprocessor Systems for Database Management, Advanced Database Machine Architecture, D.K. HSIAO Editor, Prentice-Hall,, 1983, pp. 36-86.

[3] Babb, E. : Implementing a Relational Database by means of Specialized Hardware, ACM Trans. Database Systems, Vol. 4, N° 1, 1979.

[4] IDM500, Reference Manual, Britton - Lee Inc., Los Gatos, California.

[5] Armisen, J.P. and Caleca, J.Y. : A Commercial Back-End Database System, Proceedings of the 7th International Conference on VLDB, Cannes, 1981.

[6] Bancilhon, F. et al. : VERSO - A Relational Backend Database Machine, Advanced Database Machine Architecture, D.K. HSIAO, Editor, Prentice Hall, 1983, pp. 1-18.

[7] Bancilhon, F. and Scholl, M. : Design of a Back End Processor for a Data Base Machine, Proceedings of ACM SIGMOD, Santa Monica, 1980 , pp. 93-93g.

[8] Gamerman, S. : Où l'on découvre que les performances des filtres dans les Machines Bases de Données ne sont pas celles qu'on croyait, Thèse de 3e cycle, Université Paris XI, Orsay, 1984.

[9] Scholl, M. : Architecture matérielle et logicielle pour le filtrage dans les Bases de Données relationnelles, Thèse d'Etat, INPG, Grenoble, March 1985.

DESIGN AND ANALYSIS OF A DIRECT FILTER USING PARALLEL COMPARATORS

P. Faudemay
Institut National de Recherche en Informatique et Automatique
Le Chesnay, France

P. Valduriez
Microelectronics and Computer Technology Corporation
Austin, Texas

Abstract:

Advents in VLSI technology make it possible the development of fast hardware filters based on parallel comparators without compilation. We propose a new solution for a direct filter implementation that is efficient and extendible. It is based on a comparator array and a distributed logic for solving boolean connectors. The filter realization is feasible using current NMOS technology in an economical way. Within a few years, up to a few hundred comparators could be integrated on a single chip. At the same time, the number of predicates that can be processed by a board can vary from 256 to a few thousand. Such a high number of predicates permits the efficient processing of important database operations. A prefilter, realized by a specialized component, extends the functionality of the filter. An analysis of our filter and comparisons with compiled filters, in particular for the case of selections and semi-joins, shows the superiority of the direct filter in various situations. These two operations are very useful in a relational database machine.

Keywords:

Database Machine, Compiled Filtering, Direct Filtering, Relational, Selection, Semi-join, Parallel Comparators, VLSI.

1. INTRODUCTION

The idea of using filters in a database machine is almost as old as the idea of a database machine. Filters introduce many enhancements in the execution of database functions. However they substantially differ from one another by their functionality and design. The prime function of a filter is to select in a file a subset of records that satisfy a search predicate. In a relational system, it typically realizes unary operators that are very frequent (restriction + projection without duplicate elimination). This function can be extended to the evaluation of memory bucket addresses that will receive the records (distributed sorting), or of mark bits associated with the selected records [SALT83]. Proposals have also been made for doing binary operations on sorted files [BANC82]. In this paper we will focus only on selection from a single file which we believe to be the operation which is most efficiently implemented by filters.

In a classical system the I/O time for selection is linearly proportional to the size of the operand file while the CPU time is proportional to the query complexity. The I/O time can be reduced substantially by developing access paths to data. Filter operators decrease the CPU time. In fact, adequate hardware filters permit to make the time to perform selections independent of query complexity. However, their implementation is often costly in terms of number of boards and components. The recent advent of VLSI technology can now be applied usefully to build filters with a better cost/performance ratio.

Initially, filters were associated with a secondary memory medium, transforming it to an associative memory [BABB79, COPE73, BANE79, OZKA75]. Performance enhancements were attempted by implementing filters in MISD, SIMD, and MIMD modes. However, disk technology evolutions seem to indicate that only the MISD (or simply SISD) mode is viable [BORA83]. Attaching a filter to a disk controller provides the capability of decreasing channel traffic and main memory utilization. The possibility of using large RAM memories in database machines requires new algorithms for performing database functions [DEWI84]. The selection of data already in main memory can become a critical operation since CPU time is not negligible. Hopefully, this can be optimized by a very fast filter. Two main classes of hardware filters actually exist. The first class is compiled filters using a finite state automation (FSA) and a hardware structure based on current components [BANC83], or a multi-level search table using a binary trie [TANA83]. A compiled filter adds a processing overhead (compilation of the search predicates) that is rapidly made up when query complexity and file size increase. The second class is filters using comparators, where the number of predicates is fixed in hardware and limited to only a few predicates. The software is relatively simpler. Certain filters are hybrids of these two classes and use a compiled automaton together with comparators [HASK83].

The use of VLSI technology makes it possible to develop a direct filter--as opposed to a compiled filter--with a large number of predicates. If it is attached to a disk controller such a filter will be more efficient than a compiled filter, provided the size of the operand file is not too big (several pages) or is restricted by an adapted access method such as predicate trees [VALD84a]. This intuitive prediction would also be true for filtering a larger file in main memory, since the compiling time becomes more critical, the access in memory being faster. If the number of predicates that can be accepted is augmented to 1000, then semi-joins of large relations can be drastically improved [VALD84b]. Semi-join is an important relational operator since it can be used as a building block to the most expensive operation (join). Therefore, speeding up semi-join will also speed up the join operation. Semi-join could be viewed as a generalization of selection where comparison values span a relation attribute (join attribute). Besides performance improvements, a direct filter provides for the replacement of a complex hardware by a simple and repetitive structure, that can be realized through a few chips. The implementation of a silicon filter is also helpful for handling unformatted data, such as texts, without compilation with a conventional processor (which slows down the overall throughput) and without using a complex hardware.

In this paper, we propose a new solution for implementing a direct filter with parallel comparators. This solution is compatible with actual capabilities of VLSI technology and extendible according to future technological improvements. The filter design is based on a regular structure that can be repeated on a single chip or with several similar chips on a board. The implementation will yield significant performance enhancements for classical selections as well as for semi-joins. Finally, the number of chips for the filter processor is low compared to many others.

The filter implementation is presented in section 2. It is based on a comparator array and a distributed logic for solving boolean connectors. Several comparators operate in parallel when reading bytes of a same attribute. The distributed logic exhibits some similarity with systolic arrays [KUNG80]. However, each comparator only requires a few transistors and the connection with a successor is limited to two wires. Moreover, our filter acts in an asynchronous fashion as opposed to a pipeline strategy. The management of a prefilter by a specialized component is also discussed. It extends the functionality of the filter to handle various attribute types and formats, notations, addressing of result records, and large size attributes. Some of its functions (buffer addressing) are implemented with current hardware by the RDBM filter [SCHW83]. Also, we propose some possible extensions of the filter functionality. Section 3 gives an analysis of our filter and a comparison with compiled filters according to the number of transistors and the size of operand files. This is discussed for the case of selections of data in RAM memory or on disk and semi-joins. These comparisons show the superiority of the direct filter in various situations.

2. FILTER DESIGN

The presentation of the filter design is given in two main parts. The first describes a comparison module (comparator) that can verify a predicate and maintain the comparison result until the end of record reading. The second part presents a sliced logic, distributed on every comparator of the filter, that integrates the individual comparison results and generates the boolean value of the search expression. We will show that current NMOS technology permits to integrate at least one comparator per chip and will shortly permit from ten to a few hundred comparators per chip, with acceptable propagation delays. Therefore, a chip is made of n identical comparators, n identical evaluation logics and one controller. The number of pins is not given but remains within specific limits, independently of the number of predicates. A last subsection indicates the functions of a prefilter which can extend the capabilities of the filter. Its implementation is also compatible with current technology. Finally, the number of predicates that can be processed is between 100 and 5,000, spanning the technological capabilities from today to 1992.

2.1 The Comparators

A comparison module is illustrated in Figure 1. It applies to a record a single predicate of the form <attribute op operand-value>, or in some cases <attribute op attribute> where op is an operator in $\{<, \leq, =, \neq, >, \geq\}$. It assigns the bit value TRUE if the predicate is satisfied and the bit FALSE if the predicate is not satisfied or is currently being evaluated. A controller is devoted to initialize and activate several comparators.

A comparator requires 8 modules plus an operand memory. RA is a special byte of the operand memory that specifies the attribute number for which the comparator is active. The attribute number is broadcasted to all comparators before the distribution of the attribute values. This broadcasting is done by the prefilter. Another solution would be to maintain a table of active attributes by the controller. The register RAW is used for inter-attribute comparisons. It holds the attribute number which must be written to the operand memory.

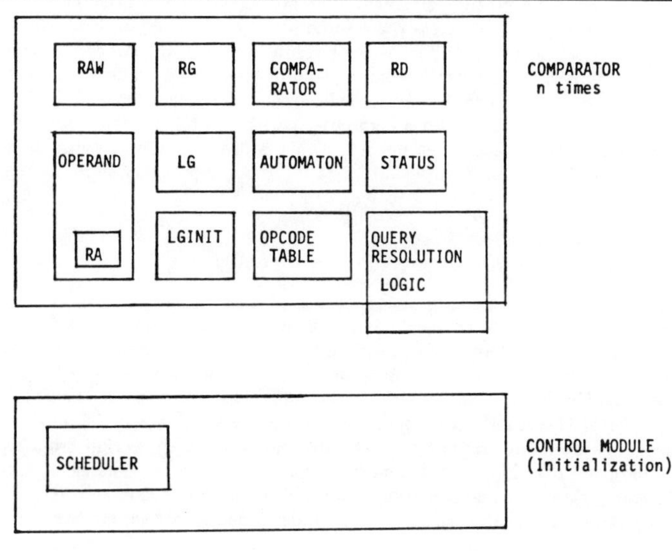

RAW, RG, RD, LGINIT, OPCODE, STATUS: registers

OPERANDE: memory

Figure 1. A Comparator and Its Environment

STATUS is a register indicating that the comparator is enabled, disabled, waiting for an attribute, or that the automaton must handle an attribute end. LR and RR are left and right registers that contain respectively one byte of the compared attribute and one byte in the corresponding operand respectively. A basic COMPARATOR reads RR and LL and gives the result $<$, $=$, or $>$. It can process one bit at a time or all bits in parallel. A length counter (LG), initialized with operand length, is decremented by one unity when each byte is processed. When LG equals 0, it delivers a bit END-OPERAND. The register LGINIT contains the operand length and initializes LG for each new record. The automaton integrates all byte comparisons and gives the result of comparing attribute and operand by generating a final state $<$, $=$, or$>$. The transition table of the automaton is shown in Figure 2. For the sake of clarity, we have not indicated the case of null values. The previous state is indicated by a row and the current state by a column. The previous state "begin" results from a record or attribute end. The current state "end (attribute or operand) and =" results from the attribute or operand end and the equality for the previous byte comparisons. According to the automaton result, a truth table OPCODE is applied to give the result TRUE or FALSE for the predicate. This table uses three bits ($<$, $=$, $>$) and is indexed by the automaton result. A typical size of a module is 54 transistors. Our calculations are based on 6 transistors per memory bit and a byte is coded by 9 bits in order to represent special characters such as the "don't care character". A rough evaluation indicates that the comparator requires approximately 100 transistors.

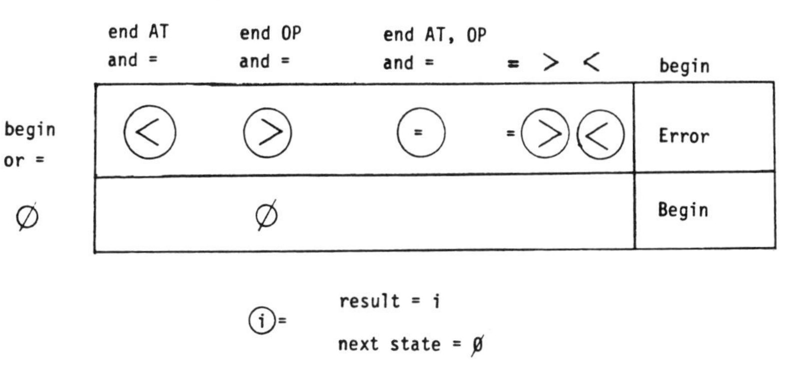

Figure 2. Transitions Table of the Automaton

In the simplest implementation, the memory containing the operand is external to the comparator and has its own counter. Bytes of different operands share this memory and are successively read into the comparator registers. Thus, with three comparators and two operands ABC and DEF, the successive bytes in memory are AD-BE-CD, where "-" means any character. In this case, one comparator remains idle. The size of the operands can be arbitrary. However, the number of comparators that can be integrated on a chip is limited by the relative speed of the external memory. For example, if the operand memory has an access time of 100 ns and the filter a cycle time of 400 ns, then at most 4 bytes of distinct operands can be processed at each cycle. The maximum number of predicates per chip is therefore 4. A better implementation incorporates the operand memory on chip. Each comparator has its own operand memory which can hold from 32 to 256 bytes. Such a comparator requires from 2500 to 20K transistors, which is easily feasible with current level of integration. The current number of transistors on a single chip can be 70K [PATT80].

The activation control of comparators is devoted to a scheduler. It permits the loading and reading of the length registers, the length counters, and the OPCODE, and activates the input and output of LR and RR. It might also employ a binary table to associate the active predicates for each attribute. This table needs m.p bits, where m is the number of attributes and p the number of predicates. It must be connected through an internal bus of p wires. Therefore, if the number of predicates is high, it is better to replace the table and its bus by using the memory byte RA, and the basic comparator as explained above. Broadly speaking, the scheduler without the table of active predicates would require less than 5K transistors.

Without considering the sliced logic for evaluating booleans, (which will be shown to require only a few transistors), the current level of integration allows from 8 to 16 comparators per chip, with minimal operand lengths. We believe this number of predicates with short operands to be more efficient than long operands with less predicates. It is always possible to represent the operand ABCDEF by the concatenation of the operands ABC and DEF. During execution by the filter, the occurrence of operand end and the state "evaluation" ("=") activates the subsequent comparator when indicated by a STATUS bit "concatenation". This bit is generated at load time by the controller. It is then possible to have a maximum operand length of 256 bytes and up to 16 predicates per chip. With expected future densities (10M transistors by 1992 [PATT80]), from 200 to 500 comparators per chip with 256 byte operands will be viable. Comparator technological needs are given in Table 1. A high number of comparators avoids reusing the same comparators for different predicates. Thus, it greatly simplifies the management of booleans as well as the initialization sequence of the filter. Furthermore, the mean number of attributes per predicate is generally low: one or two in selection requests and one in semi-joins. This avoids the need for a complex logic which limits the number of comparators.

		Comparator with 32 bytes memory	Comparator with 256 bytes memory
	trans per comparator	2500	20K
1985	comp. per chip	8-16	
	comp. per board	128-256	
1992	comp. per chip		200-500
	comp. per board		2,000-5,000

Table 1. Comparator Needs

2.2 The Sliced Logic for Query Resolution

A sliced logic, distributed on every comparator, evaluates boolean results calculated by individual comparators according to predicate connectors. The comparator array produces a bit array with one element per comparator. This array must be evaluated according to a connector array that describes for each predicate its connection (OR, AND) with the next predicate. The predicates are ordered in the search expression in conjunctive or disjunctive normal form. This last form is better suited when the number of predicates is large. Nevertheless, the mapping from one form to another can be done by applying the rule:

$$(A \wedge B) \vee (C \wedge D) = \overline{(\bar{A} \vee \bar{B}) \wedge (\bar{C} \vee \bar{D})}$$

The information about connector priority must be broadcasted at load time to all comparators.

The two arrays (comparators and connectors) will generate a result bit, whose calculation is done using a sliced logic distributed on each comparator. A slice of this logic local to a comparator is a query resolution module as shown in Figure 3. This logic module has four binary inputs and two binary outputs. MONIN is the current value of the monomial while RESIN is the current value of the global result. PRED is the actual value of the predicate and CONNECT the connector. After evaluating the inputs, MONOUT contains the new value of the monomial while RESOUT gives the new global result. The truth table associated with a logic module is given in Figure 4, where a monomial is supposed to be a conjunction.

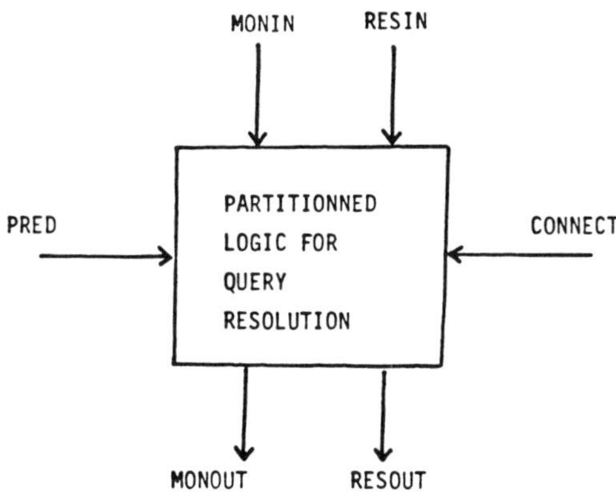

Figure 3. Scheme for Query Resolution

RESIN	MONIN	PRED	CONNECT	Result MONOUT	RESOUT
0	0	0	0	0	0
0	0	0	1	1	0
0	0	1	0	0	0
0	0	1	1	1	0
0	1	0	0	0	0
0	1	0	1	1	0
0	1	1	0	1	0
0	1	1	1	1	1
1	-	-	-	-	1

Figure 4. Truth Table of the Partitioned Logic for Query Resolution (with priority of AND)

The algorithm of a logic module is now detailed, for the case of a disjunctive normal form of the selection expression (the other case can be easily deduced). The boolean value TRUE is represented by 1, while FALSE is represented by 0. The connector OR is represented by 1, while AND is represented by 0. For the first predicate of the expression, the inputs MONIN and RESIN are initialized to 1 and 0, respectively. The current value of the monomial indicated by MON, is MON = MONIN and PRED. MONOUT is set to MON if the connector is AND or set to 1 if the connector is OR. The signal RESOUT equals RESIN if the connector is AND, and RESOUT = RESIN or MON. The boolean calculation process associated with a comparator is presented in Figure 5.

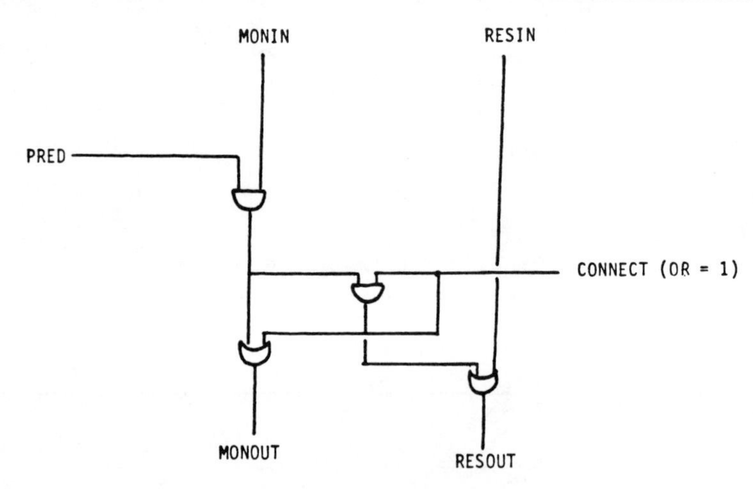

Figure 5 Query Resolution Module

The individual comparison results are integrated by applying connectors. The gate delays used for connectors permit the evaluation of the maximum number of predicates to be accepted in the same monomial. If the maximum number of predicates in a monomial is a small portion of the total number of predicates, then the query resolution uses many ORs. In this case, the signal generated from MONIN and all PREDs crosses about one gate (an OR gate) by comparator. With a gate delay of 2 ns per gate, the delay of the query resolution module for 100 predicates is 200 ns. During this time, all the signals PRED must remain stable. Thus the comparison results can be evaluated by the comparison module in about 200 ns, with a basic time of 400 ns for reading in main memory. With a cycle time of memory ranging from 200 to 800 ns, the maximum size for an arbitrary expression ranges from 60 to 300 predicates. To go further, it would be necessary to group together the RESOUTs of each series of 100 comparators by parallel ORs. The main advantage of a disjunctive normal form is that processing of semi-joins (that only require OR) is favored. Probably, the gate delay times will decrease in the future, but memory read times and cycle times will also decrease in a similar way. Thus, the limit of 60 to 300 predicates per conjunctive monomial appears to be fixed with this approach. Nevertheless, with parallel ORs, the maximum number of predicates could be more than one thousand. Practically, the maximum number of predicates could now be 256 by board (16 chips of 16 comparators each plus the output buffers and the prefilter). Such a large number of predicates is very useful for textual searching and for semi-joins.

2.3 The Prefilter

The prefilter supports three main functions. In order to not slow down a fast filter, it is likely to realize these functions using VLSI technology. Considering the importance of its functionality in a database machine, the prefilter should be an integrated part of the filtering processor as shown in Figure 6. We do not give the details of the hardware organization. Some of its functions are implemented with current hardware of existing filters [BANC83, SCHW83] but it generally requires several boards. Their functionalities are also increased in our version to enhance flexibility. We summarize the prefilter functions as follows:

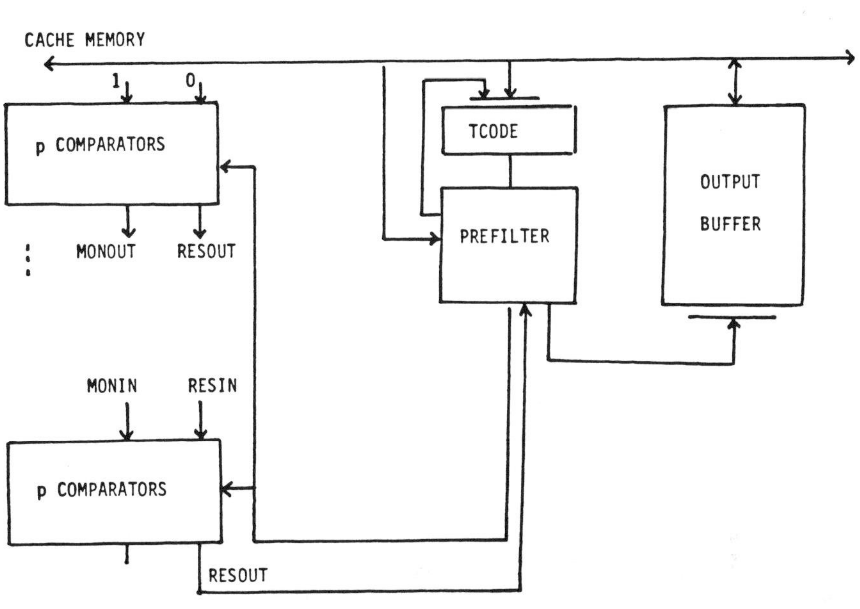

Figure 6. Filter Processor

(a) transcoding (done by the TCODE memory indexed by the data and by the prefilter), length counting and byte permutation for the management of numerical terms.

(b) detecting ends of records, attributes, or textual terms for activating the control signals of comparator chips (each having p comparators).

(c) management of input and output buffers. The input buffer is not indispensable since the filter can directly access a main memory. But in the case of a sequential input from RAM or disk, an output buffer is necessary. It keeps the result records until the end of each evaluation. The management of an input buffer permits skipping of attributes that are not needed for the evaluation.

2.4 Extensions

To complete the functionality of the direct filter, five possible extensions can be considered. These are:

(a) inter-attribute comparisons. The comparators must be able to write in the operand memory, as soon as the boradcasted attribute number is the number contained in a special attribute register, activated by STATUS. This register is represented by RAW in Figure 1.

(b) management of long texts, for example with length less than 64K bytes, where a text attribute is given in format 'length-value', the length being encoded in one byte.

(c) textual search, expressed in disjunctive normal form with the possibility of fixed and variable length "don't care" characters within each operand. With 256 operands, a filter could search up to 30-60 expended predicates, which is a nice number for practical applications.

(d) records notation [SALT83] and addressing of records in memory buckets according to a bit string that represents the verified set of predicates. It may also help for the parallel execution of several queries with the same processor.

(e) filtering of bit strings contained in a directory file according to a mask representing a set of logical page addresses. This is particularly useful for the implementation of the access method based on predicate trees [GARD84].

3. EVALUATION

It is interesting to compare the direct filter with a compiled filter, based on indexed or dichotomic automata. In this section, we compare these two methods for selection and semi-join. We suppose that both filters are hardware implemented and work "on the fly", i.e. process data at a rate equal to the arrival rate of bytes. We have shown that this is possible with current technology for the direct filter. We also admit that the number of predicates of the compiled filter is always at least equal to that of the search expression, while it varies for the direct filter according to the technology. This assumption does not change the magnitude order of the result but should be further refined for the evaluation of semi-joins. The compilation time of the compiled filter is supposed to be equal to twice the time of a fast sort of predicates (post order sort) in the case of a few predicates and equal to the expression given by [HOLL83] on PDP11-40 for 120 predicates. Obviously, these times will decrease with future technology as well as enhanced memory access times. The result is a compilation time of 200 ms for several predicates and 7 sec for 1000 predicates.

The comparison of both methods has been done in case of a selection among a file. The parameters and formulas used in the evaluation are given in the Appendix. This selection is optimized using an access method which selects a subset of the file which can be one page, 0.1 or 0.3 of the number of pages. The gain in using the direct filter as a function of the number of records in the operand file is illustrated in Figure 7. It varies from a factor 6 to 1.3 when the file is on disk. With a file in main memory, the improvement ratio is from 26 to 2.6 (not presented in Figure 7). It is also significant without any access path (sequential scan).

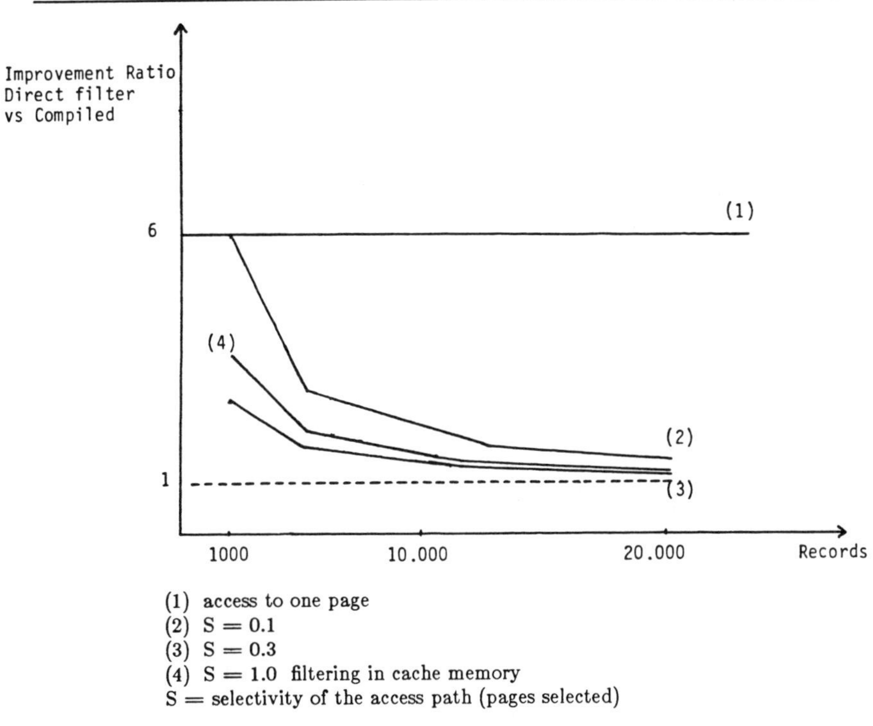

(1) access to one page
(2) S = 0.1
(3) S = 0.3
(4) S = 1.0 filtering in cache memory
S = selectivity of the access path (pages selected)

Figure 7. Selection with an Access Path

The comparison of the methods have also been done for the case of semi-join. This operator serves in the optimization of joins [VALD84b]. The operation is done in two steps. The first one is a selection, for reading join attribute values in a first file and constructing join predicates. The second one completes the semi-join by selecting records in a second file that satisfy the disjunction of predicates. This next step can require several passes for the direct filter if the number of join predicates is greater than the number of comparators. Figure 8 shows the improvement ratio given by the direct filter versus the total number of transistors for the filter. The files are supposed to have same cardinality. The gain with the direct filter increases as soon as the number of comparators (that is function of the number of transistors) becomes equal or greater than the number of records in the first relation. For a semi-join of 10,000 x 10,000 records, the gain only appears at 120 K transistors (corresponding to 512 predicates in the filter) but this number will exceed 5 by 1990. For a semi-join with data in the main memory, the superiority of a direct filter is even greater. Presently, its speed would be estimated at about 4 times that of the compiled filter, and the gain is about 48 sec. For a semi-join of 1,000 x 1,000 in 1988-1990 (1,000 comparators by filter) the gain would be a factor of 88 (or 7 sec.). This semi-join method should also be compared with other software or hardware methods. Except for the case of high join selectivity where hashing methods could be better, we believe this method will always be superior.

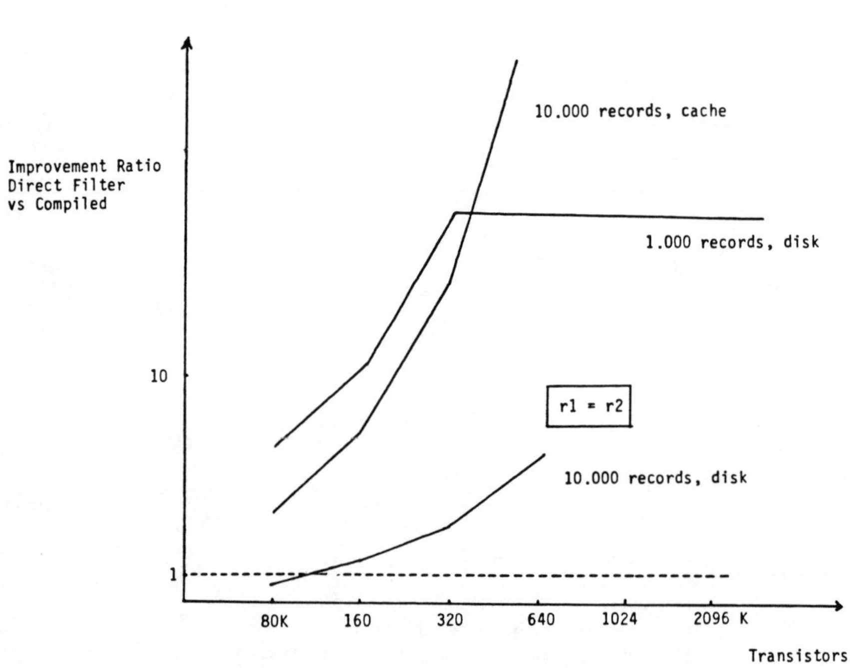

Figure 8. Semi-joins

4. CONCLUSION

The hardware filter, presented here, is based on a simple and repetitive structure that organizes comparators in parallel and avoids the compilation approach. This structure is well suited for implementation using VLSI technology and will take advantage of expected developments in the number of transistors per chip. The regular structure permits to interconnect in a similar and economical fashion several chips on a board. With current technology, it can evaluate simultaneously more than two hundred predicates on relational attributes or several tens of terms in a text. Actually, the number of comparators that could be integrated on a board is 256 (16 chips of 16 comparators). We also presented the functions that could be added using a hardware prefilter. The prefilter permits to enhance functionality, flexibility and performance of the filter, by managing the control and the data of comparators. It can also be built with component technology and should be an integrated part of the filtering processor.

Significant performance enhancements, in comparison with compiled filtering, can be expected. We showed the improvement ratio of the direct filter in case of selections of data on disks or in main memory and in case of semi-joins for average files. The increase in the number of transistors per chip will allow processing between one hundred and a few thousand predicates. This will permit the application of such a filter to semi-joins for very large files and to textual search of arbitrary complexity.

Acknowledgements: The authors want to thank the members of the SABRE project, particularly G. Gardarin and Y. Viemont, for their helpful comments and fruitful discussions. This work has been supported by INRIA.

5. REFERENCES

[BABB79] Babb, E., "Implementing a Relational Database by Means of Specialized Hardware", ACM Trans. on Database Systems, vol. 4, no. 1, March 1979, pp. 1-29.

[BANC82] Bancilhon, F., Richard, F., School, M., "On Line Processing of Compacted Relations", 8th International Conf. on VLDB, Mexico, September 1982.

[BANC83] Bancilhon F., et al., "VERSO: A Relational Back-End Database Machine", Advanced Database Machine Architecture, Ed. by D. Hsiao, Prentice Hall, 1983, pp. 1-18.

[BANE79] Banerjee, J., Hsiao, D. K., and Kannan, K., "DBC -- A Database Computer for Very Large Databases", IEEE Trans. Computers, vol. C-28, no. 6, June 1979.

[BORA83] Boral H., DeWitt, D. J., "Database Machines: An Idea Whose Time Has Passed? A Critique of the Future of Database Machines", IWDM, Munich, Springer Verlag Ed., September 1983.

[COPE73] Copeland, C. P., Lipovski, G. J., and Su, S. Y. W., "The Architecture of CASSM: A Cellular System for Non-Numeric Processing", Proc. First Annual Symposium on Computer Architecture, December 1973, pp. 121-128.

[DEWI84] DeWitt, D. J., et al. "Implementation Techniques for Main Memory Database Systems", ACM-SIGMOD Conf. Boston, June 1984.

[GARD83] Gardarin, G., Bernadat, P., Temmerman, N., Valduriez, P., Viemont, Y., "Design of a Multiprocesor Relational Database System", IFIP World Congress, Paris, September 1983.

[GARD84] Gardarin, G., Faudemay, G. P., Valduriez, P., Viemont, Y. "The Content Addressable Page Manager of SABRE", Submitted to ACM Trans. on Database Systems.

[HASK83] Haskin, R. L., Hollaar, L. A., "Operational Characteristics of a Hardware-based Pattern Matcher", ACM Trans. on Database Systems, vol. 8, no. 1, March 1983.

[HOLL83] Hollaar, L. A., et al., "Architecture and Operation of a Large, Full-Text Information-Retrieval System", Advanced Database Machine Architecture, ed. by Hsiao, D. K., Prentice-Hall, 1983, pp. 256-299.

[KUNG80] Kung, H. T., Lehman, P. L., "Systolic (VLSI) Arrays for Relational Database Operations", Proc. ACM-SIGMOD Conference, 1980, pp. 105-116.

[OZKA75] Ozkarahan, E. A., Schuster, S. A., Smith, K. C., "RAP--An Associative Processor for Data Base Management", Proc. AFIPS, vol. 44, 1975, pp. 379-387.

[PATT80] Patterson, D. A., Sequin, C. H., "Design Considerations for Single-Chip Computers in the Future", IEEE Trans. Computers, vol. C-29, no. 2, February 1980, pp. 108-109.

[SALT83] Salton, G., Fox, E. A., Wu, H., "Extended Boolean Information Retrieval", Comm. ACM, vol. 26, no. 12, December 1983, pp. 1022-1036.

[SCHW83] Schweppe, H., et al., "RDBM--A Dedicated Multiprocessor System for Database Management", Advanced Database Machine Architecture, ed. by Hsiao, D. K., Prentice-hall, 1983, pp. 36-86.

[TANA83] Tanaka, Y., "A Data-stream Database Machine with Large Capacity", Advanced Database Machine Architecture, ed. by Hsiao, D. K., Prentice-Hall, 1983, pp. 168-202.

[VALD84a] Valduriez, P., Viemont, Y., "A Multikey Hashing Scheme Using Predicate Trees", ACM-SIGMOD Conf., Boston, June 1984.

[VALD84b] Valduriez, P., Gardarin, G., "Join and Semi-join Algorithms for Multiprocessor Database Machines", ACM Trans. on Database Systems, vol. 9, no. 1, March 1984.

APPENDIX

Evaluation parameters and formulas

I. Selection with access paths

(a) The following parameters are needed:

S: selectivity factor of the access path,
r: cardinality of operand file (before access path selection),
L: record length (in bytes),
t: read time of a 20K bytes page from disk (including access time) or from main memory,
P: page length, in bytes,
k: compilation time of a predicate,
c: minimum compilation time (for initialization),
p: number of predicates in the search expression.

(b) Improvement ratio of the direct filter

The improvement ratio, noted IR, brought by the direct filter is the execution time of the selection by the compiled filter over the execution time by the direct filter. We do not consider the time for producing the result records. We suppose that the result records are produced in parallel with the read time, as done by our prefilter. The execution time of the compiled filter is then the time for compiling predicates and the time for reading the operand file. The compilation time is c + k.p. The reading time is $\lceil S.r.L \,/\, p \rceil.t$, where $\lceil a \rceil$ designates the smallest integer equal or greater than a. The execution time of the direct filter is the same as that of the compiled filter. Thus, we have:

$$\mathrm{IR} = \frac{\lceil S.r.L/P \rceil .t + c + k.p}{\lceil S.r.L/P \rceil .t}$$

The values of parameters have been fixed in Figure 7 as follows:

L=100, P=20K, t=40 ms (disk pages) or 8 ms (memory pages), K=6.6 ms, p=4, c=180 ms.

II. Semi-join

(a) The following additional parameters are needed:

r1: cardinality of file R1 (number of records),
r2: cardinality of file R2,
x: number of predicates per K transistors in the direct filter,
T: number of K transistors of the direct filter.

(b) Improvement ratio of the direct filter

IR is defined as in the case of selection. Processing semi-join of R2 by R1 requires reading R1 for selecting join attribute values and then reading R2 for completing the operation. The time for writing the result is ignored for the same reason as in case I. Reading R1 in both methods is t.r1.L/P. With compiled filter, the compilation time is k.r1 + c and the time for doing the semi-join is t.r2.L/P. Note that the semi-join by a compiled filter is supposed to require only one pass among R2. The time for performing semi-join with the direct filter is the time for reading R2 multiplied by the number of passes, which is greater than 1 if the number of predicates accepted is less than the number of join attribute values in R1. This number of passes is $\lceil r1/x.T \rceil$. Thus, we have:

$$\mathrm{IR} = \frac{t.r1.L/P + c + k.r1 + t.r2.L/P}{(t.r1.L/P) + \lceil r1/x.T \rceil .t.r2.L/P}$$

The values of parameters in Figure 8 have been fixed as follows: x=3.02.

HITHER HUNDREDS OF PROCESSORS IN A DATABASE MACHINE†

Lubomir Bic
Robert L. Hartmann
Department of Information and Computer Science
University of California, Irvine
Irvine, CA 92717

ABSTRACT: In a recent paper titled "Wither Hundreds of Processors in a Database Machine?", Agrawal and DeWitt demonstrated that, in order to exploit large numbers of processors in a database machine, the I/O bandwidth of the underlying storage devices must significantly be increased. One way to accomplish this is to use multiple parallel disk units. The main problem with this approach, however, is the lack of a computational model capable of utilizing any significant number of such devices. In this paper we discuss the implementation of a data-driven model (presented at last year's workshop) on a simulated architecture. It will be shown that this model is capable of exploiting the potential I/O bandwidth of a large number of disk units as well as the computational power of the associated processors.

1. Introduction

In a recent inspiring paper, "Wither Hundreds of Processors in a Database Machine?", Agrawal and DeWitt /AgDeW84/ have demonstrated that the main limitation to parallelism in database machines is the available I/O bandwidth provided by the underlying disk subsystem containing the database; unless that problem is tackled, the use of hundreds of processors does not seem justified. This has been shown to apply to conventional disk drives as well as to those with parallel readout capabilities.

One approach to increase the potential I/O bandwidth is to replace a single large disk with several smaller units. The main problem with this approach is the lack of an adequate database model which would permit the exploitation of any significant number of parallel disk units. In particular, network-oriented models such as DBTG /TaFr76/ operate at a too low level of interaction to exploit parallelism. In this case the user (application program) is viewed as a 'navigator' who guides a sequential thread of computation through the database. The relational model, on the other hand, permits high-level non-procedural queries to be formulated in the form of relational algebra or relational calculus expressions. However, in order to avoid comparing each element of one relation against all elements of the other, it requires that for operations involving two relations, such as join or set difference, the relations be sorted or otherwise preprocessed. These requirements place severe limitations on the number of parallel disk units since some form

†This work was supported by the NSF Grant MCS-8117516: The UCI Dataflow Project.

of centralized control is necessary to coordinate their operation.

At last year's workshop, IWDM-3, we presented a data processing model based on the principles of data-driven computation /COM82, TBH82/, which we claimed to be suitable for highly-parallel database processing /BiHa83a/. To support this claim, we have implemented the model on a simulated dataflow architecture. The results of our experiments are presented in this paper, which is organized as follows: Section 2 briefly surveys the proposed model and its mapping onto an architecture; Section 3 describes the major components of the simulator and the relevant assumptions made for the performed experiments; finally, Section 4 presents the results of these experiments and discusses their significance.

2. The AG-Model

The proposed database model is referred to as the *Active Graph Model*, abbreviated as AG-Model. (The justification for this name will be given below, in Section 2.2.) The following paragraphs give only a brief overview of the AG-Model and its mapping onto an architecture; more detailed descriptions may be found in /BiHa83a, BiHa83b, Har85/.

2.1 Data Representation

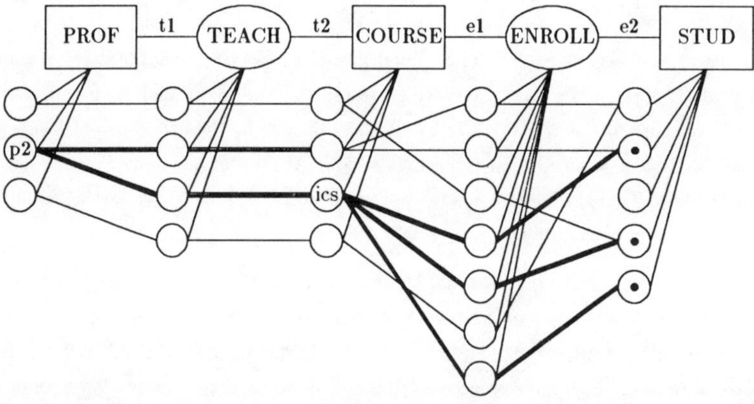

Figure 1

The AG-Model views data as a network of nodes and arcs. Similar to the Entity-Relationship model /Chen76/, nodes are organized into sets of *entities* and *relationships*. All nodes within a set are implicitly connected to a *master node* for that set. Each node consists of a *key*, which is unique within a set, and data values called *attributes*. Relationship nodes connect entity nodes via arcs, referred to as *roles*. More than one relationship may be defined between any two entity sets. Figure 1 shows a sample database consisting of the entity sets PROFessors, COURSES, and

STUDents, connected via the relationship sets TEACH and ENROLLment. (Role names are not specified.)

2.2 Dataflow View of Processing

The main departure of the above model from conventional models is the way queries are processed. The database graph is not merely a passive representation of data stored on a secondary storage medium. Rather, each node of the graph is an ***active*** component (hence the name 'Active Graph'), capable of receiving, processing, and emitting messages called ***tokens***, traveling asynchronously along the graph arcs. Tokens are the carriers of queries as well as the resulting data values extracted from the database graph. Since each node processes tokens asynchronously, computation is distributed throughout the network without the need for any centralized control.

A complete high-level query language, equivalent in its expressive power to the relational algebra /Har85/, has been developed for the AG-model. Each query is transformed into a collection of tokens which are injected into the database graph. According to well defined rules, tokens propagate through the graph until the nodes satisfying the given query are located and their attribute values extracted from the graph. To illustrate this principle, assume that we wish to retrieve the IDs and names all students enrolled in a course with subject='ics' taught by a professor with name='p2'. Formally, this request has the form:

$$PROF[NAME='p2'],\ TEACH[\ ],\ COURSE[SUBJ='ics'],\\ ENROLL[\ ],\ STUD[\mathbf{export}(ID, NAME)]$$

To answer this query, a ***restriction*** token is injected into the master node of each involved set, from where it is replicated to all member nodes. For example, a token carrying the restriction 'NAME=p2' is injected into the node 'PROF' and is replicated to all elements of that set. When all nodes have processed their restrictions, tokens, referred to as ***sweep*** tokens, are propagated along existing arcs through the sequence of sets PROF through STUD; each sweep token is forwarded by a receiving member node only if that node satisfies its corresponding restriction. In Figure 1, heavy lines indicate the flow of sweep tokens corresponding to the above query. Nodes in the last set, STUD, that receive a sweep token satisfy the given query. Each of these places the values of the specified attributes 'ID' and 'NAME' onto a ***result*** token, which is propagated to an output device.

2.3 Mapping of the AG-Model onto an Architecture

In the original paper /BiHa83a/, the architecture considered for the AG-Model assumed the existence of high density Random Access Memory (RAM) to hold the entire database. While this approach may become feasible in the future through further advances in VLSI and VHSIC technology, the use of current state-of-the-art solid state memories does not seem practical for this purpose – a sufficiently large database (10^{10} to 10^{12} bytes) would be prohibitively expensive, consume vast quantities of power, and probably be volatile.

Recently, there has been a dramatic decrease in the cost per bit of small (5 1/4 inch winchester) disk drives, which permit us to explore new alternatives. The latest versions of these devices provide access times comparable to those of larger units while maintaining a similar cost per bit ratio. The following table gives some comparative information in support of this observation.

	large	small
cost/unit	\$70K	\$2K
capacity	$2.5 * 10^9$	$6.8 * 10^7$
cost/byte	.0026¢	.0029¢
access time	24 msec	43 msec
no. of actuators	4	1
no. of units for 10^{10}B	4	133
no. accesses/msec	16/24 = 0.66	133/43 = 3.09
typical unit	IBM 3380	Fujitsu M2243AS

According to the above table, 4 of the large disks versus 133 of the smaller units are needed to hold a database of 10^{10} Bytes. Assuming that each of the large units has 4 independent actuators, the total number of accesses per millisecond is 16/24 = 0.66; in the case of the smaller disks this number is 133/43 = 3.09. Thus, while the cost per byte of storage increases only by approximately 10%, the maximum access rate increases by a factor of 5.

Based on the above observations we have implemented the AG-Model on a simulated computer architecture with the following characteristics:

A collection of n processing elements (PEs) are arranged into a k-dimensional array. Both the number of PEs as well as the number of dimensions were varied during the simulation runs to determine their effect. To simplify subsequent discussion, we shall assume k to be 2, i.e., the architecture is a square array, where each PE is connected to its four nearest neighbors. Each PE is in control of a separate disk unit and is equipped with local primary memory, used for program storage, token buffers, and disk cache. The amount of memory available for disk cache is assumed to be very small (about 3%), relative to the disk space allotted for node storage. Thus disk performance is the major factor determining the access time to nodes.

For reasons of reliability, the space on each disk is divided in half; one half contains data belonging to the owner PE while the other contains a copy of the data belonging to its nearest neighbor. Thus, in the the case of a PE/disk failure, the neighboring PE may resume the work of the failed component.

Input and output, which comprises the injection of tokens and the transport of results to the outside of the system, is accomplished via specialized interface processors, attached to a small subset of PEs.

The database graph is mapped onto the architecture as follows: Each node (master or data) is randomly assigned to one of the PEs through use of a hashing function applied to the node's unique key. Therefore, data is distributed in a uniform fashion over the entire processor array.[1] The unique key and the hashing function provide a method of direct access to a node when the key value is known.

The speed of token propagation along the graph arcs is a critical factor and must therefore be implemented efficiently. As mentioned in Section 2.2, we can distinguish the following three kinds of tokens:

1. *Restriction tokens.* A copy of the same token is replicated by a master node to all its member nodes. The number of such tokens may potentially be very large.
2. *Result tokens.* The master node is receiving a large number of different tokens, each arriving from one of its member nodes. The number of these tokens may also be very large. Furthermore, it may be necessary to perform sorting or some aggregate operations, such as calculating averages, minima, or maxima, on the resulting values.
3. *Sweep tokens.* These are exchanged among member nodes of different sets on a one-to-one basis along existing arcs. Their number is relatively small; it corresponds to the typical join ratio of two relations.

For each of the above three situations we employ a different scheme for token propagation to minimize the communication overhead:

1. To replicate a restriction token to all elements of a set S, a scheme called *flooding* is used which replicates the token as follows. From the PE holding the sending node the token is replicated first in only one direction, say horizontally. Each PE in that row then replicates the token vertically along the corresponding column thus 'flooding' the entire PE array. Each PE then treats the received token as if a separate copy had arrived for each node of the set S. Note that the number of transmissions is proportional to the number of PEs rather than the number of nodes comprising the set S.
2. To return a large number of result tokens to a single node a scheme called *draining* is used, which accomplishes the reverse function of flooding. PEs of the last row receiving the flooding tokens return the results along the respective columns until the originally first row is reached.

[1] It should be noted that the use of hashing is necessary only to assign graph nodes to PEs but not to distribute data over each disk. Rather, each PE could maintain nodes belonging to the same set in a sequential order, possibly with indices, to increase the utilization of its disk unit. To simplify the simulator, however, we have assumed the worst case, i.e., a random distribution of all nodes throughout each disk; the only optimization employed was disk arm scheduling, which orders accesses to nodes according to disk addresses to minimize seek time.

In this row tokens are propagated horizontally toward the PE containing the master node. Since all PEs within the array are involved in the draining process, aggregate operations as well as sorting of values can be performed very efficiently. Consider, for example, the situation where the total of all results is to be calculated. During the draining process, each PE determines the total of the values produced internally, which it then combines with the total reported to it by its immediate neighbor; this result is then forwarded to the next PE.

3. Sending and receiving sweep tokens along arcs between selected subsets of nodes must be performed on an individual basis. The PE holding the sending node determines the i and j coordinates of the PE holding the receiving node. Based on that information and its own position within the array it determines which of its four neighbors has the shortest geometric distance to the destination PE, and sends the token in that direction. This operation is repeated by each PE receiving the token until the final destination is reached.

3. The AG-Simulator

To test architectural ideas and to evaluate the performance of the the proposed database system, we have implemented the AG-Model on a simulated architecture. The complete software package, henceforth referred to as the *AG-Simulator*, consists of approximately 8000 lines of SIMULA code executing on a VAX-11/780.[2] The following sections describe the overall structure of the simulator and the assumptions made during its construction.

3.1 Hardware Components

The AG-Simulator implements all major components of the architecture; these include:

- the processor
- the memory system (cache and disk)
- the bi-directional inter-PE communication ports
- the interface processor ports for I/O.

The communication ports and disk memory operate asynchronously with respect to the processor and each other.

3.2 Software Components

The complete set of token processing and communication algorithms comprising the AG-Model was actually implemented on the simulated architecture. A synthetic database, with nodes

[2] VAX is a registered trademark of Digital Equipment Corporation

consisting of a key and a single attribute, was created. For attribute values, uniformly distributed random numbers were used; this permits queries to select different subsets from a given set by choosing a range with a fixed span and random endpoints. All algorithms for sending and receiving tokens and for processing these against the synthetic database were implemented as if a physical machine architecture were available. The simulator accepts user queries, transforms these into tokens injected into the database graph, carries out all token propagation and processing, and reports results as well as statistics on performance.

Timing Assumptions. For the simulated components of the architecture the following assumptions were made:

The time required to access an isolated node is assumed to be the average disk access time, 30ms.[3] If more than one data node of the same set is to be accessed by an operation, the time for the second through the last access is calculated using one of two formulas given below. Two assumptions were made based on an analysis of typical disk drive characteristics. First, the cylinder to cylinder plus rotational access time is half the average access time. Second, the nodes are spread uniformly over the allotted cylinders (500 per disk). (As already mentioned in footnote 1, the second assumption represents a worst case – clustering would, in most cases, considerably reduce access time as more than one node could be accessed during each disk operation.)

The two formulas used to calculate the access time t to a node are:

(1) when the number of nodes to be accessed is less than the number of cylinders:

$t = MeanAccessTime - (MeanAccessTime/2 * NumberOfNodes/500)$,

(2) when the number of nodes is greater than the number of cylinders:

$t = MeanAccessTime/2 * 500/NumberOfNodes$.

The first formula decreases the value of t as the number of nodes increases: with a small number of nodes, t is close to the mean access time; when the number of nodes approaches 500 (one per cylinder), t is one half the mean access time. This value is the track-to-track seek time plus the rotational delay for this class of disk. The second formula, used when the number of nodes exceeds the number of cylinders, then decreases the time t even further, since more than one node are accessed during each disk operation.

Processing time is perhaps the most critical of all assumptions. Fortunately, since all communication and token processing algorithms were actually implemented, the corresponding times can be measured rather than estimated. These values are then multiplied by a constant factor to account for the fact that each of the actual PEs would be (16 bit) micro-processor rather than the VAX-780 CPU executing the simulator.

[3] This is the average access time to half the disk; the second half, containing a backup copy of data belonging to the neighboring disk, is accessed infrequently.

The following times were typically observed and were used in all simulation runs presented in this paper. (None of these include any disk access times.)

1. Time to relay a token: 1 MS.

   This is the time required to service the interrupt, decide if the token is for the current PE, and initiate transmission to the next PE.

2. Time to broadcast a token: 3.5 MS.

   This is the time to decide in which direction (dimension) a copy of the current token must be sent, make the copy and send it.

3. Time to process a token: 4.5 MS.

   This is the time to perform the necessary operations on a token according to its type (restriction, sweep, or result token).

4. Simulation Results

This section describes the results of the simulation experiments carried out to determine the performance and the dynamic behavior of the AG-Model under the assumptions described above.

4.1 Performance Evaluation Methodology

We have followed the methodology for evaluating database systems proposed by Boral and DeWitt /BoDeW84/. The basic structure of the synthetic database as well as the proposed four query types and the query mix were adopted from this paper:

- Query type I is a direct access of a single node using a key. In the implementation of the AG-Model, hashing is used instead of indexing.
- Query type II selects 1% of a given set.
- Query type III selects 10% of one set and joins the resulting subset with another set. In our case, no indices are used; rather, a join is functionally equivalent to sending sweep tokens from selected elements of one set to another.
- Query type IV is the same as query type II except the selection rate is 10%. In addition, this query performs some aggregate function; we have chosen to perform sorting on the final results.
- Finally our query mix is the one suggested in /BoDeW84/: 70% of type I, 10% of type II, 10% of type III, and 10% of type IV queries.

4.2 Parametric Variation Experiments

We have carried out the following four series of experiments to test various aspects of the proposed system.

4.2.1 Architecture Topology Variation

As mentioned in Section 2.3, the architecture assumed for the proposed system is a k-dimensional array of processing elements. The first set of experiments was intended to investigate the effects of varying the number of dimensions, k. The primary objective was to confirm our intuitive assumption that, once a 'reasonable' number of physical links are established among PEs, adding new connections has little impact on improvement in performance.

We can distinguish the following three major phases of each query: (1) flooding of the array, which sends restriction tokens to all PEs, (2) exchange of sweep tokens among nodes of the involved sets, and (3) draining of the array, which collects the results. Let us consider these in turn:

1. *Flooding*: Figure 2(a) shows the correlation between the number of dimensions and the flooding time: the improvement is dramatic when increasing the number of dimensions from 1 to 2, as represented by the distance between the solid and the dashed curves; it becomes less important when a third dimension is added. (Note that the time to flood the array is completely independent of the database size, the query type, or the disk performance.)

2. *Propagation of sweep tokens*: Each sweep token is propagated along the shortest geometric distance from the sending to the receiving node. Since the distribution of nodes over PEs is random, each sweep token will travel a distance corresponding to the average path length within the array. This distance is plotted in Figure 2(b) for the three different dimensions. The resulting curves are similar to those for the array flood times (Figure 2(a)): the improvement between 1 and 2 dimensions is dramatic but diminishes when a third dimension is added.

3. *Draining*: The time to drain the array obviously depends on the number of results to be returned. If this number is very small, the time to drain the array is essential the same as the array flood time (Figure 2(a)). If the number of results is large, the time to complete the query will be limited by the speed of the IO device designated to (sequentially) output all results. (This, of course, does not prevent other queries to proceed in parallel, thus utilizing the available resources.)

In summary, we observe that in all three cases the effect of increasing the connectivity of the PE array diminishes rapidly. Considering the fact that each new dimension requires two communication links to be added to every PE, the improvement from two to three dimensions appears already quite marginal. Based on this observation, we have restricted all subsequent experiments to only two-dimensional arrays of PEs.

4.2.2 Problem Size Variation

The next set of experiments is intended to study the effects of varying the amount of work handled by each PE, on the request processing time. For that purpose, we consider an array of 9 PEs (3 × 3) and vary the set size from 10 to 1000; (the number of nodes per PE thus varies from 1.1 to 111.) Figure 3(a) shows the mean processing time for three different types of queries.[4] While a very slow increase is observed for queries of Type I, it becomes almost linear for queries of Type II and III; that is, the mean processing time for the latter types is directly proportional to the problem size.

At a first glance, this result does not seem to represent any major breakthrough in performance, since a conventional database machine displays a similar degradation in response time. We must, however, consider the amount of resources actually utilized to process each query. This is shown in Figures 3(b) and 3(c) for secondary memory and for the PEs, respectively. As expected, for queries of Type I, most (90%) of the available I/O bandwidth as well as the processing time is unused. For queries of Type II and III, disk utilization rises to a maximum of approximately 75% and then decreases slightly; this is due to a decrease in average seek time as the density of nodes on the disks increases. The available processing power is even less utilized; with 100 nodes per PE, over 60% is still unused.

In summary, we observe that, for queries of Type I, the mean processing time remains nearly constant; that is, all disks except one and almost all PEs are unused. For other query types the mean processing time increases linearly with the problem size, however, even in the relatively small array of only 9 PEs, much of the available I/O bandwidth (> 35%) as well as the computing potential (> 60%) is still unused. (This unused capacity may be exploited by increasing the number of simultaneous queries, as will be discussed in Section 4.2.4.)

4.2.3 Array Size Variation

The purpose of this series of experiments is to investigate the effects of increasing the array size, i.e., the number of PEs. Ideally, the mean processing time for a query should increase only slightly (due to longer communication paths within the array), while the unused I/O bandwidth and the PE idle time should increase in proportion with the array size. To confirm this assumption, we have varied the array size from 4 to 1000 PEs, while keeping the set size and the queries constant. The resulting mean processing time for a query is plotted in Figure 4(a). We observe that by increasing the number of PEs from 9, (which was the size assumed in the previous experiment), to 1000, i.e., by two orders of magnitude, the mean processing time for a query does not show any dramatic changes; it decreases first as more disk units and PEs are added and then rises again due to longer communication paths within the array. (Note that a logarithmic scale is used in Figure 4(a).)

---

[4] These experiment were carried out with a multiprogramming level of two, i.e., two queries were executing simultaneously.

While the above changes in query processing time are rather insignificant, the increase in unused I/O bandwidth and PE time is dramatic, as shown in Figure 4(b) and 4(c), respectively; with 300 PEs, both values are nearly zero.

4.2.4 Multiprogramming Level Variation

The previous experiments have shown that increasing the number of PEs does not have any significant adverse effect on the mean query processing time. Our objective now is to show that the unused I/O bandwidth and the computational power may usefully be exploited for simultaneous processing of other queries. For that purpose, we return to the original array of nine PEs, and vary the number of simultaneous queries (selected from the mix suggested in /BoDeW84/) from 1 to 16. Figure 5 shows that, even in the case of nine PEs, where resource utilization is relatively high (Figures 3(b) and 3(c)), the system throughput increases from 1.3 to approximately 3 queries per second.

5. Conclusions

The objective of this paper was to demonstrate that the use of hundreds of processors in a database machine is feasible, provided the I/O bandwidth of the secondary storage medium is increased accordingly, as pointed out in /AgDeW84/. To accomplish the latter, we proposed to replace each large disk with a number of smaller units, each connected to an independent processor. By employing a database model (the AG-Model) suitable to parallel processing, we have shown that the potential I/O bandwidth and the associated computational power of the PE array may usefully be exploited.

We have implemented the AG-Model on a simulated architecture. Due to limitations imposed by the simulator (a typical simulation run producing one data point for the plotted curves consumed between 2 and 10 hours of VAX-11/780 CPU time) we were forced to accept a number of restrictions. In particular, (1) the size of the array had to be kept very small; for example, to place any significant load on individual PEs, only 9 were used for the problem size variation experiments (Figure 3(a)-(c)); (2) the distribution of data nodes over the disks was assumed to be random; a better memory management scheme would significantly improve the utilization of the available I/O bandwidth; (3) in an actual implementation, queries referring to the same sets could reduce the number of disk accesses significantly by using a cache, as discussed in /BeDeW84/; we did not exploit this potential of data sharing in the simulator.

Despite the above adverse assumptions, the obtained results are quite encouraging — the proposed system is capable of utilizing the available I/O bandwidth and the computational power of a significant number of asynchronously operating processing elements.

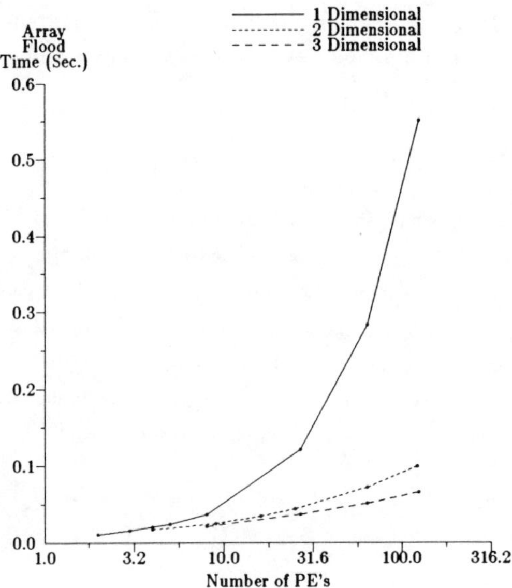

Fig. 2(a). Dimensionality Effect on Flood Time

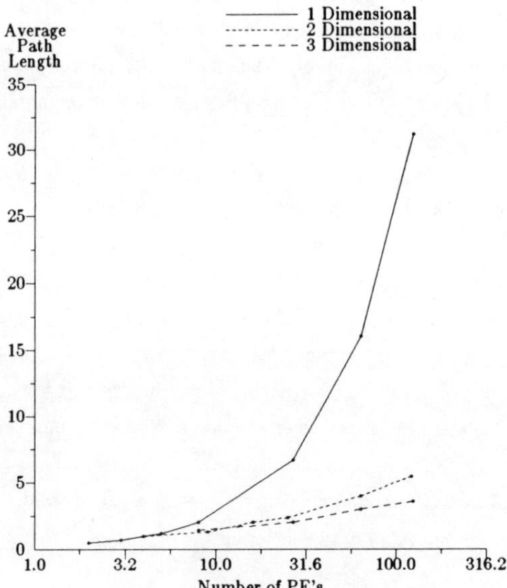

Fig. 2(b). Dimensionality Effect on Path Length

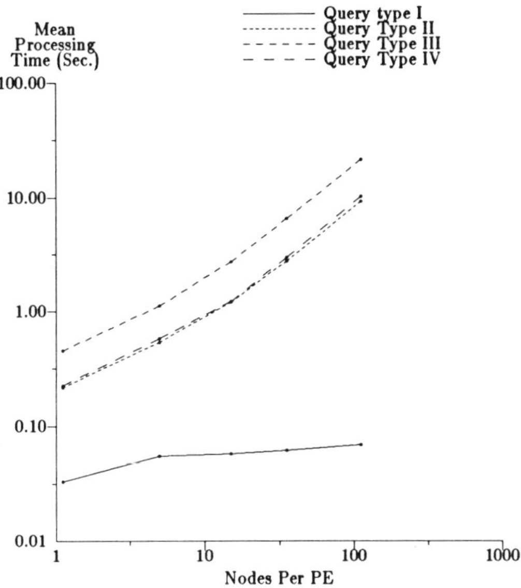

Fig. 3(a). Problem Size Effect on Processing Time

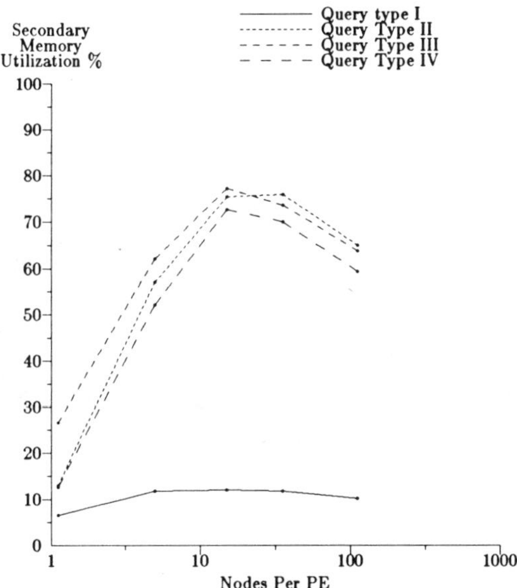

Fig. 3(b). Problem Size Effect on Disk Utilization

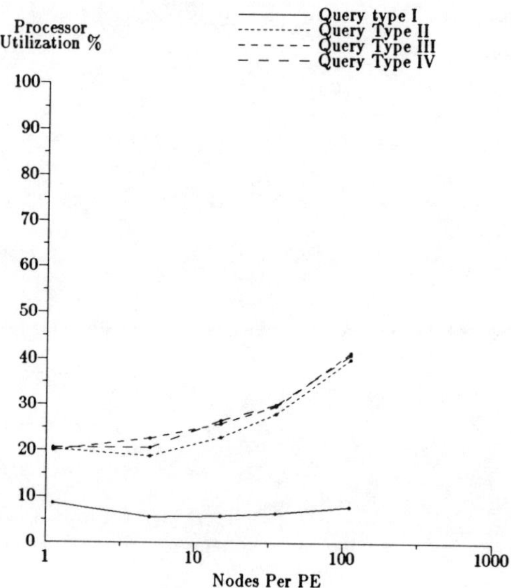

Fig. 3(c). Problem Size Effect on Processor Utilization

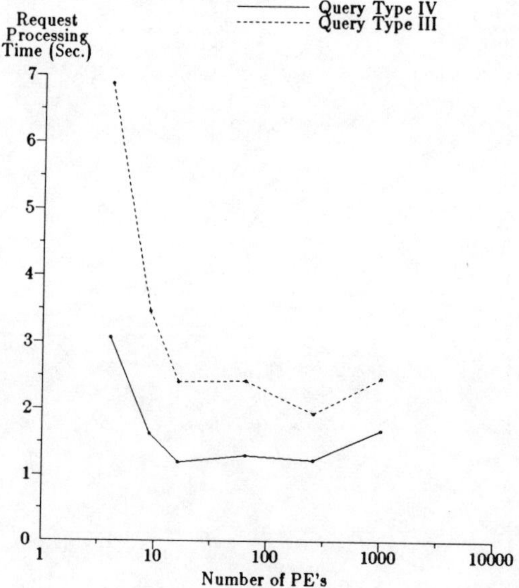

Fig. 4(a). Array Size Effect on Processing Time

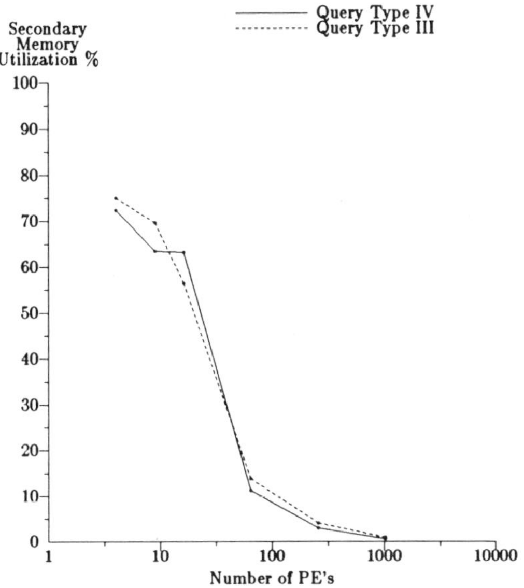

Fig. 4(b). Array Size Effect on Disk Utilization

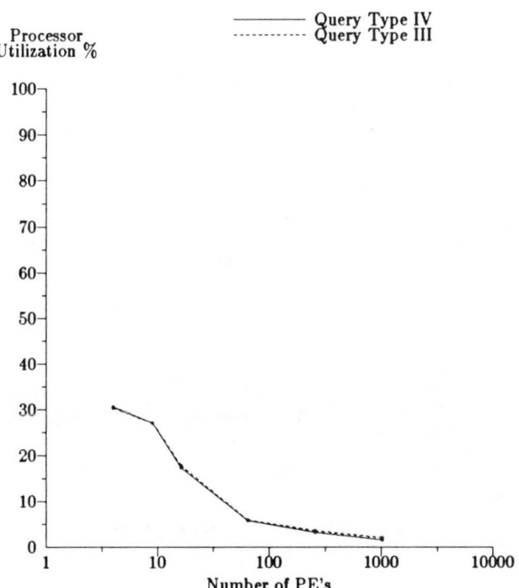

Fig. 4(c). Array Size Effect on Processor Utilization*

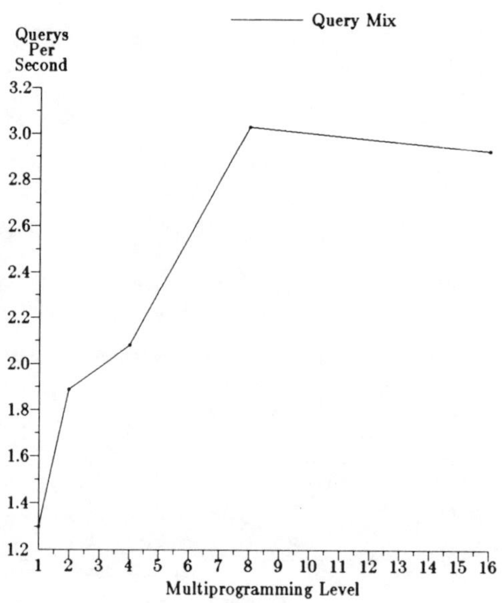

Fig. 5. System Loading Effect on Throughput

References

/AgDeW84/ Agrawal, R. and DeWitt, D. J.: "Whither Hundreds of Processors in a Database Machine?," Int'l Workshop on High-Level Architecture, Los Angeles, California, 1984.

/BiHa83a/ Bic, L., Hartmann, R.: "A Network-Oriented Dataflow Database", Proc. Int'l Workshop on Database Machines (IWDM-3), Munich, 1983

/BiHa83b/ Bic, L., Hartmann, R.: "The Active Graph Database Model", Proc. 2nd Int'l Conf. on Databases (ICOD-2), Cambridge, U.K., August 1983

/BoDW81/ Boral, H. and DeWitt, D. J.: "Processor Allocation Strategies for Multiprocessor Database Machines," ACM Trans. Database Systems, Vol. 6, No. 2, June 1981, pp. 227-254.

/BoDeW84/ Boral, H. and DeWitt, D. J.: "A Methodology for Database Performance Evaluation," ACM 0-89791-128 August 1984.

/Che76/ Chen, P.: "The Entity - Relationship Model: Toward a Unified View of Data," ACM TODS, 1,1, March 1976

/COM82/ COMPUTER, Special Issue on Dataflow Systems, 15,2, Feb. 1982

/Har85/ Hartmann, R.: "The Active-Graph Database Machine," PhD Thesis (in progress), Dept of ICS, University of California, Irvine, 92717

/TaFr76/ Taylor, R. W., Frank, R. L.: "CODASYL Data Base Management Systems," ACM Computing Surveys, Vol.8, No.1, March 1976

/TBH82/ Treleaven, P. C., Brownbridge, T. R., Hopkins, R. C.: "Data-Driven and Demand-Driven Computer Architecture," ACM Computing Surveys, 14,1, March 1982

The Silicon Database Machine

M. D. P. Leland
W. D. Roome

AT&T Bell Laboratories
Murray Hill, New Jersey 07974

ABSTRACT

This paper describes the design of the hardware and software for a multiprocessor, silicon memory, database machine—the SiDBM. The entire database resides in stable silicon memory; there are no disks. The processors are functionally specialized, with relation managers, host interfaces, query managers, and query processors. The processors are tightly coupled, and the silicon memory is shared and is directly addressable by all of them. The SiDBM supports a relational model, and allows concurrent transactions and queries. The number of processors and the database size can be selected to suit the application; the expected range is 3 to 16 processors, and 100 megabytes to 2 gigabytes of data. This paper also gives some preliminary performance results for the SiDBM.

1. Introduction

The structure of a traditional database management system (DBMS) has been strongly influenced by the nature of the disks used to store the data. For example, because disks are block-oriented with a long access time, a high-performance disk-based DBMS must cluster related data in the same block. If, while processing a query, a DBMS needs data in another disk block, the DBMS must suspend that query, and work on another while waiting for the block. Furthermore, because a disk block must be updated as a whole, a disk-based DBMS must choose an updating scheme that minimizes the number of blocks which must be updated.

One way to improve performance is to store the data in directly-addressable silicon memory, instead of disks. Silicon-based storage has many advantages for a DBMS:

- The database can be easily shared among several processors.
- Locality is no longer important: records can be placed anywhere.
- Different indexing methods, such as binary trees or hashing schemes, become practical.
- Query optimization is simpler: there is no need to consider disk access time.
- Scheduling is simpler: each task can be run to a natural stopping point.
- Updating is simpler: it's practical to update individual words in records.
- Response time and throughput become much more predictable and repeatable.
- Silicon memory is much less sensitive to dust and vibration.

This paper describes the design of a multiprocessor, silicon memory, back-end database machine—the SiDBM. Our goal is to make the SiDBM at least 10 times faster than a conventional disk-based DBMS. The processors are tightly coupled, and the silicon memory is directly addressable by all of them. The SiDBM uses a relational model, and allows multiple, concurrent transactions. The SiDBM allows update transactions as well as read-only queries; we feel that good update performance is as important as good query performance. The number of processors and the database size can be selected to suit the application; the expected range is 3 to 16 processors, and 100 megabytes to 2 gigabytes of data.

Silicon memory has two disadvantages: it costs more, and it needs continuous power to maintain the data. As for the first, the cost of silicon memory is decreasing faster than that of disks; even if silicon memory isn't cheaper than disks, for many applications, the increased performance should compensate for any additional cost of silicon memory. Furthermore, silicon memory will benefit from new high-density packaging technologies, such as wafer-scale integration. As for the second problem, silicon memory can be made stable either by using batteries to maintain power, or by using disks to shadow the silicon memory.

Before describing what the SiDBM is, it is important to note what it is not. First, it is not a distributed database management system: it is a backend database machine that uses multiple processors to improve performance. Of course, the SiDBM could be a component in a distributed database management system.

Second, our silicon memory is not a cache for a disk, nor is it an I/O device whose blocks must be copied to and from primary memory. Our silicon memory is a single-level store that is an extension of the primary memory of the processors, and has the same access characteristics as primary memory. We really are assuming that the entire database fits in silicon memory, and that the silicon memory is stable.

Section 2 describes the logical structure of the SiDBM, and Section 3 compares the SiDBM to other database machine work. Section 4 describes the SiDBM hardware. Sections 5 and 6 describes the components of the SiDBM: the Relation Managers (RMs), and the Query Manager (QM) and Query Processors (QPs). Section 7 describes our prototype, and gives some performance results. Section 8 gives some conclusions, and plans for future work.

2. Logical Structure

2.1 Processors and Memories

The SiDBM has the following processor components:

- HI Host Interface: communicates with the outside world (host computers, etc.).
- QM Query Manager: translates requests from HIs into tasks for QPs and RMs.
- QP Query Processor: executes tasks for a query, as directed by the QM.
- RM Relation Manager: gatekeeper for a set of relations.

These processors are connected to the following memory components, as shown in Figure 1:

- SM Stable Memory: directly-addressable memory holding the database.
- CM Communications Memory: used for communication between processor components.

Each processor has some local memory, on the order of 512 Kbytes. Local memory accesses do *not* go over the global interconnect. This local memory holds the processor's instruction text, stacks, and local data. The HI processors can have devices, such as communication lines or network connections. As with the local memory, device accesses do not use the global interconnect. The other processors do not have devices.

The SM holds the database itself, and takes the place of a disk. As the name implies, the memory is stable over crashes; at worst, the word being written during a crash will be lost. The SM appears in the address space of each processor; it is directly addressable, just like the processor's local memory. The SM can be read by any processor, but can only be written by the RM processors (this is enforced by memory mapping hardware in each processor). The SM is the only stable memory; the processors' local memories are not stable.

The CM also appears in each processor's address space, and is used for communication between the processors. The CM differs from the SM in that it is not stable, and it can be written by any processor. The CM is logically partitioned among the processors; currently 64 Kbytes are assigned to each processor.

The SiDBM is essentially a shared memory multiprocessor; in fact, our prototype uses a standard bus for the interconnect, and single-board computers (with on-board memory) for the processors. However, the SiDBM differs from a conventional shared memory multiprocessor in that most of a processor's accesses are to its own local memory, so that the load on the interconnect is much less (we will return to this point in Section 4.3).

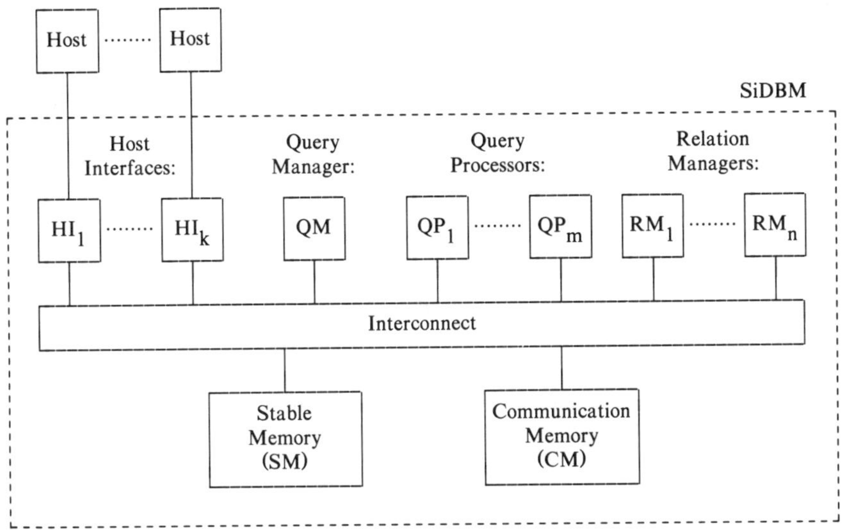

Figure 1: Logical structure of the Silicon Database Machine.

2.2 Interprocessor Communication: Tasks and Streams

Each processor has a simple multi-tasking executive that multiplexes that processor among a small set of *tasks* (say 1-20). Each task is a simple thread of control running through the permanently resident instruction text of that processor. Each task has its own stack, and tasks can be created and destroyed dynamically. All tasks on a processor share the same address space; they are mutually cooperative, rather than mutually suspicious.

The basic interprocessor communication mechanism is a *stream*. A stream is a queue in CM, with a simple producer-consumer protocol. A sender or receiver first acquires a lock on the stream, adds or removes data, and then releases the lock. The lock is held so briefly that a task just spins (loops on a "test-and-set" instruction) if the stream is already locked.

Any task that knows the address of a stream can send data to that stream, or can receive data from it. Thus streams can be many-to-many, although most streams are one-to-one or many-to-one. For example, the QM creates a stream at a known address; an HI sends a request to the QM by sending data to that stream. The request may include the address of a stream back to the HI.

In general, each processor creates a request stream to itself, and has a "dispatcher" task that reads requests from that stream. In the QM and the RMs, the dispatcher task handles each request itself. For the QPs, the dispatcher task creates a new task to handle each request.

2.3 Host Interfaces

Each HI gets requests from the outside world—directly connected terminals, a host computer, a connection to a local area network (LAN), etc. The HI translates that information into requests for the QM, and places those requests in the QM's command stream. The HI then waits for a reply, which could come from the QM or from one of the other processors. The reply may contain pointers to one or more records in the SM; the HI accesses those records, and outputs them in the desired format.

Some HIs might simply forward requests from host computers; others might run complex application programs. A host computer might even be connected directly as an HI. However, any HI that runs general user programs will need a more complex operating system, to protect both the database from the user programs, and the user programs from each other. This paper will not describe the HIs in any detail.

2.4 Query Manager and Query Processors

The QM waits for requests in its command stream. The QM translates each request into a network of simple operations, such as select, join, sort, project, and aggregate, and assigns those operations to the QPs and RMs. The operations are connected via streams, over which are sent pointers to records in the SM, and other data. In general, the records themselves are not moved.

2.5 Relation Managers

Each RM is the gatekeeper for a set of relations, and provides transaction-oriented read/write access to the records in those relations. A transaction can span several RMs, in which case those RMs cooperate via a two-phase commit protocol [Gray 1978, Lai and Wilkinson 1984] to ensure that all either they all commit the transaction or else none of them do. Except for that, each RM operates independently.

Records can be accessed by key or by secondary index; each RM uses and maintains its own indexes. Each RM allows multiple readers and writers, and handles concurrency control and crash recovery. Each RM provides select and update operations, but does not provide other relational operations such as join or project. For select requests, an RM returns addresses of records in the SM; those addresses are guaranteed to be valid for the duration of the requesting transaction, but no longer.

The relations in the database are partitioned among the RMs, as determined by the system administrator. The administrator also logically partitions the stable memory among the RMs; each RM independently manages the data structures (records, indexes, free space, etc.) in its partition. The result is that an RM can access or update the data structures in its SM whenever it wants to; an RM does not contend with other processors for locks on shared data structures.

2.6 A Simple Example

As an example, here is how the SiDBM handles the following selection query:

range of x is Employees
retrieve into Temp (x.all) where x.name = "Smith"

Let's suppose that relation *Employees* is managed by Relation Manager *rm1,* and relation *Temp* is managed by *rm2.* After first receiving this query from its host (or whatever), a Host Interface does the following:

- creates a "reply" stream to itself (allocated from the HI's CM partition);
- sends the query, along with the reply stream's address, to the QM's request stream;
- waits for a reply message to arrive on the reply stream;
- and finally sends the appropriate response to the requesting host.

After receiving the query on its request stream, the QM does the following:

- parses the query and determines that this is a simple selection request;
- determines that *Employees* and *Temp* are managed by *rm1* and *rm2*, respectively;
- selects a QP to handle this request—say *qp1;*
- and sends the parsed query and associated data to *qp1's* request stream.

After receiving that request, the dispatcher task on *qp1* starts a new task to handle that request. This new task does the following:

- creates its own reply stream, from its own CM partition;
- sends start transaction requests to *rm1* and *rm2*, and waits for replies;
- sends a read request to *rm1*, specifying the search expression (name = "Smith") and the address of its reply stream;
- reads record pointers from its reply stream, and sends an add request to *rm2* for each record;
- after getting end-of-file on its reply stream, sends commit requests to *rm1* and *rm2;*
- sends a "done" message to the HI, on the HI's reply stream;
- sends a "done" message to the QM, on the QM's request stream (so that the QM knows that *qp1* is available for more work);
- and finally frees its reply stream created earlier, and terminates itself.

After getting the read request, *rm1* does the following:

- finds all records that match the search expression (using an index on the name field, if one exists, or else using linear search);
- sends pointers to those records over *qp1's* reply stream;
- locks these versions of those records in place for the duration of this transaction;
- and sends an end-of-file indicator on the reply stream when done.

After getting each add request, *rm2* does the following:

- allocates space from its SM partition for the new record;
- copies data from the existing record into the new record;
- arranges for the new record to become permanent if and only if the transaction commits;
- sends a reply to *qp1*.

The RMs handle the start transaction and commit requests similarly.

2.7 Observations

You should notice the following points about the SiDBM architecture:

- There is little copying of records; in general, processors exchange pointers to records rather than records themselves. Thus in the above example, *rm1* sends pointers to *qp1*, and *qp1* gives those pointers to *rm2*.

- The use of shared memory is very disciplined: each piece of CM is "owned" by some processor, and another processor can update that piece only if "granted" permission by the owner (this is only an informal software convention; the SiDBM is not a true capability-based system). In the example, *qp1* grants *rm1* permission to use *qp1's* reply stream by sending the address of the reply stream in the request to *rm1*.

- There is little contention for shared memory: the only place where the classical mutual exclusion problem occurs is when acquiring a lock on the data structures associated with a stream.

- The interconnect usage is relatively low, because it is only used for references to SM or CM. All instruction fetches, stack references, and local data fetches—in short, at least 80% of each processor's memory references—do not involve the global interconnect.

- The system administrator can engineer the SiDBM to a particular application by selecting the number of HIs, the number of QPs, the number of RMs, the amount of SM, and how the relations and SM are partitioned among the RMs. For example, if there are many complex queries, the system administrator might select one RM and a lot of QPs. If there are a many simple retrieval requests and many relations, the system administrator might select a lot of RMs and only a few QPs.

3. Comparison With Other Work

3.1 Disk-Based Search Devices

Many proposed database machines have been based on search devices tightly coupled to disks. These include RAP [Schuster 1979, Langdon 1978], CASSM [Su 1979], CAFS [Maller 1979], and DBC [Banerjee 1978 and 1979, Kannon 1978, Menon 1980]. Typically a search device is attached to each disk head, and they can scan all records in a cylinder in one disk revolution [Roome 1982]. Another approach, used in IDM with the database accelerator [Epstein 1980], VERSO [Bancilhon 1983], DBMAC [Missikoff 1983], and SABRE [Gardarin 1983]. is for fast, special-purpose hardware to scan (possibly multiplexed) data as it is read from the disks.

For a silicon database, the equivalent approach would be to integrate the searchers with the memory devices. Unfortunately, thousands of searchers are required to match the performance of a simple indexing scheme. To see why, consider the following simple analysis. Suppose that there are n records, where n is in the range of 1,000 to 1,000,000. If there are m searchers, each of which can test one record in one time unit, the parallel searcher approach takes t_p time units to locate the desired records, where

$$t_p = n/m.$$

Now consider a simple indexed search, using a single, conventional processor. Using a height-balanced binary tree index, a search takes at most $1.44\log_2 n$ comparisons [Knuth 1973]. Let's suppose that this processor can do one comparison in 10 time units (i.e., we assume that the specialized search devices can test records 10 times faster than a general purpose processor). Then an indexed search takes t_i time units, where

$$t_i = 14.4\log_2 n.$$

To determine the number of searchers required to equal the performance of an indexed search, we set $t_p = t_i$ and solve for m. Thus a database with 1,000,000 records requires approximately 3500 searchers. Perhaps more interesting than the actual number of searchers is the observation that, for n in the range of 1,000 to 1,000,000, the parallel searcher approach requires one searcher for every 150 to 300 records to equal the performance of a simple indexing scheme. That implies one searcher for every one or two memory chips. Thus the parallel searcher approach first requires solving a challenging VLSI problem, and then solving the problem of connecting several thousand searchers in a network. For this reason, we choose not to explore the parallel searcher approach.

3.2 Multiprocessor Database Machines

Proposed multiprocessor database machines use either standard processors or specialized hardware to perform the database functions. Machines using standard processors include DIRECT [DeWitt 1979, Boral 1981, Bitton, Boral, et al 1983], DSIS [Lien 1981], Jasmin [Fishman 1984, Lai 1984], DBMAC [Missikoff 1983], and SABRE [Gardarin 1983]. All of these machines differ from the SiDBM in significant ways. All store the database on disk, and use much of their processing power to manage these disks. Several of these machines do have shared memory, but either it is not directly addressable, so large amounts of data must be copied to or from local memories, or else management is shared by all processors, so that locking mechanisms must be used to avoid conflicts in memory accesses.

For example, the DIRECT database machine has a large set of processors, each with private memory, that operate on records in a large shared page cache. DIRECT stores data on disk, and stages it into the cache. The DIRECT processors cannot address the cache directly; they must copy pages into their local memory. The DIRECT processors have a limited address space, and can only hold three pages at a time. Finally, DIRECT has a central controller that manages the page cache; the controller assigns pages to processors as a query executes (our QM participates in the setup, but not the execution, of a query). Analysis of DIRECT [DeWitt and Hawthorn 1981, Agrawal and DeWitt 1984] has shown that there are two bottlenecks: the central controller, and the transferring of data from disk into the page cache. These problems do not exist in the SiDBM.

Our query processors are similar to the stream processors in DSIS [Lien 1981]. However, we have chosen a different set of primitive operations, and our interconnection mechanism is different.

The layered structure of the SiDBM is similar to that of Jasmin [Fishman 1984, Lai 1984]. The differences are that Jasmin is disk-based, and does not use shared memory for interprocessor communication. The silicon memory allows our Relation Manager to combine the functions of Jasmin's Record Manager and Intelligent Store components. Also, while Jasmin creates a network of tasks to process a query, all the tasks for a query run on the same processor.

In addition to the differences mentioned above, DBMAC [Missikoff 1983], and SABRE [Gardarin 1983] use some on-thc-fly filtering of data as it is read from disk. DBMAC also stores its database very differently than the SiDBM.

The proposals to use specialized hardware for database operations include RDMB [Schweppe 1983], IQC [Sekino 1983], and the data-stream database machine proposed by Tanaka [1983]. The SiDBM uses standard processors, although the design is modular enough that specialized engines could replace one or more of the QPs in the future.

Another proposal for specialized hardware [Hsiao 1983] uses many simple processors to do a single primitive operation. The SiDBM differs from this massively parallel approach by using large-grained parallelism (the QPs) in query processing, with each of the primitive operations required in a query done on one processor.

3.3 Multiprocessors

The SiDBM is essentially a shared memory multiprocessor [Enslow 1977], and is similar to C.mmp [Wulf 1974] with its hierarchy of busses. Pure shared memory multiprocessors have two problems: the interconnect becomes a bottleneck, and the processors are constantly getting locks on shared memory. The SiDBM avoids the first problem because most of each processor's memory references are to its own local memory, which it can access without contending for the interconnect. In particular, instruction fetches are always local.

The second problem is avoided by very controlled use of shared memory. For example, only an RM can update the SM—and an RM can only update the SM partition assigned to it. Thus an RM doesn't have to acquire locks every time it accesses data structures in its SM. As mentioned earlier, the *only* place where the classical mutual exclusion problem occurs is when sending or receiving data from a stream.

3.4 Main Memory Database Machines

In the SiDBM, we assume that *everything* always fits into memory. That is, all relations are in the SM, and all transient data necessary for the query processing (e.g., arrays of pointers to records being sorted) fits in the local memories of the QPs. Thus our implementation strategies differ from those discussed by DeWitt et al [1984], which assume that data must be paged to and from disk.

The Massive Memory Machine, or MMM [Garcia-Molina 1984], is another proposal to use a large amount of main memory. However, the MMM is envisioned as a single processor, with standard disk drives. Although it could be used for database applications, it is not designed solely for them, as is the SiDBM. Furthermore, the MMM does not have the parallelism which the SiDBM has in the QPs and RMs.

Another approach is to replace the disks in a conventional DBMS with high-speed silicon-based I/O devices (i.e., "RAM disks"). This approach gives a large performance improvement with no significant software changes. Of course, such a DBMS would cost the same as the SiDBM, because the major cost is in the silicon memory. However, the RAM disk approach still treats silicon memory as a block-oriented device, whose blocks must be copied to and from a primary memory cache. Also, it is not clear how this approach would use multiple processors. Thus, given equivalent processors and memories, the SiDBM will be inherently faster than a RAM disk DBMS. The SiDBM wouldn't be 10 times faster—but since the costs are the same, the SiDBM wouldn't have to be.

4. Hardware

This section gives a high-level description of the hardware we would like to use to build the SiDBM. Instead of building such a system immediately, we have constructed an initial prototype, using off-the-shelf hardware, as described in Section 7. This prototype is close enough to the desired hardware that we can develop the software and can demonstrate the feasibility of the SiDBM.

4.1 Processor Components

The top half of Figure 2 shows a block diagram of a processor component—a QM, QP, RM, or HI. Each processor has a local processor bus, which connects the CPU to local memory, devices, and an interface module for the global interconnect. Local memory and device references are handled by the processor bus, without involving the interface module.

Rather than having a separate CM module on the interconnect, the CM has been distributed among the processors. The CM partition assigned to a processor is attached to that processor's interface module; the CM itself is the logical union of all these partitions.

The processor interface module acts as a slave on the local processor bus, responding to requests within the address ranges assigned to the SM and CM. If the request is for that processor's CM partition, the interface module accesses the attached memory, and returns the data via the local bus. Such accesses do not involve the interconnect. If the request is for another processor's CM partition, or for the SM, the interface module forwards the request to the interconnect, and returns the response. Thus each interface module acts as both a master on the interconnect, for SM and foreign CM references, and as a slave, responding to requests for its portion of the CM.

Distributing the CM over the processor components has two advantages over the alternative approach of having one CM module attached to the interconnect. First, the distributed approach automatically grows the CM as processors are added. Second, the distributed approach decreases the load on the interconnect, because a processor can reference its own CM partition without using the interconnect. Note that as far as the SiDBM software is concerned, there is no difference between these approaches.

The local memory and devices occupy the high and low megabyte of the processor's address space. Assigning one megabyte of address space to the CM, with a 64 Kbytes partition per processor, allows up to 16 processors. The remainder of the address space is assigned to the SM.

There are two possible ways to package the processor components. The first is to use a card cage and bus for the processor's local bus. The processor and local memory would occupy one or more boards, and the processor interface and CM partition would be packaged as one board with a connection to the interconnect. This packaging would be best for the HIs, since it allows arbitrary device boards to be added. The other packaging would put the processor, its local memory, the processor interface, and the CM partition all on one board that plugs directly into the interconnect. This would be best for the QM, QP, and RM components, which have no devices.

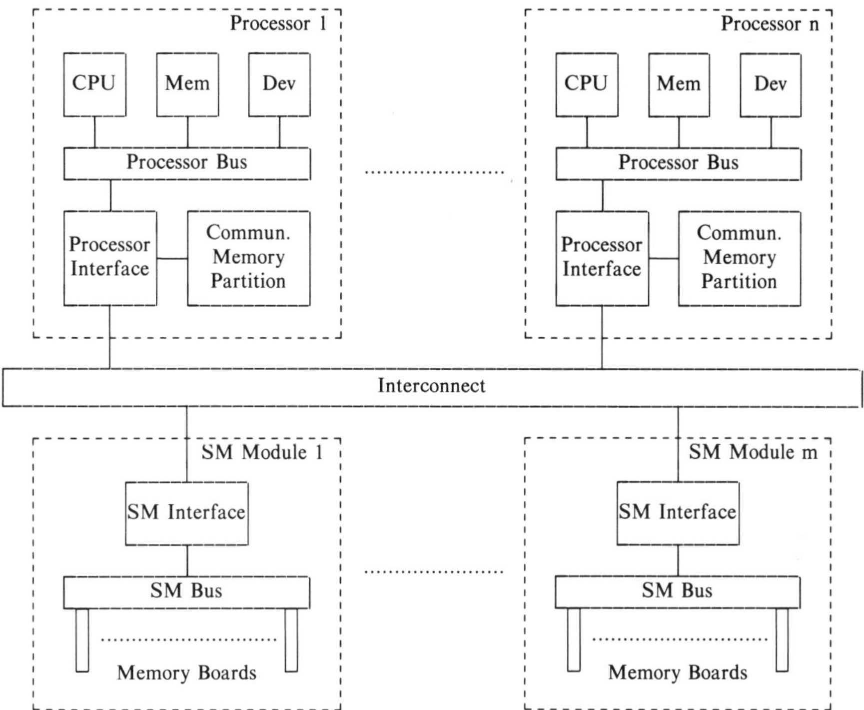

Figure 2: Block Diagram of Silicon Database Machine.

4.2 Stable Memory

Physically, the SM is partitioned into modules, as shown in the lower half of Figure 2. Each module contains a special bus, loaded with memory boards, and an SM interface board that connects the SM bus to the interconnect. The interface acts as a slave on the interconnect, listening for requests for its associated memory boards, and acts as a master—the only master—on the SM bus. The SM interface board could also provide a cache. The memory boards on the SM bus are the only boards that need uninterruptible power. The physical partitioning of the SM into modules is independent of the logical partitioning of the SM among RMs, although logically partitioning the SM by modules might simplify administration.

4.3 Interconnect

There are several possibilities for the interconnect fabric: a bus, a general crossbar, or a partial crossbar (see below). We think that a bus is sufficient, because at least 80% of each processor's memory references should be local—instruction fetches, stack references, or other local data. Thus n of our processors present about the same load as a conventional multiprocessor with $.2n$ processors. Since a bus can usually handle two to three conventional processors, it should handle 10 to 15 of our processors.

Our experience with the prototype supports this assertion. As described in Section 7.2, bus contention caused less than a 3% performance degradation in a six processor load test (three QPs feeding update requests to three RMs).

If bus contention does prove to be a problem, we could provide a direct connection from each RM to the SM modules assigned to it. This "partial crossbar" would be considerably cheaper than a full crossbar.

5. Relation Manager

5.1 Interface

The RMs provide transaction start, commit, and abort requests, as well as select (read) and update (write) requests. The RMs guarantee that transactions are serializable, and that commits are atomic and permanent [Gray 1978]. After a crash, the RMs abort any active, uncommitted transactions. A transaction can span several RMs, in which case those RMs cooperate at transaction start and commit time to ensure serializability, atomicity, and permanence. Other than that, each RM operates independently. The algorithms for multi-RM transactions have not yet been implemented, but are similar to those designed for Jasmin [Lai and Wilkinson, 1984]; they will not be described here. The remainder of this section describes the independent operation of each RM.

For a select request, a client (QP, QM, etc.) specifies a transaction, a relation, a search expression, and a stream. The RM uses that stream to return pointers to all records in that relation which match that expression. The client can use those pointers to access those records for the duration of the transaction. Expressions are currently limited to the AND of one or more simple predicates, each of which tests a single field. Currently supported predicates include equality tests (*field = constant value*), prefix tests, and range tests (*low value* $\leqslant$ *field* $\leqslant$ *high value*).

If one of the fields in a search expression is indexed, the RM uses that index to locate the records. Because the RM uses binary tree indexes, the records are returned in ascending order on that field. If the search expression involves several indexed fields, the client can specify which one to use; this also allows the client to specify a sort order. Otherwise the RM decides which index to use. If the search expression does not involve any indexed fields, the RM just tests all records in the relation.

For updates, clients do *not* directly modify records. Instead, a client sends an update request to the RM, specifying the relation, a pointer to the current version of the record (as returned by an earlier select request), and a pointer to a new version. The RM copies the new version into stable memory, and arranges for that version to become current if and when the transaction commits. The RM does not alter the current version yet; however, subsequent select requests for that transaction will return a pointer to the new version.

5.2 Concurrency Control

The RM uses an optimistic concurrency control scheme [Roome 1982, Kung 1981]. The RM ensures that each transaction sees a consistent snapshot of the database, as of the time the transaction started. The RM allows a transaction to commit if and only if, at commit-time, every record read by that transaction is still current in the database. A transaction sees its own updates. The RM uses a versioning mechanism to implement this concurrency scheme, with automatic garbage collection for unneeded old versions.

The advantages of the optimistic concurrency control scheme are uniform response time for requests, and simplification of the RM internals. We feel that these compensate for the disadvantages of transaction interference, and the extra space for the multiple versions. In any case, the RM could be revised to use a conventional locking scheme, if that seems appropriate.

5.3 Implementation Techniques

The RM links all versions of a record together: this includes the current version, some old versions, and some new versions. All versions are indexed, using a height-balanced binary tree for each indexed field [Knuth 1973].

For each transaction, the RM keeps a read-list and a write-list, containing pointers to all records read or written by that transaction. The write-lists are in the SM; the read-lists aren't. For a select request, the RM uses an index to find the matching record versions, and returns those versions that the transaction should see. For an update request, the RM allocates space in the SM for a new version, copies the data, and updates the indexes. The index updating is done in parallel with the client.

For a commit request, the RM first validates the transaction [Kung 1981], and then commits or aborts it. To validate a transaction, the RM verifies that all records read by the transaction are still current. This is very simple: the RM just checks the status field of each record on the transaction's read-list; this takes a few instructions per record. To commit a transaction, for each record on the transaction's write-list, the RM marks the current version as an old version, and makes the new version current. To abort a transaction, for each record on the transaction's write-list, the RM unlinks the record from the indexes, and frees its space.

The RM *retires* a committed transaction T by freeing the old versions of all records updated by T. The RM retires T when all transactions that started before T committed have committed or aborted; after that, no other transaction will ever need those old versions. We need the write-list for transaction T to locate the old versions; thus the RM maintains write-lists for all committed but unretired transactions.

5.4 Recovery

There are two aspects to crash recovery: recovering from processor crashes, and recovering from media failures. In a processor crash, if the RM was updating a word of the SM, that word may be lost, but the rest of the SM survives. In a media failure, some or all of the SM is lost (this is analogous to a disk head crash). The RM uses different techniques to recover from these failures.

First consider processor crashes. On recovery, the RM first aborts all active but uncommitted transactions, and then retires all committed but unretired transactions. This is possible because the write-lists are kept in the SM.

There is one additional consideration. Suppose that when updating a record, the processor crashes after allocating space for the new version (i.e., after updating the free list data), but before adding that record to the transaction's write-list. If we weren't careful, all knowledge of that space would be lost. To avoid such problems, the RM uses internal transactions to take the SM from one recoverable state to another. When starting such a set of updates, the RM saves the old values in an "undo" log [Gray 1978]. When the SM is again in a recoverable state, the RM discards the undo log. When recovering, the RM first examines the undo log, and undoes the updates that were in progress, if any. Only one internal transaction can be active at a time, which simplifies the undo log considerably. Also, note that log entries are for small parts of records, such as 4 byte pointers, rather than for entire records.

There are two ways to handle media failure: either duplicate the SM, or provide shadow disks. Either method can be done by the SM hardware, without changing the RM. For the shadow disk method, all changes would be saved in a stable, duplicated memory buffer (a "redo" log [Gray 1978]). A disk driver (part of the SM, not the RM) would scan this log to find dirty pages, and would write them out to disk. When the write completed, the disk driver would remove the entry from the log.

6. Query Processing: The Query Manager and Query Processors

6.1 The Query Processors

Each Query Processor (QP) is a specialized engine that implements the primitive operations of relational algebra (e.g. select, project, sort, join) [Codd 1970]. Each QP has a request stream, on which the Query Manager (QM) sends a parameterized description of each operation that that

QP is to perform. A dispatcher task on each QP reads that QP's request stream, and creates a new task for each operation. The task terminates when the operation is complete. These tasks all compete for the processor.

The QPs use streams for communication. Each primitive reads one or two input streams, and produces one output stream. A "logical record" in one of these streams consists of a number of pointers to (physical) records in the stable memory, and (optionally) of some immediate values. For example, pairs of pointers are used in the output af a join operation; immediate values are used in the results of aggregate operations such as sum or average.

In the prototype, the QP primitives are implemented in software. The design is modular; in a full-scale machine, specialized processors (e.g. sorting engines) might be used in some or all of the QPs.

6.2 The Query Manager

The Query Manager (QM) orchestrates the action of the QPs. The QM takes a parsed query from an HI and translates it into network of primitives to be executed by the QPs. The QM also sets up descriptions of the input and output streams to be used by the QPs. The QM sends start transaction requests to the RMs, sends request for operations to the QPs, and (if all goes well) asks the RMs to commit transactions.

The QM optimizes the queries so that they can be performed efficiently. Query optimization in the SiDBM differs both from that in conventional, disk-based database machines and from that in distributed databases [Rothnie 1977]. The QM does not need to consider disk access time, but it must consider other factors in assigning primitives to QPs. These factors include the load on the QPs from other queries, the load from this query, and when, during the execution of this query, processing will be required. In distributed databases, the data in any relation is distributed. In the SiDBM, queries are processed in a distributed manner, by cooperating QPs, but the data is centralized and only pointers to it are passed between QPs. Thus, the SiDBM does not need to consider issues of minimizing data transfer between processors.

The query optimization has not yet been designed or implemented. We plan to experiment with different strategies for optimization. The issues we will study include:

- How should the operations in the parsed query (from the HIs) be rearranged for efficiency? What information (e.g. statistics from the RMs) is necessary for this rearrangement?
- How should the QM assign specific QPs to particular operations?
- How much optimization can the QM do without becoming a bottleneck?
- How should the primitive operations be done by the QPs? For example, which method should be used for joins?

The example in the next section illustrates the operation of the QM and QPs, and points out some of the optimization decisions that the QM makes.

6.3 An Example

We use the simple join query in Figure 3a to show how the QM and QPs operate. We will assume that joins are done by a sort-merge algorithm. However, different algorithms (possibly in hardware) could be used with minor modifications to the QM's strategy. The overall interaction of the QM, QPs, RMs, and HI is the same as described in Section 2.6.

The QM receives (an internal form of) this query from an HI, and translates it into the parse tree shown in Figure 3b. This query is very simple, so only this parse tree is considered; for more complex queries (e.g. containing several joins) the QM considers alternative parses and chooses the one that it estimates will be processed most efficiently. In deciding how to process a query, the QM uses information about the relations involved. This information is kept in a "meta-relation" in the database.

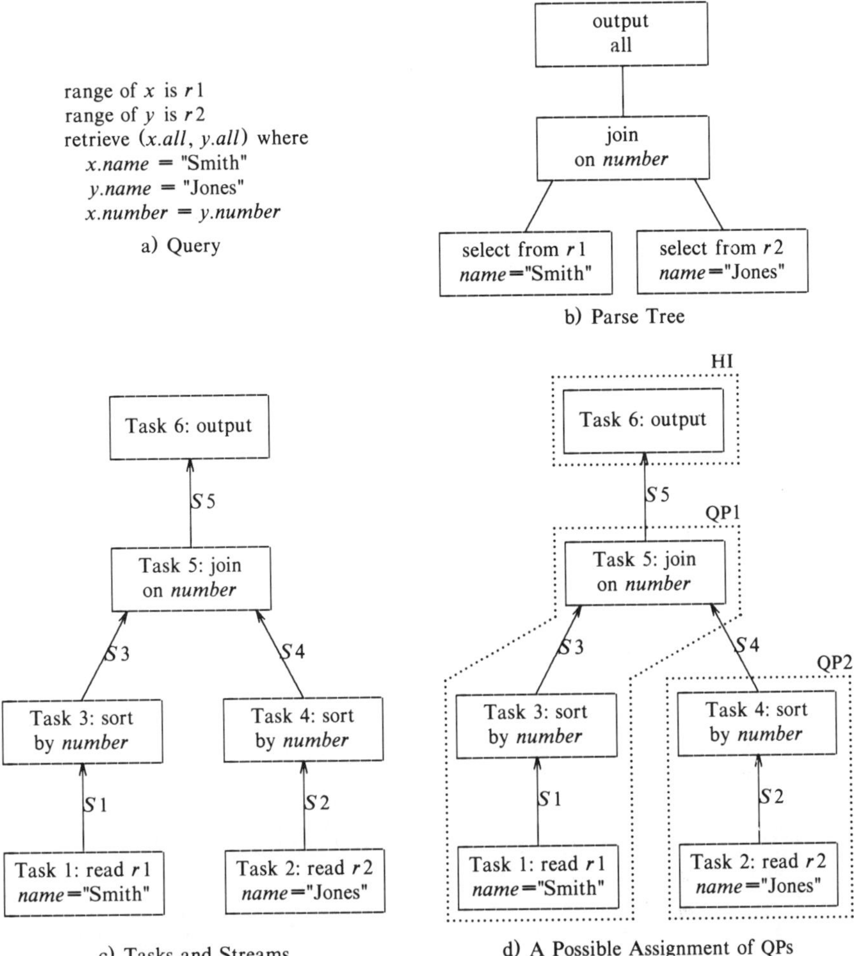

Figure 3: Processing of a Join Query

The QM translates the parse tree into primitive tasks for the RMs and QPs. In doing this translation, the QM must determine what tasks are needed to perform each operation in the parse tree. In this case, the selected pointers from relations $r1$ and $r2$ must be in order on the *number* field before the join is performed. The method for achieving this order depends on what indices exist on the *name* and *number* fields. The cases are:

- *name* not indexed, *number* not indexed: The RM cannot emit pointers in sorted order. A sorting task is necessary.
- *name* indexed, *number* not indexed: The RM cannot emit pointers in sorted order, but would use the *name* index for the selection.

- *name* not indexed, *number* indexed: The RM can emit the pointers in sorted order, with no loss of efficiency, since it must read the entire relation to select on the *name* field. A sorting task is not needed.
- *name* indexed, *number* indexed: The RM could emit pointers in sorted order, but it would have to read the entire relation to do so. Since *name* is indexed, this would be much slower than simply using the *name* index for the selection. The QM must determine which is more efficient: for the RM to search all the records, eliminating the sorting task, or for the RM to use the *name* index, requiring a task to sort the (much smaller) set of selected records.

If the RM emits pointers in *number* field order, then Tasks 3 and 4 in Figure 3c would be omitted. We describe the most complex case (Figure 3c), where the selections from both relations must be sorted by QPs before the join is performed. Tasks 1 and 2 issue read requests to the RMs containing relations $r1$ and $r2$, respectively. Tasks 3 and 4 sort the incoming streams on *number*. Task 5 does a merge join of the sorted streams. Task 6 (on an HI) outputs the requested data.

The QM determines the inter-task streams needed to process this query, and the structure of the logical records in these streams. The streams are shown in Figure 3c. Logical records in streams $S1$, $S2$, $S3$, and $S4$ consist of single pointers, all to records with the required *name* field. The pointers on $S3$ and $S4$ are ordered by the *number* field. Logical records in stream $S5$ consist of pairs of pointers $(p1, p2)$. $p1$ and $p2$ point to records in $r1$ and $r2$, respectively, with equal *number* fields. Task 6 reads pairs of pointers from stream $S5$ and outputs the fields from both records. Thus, Task 6 can begin as soon as Task 5 produces its first output; most of their processing will be overlapped.

The QM uses information from the meta-relation, information about the load on the QPs from other assigned tasks, and knowledge of the structure of the request to make the assignment of tasks to QPs. One possible assignment is shown in Figure 3d. Although we have five tasks to assign to QPs, several of these can be assigned to the same one. Task 1 (or 2) is very short and simple, only requiring its QP to issue a select command to the RM; the RM puts the required pointers on a stream which is read by Task 3 (or 4). Thus, Tasks 1 and 3 (or 2 and 4) are assigned to the same QP. On the other hand, the two sorts are time-consuming and independent, and should proceed in parallel on different QPs. The QM attempts to estimate the sizes of the data to be sorted, and assigns the larger sort to the QP with the lighter load. The join cannot begin until the sorts are completed. Thus, no parallelism is gained by having Task 5 on a distinct QP from both Tasks 3 and 4. Assigning Tasks 3 and 5, for example, to the same QP ensures that stream $S3$ is in the local communication memory of that QP. Therefore, this stream does not make use of the global bus.

In this example, two QPs process the query much more quickly than one. Ignoring stream communication time, which is negligible, the total time for two QPs is the sum of

- the longer of
  - the select time for relation $r1$ (Task 1) plus the sort time for Task 3
  - the select time for relation $r2$ (Task 2) plus the sort time for Task 4
- the pipelined time needed for
  - the join (Task 5) and output (Task 6)

If only one QP is used, the sorts would have to be done sequentially. The time needed for the query would increase by at least the lesser sort time.

7. Performance Results

This section describes the hardware prototype for the SiDBM, and some early performance results on this prototype.

7.1 Prototype Hardware

Using a standard bus and standard single-board-computers (SBCs) and memory boards, we have constructed a prototype that is close enough to the hardware described above that we can write and test software for the SiDBM, measure response time and throughput, and investigate the load on the interconnect.

The bus in our prototype is the VMEbus [Mostek 1981], a multi-master 32-bit address and data bus. Figure 4 shows how the boards are arranged. The processor components are SBCs with an 8Mhz Motorola 68000 microprocessor and 128 Kbytes of dual-ported on-board memory. The on-board memory can be expanded to 512 Kbytes. On-board memory references do not use the VMEbus.

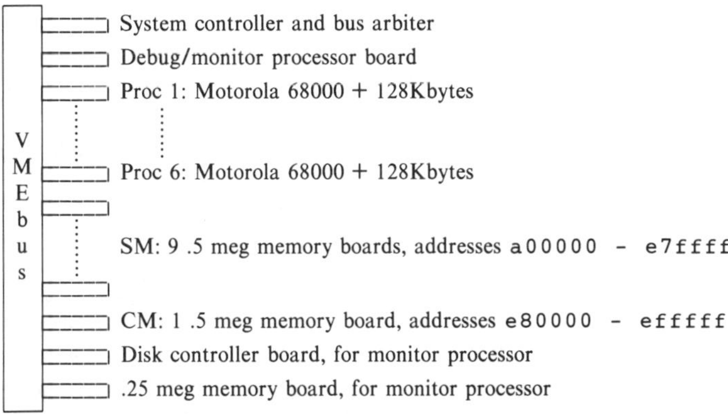

Figure 4: Board arrangement for SiDBM prototype.

The stable memory consists of ordinary memory boards, plugged directly into the VMEbus; we make them stable by saving the data on disk when powering the system down. The memory cycle time is approximately 350 ns, for both the memory boards and the on-board memory.

Instead of distributing the CM among the processors as described in Section 4.1, we used a memory board on the VMEbus for the CM, and assigned a 64 Kbyte partition to each processor. Because each processor's references to its own CM memory go over the bus, the prototype will slightly overestimate bus contention.

Our current prototype has 6 processors, 4.5 megabytes of SM, and 0.5 megabytes of CM. This is enough to generate a reasonable load, and is enough space for a test database. Unlike a disk-based DBMS, the performance of the SiDBM is relatively insensitive to the size of the database (assuming memory access times and processor speeds stay the same, of course).

The prototype also has a debugging and monitoring processor, running a simple disk-based operating system. This involves a processor board with a terminal driver, and a separate disk driver board. These are on same VMEbus as the SiDBM components. On powerup and shutdown, the monitoring processor loads and saves the silicon memory on disk, and loads programs into the SiDBM processor boards. While the database machine is operating, the monitor just acts as a terminal driver: when the user types characters, the monitor places them in a stream that an HI reads; to output characters, an HI places them in a stream read by the monitor.

The Motorola 68000 processor boards are relatively slow: a typical instruction takes 2 to 3 microseconds. There are three ways to speed up these processors. First, improve the memory mapping unit (MMU); the current one induces a wait state in each memory reference. Second, increase the clock speed to 10Mhz. And third, use a true 32-bit processor that uses a single bus cycle to access a 32-bit word; the 68000 uses two 16-bit cycles. These changes should nearly double the speed of the processors.

7.2 Wisconsin Benchmark Results

This section gives the performance of the SiDBM for the Wisconsin benchmark tests [Bitton, DeWitt, and Turbyfill, 1983]. Because the SiDBM software is not yet complete, we have only been able to run the selection tests.

Records in this database have 13 2-byte integer fields and three 52-byte string fields, for a total of 182 bytes. Memory limitations forced us to shorten the records by omitting the string fields, to give 26 byte records. This is not as significant a modification as it might seem; unlike a disk based DBMS, the performance of the SiDBM is relatively independent of the record size. To verify this we ran two tests, one against a relation with 10,000 short 26 byte records, and the other against a relation with 10,000 full-size 182 byte records. Each test ran 250 transactions, each of which read and updated 10 records. The full-sized record test took 66.0 seconds, versus 65.7 seconds for the short record test: a .5% difference. Thus we feel justified in comparing our results with short records against the published results for full-size records.

We used three of the integer fields: *unique1,* which takes on the values between 0 and $n-1$ where n is the number of records in the relation; *unique2,* which is a random permutation of the values in *unique1*, and *hundred*, which takes random values between 0 and 99. Thus selecting all records with $0 \leqslant$ *unique1* $\leqslant 99$ gives the first 100 records in a relation, and selecting records with $0 \leqslant$ *unique2* $\leqslant 99$ gives 100 records randomly scattered through the relation. The other fields are given various random integer values (e.g., the field *ten* has random values between 0 and 9).

We used relations with 10,000, 1,000, and 100 records; most tests were with a 10,000 record relation. The assignment of relations to RMs depended on the test. Unless otherwise specified, each relation was indexed on three fields, *unique1*, *unique2*, and *hundred.*

Figure 5 gives the results for the selection tests. These selected 1, 100, or 1,000 records from a 10,000 record relation into a temporary relation. The numbers are the total elapsed time, in seconds. Records were selected on the *unique2* field. Indexes were not constructed for the created temporary relation. The first three columns give the results when *unique2* was not indexed (i.e., the RM scanned all 10,000 records); the last three columns give the results when an index existed.

	Number of records selected from a 10,000 record relation					
	No index			Index		
	1	100	1000	1	100	1000
Same RM	4.1	4.5	8.8	.02	.54	5.3
Different RM	4.1	4.1	4.3	.02	.35	3.3
IDM-500, clustered index	–	21.6	23.6	–	1.5	8.7
IDM-500, non-clustered index				–	3.3	23.7

Figure 5: Elapsed time, in seconds, for selection tests.

The "same RM" line gives the results when the source and destination relations were on the same RM; the "different RM" line gives the results when they were on different RMs. The improvement by using two RMs depends on the number of records added by the destination RM: the more records added, the larger the improvement.

The line labeled "IDM-500, clustered index" gives the Bitton's results for these tests on an IDM-500 database machine with the accelerator; this was the fastest DBMS that they measured. The indexed results are for a clustered index, in which the records were stored in order of the indexed field. The "IDM-500, non-clustered index" line gives their results for a non-clustered index. Of course, only one field per relation can have a clustered index. The concept of a clustered index does not exist in the SiDBM; the SiDBM's performance is independent of which indexed field is used.

As can be seen, the SiDBM was considerably faster than the IDM-500 for all of these tests. If we use two RMs, the SiDBM is 5 times faster on the unindexed tests, and 5 to 7 times faster than the IDM-500 with a non-clustered index. The SiDBM is only 2.6 to 4 times faster for the clustered index tests. However, these tests reduce to copying a sequential set of records from one file to another; this is precisely the situation in which a disk cache works very well.

7.3 Relation Manager Tests

This section gives the results of some performance tests on the Relation Manager (RM). We were interested in the following:

- Response time for a transaction ("single-thread" tests).
- Maximum throughput, in transactions per second ("multi-thread" tests).
- The effect of the database size.
- The effect of bus contention.

To quickly summarize the results of these performance tests:

- For a 10,000 record relation, a simple read request takes approximately 6.5 milliseconds (ms), and a write takes approximately 21 ms.
- One RM can handle 6.9 transactions per second, where each transaction reads and updates five records in a 10,000 record relation.
- Increasing the number of records in a relation by a factor of 10 increases the read time by approximately 0.5 ms, and increases the write time by approximately 1.0 ms. Thus a read from a 1,000,000 record relation should take about 7.5 ms.
- Bus contention is negligible: running simultaneous load tests on three RMs gave less than a 3% degradation. I.e., three RMs give a total throughput of 20.2 transactions per second, which is 2.9 times the throughput of a single RM.

All tests were run using the Wisconsin database described above. The RMs maintained indexes on three fields, *unique1*, *unique2*, and *hundred*.

Figure 6 shows how we assigned tasks (circles) to processors (dotted rectangles). The single RM tests involved one or two driver tasks, on the *Proc1* processor, feeding requests to an RM task, on *Proc2*. The response-time tests used one driver task; the throughput tests used both driver tasks. For the throughput tests, we tried using more than two driver tasks, and we tried placing the two driver tasks on different processors; these variations did not improve the throughput. The multiple RM tests used four or six processors; the second and third RMs each had their own copies of the database. Unused processors were idle, and did not access the bus.

For the read-only tests, each driver submitted several hundred transactions. For each transaction, the driver task sent the RM a start request, several read requests, and a commit request. We varied the number of records per transaction from 1 to 10. Records were read by value of the indexed field *unique2*.

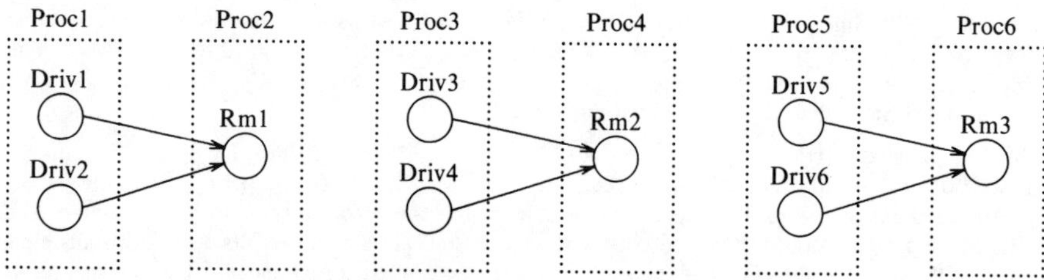

Figure 6: Task and processor structure for RM tests.

For the read-write tests, the driver task sent a write request to the RM after each read request; "10 rec/trans" means that each transaction issued 10 reads and 10 writes. The update changed the value of the indexed field *hundred*, but not the other fields. Each driver task ran one transaction at a time, and waited for the RM to reply to a request before submitting the next request. For the multiple driver tests, each driver used a different set of records, and submitted requests independently.

Figure 7 gives the response time per transaction for relations with 1,000 and 10,000 records. These tests used a single driver task, feeding requests to a single RM. These results imply that a read request takes 6.0 ms for the 1,000 record relation, and 6.5 ms for the 10,000 record relation (this includes the time for the driver task to formulate the read request and send it to the RM). Thus each power of 10 increase in the relation size adds about 0.5 ms to the time for a read request (the retrieval time increases as log$n$, where n is the number of records in the relation), so that a read from a 1,000,000 record relation should take approximately 7.5 ms.

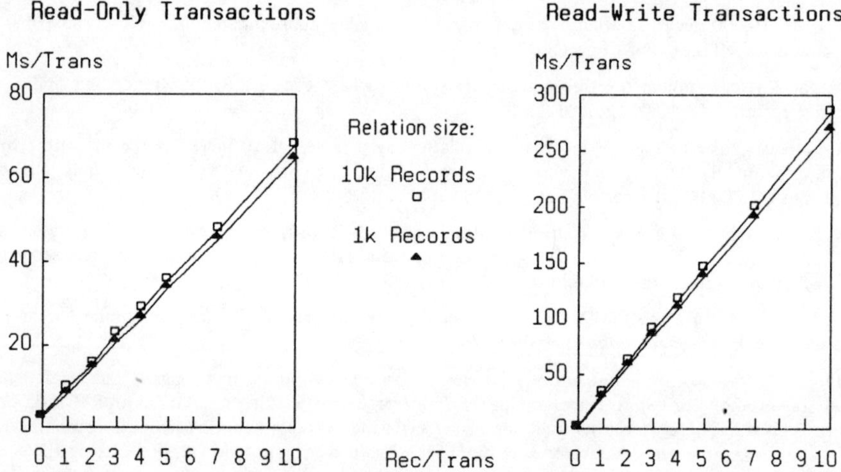

Figure 7: Transaction response time.

A write request takes approximately 20 ms for the 1,000 record relation, and 21 ms for the 10,000 record relation. Actually, this is the total amount of processing time that the RM must do for each write request. Some is done when the write request is processed, and the rest is done when the transaction commits. Much of this time is overlapped with the client. We estimate that if the RM is idle, the perceived response time for a write request—from sending that request until receiving the RM's reply—is about 5 ms.

Transaction Description	Total throughput (trans/sec)		
	1 RM	2 RMs	3 RMs
read 5 records	32.4	64.4	96.0
read and update 5 records	6.9	13.7	20.2

Figure 8: Total throughput versus number of RMs.

Figure 8 shows how the total throughput, in transactions per second, varies with the number of RMs. Transactions either read 5 records or read and updated 5 records from a 10,000 record relation. Each RM operated independently; no synchronization was needed at transaction start or commit time. Each RM was driven by two driver tasks on another processor, so that the three RM test used all six processors. Thus this test measures the degradation due to bus contention. As can be seen, adding more RMs gives an almost linear increase in throughout: for update transactions, the total throughput for three RMs is only 2.4% less than three times the throughput of one RM, and for read-only transactions, it's only 1.2% less. Thus we can conclude that, at least for three RMs, bus contention is not a problem, and that given a balanced workload, distributing relations among three RMs can triple the system throughput.

8. Conclusions and Future Work

This paper describes the SiDBM, which exploits silicon memory and multiple processors to provide a fast relational database machine, and gives some performance measurements on a prototype. From these measurements we can conclude that:

- The SiDBM is much faster than existing database machines.
- The SiDBM can use multiple processors effectively.
- Bus contention is not a problem, at least for 6 processors.

Future plans include work in the following areas:

- Query optimization algorithms, and algorithms for assignment of tasks to Query Processors.
- Algorithms for placement of relations among Relation Managers.
- Concurrency control algorithms for transactions that span several Relation Managers.
- Specialized processors for query processing tasks.

Acknowledgements

Larry Lai and Ed Lien contributed to the early design of the SiDBM. The query processors were inspired by work by Jon Shopiro.

References

Agrawal, R. and DeWitt, D.J., "Whither Hundreds of Processors in a Database Machine?," Proc. Intl. Workshop on High Level Computer Architecture, May 1984, pp. 6.21-6.32.

Bancilhon, F., Fortin, D., Gamerman, S., Laubin, J.M., Richard, P., Scholl, M., Tusera, D., and Verroust, A., "VERSO: A Relational Backend Database Machine," in *Advanced Database Machine Architecture,* D.K. Hsiao (ed), Prentice-Hall, 1983, pp. 1-18.

Banerjee, J., Hsaio, D.K. and Baum, J.T., "Concepts and Capabilities of a Database Computer," ACM Trans. on Database Systems, 3:4 (December 1978), pp. 347-384.

Banerjee, J., Hsaio, D.K. and Kannon, K., "DBC—A Database Computer for Very Large Databases," IEEE Trans. Computers, C28:6 (June 1979), pp. 414-429.

Bitton, D., Boral, H., DeWitt, D.J., and Wilkinson, W.K., "Parallel Algorithms for the Execution of Relational Database Operations," ACM Trans. on Database Systems, 8:3 (Sept 1983), pp. 324-353.

Bitton, D., DeWitt, D.J., and Turbyfill, C., "Benchmarking Database Systems: A Systematic Approach," CS Tech. Rep. #526, Univ. of Wisconsin at Madison, December 1983.

Boral, H. and DeWitt, D.J., "Processor Allocation Strategies for Multiprocessor Database Machines," ACM Trans. on Database Systems, 6:2 (June 1981), pp. 227-254.

Codd, E. F., "A Relational Model of Data for Large Shared Data Banks," Comm. of the ACM, 13:6 (June 1970), pp. 377-387.

DeWitt, D.J., "DIRECT—A Multiprocessor Organization for Supporting Relational Database Management Systems," IEEE Trans. Computers, C28:6 (June 1979), pp. 395-406.

DeWitt, D.J. and Hawthorn, P.B., "A performance Evaluation of Database Machine Architectures," Seventh Intl. Conf. on Very Large Databases, September, 1981, pp. 199-214

DeWitt, D.J., Katz, R.H., Olken, F., Shapiro, L.D., Stonebraker, M.R., and Wood, D., "Implementation Techniques for Main Memory Database Systems," SIGMOD '84: Proceedings of the Annual Meeting, June 1984, pp. 234-239.

Enslow, P.H., "Multiprocessor Organization—A Survey," ACM Computing Surveys, 9:1 (March 1977), pp. 103-129.

Epstein, R. and Hawthorn, P., "Design decisions for the intelligent database machine," Proceedings of the 1980 National Computer Conference, pp. 237-241.

Fishman, D.H., Lai, M.Y., and Wilkinson, W.K., "Overview of the Jasmin Database Machine," SIGMOD '84: Proceedings of the Annual Meeting, June 1984, pp. 234-239.

Garcia-Molina, H., Lipton, R.J., and Honeyman, P., "A Massive Memory Database System," Tech. Report 314, Dept. of EE and CS, Princeton Univ., September 1983.

Gardarin, G., Bernadat, P., Temmerman, N. Valduriez, P., and Viemont, Y., "SABRE: A Relational Database System for a Multimicroprocessor Machine," in *Advanced Database Machine Architecture,* D.K. Hsiao (ed), Prentice-Hall, 1983, pp. 19-35.

Gray, J.N., "Notes on Database Operating Systems," in *Operating Systems: An Advanced Course,* R. Bayer et al (ed), Springer-Verlag, 1978, pp. 393-481.

Hsiao, C., "Highly Parallel Processing of Relational Databases," Ph. D. Thesis, Purdue University, Department of Computer Sciences, Aug. 1983.

Kannon, K., "The Design of a Mass Memory for a Database Computer," Proc. Fifth Annual Symp. on Computer Architecture, April 1978, pp 44-51.

Knuth, D.E., *The Art of Computer Programming: Volume 3/Sorting and Searching,* Addison-Wesley, 1973.

Kung, H.T., and Robinson, J.T., "On Optimistic Methods for Concurrency Control," ACM Trans. Database Systems, 6:2 (June 1981), pp. 213-226.

Lai, M.Y., and Wilkinson, W.K., "Distributed Transaction Management in Jasmin," Proc. of the Tenth International Conf. on Very Large Databases, August 1984, pp. 466-470.

Langdon, G.G., "A Note on Associative Processors for Database Management," ACM Trans. Database Systems, 3:2 (June 1978), pp. 148-158.

Lien, Y.E., Shopiro, J.E., and Tsur, S., "DSIS—A Database System with Interrelational Semantics," Seventh Intl. Conf. on Very Large Databases, September, 1981, pp. 465-477.

Maller, "The Content Addressable File Store—CAFS," ICL Technical J., November 1979, pp. 265-279.

Menon, M.J. and Hsiao, D.K., "The Access Control Mechanism of A Database Computer (DBC)," ACM Fifth Workshop on Computer Arch for Non-Numeric Processing, March 1980, pp. 17-28.

Missikoff, M. and Terranova, M., "The Architecture of a Relational Database Computer Known as DBMAC," in *Advanced Database Machine Architecture,* D.K. Hsiao (ed), Prentice-Hall, 1983, pp. 87-108.

Mostek Corp, Motorola Inc and Signetics/Philps, *VMEbus Specification Manual,* 1981.

Roome, W.D., "The Intelligent Store: A Content-Addressable Page Manager," Bell System Tech. J., 61:9 (November 1982), pp. 2567-2596.

Rothnie, J.B., Jr., and Goodman, N. "A Survey of Research and Development in Distributed Database Management," Proc. of International Conference on VLDB, Oct. 1977, pp. 48-62.

Schuster, S.A., Nguyen, H.B., and Ozkarahan, E.A., "RAP.2—An Associative Processor for Databases and Its Applications," IEEE Trans. Computers, C28:6 (June 1979), pp. 446-458.

Schweppe, H., Zeidler, H.Ch., Hell, W., Leilich, H.-O., Stiege, G., and Teich, W. "RDBM: A Dedicated Multimicroprocessor System for Database Management," in *Advanced Database Machine Architecture,* D.K. Hsiao (ed), Prentice-Hall, 1983, pp. 36-86.

Sekino, A., Takeuchi, K., Makino, T., Hakozaki, K., Doi, T., And Goto, T., "Design Considerations for an Information Query Computer," in *Advanced Database Machine Architecture,* D.K. Hsiao (ed), Prentice-Hall, 1983, pp. 130-167.

Su, S.Y.W. et al, "Architectural Features and Implementation Techniques of the Multicell CASSM," IEEE Trans. Computers, C28:6 (June 1979), pp. 430-445.

Tanaka, Y., "A Data-Stream Database Machine with Large Capacity," in *Advanced Database Machine Architecture,* D.K. Hsiao (ed), Prentice-Hall, 1983, pp. 168-202.

Wulf, W., Cohen, E., Corwin, W., Jones, A., Levin, R., Pierson, C., and Pollack, F., "HYDRA: The Kernel of a Multiprocessor Operating System," Comm. of the ACM, 17:6 (June 1974), pp. 337-345.

Database Machine FREND

Sadayuki Hikita, Suguru Kawakami, Hiromi Haniuda
Systems Research Laboratory, OKI Electric Industry Co. Ltd.,
4-10-12 Shibaura, Minato-ku, Tokyo 108, Japan

Abstract

Relational database machine FREND is presented in this paper. Different from conventional database machines, FREND has been developed for composing distributed systems in accordance with personal computers and a local area network. Since it consists of a16-bit micro-processor and small disk units, FREND is a small scale and cost-effective database machine. Overview of FREND is described. Then processing structure and optimization of query processings are explained. In order to demonstrate that FREND could apply to practical usage, its performance is evaluated finally.

1. Introduction

The relational data model[1] and the development of semi-conductor technology encouraged the research and development of database machines. Although a lot of database machines have been proposed[2,3,4], only a few machines are used in a commercial market[5]. This is because most of them are not superior to database management systems implemented by software in general purpose computers. Especially, special purpose hardware such as join processors increases hardware costs.

By virtue of development of semi-conductor technology, high-performance micro-processors are inexpensively available these days and those processors will be frequently replaced by new versions. Even for database machines, a lot of functions must be implemented by software. If those software are tightly coupled with hardware or processors, most of software must be revised when those are replaced by new versions. Therefore database machines should be designed to enjoy the development of memory technology, micro-processor technology and disk technology.

FREND (Flexible Relational Database Machine) adopts a 16-bit general purpose micro-processor. Its software is designed as a layered module structure and coded in a high leveal language. Therefore, most programs for database managements of FREND could be workable in various hardware environments.

The research and development project of database machine FREND started in 1980. Based on prototype FREND, the first commercial version called db-1 has been sold since 1983 in Japanese market. Its target host computers are assumed to be personal computers which are connected through communication lines, such as local area networks.

In chapter 2, overview of database machine FREND is presented. Chapter 3 describes configuration of FREND. The processing mechanisms are explained in chapter 4. Finally the performance is evaluated in chapter 5.

2. Overview of FREND

A lot of kinds of main-frame computers, and mini-computers have supported database management systems (DMBS). However, new DBMS market have emerged in the market of personal computers. The discrimination of DBMS markets are roughly shown in Fig. 1. A large gap between the DBMS market of personal computers and the one of mini-computers can be found. Relatively expensive mini-computers must be requested to support DBMS. On the other hand personal computers will become more powerful, then they will be able to fill this gap to some extent. However, they could not support shared databases, because they would be designed for personal use, not for shared use. FREND is the best suited to bridge the gap and to support shared databases.

Database machine FREND was designed to be shared among small computers such as personal computers and to compose distributed systems[6] with personal computers and with networks. Personal computers, work as hosts of FREND, easily utilize databases in FREND through a communication network, such as through a local area network. Various kinds of those computers only have to install the routine for FREND interface if they want to be host computers of FREND. This routine is an adapter program between application programs and FREND. It provides all commands of FREND and is so small that it is portable to other computers without efforts. Application programs in host computers can access shared databases in FREND by subroutine calls as if they were in their computers.

The SEQUEL[7] like commands are provided with FREND. When an application program wants to access to database in FREND, it sets a command code and parameters in a predefined format. This command is sent to FREND after the interface routine is activated by a subroutine call. The results are returned back to the interface routine in the host computer. In this way, an application program has a tuplewise interface with the interface routine.

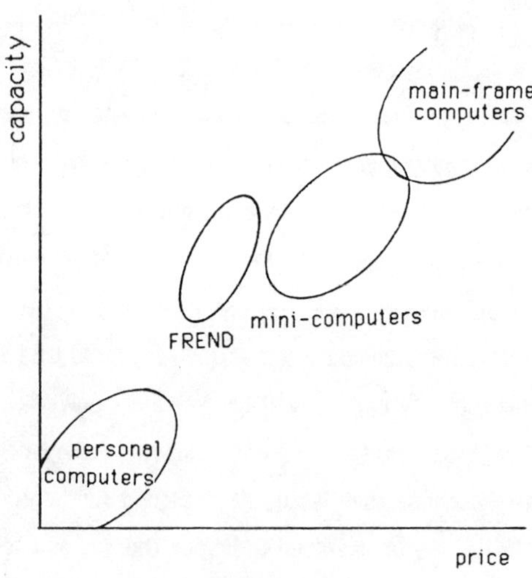

Fig. 1 DBMS markets

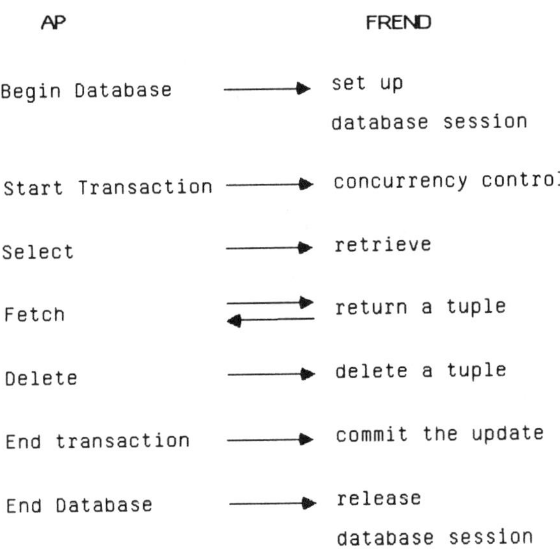

Fig. 2 An example of a command sequence

A sequence of commands of a job could not be partially completed, but must be committed as an atom. This is controlled by a transaction. There may be concurrent transactions running in FREND, each of which declares the beginning and the end of it. FREND controls the concurrency and commitment[8] by a transaction. FREND controls the concurrency at the beginning of a transaction, and provide the shared mode lock and the exclusive mode lock. Because FREND does not commit an update before the declaration of End Transaction, the update is aborted when failure occurs before End Transaction. An example of a sequence of commands between an application program and FREND is shown in Fig. 2.

3. Configuration Of FREND

3.1 Hardware configuration

The hardware configuration of FREND is shown in Fig. 3. FREND consists of a 16-bit micro-processor, small disk units, RS232-C interfaces and IEEE-488 bus interfaces. Communication between FREND and host computers is done through up to eight RS232-C serial lines or an IEEE-488 bus.

The database processor executes all functions of FREND. It not only controls database management, but also controls commumnication between FREND and host computers, and also controls data transfer between a disk memory and a main memory. Intel 8086 is used for the processor and it runs special purpose operating system tuned for real time processing.

One megabyte memory is equipped for FREND. All programs of FREND work in the main memory without roll in / roll out overhead. 64 KByte of it is used for database buffering in which size of pages is 1 KByte. A disk controller controls up to 4 disk units in which 40 MByte or 80 MByte, 8 inch small disk units can be alternatively selected.

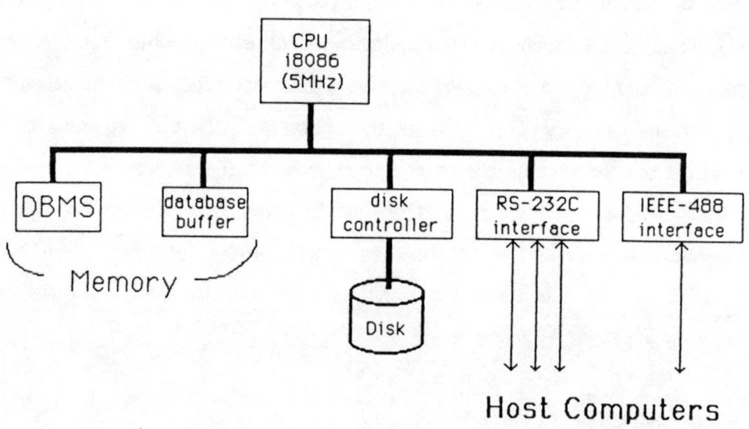

Fig. 3 Hardware configuration

3.2 Software configuration

FREND consists of five processing modules; External Interface Program (EIP), Multiple Relation Manager (MRM), Single Relation Manager (SRM), File Access Manager (FAM) and Database Support Program (DBSP). EIP controls database communication, say database session, between FREND and host computers. When personal computers, those could be said to be host computers, want to access to FREND, they must set up database session before sending queries. After completion of accesses, the database session must be cleared. DBSP supports maintenance works of FREND, such as controls of start / stop services, volume copies of disk units and so on. Other three modules execute kernel functions of the database management system. Those modules organize layered processing structures. Those are shown in Fig. 4.

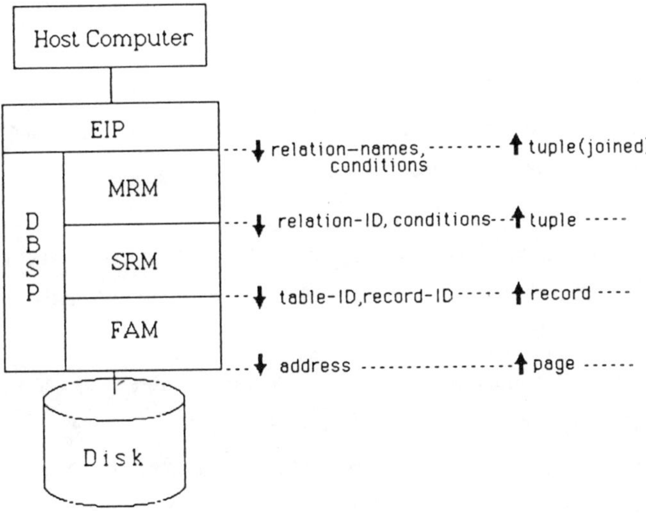

Fig. 4 Software configuration

MRM provides functions of defining and manipulating relations. MRM receives queries from personal computers and analyzes them. All names, queries specify, are converted into internal names such as relation identifiers, attribute identifiers. If queries contain join operations, it optimizes execution strategy based on nested loops algorithm[9,10]. The optimization is explained in section 4.1. MRM handles all kinds of data as relations uniformly; they include not only relations users define, but also relations of system data such as definition information of relations, security informations and so on. This results in simplification of programs of MRM.

SRM provides functions of manipulating single relation. SRM receives a query from MRM in which all names used in a query are converted to identifiers and in which target relation is limited to one relation per query. Since MRM decomposes join-queries into single-relation-queries and sends them one by one based on nested loops algorithm, SRM only has to handle single relation. A relation is composed of a set of tables; a table of relation itself and tables of indexes. This is shown in Fig. 5. SRM handles all kinds of data as tables uniformly. A table consists of a set of fixed length records. The information transferred from SRM to FAM includes both table identifier and record identifier. SRM also optimizes access paths of a single relation. FREND provides two kinds of indexes for users; B tree index and hashing index. Optimal access path is decided according to conditions specified by a query, which is explained in section 4.2.

FAM provides access method for SRM in which table and record indentifiers must be specified by SRM. FAM converts those identifiers into a physical address. Physical addresses are completely virtualized from SRM. FAM also maintains database virtual storage and allocates some parts of the main memory to database buffers. In order to control commitment, FAM uses the method based on shadow[11]. By virtue of this method, databases are recovered consistently from system failures or abortion of transactions without interventions of maintenance personnel.

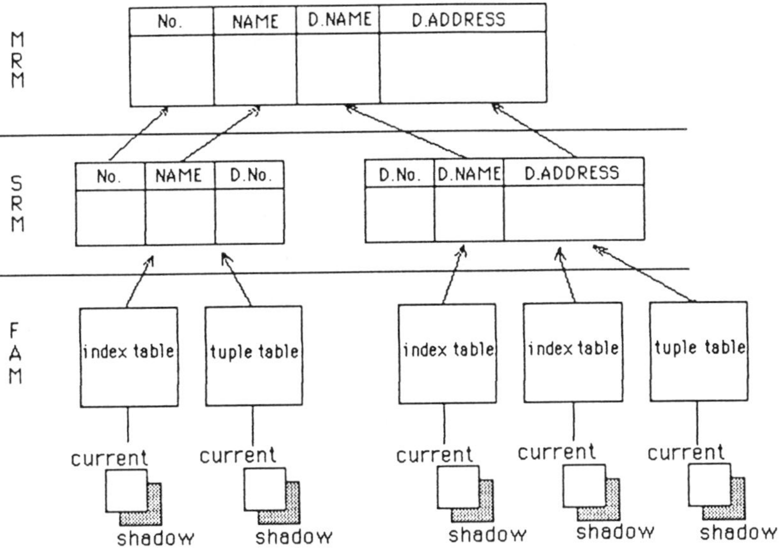

Fig. 5 Data structures

4. Processing Mechanism

4.1 Join strategy

FREND executes join opreations based on nested loops algorithm. Users can alternatively specify B-tree indexes or hashing indexes when they define relations and their attributes. We assume that FREND would be used in environments where indexes are always defined to all relations and they are accessed through those indexes. When B tree indexes are accessed, sort-merge joins algorithm[9,10] would be effective. However, in FREND users may sometimes define hasing indexes and access databases through them. Hashing index is useless for sort-merge joins algorithm, because join attributes should be sorted before join operations. Nested loops algorithm works well both on B tree indexes and hashing indexes. Furthormore, in case of three way joins, a temporary relation; a resultant relation of the first join operation, must be always sorted before the second join operation in sort-merge joins algorithm. In these situations, nested loops algorithm might work faster than sort-merge joins because a temporary relation does not occur in that algorithm.

In the relational data model, sequences of join operations can be interchangeable. These sequences much influence the join processing time. FREND parses a query and get all possible join sequence trees. Then an optimal tree is selected according to following rules.

1. Select a tree which includes as much indexes as possible.
2. If a single tree could not be selected, but several trees are selected by rule 1, select a tree in which a costly join operation such as joins without indexes, is executed in a loop as out as possible.

The example of the optimization is shown in the followings. We assume there is a query shown below.

```
SELECT    SNAME
FROM      S
WHERE     CITY="New York"
AND         P* IN
     ( SELECT  S*
       FROM    Y
       WHERE   QUANTITY>="200"
       AND      P* IN
          ( SELECT   P*
            FROM     P
            WHERE    PNAME="BOLT"
            AND      SIZE="20"        ))
```

Now we assume indexes are defined on three attributes; Y.S*, P.P* and S.CITY. If relation S is at the outermost loop and relation P is at the innermost loop, join operation would be most effectively executed by virtue of indexes. On the other hand, if relation P is at the outermost loop and relation S is the innermost loop, then indexes could not be used in join operations which results in the worst response. Furthermore, since an index is defined on S.CITY, restriction operations are effectively executed when relation S is at the outermost loop. As a result, FREND automatically navigates the sequences of join operations such that relation S is executed at the outermost loop and relation P is at the innermost loop.

4.2 Access path selection of a single relation

A lot of indexes can be defined on attributes of a relation. There are two types of indexes; B tree index and hashing index. Usually B tree indexes would be selected, however, in special cases such that all records are accessed only by key attribute such as account number, and queries always specify with "=" condition, hasing indexes would be selected. SRM selects an optimal access path according to conditions specified by queries. Priorities are shown below from higher one to lower one.

1. hasing index on which a query specifies with "=" condition
2. B tree index on which a query specifies with "=" condition
3. B tree index on which a query specifies with conditions other than "=" condition
4. hasing index on which a query specifies with condition other than "=" condition
5. relation scan when none of indexes are specified by conditions of a query

4.3 Commitment control and buffering

In order to undo the uncommitted data, FREND adopts the method based on shadow. When a page is to be updated, the contents of it is copied to a new page called current. Updates are done only in current pages, not in shadow pages. When a transaction is completed, those shadow pages are discarded. If transaction could not be completed, those current pages are discarded and shadow pages are returned to be current.

FAM controls the main memory as database buffers. In order to enhance the hit ratio, those buffers are separately controls according to types of data. All database buffers works based on LRU algorithm. Therefore updated data are not instantly written back to disk storage. When a transaction is committed, all updated data are written back to disk storage and shadow data are discarded. In such applications these tuples are consecutively updated, the method FREND adopts works very effectively.

5. Performance

5.1 Assumptions

Performance evaluation is done by referring[12]. Response time is measured by an internal hardware timer equipped in FREND which measures only the query execution time of FREND itself. Before every measurement the database buffers (64 KBytes) is cleared. The measured time does not include communication overhead, nor personal computer overhead.

Following relations are used for the evaluation. Each tuple consistes of 4 attributes. One of them is 4 byte integer. This attribute is a primary key of a relation. Six types of evaluation are shown below.

Test I: 50 tuples are selected from ten thousand tuples of a relation. Length of tuples are changed from 10 to 1000 Bytes.

Test II: 50 tuples are selected from a 100 tuple relation to a 40000 tuple relation. Length of tuples is 182 Bytes each.

Test III: 1000 tuples, 182 Bytes each is added to a 1000 tuple relation. Index overhead is measured from 0 to 8 indexes.

Test IV: 1000 tuples are selected from a relation with 10000 tuples. Each tuple is 182 Bytes in length.

Test V: Join query of two relations is executed, each of which has 10000 tuples. Result of join operations outputs 1000 tuples, 182 Bytes each.

Test VI: Join query of three relaions is executed, each of which has 10000 tuples. Result of the join operation outputs 1000 tuples, 182 Bytes each.

Six types of queries are shown in appendix A.

5.2 Effects of indexes

Results of Test I and Test II are shown in Fig. 6 and Fig. 7 respectively. In both tests, an index is used as an access path. Although cardinality of relations increases from 100 to 40000 (400 times), processing time only increases from 1 to 1.4 (1.4 times). Furthermore, although length of tuples increases from 10 to 1000 (100 times), but processing time only increases from 1 to 1.6 (1.6 times). Because of an index, processing time does not increase linearly to the cardinality of a relation or the length of a relation.

On the other hand, the overhead of index maintenance is measured in Test III. Fig. 8 shows processing time of insertion vs. the number of indexes. Most processing time of insertion can be said to maintain indexes. Especially when a relation has more than 5 indexes, this trend become more definite. Therefore, index attributes should be selected carefully according to retrieval / update ratio.

5.3 Effects of the database buffers

Results of Test IV, Test V and Test VI are shown in Fig.9, Fig.10 and Fig.11 respectively. There is no difference between the disk access time when one tuple is output and the one when five tuples are output. This means the database buffers work well, and the hit ratio of database buffers is high.

Fig. 12 shows data transfer time between main memory and disk unit vs. the number of tuples output. In this figure, data of Test VI (3 relation join)

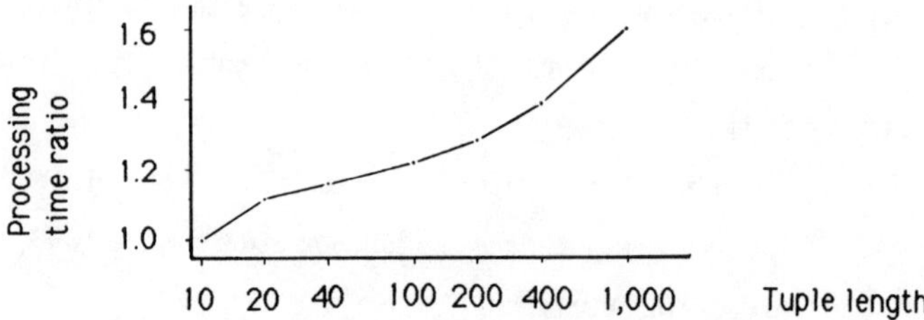

Fig. 6 Test I (Tuple length vs. processing time ratio)

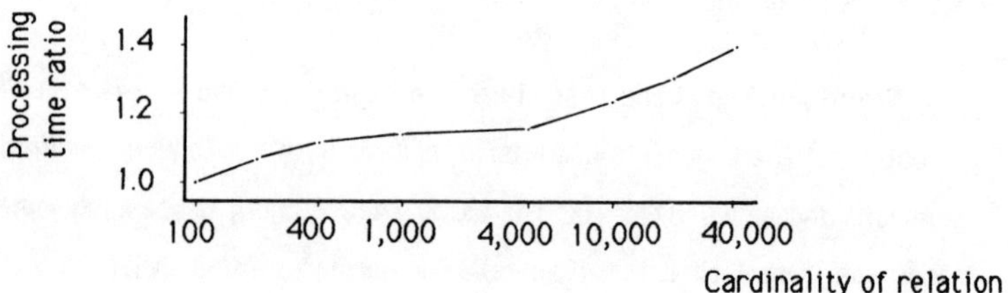

Fig. 7 Test II (Cardinarity vs. processing time ratio)

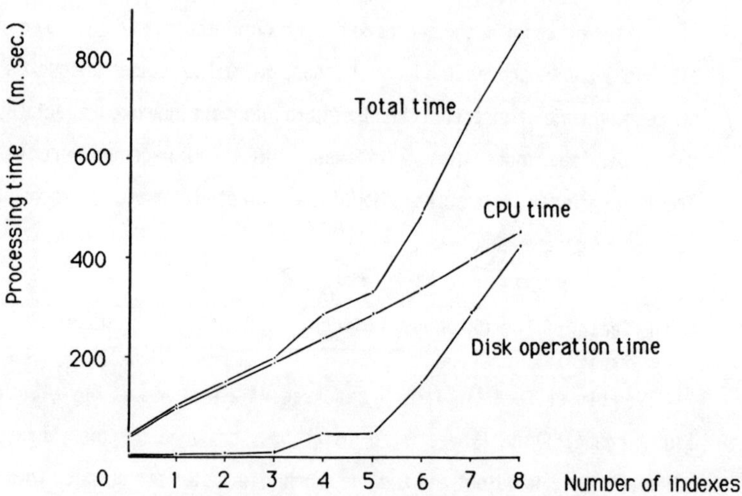

Fig. 8 Test III (Overhead of index maintenance)

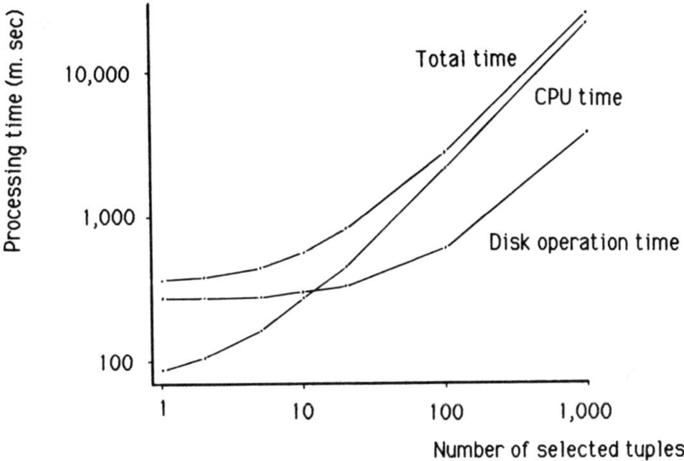

Fig. 9 Test IV (Selection from a relation)

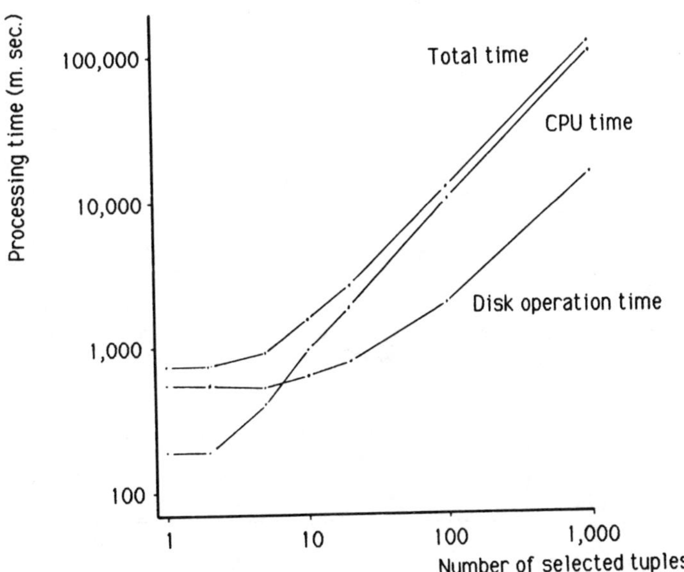

Fig. 10 Test V (Join of 2 relations)

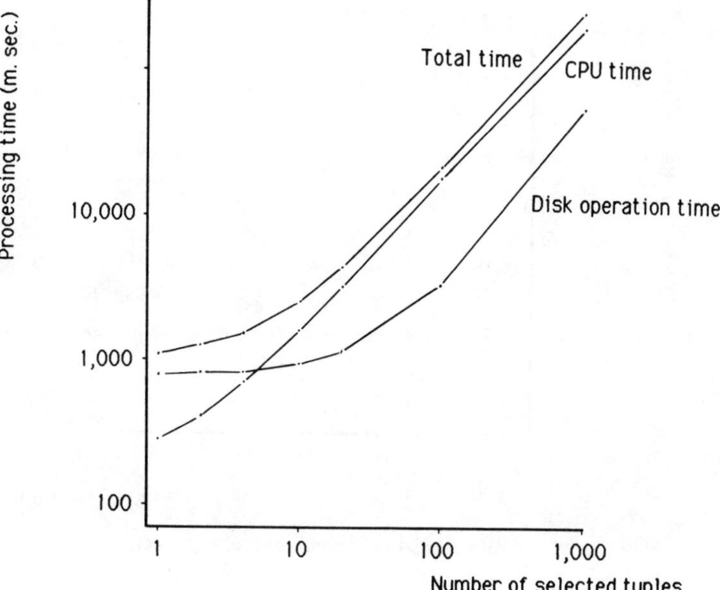

Fig. 11 Test VI (Join of 3 relations)

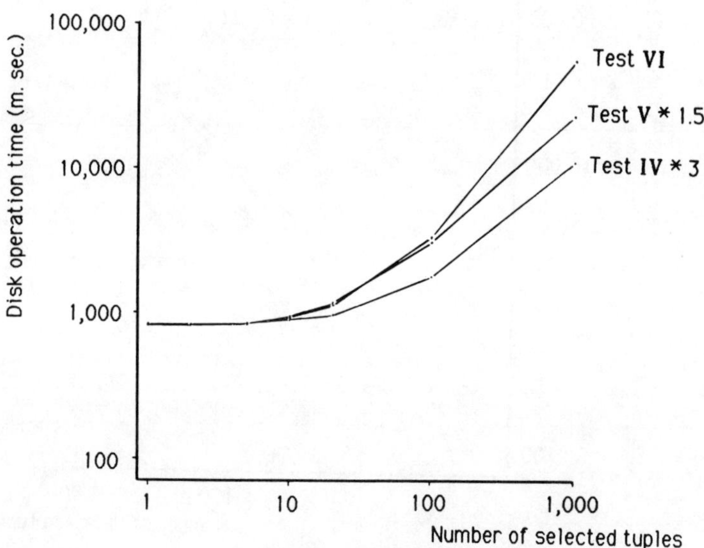

Fig. 12 Comparison among normalized disk access time of Test IV, V and VI

is plotted, however, data of Test **V** (2 relation join) is multiplied by 1.5 and data of Test **IV** (selection of a relation) is multiplied by 3.

When less than 5 tuples are selected, disk access time of three types of data is almost equal. This means that the database buffers are large enough to join even three relations. The nested loops algorithm works well with only 64 KByte database buffers. However, when output tuples are more than 5, especially, 1000 tuples are output, Fig 12 shows that the data from Test **VI** is larger than the from Test **V** and Test **IV**. This means the database buffers are not large enough. If the database buffers are equipped with more than 64 KByte, the response time of 2-relation or 3-relation joining queries would show better performance than those shown in Fig. 10 and Fig 11.

6. Conclusion

The relational database machine FREND is introduced in this paper Performance evaluation shows better results than we expected. This would be because indexes are very effective in those test and because the database buffers work well. Furthermore, FREND adopts both special purpose operating system and database storage management system. We also assume those could enhance the performance[13,14]. In order to further enhance the performance of FREND, it must adopt a higher performance micro-processor such as 32-bit ones and have larger main memory than now. Although I / O bottleneck has not yet been completely resolved in transaction oriented applications, the future of database machine like FREND would be promising.

Appendix A

Test queries

```
Test I:    SELECT    *
           FROM      R1
           WHERE     E*<50
```

```
Test II:    SELECT   *
            FROM     R_t
            WHERE    E*<50

Test III:   do i=1 to 1000 ;
                 INSERT INTO R
                 < "----", "----", "----">
            end;

Test IV:    SELECT   *
            FROM     R_1
            WHERE    E*<1000

Test V:     SELECT   R_1.* , R_2.*
            FROM     R_1 , R_2
            WHERE    R_1.E*=R_2.E*
            AND      R_2.E*<1000

Test VI:    SELECT   R_2.* , R_3.*
            FROM     R_1 , R_2 , R_3
            WHERE    R_2.E*=R_3.E*
            AND      R_2.E*<1000
            AND      R_3.E*<1000
            AND      R_2.E*=R_1.E*
```

note: E* is a primary key of relation R_1.

References

[1] E. F. Codd, "A Relational Model of Data for Large Shared Data Banks", CACM, Vol.13, No.6, June, 1970, pp377-387.

[2] E. A. Ozkarahan, et al., "RAP-An associative processor for database management", AFIPS, Vol.44, 1975, pp379-387.

[3] D. J. Dewitt, "DIRECT-A Multiprocessor Organization for Supporting Relational Database Management Systems", IEEE Trans. on Computers. Vol.C-28, No.6, 1979, pp.395-406.

[4] Y. Tanaka, "A Data Stream Database Machine with Large Capacity", Proc. of the international workshop on Database Machines, Aug. 1982, pp.173-231.

[5] R. Epstein, et.al., "Design decisions for the intelligent database machine", AFIPS, Vol.49, 1980, pp.237-241.

[6] S.Hikita, et.al., "Stepwise Approach to Distributed Database System by Database Machines", 1985 ACM Symposium on Small Systems,1985 to appear.

[7] D. D. Chamberlin, et.al., "SEQUEL 2: A Unified Approach to Data Definition Manipulation and Control", IBM J. RES. DEVELOP, November, 1976, pp.560-575.

[8] S.Hikita, et.al., "Extended Functions of the Database Machine FREND for Interactive Systems",1984 IEEE Workshop on Vusual Languages,1984, pp.66-71.

[9] M. M. Astrahan, et.al., "System R: Relational Approach to Database Management", ACM TODS, Vol.1, No.2, June 1976, pp.97-137.

[10] W. F. King, "Relational Database Systems: where we stand today", IFIP, 1980, pp.369-381.

[11] R. A. Lorie, "Physical Integrity in a Large Segmented Database", ACM TODS, Vol.2, No.1, 1977, pp.91-104.

[12] D. Bitton, et.al., "Benchmarking Database Systems A Systematic Approach", Proc. of VLDB, 1983, pp.8-19.

[13] M. Stonebraker, et.al., "Performance Enhancements to a Relational Database System", ACM TODS, Vol.8, No.2, 1983, pp.167-185.

[14] M. Stonebraker, "Operation System Support for Database Management", CACM, Vol.24, No.7, 1981, pp.412-418.

Memory Management Algorithms in Pipeline Merge Sorter

Masaru Kitsuregawa *
Shinya Fushimi **
Hidehiko Tanaka **
Tohru Moto-oka **

* Institute of Industrial Science
The University of Tokyo

** Faculty of Electrical Engineering
The University of Tokyo

ABSTRACT

In this paper we discuss the problems on memory management algorithms for pipeline merge sorter. This hardware sorter can sort the data stream following its flow, which means memory space must be managed in keeping up with the flow of the stream.

We present three different memory management algorithms: Double Memory Method, Pointer Method, and Block Division Method. Double memory method is very simple but its efficiency is low, 50%. Pointer method attains relatively high efficiency but it requires more sophisticated logic in a processor. The block division method, which is a new algorithm we propose, is shown to be a generalized algorithm for the others. The memory is divided into blocks of fixed size and the block level management is performed, while the other two employ record level management.

New storage optimization scheme, "String Length Tuning Algorithm" is also proposed. With this algorithm the data stream of any record length can be sorted efficiently, while most of the hardware sort algorithm proposed so far can sort efficiently only the records with fixed length determined by hardware. For example, 2-way sorter with optimization degree 6 attains about 0.99 memory efficiency.

1. Introduction

The sorting is the most fundamental and also the frequently used operation in computer system. Due to its heavy computational cost, the development of the specialized hardware sorter is researched extensively. The improvement of semiconductor technology is another reason to stimulate its development.

For such application as data base processing, where very large amount of data must be handled, we cannot expect the data is ready in main memory at the start of sorting. Usually data is stored over the secondary storage devices and need to be transferred from disk to main memory at first. This data transfer time causes large overhead. Therefore possible solution is to utilize this data transfer time for sorting. Several types of $O(N)$ time hardware sorter, which can sort the data stream following its flow, are proposed: Pipeline bubble sort[1], Rebound sort[2],Parallel enumeration Sort[3], Pipeline heap sort[4], Pipeline merge sort[5]. In these sorters, data transfer and sorting can be overlapped each other. The first three algorithms use N processors to sort N records, whose hardware cost would be crucial for large N. The last two use only log N processors. In these sorters, it is easy to implement flexible control mechanism in processors, since the cost of logic is much reduced. Among last two, since the latter has independent input and output ports, it can realize the file level pipeline processing, namely, the next file can be input for sorting while the current file is being output. It is suited for the continuous sort operation. In the former one, input and output port are shared.

In this paper, we focus on the pipeline merge sorter, especially we discuss its memory management algorithm. This sorter is data stream oriented sorter, which means its memory management also must be performed keeping up with the flow of the stream.

After we briefly describe the pipeline merge sort algorithm in section 2, three different memory management algorithms: Double memory method, Pointer method, Block division method, are described in section 3. The block division method, which is a new algorithm we propose here, is shown to be a generalized algorithm for the other two. Its cost is evaluated in detail. In section 4, we propose the novel memory optimization algorithm for the changes of record length. Most of the hardware algorithm proposed so far can sort efficiently only records of given size which is fixed by hardware. Our algorithm attains very high memory efficiency for records of any length. We call it "string length tuning algorithm".

We have already implemented the pipeline merge sorter version 1. It can sort the data stream of 3Mbytes/sec, which is the highest data transfer rate of the currently available disk. In [6] detail register transfer level description and hardware organization is presented.

The authors are also developing the high performance relational algebra machine GRACE. The sorter reported here is a fundamental element in GRACE.

2. Pipeline Merge Sorter

2.1. Pipeline Merge Sort Algorithm[5]

The organization of the sorter is shown in Fig.2.1, where $n(=\log_K N)$ identical processors are connected linerly. N is the total number of the records to be sorted. Each processor has the capability of K way merge operation. The i-th processor is attached the memory bank with the capacity of $(K-1)K^{i-1}$ records.

The sorting process overview is depicted in Fig.2.2. The input stream is led into the first processor and the output stream is output from the last processor. This is a stream oriented sorter which can sort the records keeping up with the flow of the input data stream. The i-th processor merges K strings, sent from the (i-1)-th processor, each of which consists of K^{i-1} records, and outputs the merged string of K^i records to (i+1)-th processor. As is shown in Fig.2.2, where K is equal to 2, each processor begins its merging operation when the first record of the K-th string enters after the loading of K-1 strings in its own memory bank. In this figure the unit of pipeline is not clear; it can be a record, a byte, a bit, and so forth.

Performance of the sorter can be measured by the sorting time and the necessary memory capacity. In this sorter the total sorting time amounts to $2N+\log_K N-1$, where 2N corresponds to the input and output time of the stream. The second term is pure overhead time which is very small compared to the another term. $\mathrm{Log}_K N-1$ corresponds to the flush time of the pipe. In this pipeline the number of segments is logN. The first item to be output has to run through the segments of pipe after all the records enter the sorter.

The necessary capacity of the memory bank depends on the memory management algorithm. But in principle the space of N records would suffice except the auxiliary data structure which is discussed in more detail in the following section. To sum up, $\log_K N$ processor can sort N records in $O(N)$ time with the $O(N)$ memory space. This means the pipeline merge sorter can sort the data stream very efficiently.

2.2. Merge Processing in a Processor

Each processor iterates the merge operation of the strings sent from the preceding processor. This operation can be divided into the following three phases, between which the internal state transition occurs. The state transition diagram is shown in Fig.2.3.

Phase 0: In this state the first K-1 strings sent from the previous processor are loaded into the memory.

Phase 1: In this state a processor merges the entering K-th string with the K-1 strings in the memory and outputs the merged string to the following

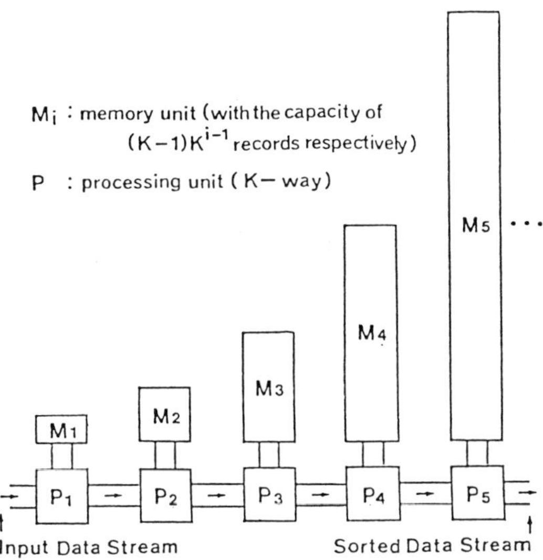

Fig.2.1 Organization of Pipeline Merge Sorter

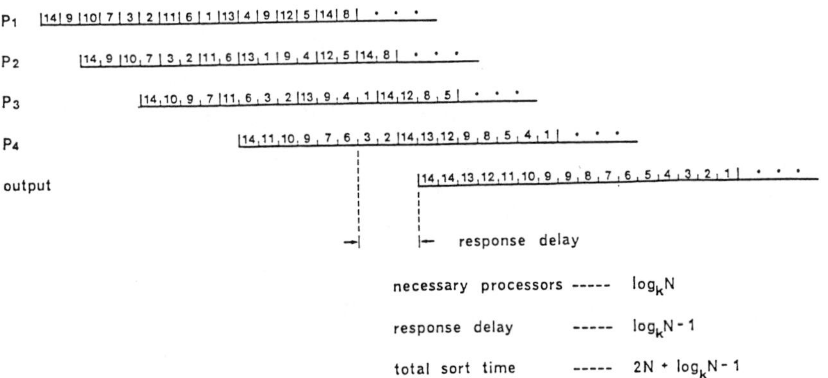

Fig.2.2 Sorting Process Overview

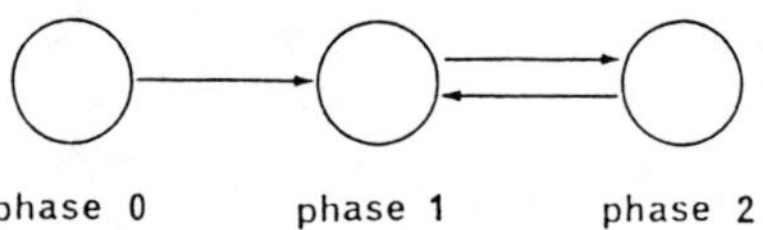

Fig.2.3 State Transition of a Processor

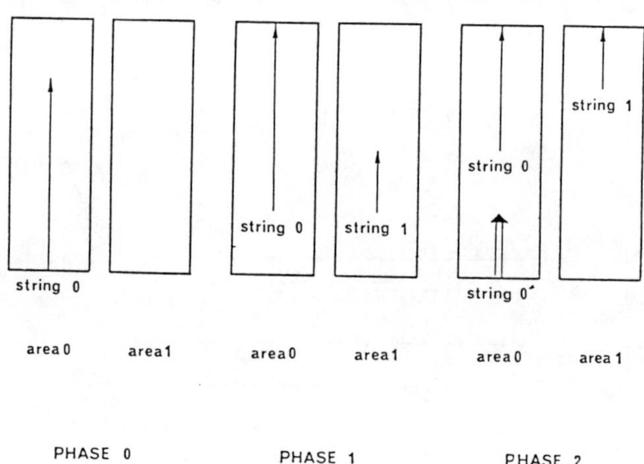

Fig.3.1 Memory Management by Double Memory Method

processor. After the whole input of the K-th string, the internal state transits to phase 2.

Phase 2: In this state a processor continues to merge the K strings which remain in the memory and at the same time loads the next K-1 strings in the memory. When all the K-1 strings are loaded in the memory, simultaneously the merging operation of the current K strings is also completed, the internal state transits to phase 1.

Each processor works in pipelined fashion. The string merge operation controlled so that the input data stream is not disturbed at all.

3. Memory Management Algorithm in Pipeline Merge Sorter

As shown from the above description, the algorithm of pipeline merge sort is very simple. Processors works based on the small 3-state transition table. Now we proceed the memory management problems.

After the initial loading in phase 0, a processor inputs one record, compares it with its own record and outputs the larger or smaller record to the following processor. Therefore the necessary memory space is constant during the operation since each processor inputs one record and at the same time outputs one record. This is due to the pipeline processing feature of this algorithm. The sequence to fetch the heads of both strings, however, is random. Therefore it is insufficient to store the input record in the area previously occupied by the the merge top record of the strings already stored in a processor. It is necessary to keep the sorted sequence in the memory. Here we propose the three different memory management algorithms. Two-way merge and ascending sorting are assumed in the following description. It should be noticed that the record length is assumed to be fixed.

3.1. Double Memory Method

A processor need to handle three logically distinct strings. Namely, as described in 2.2, a processor in phase 2 merges two strings in its memory and also input the records for the next string. The most simple memory management method is to provide each string with a memory space sufficient to hold a whole string, which means three times as large as the actually used memory area is required. In double memory method, however, the area twice as large as the pure capacity is used. Fig.3.1 shows the conceptual diagram of this method. The memory of each processor is divided into two areas: area 0 and area 1. In phase 0, the string 0 is stored in area 0. Thereafter in phase 1 the string 1 is input and compared with string 0 in area 0. The first record of string 1 is compared with the head record of string 0 in area 0. If the record of string 0 is larger than that of string1, the input record is stored in the first location of the area 1. The location is maintained simply by the address counter. Otherwise, the record of string 1 is directly output to the next processor. At the same time, the address counter is incremented. While the records of string 1 is smaller than the top record of string 0, only the counter is incremented. The records of string 1 is sequentially stored in area 1. Its location is fixed. As the merge operation proceeds, the initial parts of the both strings are consumed. That is, the bottom region of both areas are released, which is shown in the figure. When all the records of the string 1 are taken into the processor, the last record is stored at the ceiling of the area 1. The number of records remaining in the two areas is equal to the length of one string. Namely empty room with the capacity of one whole string is spread over two areas. In phase 2 strings in two areas are merged while a new string enters the processor. This string is stored in the area 0(or area 1). The last portion of the figure depicts this situation. The tail of the new string is getting up with the head of the string 0 which is used in current merge operation. If two strings meet in area 0, there would arise a memory overwriting problem. It is apparent, however, that these two strings never meet together. The sum of the remaining records of two strings being merged and the records of entering string amounts to the size of a whole string, namely K^{i-1} records. Therefore the distance between the tail record of incoming string and the head record of the remaining string 0, where we use area 0 for the new string, is the number of the remaining records of string 1. Thus incoming string could be next to the string 0, but never overwrite it. This suggests that two strings can share the area. As the comparison goes on, the string 0 and 1 shrink. At the same time when all the records in the memory are merged and output completely, the records of the next string are prepared in the area 0.

This algorithm shows that two string areas are sufficient for pipeline merge sorter which handles three logically different strings. The control mechanism of this memory management algorithm is very simple and easy to implement. But the large problem inherent to this algorithm is low memory efficiency of fifty percent.

3.2. Pointer Method

In this pointer method, the records are stored in the form of the linked list. Each record has the pointer part and records are linked to maintain the sorted sequence.

In phase 0, during the loading of records of string 0 the records are chained together. In phase 1 and 2, the input record is stored in the area which is previously occupied by the the merge top record of either string. Only the pointer part is updated. Efficient pointer manipulation mechanism not disturbing the pipeline processing, is required in this method. If the record length is short and comparable with that of the pointer, the memory space required for pointers are not ignored. For the relatively long record, however, this method attains sufficient memory efficiency.

In our pilot system, we implemented the sorter using this pointer method.

3.3. Block Division Method

This is an algorithm midway between the previous two methods, which will be clarified later. The memory space is divided into fixed-size blocks, each of which has the capacity of several records. The size of a block is multiple of the record length. Here one block exactly contains s records. Fig.3.2 shows the logical view of the memory. It is divided into l blocks and two auxiliary blocks are supplemented. Thus $s \times l = (K-1)K^{i-1}$ holds. Within a block records are stored in sorted sequence in the similar way to double memory method and inter-block sequence is maintained by another auxiliary data structure such as pointers in pointer method. Memory space is managed at block level.

In phase 0, when records of the initial string begin to enter the processor, one block is allocated and first s records are stored there sequentially. Another block is allocated when the $(s+1)$-th record comes in. Thus all the records of string 0 is stored over l blocks. At the end of phase 0, there remains auxiliary two blocks. In phase 1, one of two blocks is allocated for the new string and the strings are compared each other. When s records enter the processor, allocation for another block occurs. The block whose records are all used up for comparison is returned as empty block. The block consumption sequence is random, which is maintained through another data structure. Fig.3.3 shows the sorting process in block division method. In this example each of strings is divided into four blocks and denoted by A1, A2, A3, and A4, and B1, B2, B3, and B4 respectively. A1', A2', A3' and A4' are new strings in phase 2. Fig.3.4 shows the movement of the head of strings. In phase 2 the blocks of two strings are compared, while the new string is stored in empty blocks generated dynamically during the merge operation. It should be noticed that large number of blocks are not required but only two auxiliary blocks are sufficient. Namely the following observation holds.

> If $l + 2$ blocks are prepared, where l is the number of blocks occupied by a string, at least one empty block is generated after one block is processed.

This is obvious from the Fig.3.5 which shows the empty block generation process. It is two merge top blocks that could not be fully filled with records. Therefore one more block must be prepared. Since it is unpredictable which block of these partially filled two will be used up, input records cannot share the block. They might

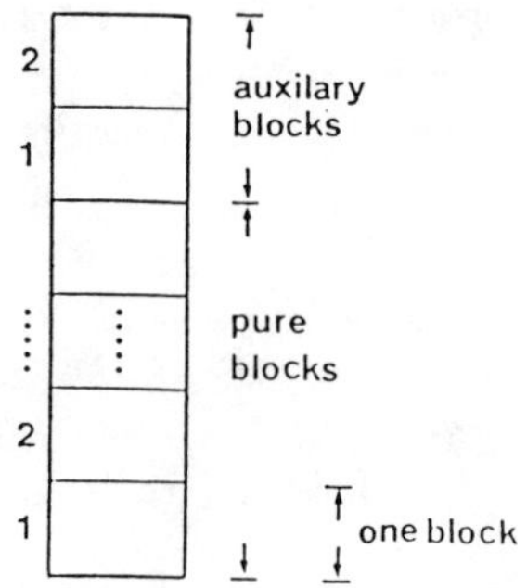

Fig.3.2 Memory Management by Block Division Method

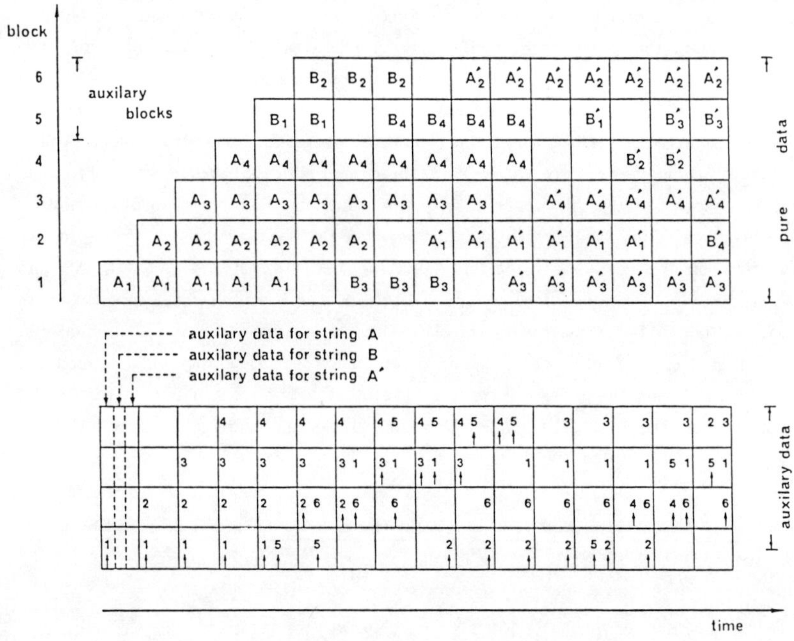

Fig.3.3 Sorting Process in Block Division Method

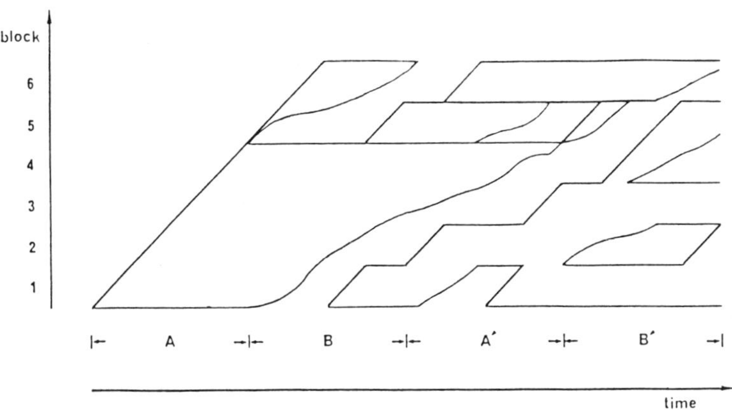

Fig.3.4 String Head Position Trace of Block Division Method

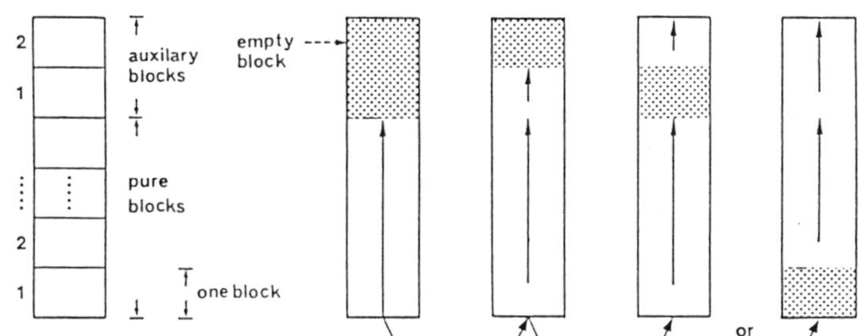

Fig.3.5 Empty Block Generation after Each Block Input in Block Division Method

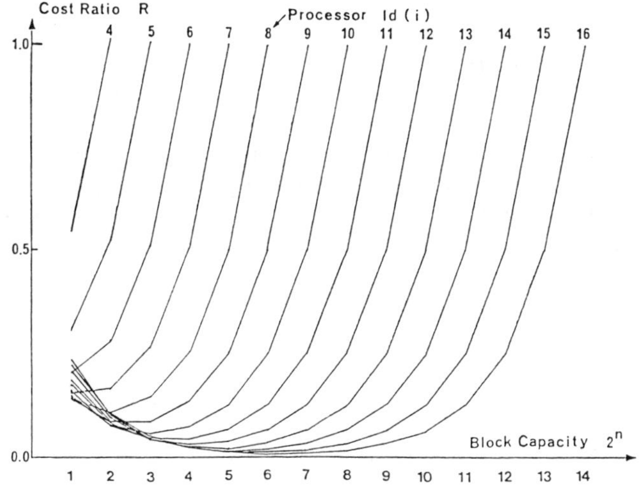

Fig.3.6 Auxiliary Memory Cost Ratio vs Block Capacity

overwrite the merge top record. Therefore another block has to be used for entering record. Thus two auxiliary blocks are necessary and also sufficient.

In the above description the additional data structure to maintain the sorted sequence of blocks is assumed. For this data structure, we can apply three methods shown in the previous sections recursively. That is, it is possible to have additional data for additional data. The amount of data, however, is much small. Therefore simple data structure seems to be adequate. Since the pure data for this additional data is pointers for start address of the block, record length is very short. Double memory method is appropriate for the additional data in block division method.

Here we reconsider the characteristics of the algorithm. Suppose a block have the capacity of one record. Either of two merge top blocks is freed after each block input since a block is a record. Therefore only one auxiliary block is sufficient. The auxiliary data structure is associated with each record. If it is used as a pointer, this corresponds to pointer method. Suppose the number of the block be one, which means no split is made. Three string areas are used in this case, which corresponds to the most brute force method explained previously. If the string consists of two blocks, the required memory is same as double memory method. Thus block division method is thought to be generalization of the other two algorithms.

3.4. Generalization from 2-way to K-way

Two-way merge sort was assumed in the previous discussion. The algorithms can be generalized from 2-way to K-way easily. With K set large, the number of banks necessary for constructing a sorter of a given capacity can be reduced, though the processing power must be enhanced. Each of three methods is modified as follows

Double memory method

$2\times(K-1)$ string areas are sufficient for K-way merge sort

Block division method

$(K-1)\times l + K$ blocks are sufficient where one string is divided into l blocks.

Pointer method is not affected. The proof is straight forward.

3.5. Cost Analysis of the Block Division Method

We have not mentioned how to determine the block capacity in block division method. K more blocks and additional data structure are required in addition to the pure data memory. The optimal block capacity is obtained as follows. Double memory method is assumed to be used for additional data structure. Here we formalize the required memory capacity.

degree of merge (K way):

$$K = 2^a$$

record length:

$$M\text{(bits)}$$

pure memory capacity:

$$(K-1)K^{i-1} = (2^a-1)\cdot 2^{a(i-1)} \qquad \text{(records)}$$

number of block division:

$$l = 2^b$$

capacity of a block:

$$K^{i-1}/l = 2^{a(i-1)-b}$$

number of auxiliary blocks:

$$K$$

capacity of auxiliary blocks:

$$(K^{i-1}/l)K = 2^{ai-b}$$

Using the above formula, we obtain

total pure memory capacity:

$$(K-1)K^{i-1} + (KK^{i-1}/l)\cdot K$$

$$= (2^a-1)\cdot 2^{a(i-1)} + 2^{ai-b} \qquad \text{(records)}$$

$$= M\{(2^a-1)\cdot 2^{a(i-1)} + 2^{ai-b}\} \qquad \text{(bits)}$$

total number of pure data block:

$$(K-1)l + K = 2^{a+b} + 2^a - 2^b$$

pointer length to maintain the block sequence:

$$\left\lceil \log_2\{(K-1)l + K\} \right\rceil \qquad \text{(bits)}$$

$$= \begin{cases} a+b & (a \leqq b) \\ a+b+1 & (a > b) \end{cases}$$

number of memory areas for additional data:
(double memory method)

$$2(K-1) = 2(2^a-1)$$

number of records in one area:

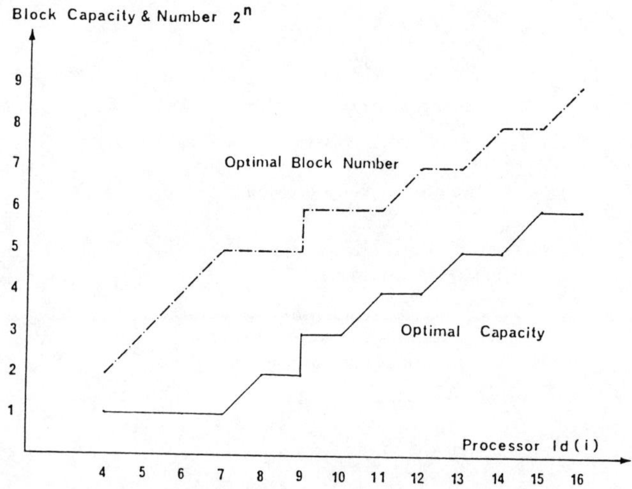

Fig.3.7 Optimal Block Capacity

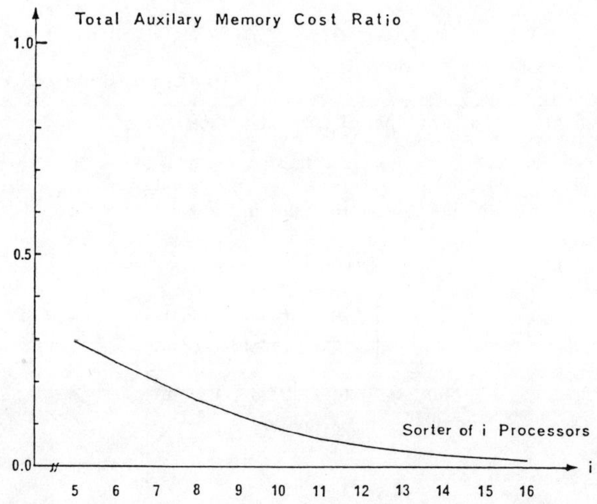

Fig.3.8 Total Auxiliary Memory Cost Ratio for Optimal Block Division

$$l = 2^b.$$

Then we have

required capacity for additional data:

$$\left\lceil \log_2\{(K-1)l + K\} \right\rceil \cdot 2(K-1)l$$

$$= \begin{cases} (a+b)\cdot 2(2^a-1)\cdot 2^b & (a \leqq b) \\ (a+b+1)\cdot 2(2^a-1)\cdot 2^b & (a > b) \end{cases}$$

total memory capacity:

$$C(M,K,l,i) \qquad \text{(bits)}$$

$$= C(M,a,b,i)$$

$$= M\{(2^a-1)\cdot 2^{a(i-1)} + 2^{ai-b}\}$$

$$+ \begin{cases} (a+b)\cdot 2(2^a-1)\cdot 2^b & (a \leqq b) \\ (a+b+1)\cdot 2(2^a-1)\cdot 2^b & (a > b) \end{cases}$$

cost ratio of additional memory to total memory capacity:

$$R(M,a,b,i)$$

$$= C(M,a,b,i)/M(2^a-1)\cdot 2^{a(i-1)} - 1$$

Thus we can determine the optimal block capacity, given the record length and K. Fig.3.6 shows the behaviour of cost function for the processors of each stage, where $M = 8$ byte and $K = 2$. Fig.3.7 gives the optimal block capacity of each stage. Fig.3.8 shows the total cost of the sorter consisting of i processors. If we adopt pointer method for such short records, the cost of pointer becomes dominant. The block division method, however, makes the auxiliary data cost reduced to only a few percentage.

4. Optimizing Storage Utilization of Sorter for Variable Record Length

4.1. Variable Record Length

In general, we lose some flexibilities at the expense of the high performance when some function is implemented by hardware. Sometimes overhead caused by such a "hard"ware becomes intractable. As for sorting, the *length of record* and the *number of records* to be sorted are examples concerning on such flexibilities. Suppose the sorter is designed to sort N records having common length L. Then we must take some higher level control to sort Y records having length X using the sorter when $Y \neq N$ or $X \neq L$, especially when $Y > N$ or $X > L$. For example, the external sort-merge technique is one of the possible techniques to sort Y records using the sorter when $Y > N$. Digital sort scheme or encoding/decoding of records are those for the case $X > L$.

As for the pipeline merge sorter, we have already proposed the technique called *pipelined connection of multiple pipeline merge sorters* to sort more records than N[7]. This makes it possible to sort $Y(>N)$ records by linearly connected sorters. For the case $Y < N$, the control scheme to sort Y records faster than $O(N)$ time has also been developed[8]. Therefore, the algorithm to sort records having different length from L is focused here, while in previous sections we assume the length of records are fixed. The algorithm aims at giving the users flexibility on record length, i.e., releasing users from the higher level control to sort records of various lengths.

It is assumed here that X is shared by the records belonging to the data stream to be sorted. More precisely, X is fixed through each data stream, but may be different from data stream to data stream. From the practical point of view, this assumption is not meaningless at all, because a number of files are created and maintained in the fixed record format in the ordinary computer system. It is the future problem to find the elegant control scheme to sort records whose lengths are different from record to record even in one data stream. (One can easily imagine that NP-completeness appears when some optimization is attempted against this problem.) As the readers will see, however, even if the record length is fixed in the data stream, no slight change of control can be sufficient.

4.2. Naive Algorithm and Its Drawbacks

Let X be the actual record length of the incoming stream and let L be the record length presumed in the hardware design stage of the sorter. Recall that L is used to determine the pure memory capacity of each processor; the i-th processor P_i has its own memory whose size is actually $K^{i-1}(K-1)L$. To examine what happens when $X \neq L$, first consider the case $0 < X < L$. In this case, the basic pipeline merge sort algorithm can be applied without any modification. The only difference from the case $X = L$ is that large and many unused memory areas are produced in each stage of processors. We cannot utilize such areas in principle: assuming that the sorter consists of n processors, if we fill up such empty areas with incoming records, the sorter becomes to hold and sort more than K^n records. This contradicts the fact that the maximum number of records the sorter with n processors can sort is at most K^n.

Next consider the case $X > L$. Due to the recursive structure of our sorter, it is sufficient to consider the restricted range of X. For example, suppose X exceeds KL but is smaller than K^2L. If we skip P_1, advance indices of processors by one, and write L for KL, then the problem is reduced to the same as in the case that $L < X < KL$ and that processor configuration begins at P_1. Similarly, when $K^2L \leqq X < K^3L$, we skip first two processors, advance indices by two, and write L for K^2L, and so forth. Note that since memory capacity becomes exponentially large, ignoring first some processors hardly affects the memory utilization of the sorter on the whole.

Then, the *logical first processor*, as opposed to the actual first processor, is defined as the leftmost processor P_i in the processors of linear configuration such that $X \leqq K^iL$ holds for given record length X. Renumbering successively, the *logical* i*-th processor* is generally defined. With this renaming, predefined record length L is analogously arranged in such a way that we write L for K^iL when the logical first processor is P_i. Hereafter, the logical first processor is simply referred to as the first processor or P_1 and the similar modification is applied to the (logical) i-th processor. The first $i-1$ processors are always skipped, if P_i is logically first. Thus, it is sufficient to consider the limited condition on X that $L < X < KL$ and assume that the i-th processor P_i has the memory of size $K^{i-1}(K-1)L$. These are assumed throughout the remaining part of this paper.

Now suppose X be a little bit longer than L, say $X = 1.1L (< KL)$ (Note that we always assume that indices of processors and record length L are *logical* in the sense of the above paragraph). Then, we must give up performing K-way merge in P_1 because X is a little larger than L, so that P_1 cannot accommodate K-1 records in its memory. Here we should take some means to process such a data stream. Natural but easygoing way seems that we skip the (logical) first processor P_1 and use P_2 as P_1, P_3 as P_2 and so on. Then, since P_2 has enough capacity to store K-1 records in general under our assumption $L < X < KL$, we can proceed sorting process in the practically same manner as described above. This means the logical first processor is skipped and the logical second processor is taken as the entrance. (In terms of the actual indices of processors, the sorting is executed with skipping the first i processors where i is the smallest number such that $X \leqq K^iL$.) As a result, the situation becomes equivalent to the case $0 < X < L$. Such a technique is later referred to as *naive algorithm*. Although no serious change of control may be necessary to implement it, it is easy to see that the unused area grows exponentially as the stage of processor goes ahead. Applying this algorithm, the efficiency of storage utilization η^0 is given by $X/(KL)$. In particular, $\eta^0 = X/(KL) = 1.1/2 = 0.55$ in the example. To understand how much the memory areas are wasted, consider the last processor in the sorter; its memory dominates the half capacity of the sorter's whole space, while about half of it is wasted in the example. In view of the number of records the sorter can sort, it is unfairly limited while the large area is wasted in the sorter.

Our objective in the remaining part is, *for given record length* X, *to make number of records the sorter can process maximal or near maximal by utilizing such unused areas in the memory that would be produced by naive algorithm.* This is called here *optimization of storage utilization.*

4.3. Basic Strategy for Optimization of Storage Utilization

The basic idea for optimizing memory utilization is based on the following fact:

> If, for some i, the i-th processor P_i always sends to the $(i+1)$-th processor P_{i+1} the longest string P_i can generate for given X, that is, if P_i always produces the string whose length is kept to be $\lfloor K^iL/X \rfloor$, then the memory utilization efficiencies are also kept $\lfloor K^iL/X \rfloor X/K^iL$ in all its successive processors.

It is easy to verify the assertion above: if it is possible for P_i to produce and send the longest strings that P_i can generate, the memory efficiency of P_{i+1} is kept to be $((K-1)\lfloor K^iL/X \rfloor X)/(K^i(K-1)L) = \lfloor K^iL/X \rfloor X/K^iL$. Moreover, the basic pipeline merge sort algorithm guarantees the inheritance of the memory utilization efficiency from some processor to its successors if the strings to be merged by each of them share the same string length. Consequently the assertion follows. Recalling that memory efficiency is dominated by the last some processors, the efficiency over all the processors involved in a sorter is approximately same as $\lfloor K^iL/X \rfloor X/K^iL$, which is expected to be sufficiently high if i is reasonably selected. We define the *logical space of the* i*-th processor* P_i as the memory space of size K^iL (denoted by M_i). On the other hand, the real memory P_i originally maintains, i.e., the memory space of size $K^{i-1}(K-1)L$ (denoted by M'_i), is called the *physical memory space of the* i*-th processor* P_i. Then we can express this idea in these terms as:

> If the logical space of P_i is always filled up with records as much as possible, the physical spaces of its successors keep the same utilization efficiency as that of P_i's logical space. As a result, the overall memory utilization

efficiency of the sorter is nearly equal to P_i's logical space efficiency.

If we choose P_i as the target of logical space packing, then its index i is called *optimization degree*. (Recall again that P_i means the *logical* i-th processor.) Later, we will use d to denote the optimization degree. Furthermore, *optimization of storage utilization of degree* d, or simply, *storage optimization of degree* d means stuffing the logical space of P_d with records as much as possible in cooperation with P_i $(i=1,\cdots,d-1)$. P_i $(i=1,\cdots,d)$ is *involved in the optimization*. Then the triplet (K, X/L,d) can characterize the storage optimization.

4.4. Storage Utilization Improvement

Putting off the algorithm to pack the logical space up to the next section, here we estimate the memory utilization improvement to be achieved by this technique. If we execute the storage optimization of degree d for given X, the *memory utilization efficiency* $\eta(K, X/L, d)$ common among P_d's successive processors can be written as follows:

$$\eta(K, X/L, d) = \frac{\left\lfloor \frac{K^d L}{X} \right\rfloor X}{K^d L}$$

Then the mean value of it, $\bar{\eta}(K,d)$ can be computed as

$$\bar{\eta}(K,d) = \frac{1}{(K-1)L} \int_L^{KL} \eta(K, X/L, d)\,dX$$

$$= \frac{1}{(K-1)L} \int_L^{KL} \frac{\left\lfloor \frac{K^d L}{X} \right\rfloor X}{K^d L}\,dX$$

$$= \frac{K^d}{K-1} \int_{K^{d-1}}^{K^d} \frac{\lfloor y \rfloor}{y^3}\,dy \quad \left(y = \frac{K^d L}{X} \right)$$

$$= \frac{K^d}{K-1} \sum_{i=K^{d-1}}^{K^d-1} \int_i^{i+1} \frac{i}{y^3}\,dy$$

$$= \frac{K^d}{2(K-1)} \sum_{i=K^{d-1}}^{K^d-1} \left(\frac{1}{i} - \frac{i}{(i+1)^2} \right)$$

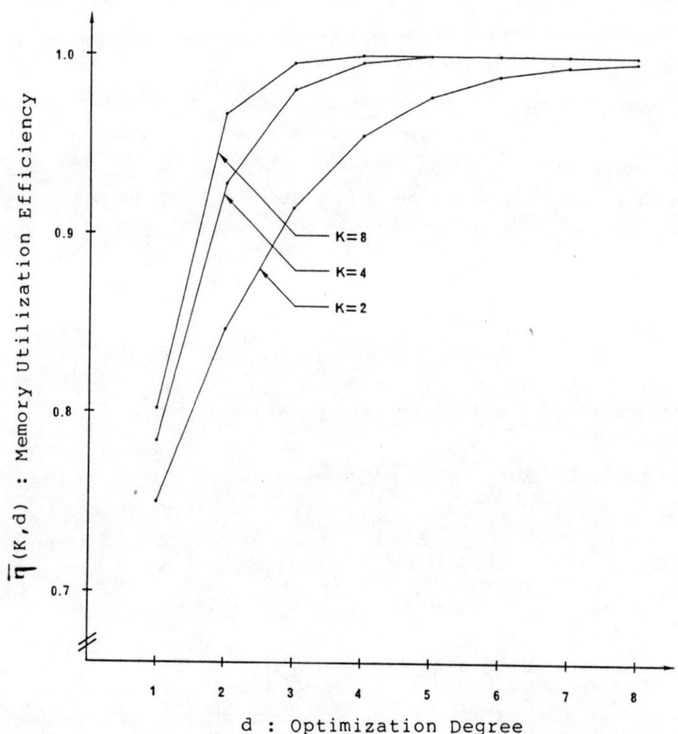

Fig.4.1 Memory Utilization Efficiency Improvement by Storage Optimization (K:K-way sort, d:optimization degree)

The behavior of $\bar{\eta}(K,d)$ is depicted in Fig.4.1 for several K's and d's. The figure shows that the sufficiently high efficiency can be obtained for relatively small d and K. Thus it is concluded that the goal we are aiming at is achieved if we get the efficient algorithm to perform stuffing the logical space.

4.5. Optimization of Storage Utilization by String Length Tuning

From the discussion in the previous section, the algorithm to conduct optimizing of storage utilization is reduced to solving the problem, for given optimization degree d, to pack the logical space of P_d with records as much as possible. Our idea to realize this is to change and adapt the string lengths dynamically at each stage of processors involved in the optimization with keeping merge way K, which is called *string length tuning.*

Let the optimization degree be d. By string length tuning, P_d's logical space must be stuffed with K strings coming from its immediate predecessor. Consider the following lemma and its corollary.

[Lemma 1]

For every positive integer m and positive real number α, there exist unique two integers l_0 and l_1 such that

$$\lfloor m\alpha \rfloor = l_0 \lfloor \alpha \rfloor + l_1 \lfloor \alpha+1 \rfloor \tag{1}$$

where $l_0 + l_1 = m$ and $l_0, l_1 \geqq 0$.

[Proof]

Lemma directly follows from that (1) and the constraint on l_0 and l_1 uniquely determine l_0 and l_1, that is, $l_1 = \lfloor m\alpha \rfloor - m\lfloor \alpha \rfloor$ and $l_0 = m - l_1$.

[Corollary 2]

For m and α as in Lemma 1, and for any integer i, l_0 and l_1 determined by (1) also satisfy the equality:

$$\lfloor m\alpha \rfloor + i = (l_0 - i) \lfloor \alpha \rfloor + (l_1 + i) \lfloor \alpha+1 \rfloor \tag{2}$$

Provided that the sorter consists of n processors, for given X, the maximum number of records that logical space of P_i $(i=1,\cdots,n)$ can store, that is, the maximal length of string P_i can generate, is called the *optimal string length of* P_i *for given* X. Then, (1) gives the following transformation of the optimal string length of P_d (length of string is expressed by the number of the records in the string).

$$\left\lfloor \frac{M_d}{X} \right\rfloor = \left\lfloor \frac{K^d L}{X} \right\rfloor$$

$$= l_0^{d-1} \left\lfloor \frac{K^{d-1}L}{X} \right\rfloor + l_1^{d-1}\left(\left\lfloor \frac{K^{d-1}L}{X} \right\rfloor + 1 \right)$$

$$= l_0^{d-1} \left\lfloor \frac{M_{d-1}}{X} \right\rfloor + l_1^{d-1}\left(\left\lfloor \frac{M_{d-1}}{X} \right\rfloor + 1 \right) \qquad (3)$$

where $l_0^{d-1} + l_1^{d-1} = K$.

The recursion (3) manifests that for given X, the logical space of P_d can be packed if its immediate predecessor P_{d-1} can generate l_0^{d-1} strings of P_{d-1}'s optimal length and l_1^{d-1} strings of the optimal length plus 1. If we expand (3) recursively, then we have

[Basic string length tuning algorithm]

$$\left\lfloor \frac{M_d}{X} \right\rfloor = l_0^{d-1} \left\lfloor \frac{M_{d-1}}{X} \right\rfloor + l_1^{d-1}\left(\left\lfloor \frac{M_{d-1}}{X} \right\rfloor + 1 \right)$$

$$= L_0^{d-1} \left\lfloor \frac{M_{d-1}}{X} \right\rfloor + L_1^{d-1}\left(\left\lfloor \frac{M_{d-1}}{X} \right\rfloor + 1 \right)$$

$$= L_0^{d-1}\left\{ l_0^{d-2} \left\lfloor \frac{M_{d-2}}{X} \right\rfloor + l_1^{d-2}\left(\left\lfloor \frac{M_{d-2}}{X} \right\rfloor + 1 \right) \right\}$$

$$+ L_1^{d-1}\left\{ (l_0^{d-2} - 1) \left\lfloor \frac{M_{d-2}}{X} \right\rfloor + (l_1^{d-2} + 1)\left(\left\lfloor \frac{M_{d-2}}{X} \right\rfloor + 1 \right) \right\} \qquad (\text{ by } (2))$$

$$= \left(L_0^{d-1} \cdot l_0^{d-2} + L_1^{d-1}\left(l_0^{d-2} - 1 \right) \right) \left\lfloor \frac{M_{d-2}}{X} \right\rfloor$$

$$+ \left(L_0^{d-1} \cdot l_1^{d-2} + L_1^{d-1}\left(l_1^{d-2} + 1 \right) \right) \left(\left\lfloor \frac{M_{d-2}}{X} \right\rfloor + 1 \right)$$

$$= L_0^{d-2} \left\lfloor \frac{M_{d-2}}{X} \right\rfloor + L_1^{d-2}\left(\left\lfloor \frac{M_{d-2}}{X} \right\rfloor + 1 \right)$$

$$= \cdots\cdots$$

$$= L_0^{1} \left\lfloor \frac{M_1}{X} \right\rfloor + L_1^{1}\left(\left\lfloor \frac{M_1}{X} \right\rfloor + 1 \right) \qquad (4)$$

where

$$\begin{cases} L_0^{i-1} = l_0^{d-1} & (i=d) \\ L_0^{i-1} = L_0^i \cdot l_0^{i-1} + L_1^i (l_0^{i-1} - 1) & (1 < i < d) \end{cases}$$

and

$$\begin{cases} L_1^{i-1} = l_1^{d-1} & (i=d) \\ L_1^{i-1} = L_0^i \cdot l_1^{i-1} + L_1^i (l_1^{i-1} + 1) & (1 < i < d) \end{cases}$$

As a result, the logical space of P_d can be packed if the first processor P_1 can generate strings of its optimal length or one more long according to (4). Since the number of records in the string P_1 produces equals to P_1's merge way, this can be restated as:

[Theorem 3]

For given X, the storage optimization of degree d can be achieved if the first processor P_1 repeats merges in $\lfloor KL/X \rfloor$- or $(\lfloor KL/X \rfloor + 1)$-way according to the sequence determined by (4).

Note that the first d processors require additional memories because they must hold more records than their physical spaces can do. Such additional memories, however, amount to sufficiently small size, which is beyond the scope of this paper.

Some readers may be puzzled because P_1 performs merges in two different merge ways, neither of which equals to K. This claim seems to partially contradict to our design scheme that only the string lengths are variable. But if we regard m-way merge ($m<K$) in P_1 as K-way merge between m strings of length 1 and $K-m$ strings of one less length than it, i.e. 0, then we can still say that by the string length tuning algorithm of the optimization degree d, all processors including P_1 always execute K-way merge while only the first d processors process variable length strings. Actually, (1) determines l_0^0 and l_1^0 as

$$l_1^0 = \left\lfloor \frac{KL}{X} \right\rfloor \quad \left(\left\lfloor \frac{L}{X} \right\rfloor = 0 \text{ by } X > L \right)$$

and

$$l_0^0 = K - l_1^0$$

respectively.

For the comparison, let's return to the example in section 4.2, where $K=2$ and $X=1.1L$. If we apply the storage optimization of degree 3, $\eta(2, 1.1, 3)$ reaches $7.7L/8L=0.9625$ while that of naive algorithm is 0.55. Fig.4.2 gives the snapshot of the sort processing view, where five processors are used. As you can see, 27 records are packed into the memory space of the sorter when the string length tuning algorithm is employed, while the naive algorithm kills the first processor and accommodates only 15 records. Fig.4.3 give the pipeline processing overview of the length tuning algorithm for this example.

4.6. Discussion

So far we discussed the case where the length of the actual record is larger than that of the originally designed length. Here we consider the case where the record is shorter than it. Since the maximal number of the record which the sorter can sort is determined by the number of the processors, we have to prepare additional processors. When a processor is built on LSI, its cost would be very inexpensive. We can add a number of processors with small capacity of memory at the front end. These processors are usually bypassed, and used only when very short records are input.

Thus by employing the string length tuning algorithm, very high memory efficiency is achieved for any length of records.

5. Conclusion

In this paper, we presented the three different memory management algorithms for pipeline merge sorter. Double memory method is very simple but its efficiency is 50%, while the other two require more sophisticated logic in processor but keeps much higher efficiency. The block division method, which is a new algorithm we proposed, was shown to be a generalized algorithm for the others. The memory is divided into blocks of fixed size and the block level management is performed, while record level in pointer method and string level in double memory method.

New storage optimization scheme, " String Length Tuning Algorithm" is also proposed. With this algorithm the data stream of any record length can be sorted efficiently, while most of the hardware sort algorithm proposed so far can sort efficiently only the records with fixed length determined by hardware. For example, 2-way sorter with optimization degree 6 attains about 0.99 memory efficiency.

The pilot system of version 1, we have already implemented, does not employ tuning mechanism. The version 2, now under construction, has several extended control mechanism, including string length tuning, which realizes very flexible sort environment.

Due to the limited space, we cannot present the detail derivation process for the

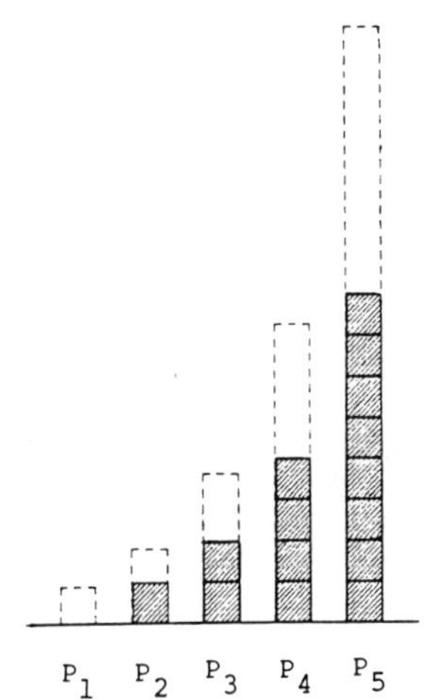

a) Naive Algorithm

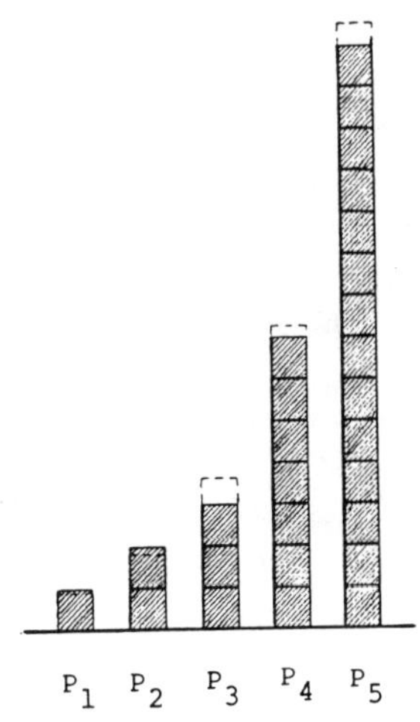

(b) String Length Tuning Algorithm

Fig.4.2 Comparison of Storage Utilization Efficiency between Naive Algorithm and String Length Tuning Algorithm (K,X/L,d)=(2,1.1,3)

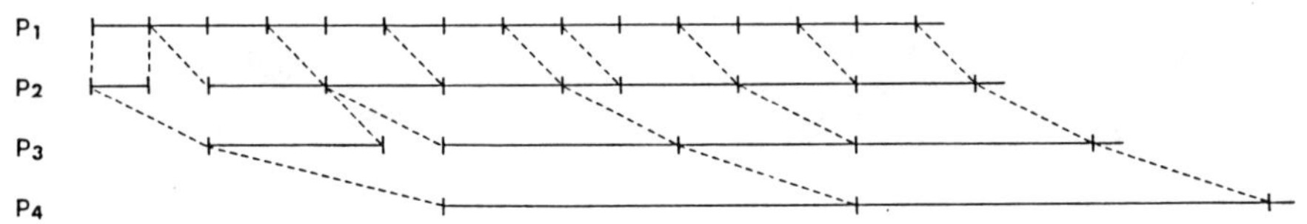

Fig.4.3 Pipeline Chart of String Length Tuning Algorithm for The Example of Fig.4.2.

auxiliary memory of string length tuning, which will be reported elsewhere.

References

1] Kung,H.T.:The Structure of Parallel Algorithms, Advances in Computer 19,Academic Press,1980.

2] Chen, T.C., Lum, V.Y. and Tung,C.:The Rebound Sorter:An Efficient Sort Engine for Large Files, Proc.4th VLDB,1978.

3] Yasuura,H.:The Parallel Enumeration Sorting Scheme for VLSI, IEEE, Trans. Comput. Vol.C-31, No.12, 1983.

4] Tanaka,Y. et.al.:Pipeline Searching and Sorting Modules as Components of a Data Flow Database Computer, IFIP 80,1980

5] Todd,S.:Algorithm and Hardware for Merge Sort Using Multiple Processors, IBM J.R&D, 22,5,1978.

6] Kitsuregawa,M.et.al:Organization of Pipeline Merge Sorter, Trans, IECE Japan, J66-D, 1983.

7] Kitsuregawa,M.et.al:Architecture of Pipeline Merge Sorter, TGEC82-83, IECE Japan, 1982.

8] Hayashi,T.:VLSI Pipeline Merge Sorter, Ms Thesis, Univ.of Tokyo, 1984.

9] Kitsuregawa,M. et.al:Architecture and Performance of Relational Algebra Machine GRACE, Int.Conf.on Parallel Processing 84,1984

10]Kitsuregawa,M. et.al:Relational Algebra Machine GRACE, RIMS Symposia on SSE, Lecture Notes in Computer Science, Vol.147, pp.191-212, 1982.

WORKLOAD MODELING FOR RELATIONAL DATABASE SYSTEMS

S. Salza, M. Terranova

Istituto di Analisi dei Sistemi ed Informatica

viale Manzoni 30, 00185 Roma, Italia

ABSTRACT

The paper presents a pragmatic approach to the workload analysis in relational database systems. A set of extensional and statistical parameters is proposed, that can be easily estimated for the permanent relations of the database, and then computed for any derived relation. In this way arbitrarily complex transactions can be analized.

Both data the data access cost and the processing cost are considered. The latter is usually neglected, but may become a relevant aspect in relational systems, and provides an important information in the design and configuration of specialized systems, like database machines.

The proposed methodology may also be valuable in database design, both at the physical and at the logical level. In fact it allows to compare on a quantitative basis different logical schema for the same application, and suggests the appropriate actions to improve the hysical data organization.

1 - INTRODUCTION

Workload modeling is a fundamental topic in database design and performance prediction. This was clear since the early systematic studies on the subject [SEVC81],[HAWT81].

The first goal is to characterize on a quantitative basis the workload in order to qualify performance statements on database systems. Furthermore the analysis of the execution cost allows to check and compare the design decisions at the logical level, taking into account their effect on the system performance. Finally detailed information on the attribute access patterns can be derived to guide the physical design of the database.

Although usually the analysis is limited to the data access cost, we decided to consider also the processing cost. In fact this may become a relevant aspect in relational systems, where the execution of some operators requires a large number of comparisons. Estimating the processing cost is an even more important problem in designing database machines, to select the appropriate configuration in multiprocessor architectures [SATV83], and/or the processing speed of hardware filters. In fact filter based systems [BANC83],[GRRT84] were conceived according to an idea that gives a central role to the processing needs.

To compute the transaction execution costs we first need to give a statistical characterization of the database, that allows to estimate the size of the result and the cost of the intermediate steps. A first proposal in this direction was made by Demolombe [DEMO80] for queries expressed in predicate calculus language. Later Richard [RICH81] introduced a set of parameters closed for Codd's algebra. More specific aspects, connected with functional dependencies and non-uniform distribution, were considered in [GEGA82], [CHRI83], [CHEU82], [ROSE81].

In this paper we propose a more pragmatic approach to the computation of the execution cost for a database application. A workload description is given that includes both the dynamical aspects (the transactions and their arrival rates) and the logical and physical organization of the database. The proposed set of parameters can easily be estimated, even in a preliminary analysis, and summarizes all the statistical information on the permanent relations. Furthermore a set of transformations is given to evaluate the parameters for the intermediate relations generated by the relational operators. The execution cost can then be computed for an arbitrarily complex transaction.

Our method can also deal with transformations of the logical schema. This is valuable in database design, where different logical schemas may be considered for the same application, and compared on the execution costs. For this purpose the workload profiles are introduced to give a concise and global characterization of the workload and to guide the improvement of the logical and physical organization of the database.

The proposed set of statistical and extensional parameters is defined in sect. 2. Sections 3 and 4 deal with the transformations introduced by the relational operators and the computation of the elementary execution costs. The logical schema transformations are considered in sect. 5, where the corresponding parameter tranformations are given. Finally, a sample case analysis is then presented in sect. 6 and 7, where the workload profiles are intoduced.

2 - THE WORKLOAD MODEL

We define a <u>database</u> as a set of <u>relations</u>, $D=\{R_i,\ i=1,..,N\}$. Each relation is a set of <u>tuples</u>, $R_i=\{r_i^j,\ j=1,..,c_i\}$, where c_i indicates the <u>cardinality</u> of the relation.

Each tuple r_i^j of R_i is an ordered set of a_i values, where a_i is the <u>arity</u> of the relation:

$$r_i^j = < r_i^j[1], r_i^j[2], .., r_i^j[a_i] >$$

(1) $$r_i^j[h] \leq V_i[h] \qquad h=1,..,a_i\ ;\ j=1,..,c_i$$

$$R_i[h] = \{\ r_i^j[h]\ ,\ j=1,..,c_i\}\quad h=1,..,a_i$$

where the multisets $R_i[h]$, containing all the values assumed by a given field in the relation tuples, are called <u>attributes</u>. The corresponding sets $V_i[h]$ are called <u>value-sets</u> and contain the distinct values.

We assume that a quantitative description of the database is given by the following parameters:

$$c_i$$
(2) $$o_i[h] \qquad i=1,..,N \qquad h=1,..,a_i$$
$$e_i[h]$$

where c_i is the relation cardinality, $o_i[h]=\mathrm{Card}(V_i[h])$ is the attribute originality and $e_i[h]$ is the attribute extension, i.e. the number of bytes used to represent the value $r_i^j[h]$.

Moreover, to represent the coupling between attributes, we introduce for every couple of union-compatible attributes the overlapping factors:

(3) $$w_{i,h}^{j,k} = \frac{\mathrm{Card}(\ V_i[h] \cap V_j[k]\ )}{\mathrm{Card}(\ V_i[h]\ )}$$

i.e. the ratio between the number of distinct values occurring in both attributes and the originality of the first attribute.

We also assume that all the transactions arriving to the DBMS belong to a set $Q=\{T_i, i=1,..,M\}$. Each transaction T_i consists of a sequence of steps that produces the result relation U_i:

(4) $$T_i = < S_i[1],\ S_i[2], .., S_i[z_i] >$$

Each step $S_i[j]$ is a relational operation (Selection, projection, join, union) and produces an intermediate relation $I_i[j]$ temporarely added to the database:

(5) $$D[j-1] \xrightarrow{S_i[j]} D[j] = D[j-1] + I_i[j]$$

where $D[0] = D$ is the original database and $I_i[z_i] = U_i$ is the result of the transaction.

A set of arrival rates $\{l_i, i=1,..M\}$ is also given, to represent the rate at which the instances of the transactions arrive to the DBMS.

3 - PARAMETER TRANSFORMATIONS

As we will see in more detail in sect. 4 the transaction execution cost can be expressed as the sum of the cost of the individual steps $S_i[j]$. Therefore we need to compute the extensional and statistical parameters for all the intermediate relations.

Our analysis is based on the following uniformity assumption:

In every relation R_i the values assumed by the fields $r_i^j[h]$ are i.i.d. random variables uniformely distributed in the sets $V_i[h]$.

As a first consequence of this, for each attribute $R_i[h]$ the multiplicities of all the values of the corresponding value-set $V_i[h]$ are identically distributed with mean $m_i[h]=c_i/o_i[h]$. Furthermore the relational operations can alter the originality of the attributes, through an uniform thinning, but do not change their overlapping factors with all the other union-compatible attributes not involved in the operation.

	CARDINALITY	ORIGINALITY
SEL	$c_S = c_1/o_1[1]$	$o_S[1] = 1$ $o_S[h] = o_1[h]\ F_h(o_1[h],c_S) \quad h\neq 1$
PRJ	$c_P = o_1[1] \quad a_P=1$ $c_P = o_1[1]\ ..\ o_1[a_P]\ (1-q) \quad a_P>1$ $q = \left(1 - \dfrac{1}{o_1[1]\ ..\ o_1[a_P]}\right)^{c_1}$	$o_P[h] = o_1[h]$
JOI	$c_J = w_{1,1}^{2,1} \dfrac{c_1\ c_2}{o_2[1]}$	$o_J[1] = o_1[1]\ w_{1,1}^{2,1}$ $o_J[h] = o_1[h]\ F_h(o_1[h],c_1\ w_{1,1}^{2,1}) \quad h\neq 1$
UNI	$c_U = q\ c_1 + c_2$ $q = 1-c_2 \dfrac{w_{1,1}^{2,1}\ ..\ w_{1,a}^{2,a}}{o_2[1]\ ..\ o_2[a]}$	$o_U[h] = o_1[h]+o_2[h]\ (1-w_{2,h}^{1,h})$

Table 3.1

Transformations for the cardinality and the originality

The complete analysis is presented in [SATE84]. The results are here summarized in table 3.1 and 3.2. where, to simplify the notation, a convenient reordering of the attributes of the operand relations R_1 and R_2 is assumed to have in the first positions the attributes involved in the operation. The same ordering is maintained in the rusult relation.

	OVERLAPPING FACTORS
SEL	$w_{S,h}^{i,k} = w_{1,h}^{i,k} \quad R_i \neq R_S$ $\qquad w_{S,h}^{S,k} = w_{1,h}^{1,k} F_k(o_1[k], c_S) \quad h \neq k$
PRJ	$w_{P,h}^{i,k} = w_{1,h}^{i,k}$
JOI	$w_{J,h}^{i,k} = w_{1,h}^{i,k} \quad R_i \neq R_J,\ h \neq 1$ $\qquad w_{J,h}^{J,k} = w_{1,h}^{1,k} F_k(o_1[k], c_1\ w_{1,1}^{2,1}) \quad h,k \neq 1$ $w_{J,1}^{i,k} = \dfrac{w_{1,1}^{2,1} w_{1,1}^{i,k} + w_{2,1}^{1,1} w_{2,1}^{i,k}}{w_{1,1}^{2,1} + w_{2,1}^{1,1}} \quad R_i \neq R_J$ $w_{J,1}^{J,k} = \dfrac{w_{1,1}^{2,1} w_{1,1}^{i,k} + w_{2,1}^{1,1} w_{2,1}^{i,k}}{w_{1,1}^{2,1} + w_{2,1}^{1,1}} F_k(o_1[k], c_1\ w_{1,1}^{2,1}) \quad k \neq 1$
UNI	$w_{U,h}^{i,k} = \dfrac{o_1[h]}{o_U[h]} w_{1,h}^{i,k} + \dfrac{o_2[h]}{o_U[h]} w_{2,h}^{i,k} + \dfrac{o_1[h]}{o_U[h]} w_{1,h}^{2,h} \dfrac{w_{1,h}^{2,h} w_{1,h}^{1,k} + w_{2,h}^{1,h} w_{2,h}^{i,k}}{w_{1,h}^{2,h} + w_{2,h}^{1,h}}$

Table 3.2

Transformations for the overlapping factors

Table 3.1 points out the reduction in the originality of the attributes not involved in the operation. To represent this we introduce the <u>compression factor</u> F_h. For instance, in the case of the select:

(6)
$$F_h(o_1[h], c_S) = 1 - p_h$$
$$p_h = (1 - 1 / o_1[h])^{c_s}$$

where p_h is computed, according to the uniformity assumption, as the probability that a given value of the attribute does not occur in the result relation.

For the projection the cardinality c_p is computed in the case of duplicate elimination (otherwise $c_p=c_1$). According to the uniformity assumption we consider the cartesian product of the value-sets $C = V_1[1]xV_1[2]x..xV_1[a_p]$, and the probability p that a given element of C does not appear in the result.

The tranformations of the overlapping factors are reported in table 3.2. In some cases the overlapping factors do not change. For the projection this happens because the originality of the attributes are not affected. In the selection the value-sets (and then their intersections) are uniformely thinned, and therefore the overlapping factors, according to their definition in (3), do not change.

Instead, when the couple of attributes belong to the result relation, the reduction of the both the originalities may reduce the overlapping factor. The amount of the reduction is then given by the compression factor.

Finally, when the join attribute is involved, the overlapping factor proportionally inherits the behaviour of the join attributes of the operand relations.

4 - TRANSACTION EXECUTION COST

The transaction execution cost depends on the physical data organization and on the algorithm used to implement the relational operators. In this paper we refer to unsorted flat files stored in fixed length blocks. This may be considered as a reference organization to give a basic estimate of the cost and to allow a measure of the improvements introduced by more sophisticated physical structures.

As far as the algorithms are concerned, we assume for the join and the union a preliminary sort of the operands. This is performed through a sort-merge having the physical blocks at the first level. This algorithm belongs to the class of separable algorithms [WHWS84], and therefore allows to split the cost between the attributes. A cost optimisation is then possible through independent actions on the single attributes. Neverthless the nested-loop algorithm is also considered because it gives a better performance for unbalanced cardinalities of the operands.

For the processing cost we restrict our analysis to the main component represented by the comparison between fields. Moreover, for large fields, we estimate the actual number of comparisons performed that may be significantly lower than the field length. For this purpose, for every relational operation, we intoduce the <u>comparison factor</u> defined as the expected number of byte compared per field comparison.

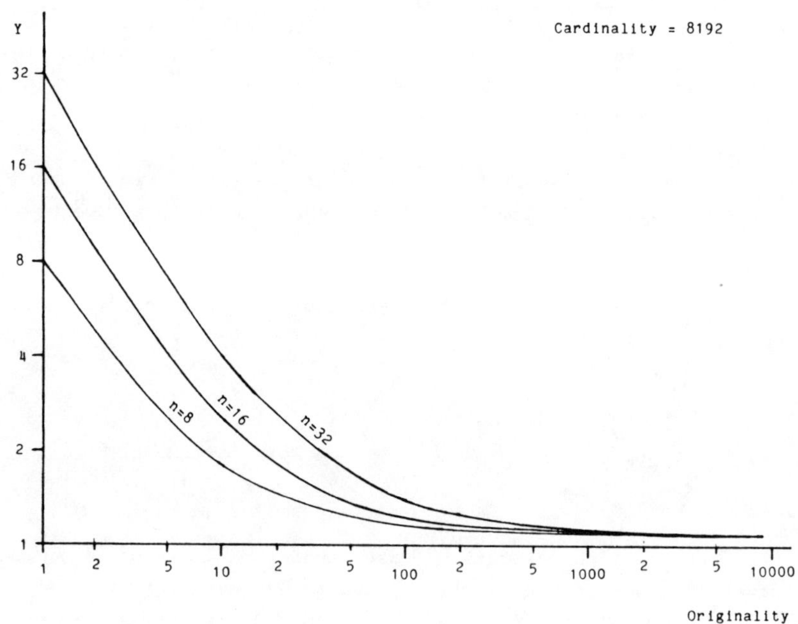

Figure 4.1
Comparison factor for the selection

In the case of the selection, let us consider a relation with cardinality c and an attribute with originality o, extension n and average multiplicity m=c/o. Among the total number of c-1 field comparisons, on the average m-1 involve identical values. In these cases n byte comparisons are needed.

For the remaining c-m field comparisons, we consider the probability q_i that the two fields match only in the first i byte. Assuming a truncated geometric distribution, and considering that a maximum of -1 byte can match:

(7)

$$q_i = (1-y) / (1-y^n)\ y^i \qquad i=0,..,n-1$$

$$q_i = 0 \qquad i \geq n$$

Therefore, for these field comparisons, an average of:

(8)

$$d = \sum_{i=0}^{n-1} (i+1)\ q_i$$

byte comparisons are needed.

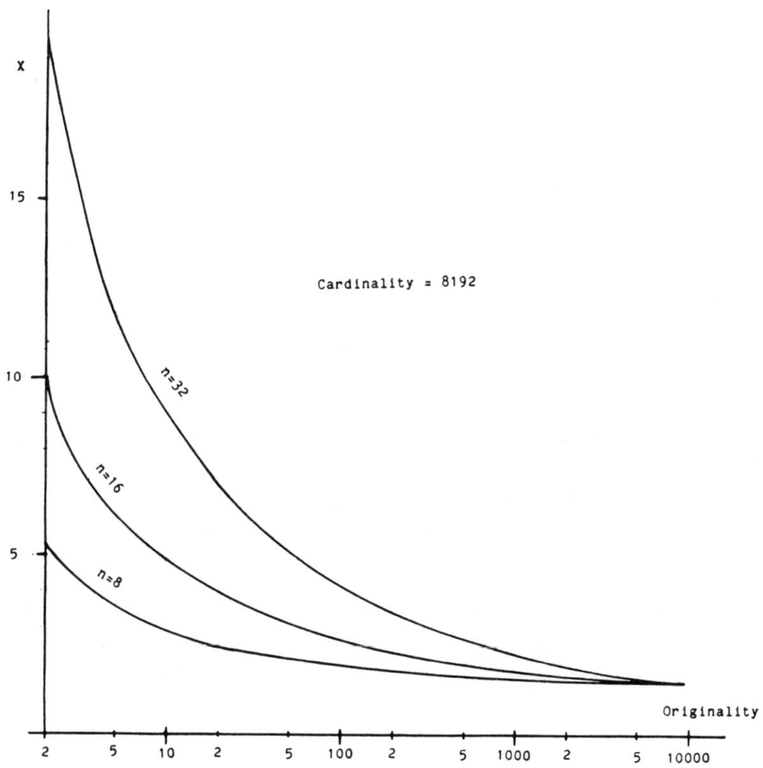

Figure 4.2
Comparison factor for the merge-join

The comparison factor for the selection is then given by:

$$(9) \qquad Y = \frac{(m-1)\, n + (c-m)\, d}{c - 1}$$

The values of Y are shown in figure 4.1 for different values of the field extension n and of the attribute originality o.

A similar approach can be used for the join and the union [SATE84]. In the sort-merge algorithm the main part of the cost is due to the preliminary sort, and the average number of byte comparisons is estimated for every level, taking into account that the matching probability increases with the ordering. Instead, for the nested loop, the comparison factor depends on both attributes and takes into account their overlapping. The values of the comparison factor for the first case, computed as an average over all the levels of the sort-merge, are shown in figure 4.2.

SEL	$P_S = c_1\ Y_1[1] \qquad B_S = E_1 + E_S$
JOI S-M	$P_J = (E_1 b_1^{\,2} + (c_1-1)\log_2(E_1))\ X_1[1] +$ $+ (E_2 b_2^{\,2} + (c_2-1)\log_2(E_2))\ X_2[1]$ $B_J = 2E_1\log_2(E_1) + 2E_2\log_2(E_2) + E_1 + E_2 + E_J$
JOI N-L	$P'_J = c_1(c_2-1)\ H^{2,1}_{1,1} \qquad B'_J = E_1 + E_1E_2 + E_J$
UNI	$P_U = (E_1 b_1^{\,2} + (c_1-1)\log_2(E_1))\ G_1[1] +$ $+ (E_2 b_2^{\,2} + (c_2-1)\log_2(E_2))\ G_2[1]$ $B_U = 2E_1\log_2(E_1) + 2E_2\log_2(E_2) + E_1 + E_2 + E_J$

Table 4.1
Execution costs for the relational operators

The execution costs for the relational operators are summarized in table 4.1, where E_i represents the relation extension in data blocks, b_i is the number of tuples per block, $Y_i[h]$, $X_i[h]$, and G_i

are the comparison factors for the selection, join and union, and $H_{i,h}^{j,k}$ is the comparison factor for the join with the nested loop algorithm.

These tables allow to compute transfer and processing cost at the step level:

$B_i[j]$: number of data block accesses during the execution of the step $S_i[j]$ of the transaction T_i.

$P_i[j]$: number of byte comparisons performed during the execution of step $S_i[j]$.

At the transaction level the execution cost is then given by:

$$(10) \qquad B_i = \sum_{j=1}^{z_i} B_i[j] \qquad\qquad P_i = \sum_{i=1}^{z_i} P_i[j]$$

Finally, considering the whole workload, we can take into account the arrival rates of the transactions and compute the overall execution cost per unit of time:

$$(11) \qquad \hat{B} = \sum_{j=1}^{M} l_i \, B_i[j] \qquad\qquad \hat{P} = \sum_{i=1}^{M} l_i P_i[j]$$

5 - SCHEMA TRANSFORMATIONS

Our analysis can also be extended to consider the effect of logical schema transformations on the execution cost. In fact for a large set of transformations it is possible to derive the new extensional and statistical parameters from the original ones.

Given a database $D=\{R_i, i=1,..,N\}$ and a set of transactions $Q=\{T_i, i=1,..,M\}$, we can consider an equivalent database $D'=\{R_i', i=1,..,N'\}$ and a set of transactions $Q'=\{T_i', i=1,..,M\}$ such that the result of corresponding transactions is the same in both cases:

$$(12) \qquad D \xrightarrow{T_i} U_i \qquad D' \xrightarrow{T_i'} U_i' \qquad i=1,..,M$$

$$U_i' \equiv U_i$$

Without substantial loss of generality, we may restrict to the equivalent databases D' that can be obtained from D by means of a schema transformation Θ having the form:

(13)
$$D \xrightarrow{\Theta} D'$$
$$\Theta = \{ t_i,\ i=1,..,N' \}$$

where t_i is a transaction that generates the relation R_i' of D' from D:

(14)
$$D \xrightarrow{t_i} R_i'$$

and, as for the ordinary transactions, t_i is a sequence of elementary steps, each consisting in a relational operation:

(15)
$$t_i = < s_i[1],\ s_i[2],..,s_i[z_i] >$$

$c_E = c_1(1-w_{1,1}^{2,1}) + c_2(1-w_{2,1}^{1,1}) + \frac{c_1\ c_2}{o_2[1]} w_{1,1}^{2,1}$
$o_E[1] = o_1[1]\ (1-w_{1,1}^{2,1}) + o_2[1] \qquad o_E[h] = o_1[h] \quad h\neq 1$
$w_{E,h}^{i,k} = w_{1,h}^{i,k}$
$w_{E,1}^{i,k} = \frac{o_1[1]}{o_E[1]} w_{1,1}^{i,k} + \frac{o_2[1]}{o_E[1]} w_{2,1}^{i,k} + \frac{o_1[1]}{o_E[1]} w_{1,1}^{2,1} \frac{w_{1,1}^{2,1}\ w_{1,1}^{1,k} + w_{2,1}^{1,1}\ w_{2,1}^{i,k}}{w_{1,1}^{2,1} + w_{2,1}^{1,1}}$

Table 5.1

Parameter transformation for the external-join

Given the description of the workload referring to the original database D and the schema transformation Θ, we can then compute the workload description referring to D'. This can be accomplished using the results of section 3, considering instead of the ordinary join the external-join [CODD79], that generates a tuple in the result also for unmatching values of the join attribute. The corresponding transformations, given in table 5.1, are derived as an extension of those of section 3, to which one must refer for the notation.

6 - A SAMPLE CASE ANALYSIS

In this section a sample case analysis is presented. Two alternative logical schemas are considered for the same database, in order to compare the execution costs.

The original description refers to a logical schema presented in table 6.1 and 6.2, where all the extensional and statistical parameters are given. An informal definition of the transactions is given in table 6.3. A complete definition would have required to specify the execution sequence, that is given, as an example, for transaction T_6 in table 6.4. For each step the table specifies the relational operation and the operands, which may be permanent or intermediate relations. In both cases the attributes are indicated by the first characters of their name and the number of the permanent relation where they originated.

An analytic account of the execution cost is presented in table 6.5. For each join the lower cost algorithm between nested-loop and sort-merge was selected. Moreover, as there was no need for duplicate elimination, the processing cost of the projections was neglected.

An alternative schema is presented in table 6.6 and 6.7. It is an equivalent schema in the sense of section 4, and can be obtained from the original one through the following transformation:

$$\theta = \{ t_1, t_2, t_3 \}$$

$$D \xrightarrow{t_1} R_1'$$

t_1 = identity(R_1)

$$D \xrightarrow{t_2} R_2'$$

t_2 = < E-JOI(R_3, 3.#ROO; R_4, 4.#ROO),
E-JOI(I_1, 4.#COU; R_1, 1.#COU),
PRJ(I_2; 3.SIZE, 4.#CLA, 1.NAME, 4.#TEA, 4.TIME)>

$$D \xrightarrow{t_3} R_3'$$

t_3 = < E-JOI(R_5, 5.#STU; R_6, 6.#STU),
PRJ(I_1; 5.#CLA, 5.#STU, 6.NAME, 6.ADDR)>

where we adopted the same notation of table 6.4.

R_1 - COURSES		**c_1 = 480**	**E_1 = 3 B**
1	<u>#COUrse</u>	$o_1[1]$ = 480	$e_1[1]$ = 4
2	NAME	$o_1[2]$ = 480	$e_1[2]$ = 20
R_2 - TEACHERS		**c_2 = 900**	**E_2 = 26 B**
1	<u>#TEAcher</u>	$o_2[1]$ = 900	$e_2[1]$ = 4
2	NAME	$o_2[2]$ = 900	$e_2[2]$ = 32
3	DEGRee	$o_2[3]$ = 5	$e_2[3]$ = 2
4	ADDRess	$o_2[4]$ = 900	$e_2[4]$ = 64
5	PHONe	$o_2[5]$ = 900	$e_2[5]$ = 12
R_3 - ROOMS		**c_3 = 240**	**E_3 = 2 B**
1	<u>#ROOm</u>	$o_3[1]$ = 240	$e_3[1]$ = 4
2	NAME	$o_3[2]$ = 240	$e_3[2]$ = 10
3	SIZE	$o_3[3]$ = 10	$e_3[3]$ = 4
R_4 - CLASSES		**c_4 = 1800**	**E_4 = 9 B**
1	<u>#CLAss</u>	$o_4[1]$ = 1800	$e_4[1]$ = 4
2	#COUrse	$o_4[2]$ = 480	$e_4[2]$ = 4
3	#TEAcher	$o_4[3]$ = 600	$e_4[3]$ = 4
4	#ROOm	$o_4[4]$ = 240	$e_4[4]$ = 4
5	TIME	$o_4[5]$ = 48	$e_4[5]$ = 4
R_5 - ENROLMENT		**c_5 = 180000**	**E_5 = 527 B**
1	<u>#STUdent</u>	$o_5[1]$ = 30000	$e_5[1]$ = 8
2	<u>#CLAss</u>	$o_5[2]$ = 1800	$e_5[2]$ = 4
R_6 - STUDENTS		**c_6 = 30000**	**E_6 = 761 B**
1	<u>#STUdent</u>	$o_6[1]$ = 30000	$e_6[1]$ = 8
2	NAME	$o_6[2]$ = 30000	$e_6[2]$ = 32
3	ADDRess	$o_6[3]$ = 30000	$e_6[3]$ = 64

Table 6.1
Sample database (schema 1)

$w_{1,1}^{4,2} = 1$	$w_{2,1}^{4,3} = \frac{11}{15}$	$w_{3,1}^{4,4} = 1$	$w_{4,1}^{5,2} = 1$	$w_{4,2}^{1,1} = 1$
$w_{4,3}^{2,1} = 1$	$w_{4,4}^{3,1} = 1$	$w_{5,1}^{6,1} = 1$	$w_{5,2}^{4,1} = 1$	$w_{6,1}^{5,1} = 1$

Table 6.2 - Overlapping factors (schema 1)

T_1 :	The name of all the students enrolled in the class of code X.
T_2 :	The name of all the student enrolled in the course of name X.
T_3 :	The address and the phone number of the teacher of name X.
T_4 :	The name of all the teachers lecturing in the course of name X.
T_5 :	The size of the classrooms where the classes of the course of name X are held.
T_6 :	The name of all the students enrolled in both the courses of name X and Y.

Table 6.3 - The set of transactions

$S_6[1]$:	SEL(R_1; 1.NAME = X)	——> I_1
$S_6[2]$:	JOI(I_1, 1.#COU; R_4, 4.#COU)	——> I_2
$S_6[3]$:	JOI(I_2, 4.#CLA; R_5, 5.#CLA)	——> I_3
$S_6[4]$:	SEL(R_1; 1.NAME = Y)	——> I_4
$S_6[5]$:	JOI(I_4, 1.#COU; R_4, 4.#COU)	——> I_5
$S_6[6]$:	JOI(I_5, 4.#CLA; R_5, 5.#CLA)	——> I_6
$S_6[7]$:	JOI(I_3, 5.#STU; I_6, 5.#STU)	——> I_7
$S_6[8]$:	JOI(I_7, 5.#STU; R_6, 6.#STU)	——> I_8
$S_6[9]$:	PRJ(I_8; 6.NAME)	——> I_9

Table 6.4 - The step sequence of T_6

TRANS.	STEP	TYPE	$B_i[j]$	$P_i[j]$	B_i	P_i
T_1	1	SEL	528	203		
	2	JOI	763	3300		
	3	PRJ	2	-	1293	3503
T_2	1	SEL	4	.5		
	2	SEL	10	1.9		
	3	JOI	530	742		
	4	JOI	2296	12375		
	5	PRJ	17	-	2857	13119
T_3	1	SEL	27	.9		
	2	PRJ	-	-	27	.9
T_4	1	SEL	4	.5		
	2	SEL	10	1.9		
	3	JOI	27	3.7		
	4	PRJ	-	-	41	6.1
T_5	1	SEL	4	.5		
	2	SEL	10	1.9		
	3	JOI	4	9.9		
	4	PRJ	-	-	18	12.3
T_6	1	SEL	4	.5		
	2	SEL	10	.9		
	3	JOI	530	742		
	4	SEL	4	.5		
	5	JOI	10	.9		
	6	JOI	530	742		
	7	JOI	13	11.5		
	8	JOI	764	948		
	9	PRJ	2	-	1867	2448.3

Table 6.5 - Execution costs (schema 1)

As some of the attributes are renamed, the last column in table 6.6 gives the corresponding attribute in the original schema. The table also contains the extensional parameters, computed from the values of table 6.1.

Comparing the execution cost in the two schemas (table 6.5 and 6.8) we note that most transactions have a simpler execution sequence in the second case. In fact schema 2 has a few large relations obtained through external-joins. Therefore in the execution sequences many joins are no longer needed or are replaced by selections. The general trend is then a reduction in processing and an increase in transfer.

R'_1 - TEACHERS		**c_1 = 900**	**E_1 = 26 B**	
1	<u>#TEAcher</u>	$o_1[1]$ = 900	$e_1[1]$ = 4	$R_2[1]$
2	NAME	$o_1[2]$ = 900	$e_1[2]$ = 32	$R_2[2]$
3	DEGRee	$o_1[3]$ = 5	$e_1[3]$ = 2	$R_2[3]$
4	ADDRess	$o_1[4]$ = 900	$e_1[4]$ = 64	$R_2[4]$
5	PHONe	$o_1[5]$ = 900	$e_1[5]$ = 12	$R_2[5]$
R'_2 - CLASSES		**c_2 = 1800**	**E_2 = 21 B**	
1	<u>#CLAss</u>	$o_2[1]$ = 1800	$e_2[1]$ = 4	$R_4[1]$
2	COURse	$o_2[2]$ = 480	$e_2[2]$ = 20	$R_1[2]$
3	#TEAcher	$o_2[3]$ = 600	$e_2[3]$ = 4	$R_4[2]$
4	ROOM	$o_2[4]$ = 240	$e_2[4]$ = 10	$R_3[2]$
5	TIME	$o_2[5]$ = 48	$e_2[5]$ = 4	$R_4[5]$
6	SIZE	$o_2[3]$ = 10	$e_2[3]$ = 4	$R_3[3]$
R'_3 - STUDENTS		**c_3 = 180000**	**E_3 = 4747 B**	
1	<u>#CLAss</u>	$o_3[2]$ = 1800	$e_3[2]$ = 4	$R_5[2]$
2	<u>#STUdent</u>	$o_3[1]$ = 30000	$e_3[1]$ = 8	$R_5[1]$
3	NAME	$o_3[2]$ = 30000	$e_3[2]$ = 32	$R_6[2]$
4	ADDRess	$o_3[3]$ = 30000	$e_3[3]$ = 64	$R_6[3]$

Table 6.6 - Sample database (schema 2)

$w_{1,1}^{2,3} = \frac{11}{15}$	$w_{2,1}^{3,2} = 1$	$w_{2,3}^{1,1} = 1$
$w_{3,1}^{4,1} = 1$	$w_{3,2}^{2,1} = 1$	$w_{4,1}^{3,1} = 1$

Table 6.7 - Overlapping factors (schema 2)

TRANS.	STEP	TYPE	$B_i[j]$	$P_i[j]$	B_i	P_i
T_1	1 2	SEL PRJ	4751 4	203 -	4755	203
T_2	1 2 3	SEL JOI PRJ	22 4762 17	2.5 742.5 -	4801	745
T_3	1 2	SEL PRJ	27 -	.9 -	27	.9
T_4	1 2 3	SEL JOI PRJ	22 28 -	2.2 3.7 -	50	5.9
T_5	1 2	SEL PRJ	22 -	2.2 -	22	2.2
T_6	1 2 3 4 5 6	SEL JOI SEL JOI JOI PRJ	22 4762 22 4762 138 5	2.2 742.5 2.2 742.5 17.5 -	9711	1506.9

Table 6.8 - Execution costs (schema 2)

7 - WORKLOAD PROFILES

The tables of the execution costs of the previous section give an analytic account of the workload characteristics. Instead the transaction profile shown in fig. 7.1 allows a quick visual comparison of the cost of different transactions, and of the same transaction in the two schemas. Moreover, to take into account the arrival rates, we can define the weighted profile, where the actual cost rate of every transaction is represented (fig. 7.2). Finally a comparison of the global execution cost in the two schemas is given in fig. 7.3.

These profiles provide a valuable information in selecting the database schema. Instead, at the physical design level, we need to consider how the accesses are clustered on the database permanent relations. We then introduce the relation access rates, i.e. the number of data blocks accessed per unit of time for every relation. Table 7.1 refers to the example of the previous section, and gives, for every transaction, the number of accesses on the permanent relations.

The last column gives the access rates (blocks/sec.) based on the transaction arrival rates in the last row.

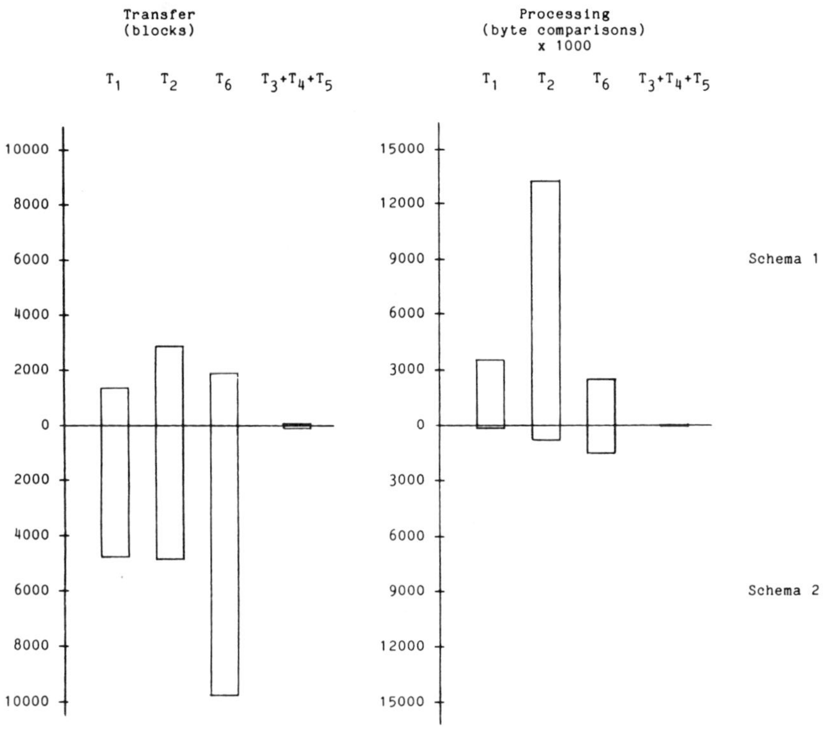

Figure 7.1 - Transaction profile

	T_1	T_2	T_3	T_4	T_5	T_6	RAR
R_1'	-	-	26	26	-	-	.52
R_2'	-	21	-	21	21	42	1.26
R_3'	4747	4747	-	-	-	9494	332.29
Rate	.03	.02	.01	.01	.01	.01	

Table 7.1 - Relation access rates (schema 2)

An even more detailed information is presented in table 7.2, where the access rate of each relation is divided among the attributes. The kind of access, i.e. the type of the relational operation, is also specified. This information may be of great help in taking actions to improve the physical data organization on a performance basis through sorting, indexing or inverting the attributes. For instance in the example most accesses are on $R'_{3.\#CLA}$, mainly for joins. An appropriate action would be to sort this attribute. This would dramatically cut both the transfer and the processing cost. A modest improvement can also be obtained acting on $R'_{1.NAME}$ and $R'_{2.COUR}$. In the latter case indexing would be more suitable than sorting as the accesses are for selection.

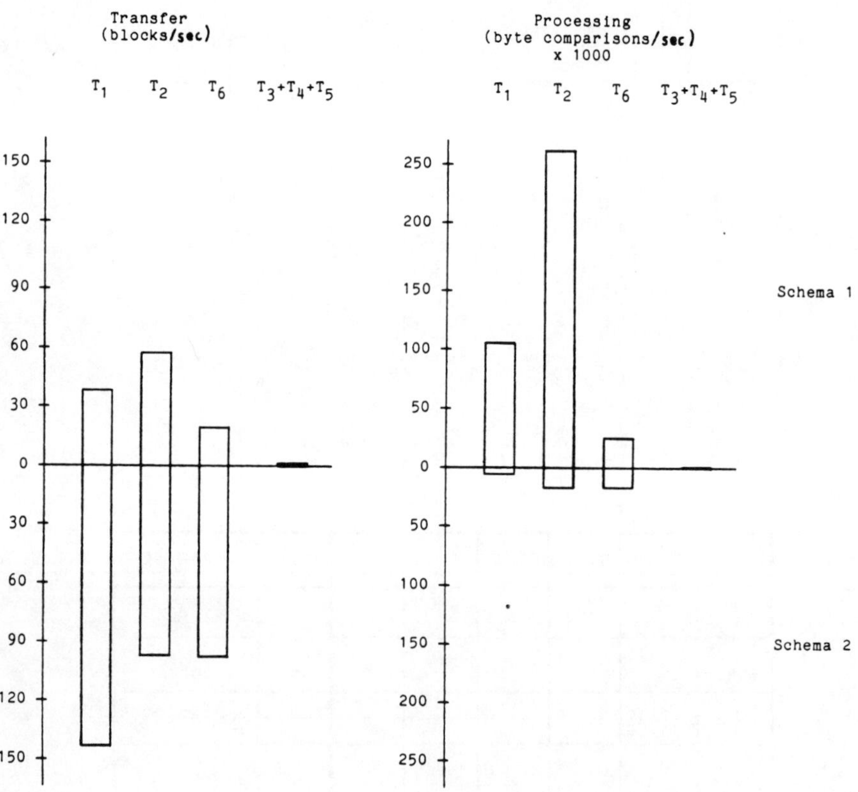

Figure 7.2 - Weighted profile

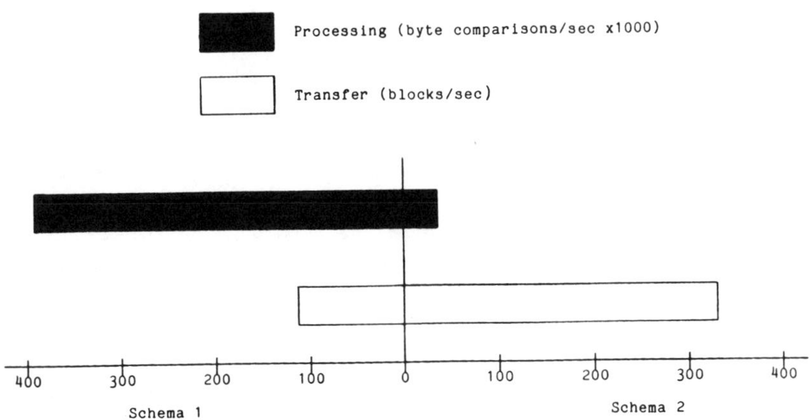

Figure 7.3 - Workload profiles.

RELATION	ATTRIBUTE	SEL	JOI
R_1'	#TEAcher	-	.26
	NAME	.26	-
R_2'	#CLAss	-	-
	COURse	1.26	-
	#TEAcher	-	-
	ROOM	-	-
	TIME	-	-
	SIZE	-	-
R_3'	#CLAss	189.88	94.94
	#STUdent	-	-
	NAME	-	-
	ADDRess	-	-

Table 7.2 - Attribute access rates (schema 2).

8 - CONCLUSIONS

In this paper we presented a method to analyze the workload of relational database systems. A simple set of parameters has been defined to represent the extensional and statistical characteristics of the relations, including coupling between attributes. The parameter values can easily be estimated for the permanent relations, and then computed for the intermediate relations through a set of transformations. In this way arbitrarily complex transactions can be analyzed.

We explicitly considered both the access and the processing cost. The latter is usually neglected but may become relevant in the design and configuration of parallel systems like database machines.

Our methodology may also be valuable in database design, both at the logical and physical level. In fact it allows to compare the execution cost for the same database referring to different logical schemas, and suggests the appropriate actions to improve the physical data organization.

REFERENCES

[BANC83] BANCILHON F. et al. : VERSO, A Relational Backend Database Machine, in Advanced Database Machine Architectures, D. K. Hsiao ed., Prentice-hall 1983.

[CHEU82] CHEUNG T. : A Statistical Method for Estimating the Number of Records in a Relational Database, Inf. Proc. Lett. Vol. 15 No. 3, Oct 82.

[CHRI83] CHRISTODOULAKIS S. : Estimating Block Transfers and Join Sizes, Proc. ACM-SIGMOD 1983, pp. 40-54.

[CODD79] CODD E. F. : Extending the Database Relational Model to Capture More Meaning, ACM TODS, Vol. 4, No. 4, Dec. 1979, pp. 397-434.

[DEMO80] DEMOLOMBE R. : Estimation of the Number of Tuples Satisfying a Query Expressed in Predicate Calculus Language, Proc. VLDB 1980, pp.55-63.

[GEGA82] GELEMBE E., GARDY D. : The Size of Projections of Relations Satisfying a Functional Dependency, Proc. VLDB 1982, pp.325-333.

[GRRT84] GONZALES-RUBIO R., ROHMER J., TERRAL D. : The SHUSS Filter: a Processor for Non-Numerical Data Processing, 11th Annual International Symposium on Computer Architecture, Ann Arbor, Michigan, Juin 84.

[HAWT81] HAWTHORN P. B. : The Effect of Target Applications on the Design of Database Machines, Proc. ACM SIGMOD 1981, pp. 188-197.

[RICH81] RICHARD P. : Evaluation of the Size of a Query Expressed in Relational Algebra, ACM SIGMOD 1981, pp. 155-163.

[ROSE81] ROSENTHAL A. S. : Note on the Expected Size of a Join, SIGMOD Rec. Vol. 11 No. 4.

[SATE84] SALZA S., TERRANOVA M. : A Methodology for the Analysis of the Workload in Relational Database Systems, Report R-97 of Istituto di Analisi dei Sistemi ed Informatica del CNR, 1984.

[SATV83] SALZA S., TERRANOVA M., VELARDI P. : Performance Modelling of the DBMAC Architecture, Proc. 3rd International Workshop on Database Machines, Munich Sept. 83, pp. 74-90.

[SEVC81] SEVCIK K. C. : Data Base System Performance Prediction Using An Analytical Model, Proc. VLDB 1981, pp. 182-198.

[WHWS84] WANG K., WIEDERHOLD G., SAGALOWICZ D. : Separability - An Approach to Physical Database Design, IEEE Trans. on Computers, Vol. C-33 No. 3, March 84, pp. 209-222

A Parallel Logging Algorithm for Multiprocessor Database Machines

Rakesh Agrawal
AT&T Bell Laboratories
Murray Hill, NJ 07974

ABSTRACT

During the past decade, a number of database machine designs have been proposed. However, these designs have been optimized only with respect to the retrieval queries, and virtually no attention has been given to the issues of recovery and its impact on the performance of the proposed machines. In this paper, we present a recovery architecture based on parallel logging for the multiprocessor-cache class of database machines and the results of the evaluation of its impact on the performance of the database machine.

1. Introduction

During the past decade, database machines have been the subject of intense research activity, and a number of database machine designs have been proposed (see the surveys in [13,21]). However, most of these designs have been optimized only with respect to retrieval queries. In reality, databases are continually updated. With update operations, a major function of the database management software is to keep the database consistent in presence of failures. This problem, referred to as the *recovery* problem, requires that a consistent state of the database objects be restored after a failure.

Database-machine designers (except for producers of commercial products such as Britton-Lee and Terradata) have virtually ignored the issue of recovery and its impact on the performance of the proposed machines. The study of recovery architectures for RAP-like associative processors in [6] is the only work in this area. In this paper, we present a recovery architecture based on *parallel logging* for the multiprocessor-cache class of database machines and its impact on the performance of the database machine.

The organization of the rest of the paper is as follows. In Section 2, we present the architecture of the multiprocessor-cache class of database machines. Our parallel logging algorithm is described in Section 3. In Section 4, we present the results of the simulation experiments to determine the characteristics of our parallel logging algorithm and its impact on database machine performance. Our conclusions are presented in Section 5.

2. Database Machine Architecture

The database machine architecture that we consider consists of a set of processors, a multi-level memory hierarchy, and an interconnection device.

Some of the processors, designated query processors, process transactions and operate asynchronously with respect to each other. One of the processors, designated the back-end controller, acts as an interface to the host processor (the processor with which a user interacts) and coordinates the activities of the other processors.

We assume that the memory hierarchy consists of three levels. The top level consists of the internal memories of the query processors. Each processor's local memory is assumed to be large enough to hold both a compiled transaction and several data pages. Mass storage devices (disks) make up the bottom level and the middle level is a disk cache that is addressable by pages. Management of pages within this cache is performed by the back-end controller.

We assume that the bottom two levels of the memory hierarchy are connected in such a way that simultaneous data transfers can occur between each of the disk drives and any page frame in the cache. A processor, designated the I/O processor, is responsible for transferring data pages between the disks and the cache. The top two levels of the hierarchy are so connected that each processor can read and write a different page of the cache simultaneously and all processors can simultaneously read the same page of the cache. See [5] for a discussion of the interconnection schemes that may satisfy these requirements.

This database machine design has been classified as a multiprocessor-cache design [8]. Examples of database machines in this class include DIRECT [7], RAP.2 [20], INFOPLEX [18], RDBM [14], and DBMAC [19].

3. Parallel Logging

Recovery has two aspects:

1. collection of recovery data during the normal execution of the transactions,
2. use of recovery data to perform necessary recovery actions in the event of a software or hardware failure.

All transactions, whether they complete or abort, incur the cost of collecting recovery data. However, only in case of a failure is the recovery data used. A recovery mechanism may make collection of recovery data relatively less expensive at the price of making recovery from failures costly. On the other hand, a recovery mechanism may make recovery from failures cheaper at the expense of incurring a large penalty during the collection of recovery data. Logging belongs to the first category whereas shadow and differential file techniques belong to the second category (see [1] for a summary of these recovery mechanisms).

A simple but important conclusion that we drew from our study of the performance of concurrency control and recovery mechanisms for centralized database systems [1] was that from the performance viewpoint the focus should be on making the normal case efficient. Thus, although transaction undos are more expensive with logging, this strategy outperformed shadow and differential file mechanisms as it places a smaller burden on transactions that complete successfully. We have in our design, therefore, optimized collection of recovery data even if it meant making recovery from a failure more expensive while insuring that recovery can still be correctly performed. In the following sections, we assume familiarity with the basic notions of logging [9, 11].

3.1 Architecture

The basic idea is to make the collection of recovery data efficient by allowing logging to occur in parallel at more than one log disk. We will show how recovery from system crashes and transaction failures can still be performed correctly without physically merging the parallel logs into one log. We assume that a page-level locking scheduler located with the back-end controller is responsible for concurrency control.

We postulate N log processors, where $N \geq 1$. Each log processor has associated with it a log disk. We assume some interconnection between the query processors and the log processors that allows any query processor to send a log fragment to any log processor. We also assume two-way communication between the back-end controller and each of the log processors.

There may be a dedicated connection between the query and log processors, or the query processors may write the log fragments to the cache and then the log processors may read the fragments from there. Later we will explore the effect of different interconnection strategies on the performance of the logging algorithm.

3.2 Data Structures

Recall that in our database machine architecture, the back-end controller is responsible for the movement of pages between the disk, the cache, and the query processors. To manage this movement, the back-end controller needs a page table. In addition to its normal contents, the page table contains status information for each page in the relation. The status information include, for example, a dirty bit to indicate that the page is to be written back to the disk. Our parallel logging algorithm requires that, for all updated pages, this status information be augmented with i) a bit, henceforth called the *log-flushed bit*, that indicates whether the corresponding log record has been written to stable storage.

and ii) an identifier, henceforth called the *log processor identifier,* that indicates to which log processor the corresponding log record was sent for writing to stable storage.

3.3 Collection of Recovery Data

To process a transaction, the back-end controller fetches the required data pages into the cache and assigns them to the query processors. We require that at the time of assigning a page, the back-end controller in addition communicates to the query processor the corresponding transaction number.

1. When a query processor updates a page, it creates a log fragment for this page in its local memory. In addition to before and after values for the updated records, the log fragment contains the transaction number and the page number of the updated page. When the page has been completely processed, the query processor selects a log processor and sends it the log fragment. The *log processor selection* algorithms is described below. The query processor then sends to the back-end controller the updated page and the identifier of the log processor to which the log fragment for this page has been sent. The back-end controller records the log processor identifier in its page-table entry for this page.

2. The log processor assembles log fragments received from different query processors in a log page. When a log page is filled up, the log processor writes it to the log disk and sends the page numbers of all the updated pages that caused this log page to be created to the back-end controller. The back-end controller in turn sets the log-flushed bit for each of these pages.

3. If the back-end controller is *forced* to flush an updated page when the cache is filled with updated pages, it first checks the log-flushed bit for the page to determine whether the log record for this page has been written to disk. If not, it sends a message to the corresponding log processor (using the log-processor id in the page table entry) to flush the log page. Only after the log processor acknowledges that the log page has been written to stable storage, will the data page be written to disk.

4. At the time of committing a transaction, the back-end controller first ensures that all the log records of the transaction have been written to stable storage by checking the log-flushed bit of the updated pages. It then sends the commit record, augmented with the *commit-number,* to any one of the log processors. This commit-number establishes the order in which the transactions have been serialized. The back-end controller can obtain the commit-number by simply appending the current time in its local clock to the current date. Another alternative would be to use a large sequential counter or append the counter to the current date. The locks held by the transaction are released only after the

back-end controller receives acknowledgement from the log processor that the commit record has been written to the log disk.

3.3.1 Log Processor Selection

Query processors use one of the following algorithms for selecting the log processor to send the current log fragment:

Cyclic selection: Each query processor cycles amongst all the log processors. That is, a query processor sends the first log fragment to the first log processor, the next fragment to the second log processor, and so on.

Random selection: Each query processor uses a random number generator (with different seeds) to generate the log processor number every time it has to send a log fragment.

Query Processor Number mod Total Log Processors selection: A query processor always sends its log fragment to the same log processor. The log processor is selected by taking the mod of its query-processor number with the total number of log processors.

Transaction Number mod Total Log Processors selection: A query processor determines the log processor number by taking the mod of the transaction number with the the total number of log processors.

Except for the fourth algorithm, log fragments of a transaction will in general be distributed over more than one log processor.

3.3.2 Comments

In our algorithm, a query processor sends a log fragment as soon as it has updated a page and the log processors are responsible for assembling log fragments into log pages. Another alternative would be that the query processors themselves assemble log fragments in their local memory and send only the full log page to the log processors. A simple analysis shows that this is not a good choice. Assume that there are 10 query processors and 1 log processor and updating a data page creates a log fragment that is 1/10 th of the size of the log page. If the second alternative were chosen then each query processor would have to update 10 data pages before sending the log page to the log processor. Thus, there may be 100 data pages in the cache waiting for the corresponding log pages to be flushed. With the first alternative, there would be 10 data pages in the cache waiting for the log page to be flushed.

From the performance point of view, it is desirable that the back-end controller not force the log processors to flush out the log page. Therefore, the page-replacement algorithm for the cache may have to be enhanced so that it it ejects an updated page with the log-flushed bit on before it replaces an updated page for which the log page has not yet been written to disk.

3.4 System Checkpoint

We require the back-end controller and each log processor to maintain a current checkpoint number in their memory. When a log processor writes a log page, it appends its checkpoint number to the log page. Subsequently, when the log processor communicates to the back-end controller the page numbers whose log records were written, it also communicates the checkpoint number. The back-end controller in turn records the checkpoint number in the page table entries of these pages. We assume that the messages are not lost and are delivered in the order they are sent.

The checkpointing is coordinated by the back-end controller. Assume that the current check point number is N. The back-end controller first records transaction numbers of all the active transactions in its memory. It then broadcasts a checkpoint initiation message to all the log processors. At the same time, it starts writing to disk those updated pages whose log records have been written with the checkpoint number N.

On receiving the checkpoint initiation message, a log processor ensures that any log disk I/O in progress is completed and the corresponding page numbers of the updated pages are communicated to the back-end controller. It then simply increments its current checkpoint number and sends an acknowledgement to the back-end controller. Incrementing the current checkpoint number signals checkpointing at that log processor. The log processor does not wait for the log page it is currently assembling to fill up or flush the partially filled log page before incrementing its checkpoint number.

After receiving acknowledgements from all the log processors, the back-end controller ensures that any updated page, whose checkpoint number in the page table is N, has been written to disk. It then sends a system checkpoint record to a predesignated log processor[1] and increments its checkpoint number. The system checkpoint record contains transaction numbers of the active transactions that the back-end controller had earlier recorded and the current checkpoint number of the back-end controller. System checkpointing completes when the system checkpoint record is written to the log disk by the log processor.

This algorithm for checkpointing does not require a complete system quiescing and the checkpointing can be performed in parallel with the normal data processing and logging activities.

1. The algorithm may easily be modified so that the back-end controller sends the system checkpoint record to any one or more than one log processors. In that case, the back-end controller will obtain from all the log processors their most recent system checkpoint records. The checkpoint record with the highest checkpoint number is the latest checkpoint record and the others may be discarded.

3.4.1 Establishing Checkpoint Locations

In our scheme, the system checkpoint record is written only on one log. In that log also, the location of the system checkpoint record need not correspond to the actual checkpoint location as the log processor may write log records while the back-end controller is flushing updated data pages for checkpointing. Thus, at the time of recovery from system crash, each log processor will have to establish the location of the checkpoint on its log.

To do so, the back-end controller obtains the most recent system checkpoint record and broadcasts it to all the log processors. Each log processor then finds its checkpoint location by scanning its log backwards from the end till it finds the first log page that has the same checkpoint number as the number in the system checkpoint record.

To avoid scanning the log backwards, a log processor may, before incrementing its checkpoint number, save a pointer to the current end of its log in a fixed place on its log disk. However, the log processor will still have to compare the checkpoint number of the log page preceding the saved address with the checkpoint number of the system checkpoint record. This is necessary as the system may fail after a log processor has written the checkpoint location to its log disk but before the back-end controller completes its checkpointing operations. If the checkpoint number of this log page is greater than the checkpoint number of the system checkpoint record, a backwards scan to the earlier checkpoint location will be required.

3.5 Recovery from System Crash

3.5.1 Winner-Loser Analysis

Each log processor makes its own list of winners and losers in parallel and sends it to the back-end controller. To do so, each log processor first establishes its checkpoint location as described in the previous section. It then initializes its loser list to all the active transactions whose numbers appear in the system checkpoint record, and then scans its log in the forward direction starting from the checkpoint location. When the log processor sees for the first time a log record for a transaction, it adds the transaction to the loser list if the transaction is not already in the list. If the commit record of a transaction is found, then the transaction is moved to the winner list from the loser list.

The back-end controller intersects the winner-loser lists received from different log processors and makes one final winner-loser list. Recall that for committing a transaction, the back-end controller sends the commit-record to only one log processor. Thus, a transaction which is a winner in any one of the lists sent by the log processors is the winner in the final list even if it is a loser in other lists.

3.5.2 Transaction Redo

The algorithm for the collection of recovery data physically splits the log in as many pieces as the number of log processors. One way of doing transaction redo would be to first merge these distributed log pieces to create one log in which the log records appear in the same order in which they would have appeared if only one log processor was used, and then perform the redo. This solution, besides being inefficient, would require that the timing information be associated with each log record, and that the clocks of the query processors be kept synchronized.

Instead, we propose that the back-end controller take one log at a time and carry out redo. While this approach is very attractive as it does not require distributed logs to be merged into one physical log, it suffers from the following problem:

The Problem: Suppose that an object X is updated from x0 to x1 by the transaction T1 and from x1 to x2 by the transaction T2, and T1 commits before T2. Furthermore, assume that the log record <x0,x1> is on the log L1 and the log record <x1,x2> is on the log L2. It has to be ensured that after redo processing, X = x2 and not x1 (which would happen if the redo processing using log L1 is done after the redo processing using log L2).

The Solution: Define a data structure <X,t(X)> where t(X) is the commit-number associated with the commit record of the transaction that updated the object X[2]. Observe that the commit-number information for the committed transactions can be collected at the same time as the winner-loser analysis. Furthermore, each log record has associated with it the transaction number and the page number that caused this log record to be created. Thus, a log record contains all the information necessary to create and access this data structure.

Transaction redo is performed using the following algorithm:

Initialize:

for all X do t(X):= 0

2. Standard techniques like hashing [16] may be used for efficient access to this data structure.

Redo Algorithm:

```
for all logs do {
    scan the log forward
    for each log record x_i with the corresponding commit-number t_i do
        if t_i < t(X) then ignore this log record
            else redo and t(X) := t_i }.
```

In the above example, assume that the commit-number of T1 is 1 and that of T2 is 2. Thus, if log L2 is processed first, then t(X) := 2 after processing the log record <x1,x2> and X = x2. Now when the log L1 is processed, the log record <x0,x1> will be ignored because the corresponding commit-number, that is 1, is less than the current value of t(X) = 2.

3.5.3 Transaction Undo

For transaction undo, the back-end controller scans one log at a time backwards. At first, it seems that the transaction undo will have a problem similar to redo.

A Hypothetical Scenario: As before, assume that an object X is updated from x0 to x1 by the transaction T1 creating the log record on log L1. Then, X is updated to x2 by the transaction T2 creating the log record on log L2. Both T1 and T2 are found to be losers in the winner-loser analysis. It must be ensured that after undo X is restored to x0 and not x1 which would happen if undo processing using the log L1 is done before undo processing using the log L2.

The Solution: This situation cannot arise with the proper locking protocol that a transaction hold its locks till commit point[3]. If T2 has updated X after T1 has updated it, then T1 must have released its lock on X. But a transaction does not release its locks before its commit record has been written to the log and T1 is a loser.

Therefore, the transaction undo can be performed simply by taking one log at a time, scanning it backwards, and restoring before values of the uncommitted updates.

---

3. As pointed out in [10], holding locks till commit point is not necessary but generally done in order to avoid cascaded undos.

3.6 Recovery from a Transaction Abort

The back-end controller determines the log processors where the log records corresponding to the pages updated by the aborted transaction exist by examining the page table entries of these pages. An updated page that has not yet been written to disk is ignored in this analysis as this page may be undone by simply discarding its updated version from the disk cache. The back-end controller then obtains the log records for the transaction from each log processor and performs the undo. The order in which the back-end controller communicates with the different log processors is immaterial as the log record for a page updated by a transaction exists only on one log. In the next section, we will describe how the algorithm for transaction undo is modified if a page may be updated more than once by a transaction, and hence different log records for the same page may exist on more than one log.

3.7 An Embellishment

A transaction frequently consists of more than one database operations. For example, in System R, a transaction consists of one or more SQL statements bracketed with Begin_Transaction and Commit_Transaction commands [11]. We will call each of these operations a transaction-step. We assume that all the steps have been numbered in the increasing order. Suppose now that a transaction updates the object X from x0 to x1 in step 1 and to x2 in step 2. It is required that at the time of transaction redo, x2 is restored and not x1. Similarly, transaction undo should restore x0 and not x1.

To handle this situation, we require that the back-end controller, at the time of assigning a data page to a query processor, in addition to the transaction number, communicates the step number also to the query processor. The query processor appends the step number along with the transaction number to the log fragment before sending it to the log processor.

For *redo processing*, the only modification required is that in the data structure <X,t(X)>, t(X) is now defined to be the commit-number appended with the step number of the corresponding transaction. In the above example, assume that during transaction redo, X is first restored to x2 and t(X) := (1,2) where 1 is the commit-number of the transaction and 2 is the step number. Subsequently, the log record created by step 1 of the transaction will be ignored as the step number appended to the transaction number for this log record, that is (1,1), is less than the current value of t(X).

Undo processing requires building a similar data structure and using an algorithm similar to that of the transaction redo. The only difference required in the algorithm is that the decision rule about when to ignore a log record is changed. For undo, the log is scanned backwards, and if the commit-number appended with the step number of the transaction that created the current log record of X is *greater than* the current value of t(X), then this log record is ignored; otherwise, the undo is performed and t(X) is updated. Thus, in the above example, if X is first undone to x0 and t(X) := (1,1), then subsequently the log record created by step 2 will be ignored as the transaction number appended with the step number for this log record, that is (1,2), is greater than the current value of t(X).

4. Performance

We performed a number of simulation experiments to determine the characteristics of our parallel logging algorithm and its impact on database machine performance. The questions that we attempted to answer from these experiments include:

- Effect of logging on the throughput of the database machine?
- When to have more than one log processor?
- Performance of various log processor selection algorithms?
- Effect of the communication medium between the query processors and log processors?
- Effect of routing the log fragments through the disk cache?
- Effect of the percentage of pages updated by a transaction?

The database machine was assumed to have 25 query processors, 100 cache frames, and 2 data disks. The query processors were modeled after VAX 11/750, and the data disks were modeled after IBM 3350 disks [15]. We also modeled parallel-access data disks as proposed by the SURE [17] and DBC [4] projects. On a parallel-access disk, all pages on the different tracks of the same cylinder may be read and written in parallel in one disk access.

A transaction was modeled by the number of pages it accesses which was assumed to be a uniform random variable in the range 1 to 250. Both random and sequential reference strings for the transaction were modeled. The write set of a transaction was assumed to be the random subset of its read set and was taken to be 20% of the pages read by the transaction. The average size of the log fragment created due to the update of a data page was assumed to be 1/10 th of the size of the data page.

Experiments were performed in the following configurations:

Conventional-Random: conventional disks and random transactions,
Parallel-Random: parallel-access disks and random transactions,
Conventional-Sequential: conventional disks and sequential transactions.
Parallel-Sequential: parallel-access disks and sequential transactions.

The details of the simulator can be found in [2]. In the following sections, we will summarize the important results from these experiments.

4.1 Effect on Database machine Performance

We used two metrics to study the impact of our parallel logging algorithm on database machine performance: i) average *execution time per page* and ii) average *transaction completion time*. The execution time per page is defined to be the time taken by the database machine to execute a given transaction load divided by the total number of data pages processed by the machine, and is a measure of the throughput of the machine. The transaction completion time is defined to be the time from the allocation of the first cache frame to a transaction to the writing of the last page updated by the transaction to disk. Table 1 summarizes the impact of logging (unit of time throughout this paper is milliseconds) assuming only one log processor.

Configuration	Execution Time per Page (ms.)		Transaction Completion Time (ms.)	
	Without Log	With Log	Without Log	With Log
Conventional-Random	18.00	17.86	7398.41	7543.20
Parallel-Random	16.62	16.50	6476.04	6649.90
Conventional-Sequential	11.01	11.39	4016.46	4333.46
Parallel-Sequential	1.92	2.05	758.06	862.24

Table 1. Impact of Logging

Although logging causes the average transaction completion time to increase, the throughput of the database machine in terms of the time taken by the machine to execute a given transaction load is not significantly degraded. With our recovery architecture, assembly of log fragments into log pages and writing them to the log disk is completely *overlapped* with the processing of data pages, and therefore, does not affect the throughput of the database machine. The effect of logging manifests itself in two ways:

i) Some updated pages are blocked in the cache for the corresponding log records to be written causing the transaction completion times to increase. The throughput is, however, not affected as the blocking of updated pages in the disk cache does not cause the disks or the processors to become idle. The blocked pages may hinder anticipatory reading of other data pages as they keep the corresponding cache frames occupied. This will happen only if cache frames are scarce and the blocked pages are large in number. In our experiments, more cache frames were available for anticipatory paging than the disks could feed, and on average, there were less than 5 pages in the cache waiting for their log records to be written to the log disk.

ii) Extra query processor time is required to create log fragments. We found in an earlier simulation of the bare (without provision for recovery) database machine [3] that, except for the parallel-sequential configuration, the query processors were very poorly utilized. Extra processing required to construct the log fragments did not increase processors' utilization significantly.

Thus, the logging did not significantly affect the throughput as the extra work required for logging could be done either in parallel with the processing of data pages or it used up the slack capacity of the database machine.

4.2 Number of Log Processors and Log Processor Selection

The most striking result from these experiments is the poor utilization of even one log disk as shown in Table 2. The rate at which the query processors update pages and hence create log fragments is just not fast enough to keep the log disk busy. We showed in [3] that the I/O bandwidth between the data disks and the disk cache severely limits the rate at which the query processors update data pages.

Configuration	Log Disk Utilization
Conventional-Random	0.02
Parallel-Random	0.02
Conventional-Sequential	0.02
Parallel-Sequential	0.13

Table 2. Log Characteristics (one log processor)

We present a simple analysis to characterize when is it worthwhile to have more than one log disk. Assume that the database machine processes a total of N pages, where $N = \Sigma |T_i|$ and $|T_i|$ is the size of the transaction T_i. The average execution time per page for the bare (without logging) database machine is E and a transaction updates u% of the data pages it accesses. The average size of a log fragment is f% of the size of a data page, and the average time to write a log page to the log disk is t. Finally, assume that the log pages may be written to the log disk in parallel with the processing of data pages by the database machine, and the execution time per page is not affected by logging. Thus, with only one log disk,

Total database machine time to process N pages = N * E
Number of log fragments = u% * N
Number of log pages = f% * (u% * N)
Time required to write the log pages to the log disk = (f% * u% * N) * t

Therefore,

$$Log\ disk\ utilization = \frac{f\,\%\ *\ u\,\%\ *\ t}{E}$$

In our experiments, f% = 10%, u% = 20%, and t = 12.61 ms. It may be verified, by substituting different values of E from Table 1, that the above equation quite accurately estimates the numbers in Table 2 for the log disk utilization. Thus, as long as the execution time of the database machine is limited by the I/O bandwidth, more than one log processor will be necessary only if the database machine has a very high degree of update activity (updates all the pages accessed, for example) or the size of the log fragments is large (physical logging instead of logical logging). However, a higher number of updated pages will require additional I/Os to write the updated pages and this may increase the value of the execution time per page. Later we will present the results of our experiments to determine whether the log disk may become a bottleneck for high values of u% while maintaining a constant value of f%.

In order to test the usefulness of parallel logging and to compare different log processor selection algorithms, we designed another experiment. From our simulation of the bare database machine [3], we had found that the utilization of the query processors was quite high when the parallel-access disks were used to process sequential transactions. We, therefore, simulated the data base machine with 75 query processors and 150 cache frames in the parallel-sequential configuration. We still assumed that there were 2 data disks and that each transaction updated 20% of pages it accessed. However, instead of logical logging, the physical logging was modeled. In physical logging, for each updated page, two log pages are written; one contains the before image and the other contains the after image of the updated page. The log disk was still assumed to be a conventional disk. The results of the experiment are summarized in Tables 3.

The average execution time per page and the average transaction completion time degrade considerably with physical logging, and using more than one log disk significantly improves the performance. The main reason for the degradation, when one log disk is used, is that the log disk becomes the bottleneck. Consequently, the log pages wait for a long time in the log-disk queue before they are written. This in turn increases the number of updated pages waiting in the cache for the corresponding log pages to be written. In our experiment with one log disk, out of 150 cache frames, on the average 129 frames were occupied by the updated pages waiting for their log records to be written, and thus only 21 frames were available for reading new data pages from data disks.

No. of Log Disks	Execution Time per Page (ms.)				Transaction Completion Time (ms.)			
	cyclic	random	QpNo mod TotLp	TranNo mod TotLp	cyclic	random	QpNo mod TotLp	TranNo mod TotLp
1	5.06	5.06	5.06	5.06	4518.07	4518.07	4518.07	4518.07
2	2.53	2.55	2.56	2.69	1999.51	2104.28	2231.98	2165.45
3	1.74	1.80	1.80	2.11	1078.94	1137.18	1135.72	1381.76
4	1.47	1.51	1.49	1.97	830.71	854.61	837.75	1137.50
5	1.33	1.35	1.32	1.96	716.28	741.73	714.12	1128.37
w/o logging	0.91	0.91	0.91	0.91	430.56	430.56	430.56	430.56

Table 3. Performance of Parallel Logging and Log Processor Selection Algorithms

Availability of fewer cache frames severely affects the performance of the parallel-access disks. As compared to the no logging case, when 5849 data disk accesses were made, a total of 25993 data disk accesses are required with logging. Furthermore, with logical logging, when a log page is written, all the corresponding updated data pages are moved to the data disk queue at the same time and if they belong to the same cylinder, they may be written to disk in one I/O. With physical logging, only one updated data page at a time is transferred to the data disk queue.

Amongst the log processor selection algorithms, performances of the cyclic, random, and query processor number mod total log processors selection are comparable, whereas the transaction number mod total log processors selection turns out to be a loser. A log processor selection algorithm should avoid congestion at some log processor while the other log processors are idle. Table 4 shows the standard deviation in the mean queue length, queue time, utilization and total I/Os at five log disks for each algorithm.

For the transaction number mod total log processors selection, the deviation in the average values at five log disks for all the four parameters is largest indicating that the log pages were not evenly distributed by this algorithm. For each algorithm, we have also tabulated the averages of the standard deviations in the queue lengths and the queue times at five log disks. The deviations in the queue length and the queue time at a log disk are largest for the transaction number mod total log processors selection indicating that this algorithm not only unevenly distributed the log pages but also the pattern of arrival of log pages at a log disk was irregular. There were too many log pages sometimes

Log Processor Selection Algorithm	Standard Deviation of the Averages				Average of the Standard Deviations	
	Q length	Q time	Utili-zation	Total I/Os	Q length	Q time
Cyclic	0.09	1.52	0.0	2.45	4.56	60.70
Random	0.40	6.07	0.01	29.67	5.07	67.99
QpNo mod TotLp	0.16	2.45	0.005	15.34	4.77	63.29
TranNo mod TotLp	1.71	27.22	0.03	141.00	16.21	220.13

Table 4. Variances in the Log Processors' Characteristics (5 log processors)

and too few the other times. The uneven usage of the log disks results in the higher values for the average number of updated pages in the cache waiting for the log records to be written.

4.3 Connection Between the Query and the Log Processors

To explore the effect of the medium connecting the log processors, we performed two sets of experiments. First we assumed a separate interconnection network between the query processors and the log processors, distinct from the interconnection network between the query processors and the cache, devoted to the task of transmitting log fragments. Experiments were performed for three different values of the effective bandwidth of the interconnection: 1.0, 0.1 and 0.01 megabytes/second. In the second set of experiments, no separate interconnection was assumed and the log fragments were routed through the disk cache.

The performance of the database machine was found to be quite insensitive to the bandwidth between the query and log processors. Recall that in our logging scheme, a log processor assembles the log fragments received from different query processors into a log page, and when a log page is filled up, it is written to the log disk. Thus, normally a log fragment has to wait in the log processor buffer before being written to the log disk. The reduced bandwidth of the interconnection increases the transmission time resulting in an increase in the average fragment waiting time which in turn causes the average the number of updated pages waiting for their log records to be written to increase. The fragment waiting time increases only marginally with a slower medium if there is a time gap between arrivals of fragments at the log processor. As shown in Figure 1, the delay in the arrival of a log fragment is absorbed in the interarrival gap.

(U: Update time T: transmission time)

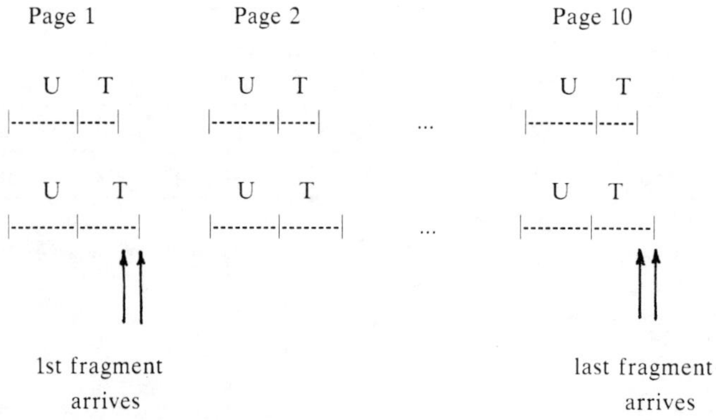

Figure 1. Effect of Slower Communication Medium on Fragment Wait Time

The performance of the database machine was not affected even when the log fragments were routed through the disk cache. Routing the fragments through the cache causes the usage of the query processors to increase and some cache frames get tied up to hold the in-transit fragments. However, the query processors or the number of cache frames are not the constraining factors for the performance of the database machine.

4.4 Percentage of Pages Updated

To see the behavior of our logging algorithm in presence of larger update activity, we increased the number of pages updated by a transaction from 20% to 50% and 80% of the pages read. The results of this set of experiments are summarized in table 5. Both the execution time and the transaction completion time increase with the conventional disks and the parallel-random configuration, but this increase was due to the increase in the number of disk accesses with the increased update activity. One log disk still remained poorly utilized (see Table 6).

Configuration	Execution Time per Page (ms.)			Transaction Completion Time (ms.)		
	20%	50%	80%	20%	50%	80%
Conventional-Random	17.86	23.22	28.59	7543.20	9716.01	11916.27
Parallel-Random	16.50	21.48	26.24	6649.90	8486.24	10203.90
Conventional-Sequential	11.39	14.47	17.98	4333.46	5325.37	6544.54
Parallel-Sequential	2.05	2.16	2.27	862.24	828.89	836.84

Table 5. Effect of Percentage of Pages Updated by a Transaction

Configuration	Total I/Os (Data Disks)			Utilization (log Disk)		
	20%	50%	80%	20%	50%	80%
Conventional-Random	59170	76840	94650	0.02	0.03	0.04
Parallel-Random	55217	71800	87874	0.02	0.03	0.04
Conventional-Sequential	59170	76840	94650	0.02	0.05	0.06
Parallel-Sequential	13761	13594	13522	0.13	0.31	0.47

Table 6. Data and Log Disk Characteristics for Higher Percentage of Updates

One surprising observation was that in the parallel-sequential configuration the number of disk accesses decreased with an increase in the percentage of updated pages, causing the average execution time and the transaction completion time to not increase appreciably. In our parallel-access disk, there are 120 pages per cylinder that can be read in one disk access. The reference string of a sequential transaction consists of physically adjacent pages on a disk. Thus, if a transaction references 100 pages, potentially all the pages can be read in one disk access. However, in one access, only as many pages as the number of free frames can be read. An I/O begins as soon as the disk becomes free, if there is a page to be accessed and a free cache frame. The number of accesses required to read all the pages of a transaction, therefore, depends crucially on how many cache frames become available at a time. When a log page is written, all the data pages waiting for the log fragments in this log page to be written become available for writing. When the update percentage is high, these pages are likely to belong to the same transaction and hence to the same cylinder and may be written in one disk access. Thus, a higher percentage of updated pages may not result in an increase in the number of disk accesses, but may cause several cache frames to become free at the same time. On the other hand, if the percentage of updated pages is low, the cache frames holding the pages that are read but not updated become free one at a time at random times. This observation suggests that 'service as soon as can' is not an appropriate strategy for the parallel-access disks and the scheduling strategies for such disks is an open area for research.

5. Conclusions

We presented a recovery architecture based on parallel logging for the multiprocessor database machines and showed how the recovery actions may be completely overlapped with the processing of data pages so that the performance of the database machine is not degraded due to recovery overhead. We also showed that the communication medium between the query processors and the log processor did not have a significant effect on the performance of logging. In particular, the performance of the logging was not degraded when the log pages were routed through the disk cache, and hence, an interconnection between the query processors and log processors devoted to communicating the log fragments is not necessary. Therefore, the parallel logging can be implemented with no modification in the hardware architecture by simply designating one or more query processors as the log processors and supplementing them with the log disks. It was also shown that the rate of processing of data pages is not fast enough to warrant more than one log disk. However, if the data processing rate is improved in the future by solving the problem of I/O bandwidth available from the mass-storage devices, then our parallel logging algorithm can be gainfully used with more than one log disk.

The parallel logging algorithm that we presented in this paper allows logging for a transaction to be performed asynchronously at more than one log disks, and yet does not require physical merging of distributed logs to recover from failures. We have also shown how to take system checkpoints in parallel with the normal data processing and logging activities. Although designed in the context of database machines, this algorithm may easily be adapted for use in any high performance database management system. For example, the main-frame computers with the main memory in the order of gigabytes are on the horizon. It will be possible to store the entire database in the main memory of such computers [12]. Our parallel logging algorithm can be gainfully used to log updates in parallel in such a high performance environment.

6. Acknowledgements

The work described here was done while the author was at the University of Wisconsin, Madison. David DeWitt, as always, provided comments, suggestions, and support. This research was partially supported by the National Science Foundation under grant MCS82-01870.

References

1. R. Agrawal and D. J. DeWitt, Integrated Concurrency Control and Recovery Mechanisms: Design and Performance Evaluation, Computer Sciences Tech. Rep. #497, Univ. Wisconsin, Madison, March 1983.

2. R. Agrawal, Concurrency Control and Recovery in Multiprocessor Database Machines: Design and Performance Evaluation, Computer Sciences Tech. Rep. #510, Univ. Wisconsin, Madison, Sept. 1983. Ph.D. Dissertation.

3. R. Agrawal and D. J. DeWitt, Whither Hundreds of Processors in a Database Machine, *Proc. Int'l Workshop on High-Level Computer Architecture 84*, May 1984, 6.21-6.32.

4. J. Banerjee, R. I. Baum and D. K. Hsiao, Concepts and Capabilities of a Database Computer, *ACM Trans. Database Syst. 3*, 4 (Dec. 1978), 347-384.

5. D. Bitton, H. Boral, D. J. DeWitt and W. K. Wilkinson, Parallel Algorithms for the Execution of Relational Database Operations, *ACM Trans. Database Syst. 8*, 3 (Sept. 1983), 324-353.

6. A. F. Cardenas, F. Alavian and A. Avizienis, Performance of Recovery Architectures in Parallel Associative Database Processors, *ACM Trans. Database Syst. 8*, 3 (Sept. 1983), 291-323.

7. D. J. DeWitt, DIRECT - A Multiprocessor Organization for Supporting Relational Database Management Systems, *IEEE Trans. Computers C-28*, 6 (June 1979), 395-406.

8. D. J. DeWitt and P. Hawthorn, A Performance Evaluation of Database Machine Architectures, *Proc. 7th Int'l Conf. on Very Large Data Bases*, Sept. 1981.

9. J. N. Gray, Notes on Database Operating Systems, in *Lecture Notes in Computer Science 60, Advanced Course on Operating Systems*, R. Bayer, R.M. Graham and G. Seegmuller (ed.), Springer Verlag, New York, 1978.

10. J. N. Gray, A Transaction Model, in *Lecture Notes in Computer Science 85, Automata, Languages and Programming*, J.W. deBakker and J. van Leeuwen (ed.), Springer Verlag, New York, 1980, 282-298.

11. J. N. Gray, P. R. McJones, B. G. Lindsay, M. W. Blasgen, R. A. Lorie, T. G. Price, F. Putzolu and I. L. Traiger, The Recovery Manager of the System R Database Manager, *ACM Computing Surveys 13*, 2 (June 1981), 223-242.

12. J. N. Gray, Practical Problems in Data Management, Invited Talk at ACM-SIGMOD 1983 Int'l Conf. on Management of Data, San Jose, California, May 1983.

13. P. Hawthorn and D. J. DeWitt, Performance Analysis of Alternative Database Machine Architectures, *IEEE Trans. Software Eng. SE-8*, 1 (Jan. 1982), 61-75.

14. W. Hell, RDBM - A Relational Database Machine: Architecture and Hardware Design, *Proc. 6th Workshop on Computer Architecture for Non-Numeric Processing*, June 1981.

15. IBM, Reference Manual for IBM 3350 Direct Access Storage, GA26-1638-2, File No. S370-07, IBM General Products Division, San Jose, California, April 1977.

16. D. E. Knuth, The Art of Computer Programming: Fundamental Algorithms, Vol. 1, 2nd edition, Addison-Wesley, Reading, Mass., 1973.

17. H. O. Leilich, G. Stiege and H. C. Zeidler, A Search Processor for Data Base Management Systems, *Proc. 4th Int'l Conf. on Very Large Data Bases*, Sept. 1978, 280-287.

18. S. E. Madnick, The INFOPLEX Database Computer: Concepts and Directions, *Proc. IEEE Computer Conf.*, Feb. 1979.

19. M. Missikoff, An Overview of the Project DBMAC for a relational machine, *Proc. 6th Workshop on Computer Architecture for Non-Numeric Processing*, June 1981.

20. S. A. Schuster, H. B. Nguyen, E. A. Ozkarahan and K. C. Smith, RAP.2 - An Associative Processor for Data Bases and its Applications, *IEEE Trans. Computers C-28*, 6 (June 1979).

21. S. W. Song, A Survey and Taxonomy of Database Machines, *IEEE Database Engineering Bulletin 4*, 2 (Dec. 1981), 3-13.

A COMPREHENSIVE ANALYSIS OF CONCURRENCY CONTROL PERFORMANCE FOR CENTRALIZED DATABASES

Werner Kiessling‡, Harald Pfeiffer

Institut für Informatik
Technische Universität München
West-Germany

Abstract

The behavior of concurrency control methods for centralized databases is investigated and evaluated on the basis of discrete-event simulation. The gained results give new insights concerning the quantitative overhead introduced by such synchronization methods. The establishment of a uniform cost measurement model enables a qualitative assessment and comparison of several competing methods, the (r, x) - , (r, a, x) - , (r, a, c) - lockprotocol and the optimistic method. In particular, valuable results concerning the effective parallelism, the tradeoff between early and late serialization, real time overhead for cycle searching and lengths of cycles are presented. The simulation series are driven by synthetic transaction workloads and also by a real reference string. Finally, the impact of these results on the selection of a suitable concurrency control method for practical applications is discussed.

Contents

---

‡Currently on leave at the University of California, Berkeley, CA 94720, sponsored by Deutscher Akademischer Austauschdienst, Wissenschaftsausschuss der NATO.

1. Introduction

The concept of a *transaction* (TA) has turned out to be the key feature for the interaction with and implementation of a modern database (DB) system. In order to improve the performance of a shared DB-system, concurrent TA-processing is mandatory (see, e.g., [2]). To process TAs of several users concurrently and consistently in a shared DB, various *concurrency control* (CC) schemes have been developed recently. These schemes hopefully increase the performance by providing a high degree of concurrency among executing TAs. However, raising the degree of concurrency also increases the probability of conflicts among TAs. Therefore it is essential to constitute the tradeoff between potential efficiency gains by higher parallelism and the involved synchronization overhead when selecting a particular CC scheme. Recently there has been a lot of research activity related to this problem, both from an analytical approach and by simulation, see, e.g., [4], [6], [9], [10], [11], [12], [14]. A comprehensive survey, covering some 30 references, can be found in [15]. The work we present in this paper is a continuation of that in [6] and summarizes results reported in more detail in [7]. By defining a suitable measurement model and conducting systematic runs, enabled by driving the simulation with a synthetic TA-workload, we will come closer to the goal of assessing and comparing the quality of CC schemes. We will also present an experiment where the simulation is driven by a reference string. Overall, answers to some interesting open problems will be given, e.g. the tradeoff between early and late serialization (addressed in [2]), or real-time overhead for cycle searching, cycle lengths, and the exhibition of an unexpected behavior of the optimistic method. Some of these results run counter to prevailing beliefs. In each case, it is shown how our results scale up to high-performance DB-systems likely to be available in the near future.

2. Description of Analyzed Concurrency Control Methods

2.1. Lockprotocols under Investigation

In this paper we analyze three well-known lockprotocols for centralized DBs, namely the (r, x) - , (r, a, x) - and (r, a, c) - protocol. All protocols support strict two-phase TAs. The names for these protocols are coined according to the employed lock modes. Their basic properties are characterized by the compatibility matrices shown in fig 1.[1] The (r, a, x) - and the (r, a, c) - protocol both aim to decrease inhibitions between read and write accesses. For (r, a, x), the new value of an object is prepared on a copy, leaving the valid value undestroyed and available for read access. The same holds for (r, a, c) , but here the newly prepared value is committed without immediately replacing the currently valid value. Thus a c-locked object has two valid values. This property can be utilized to allow consistent reads without delay by concurrent updates.

[1] For a more detailed description see, e.g., [6].

	r	x
r	+	-
x	-	-

	r	a	x
r	+	+	-
a	+	-	-
x	-	-	-

	r	a	c
r	+	+	+
a	+	-	-
c	+	-	-

+: compatible

-: incompatible

Fig. 1: Compatibilities for (r, x) - , (r, a, x) - and (r, a, c) - protocol.

Locks, which are allowed to coexist on the same objects, are called *compatible*, otherwise they are incompatible. If a lock request of a TA T is granted, then T remains *active* and can proceed in its execution, otherwise T is *blocked* or *backed up*. For (r, a, x) and (r, a, c) another operation must be requested by an updating TA, namely the *conversion* of a-locks into x-locks and a-locks into c-locks, respectively. For the (r, a, x) - protocol the conversion of all a-locks held by a TA T is requested at EOT (end of transaction) of T in a single conversion request. When this request is granted, then T can commit and release all its locks. While T is waiting in its conversion phase, T is neither active nor blocked, because it already has processed all its actions. This TA-state is referred to as *inactive*. Note that (r, x) does not produce such inactive phases. In turn, (r, a, c) likewise induces inactive phases due to a - to - c conversions. This is because after a successful conversion the respective c-locks cannot be released immediately, but only after they are no longer needed for a consistent scheduling of read-requests (c-locked objects possess two valid versions). Currently we do not support r - to - a conversions.

An internal module of the DB-system which implements a given lockprotocol is called a lock module (LM). In order to correctly fulfill its task of enforcing consistency of concurrent TAs, the LM has to decide lock requests according to the defined compatibilities. In addition, the LM must keep track of so-called *serialization conditions* SCs ([3]) among concurrent TAs.[2] These SCs are required to recognize and ensure that the desired equivalent serial schedule exists. Depending on the employed lockprotocol, different dependences among TAs are represented by SCs. Whenever read- or update-requests coincide with an already existing updater on the same object, new SCs come into existence. These arising SCs now could show up a deadlock or a violation of consistency. If due to a lock request a new SC between two TAs T_1 and T_2 is created, then this fact is denoted as *collision*[3] of T_1 and T_2. A *conflict* arises if, at a collision of T_1 with T_2, the newly introduced SC is in contradiction to already existing SCs. Note that by the compatibilities of a particular lockprotocol it is not specified *how* SCs are maintained and *when* they are checked for conflicts. (Of course this must be done before a TA's commit point.)

[2]Other customary terms for SC are follow-relationship or comes-after-relationship.

[3]What we term a collision is often called a conflict in the literature.

Maintenance of serialization conditions:

A set of SCs is conflict-free, if their transitive closure forms a partial order among concurrent TAs. The known methods for maintaining this property differ in the chosen (partial) ordering relation. We are interested in the following two:

(1) *Graph maintenance and cycle searching*:

This is the most widely used method. An SC between T_1 and T_2 is reflected by a directed arc between T_1 and T_2 in the graph. For conflict detection standard algorithms for cycle searching in graphs can be applied. The advantage of this method is that the graph reflects the required partial order in an exact way. However, its drawback obviously is the expenditure for cycle searching.

(2) *Dynamic time intervals*:

The assignment of dynamic time intervals (TIs) is an improvement of the basic static timestamp method, presented in [13]. As a comprehensive description can be found in [3], we will present only a survey here. For the TI-method the serialization order among TAs is defined as follows:

Let **R** denote the real numbers, $\mathbf{R}^*$ be $\mathbf{R} \cup \{-\infty, +\infty\}$, **I** be the set of right-open intervals [lb, ub) in $\mathbf{R}^*$ where lb, ub $\in \mathbf{R}^*$ with lb $<$ ub. Then the partial order $<_I$ on **I** is defined as:

$$[\mathrm{lb}_1, \mathrm{ub}_1) <_I [\mathrm{lb}_2, \mathrm{ub}_2) \text{ if and only if } \mathrm{ub}_1 \leqslant \mathrm{lb}_2.$$

Thus, for two time intervals $\mathrm{TI}_1, \mathrm{TI}_2 \in \mathbf{I}$ it holds:

TI_1 and TI_2 are disjoint if and only if $\mathrm{TI}_1 <_I \mathrm{TI}_2$ or $\mathrm{TI}_2 <_I \mathrm{TI}_1$.

Each TA T starts its execution with a TI = $[-\infty, +\infty)$. While T does not collide with another TA, this TI remains unchanged. To keep the right partial order between two colliding TAs their TIs are "properly" truncated, if they are not yet disjoint. Conflicts are indicated by TIs in wrong order. The advantage of this TI-method over the graph method is its simplicity and extremely low overhead cost. Its improvement over the static timestamps lies in the fact that it does not stamp a predefined total order on all concurrent TAs. Instead only an order is maintained among those TAs that have encountered at least one collision. Therefore the conflict rate is in between those for the graph and the static timestamps. Compared to the graph, this means that there might be situations where a TA is not backed up using the graph, but is backed up using TIs ("phantom" conflict).

When to check consistency:

As mentioned already, SCs can express a deadlock or an inconsistent schedule. As a deadlock is threatening only if a lock request is denied, for these collision cases we immediately create the respective SC and check for a conflict. With this strategy for the (r, x) - protocol serializability is already guaranteed by the two-phase property, such that the subsequent considerations only apply for (r, a, x) and (r, a, c), where an object can be read and updated in parallel by different TAs. In these cases the updating TA has to follow the reading TA in a serialization. In principle, the latest possible moment for materializing and checking such SCs is at the commit request of the updating TA. On the other hand, such SCs can be created at the earliest possible moment when an r- or a-lock request collides.

(1) *Late serialization at EOT*:
The disadvantage of this strategy is that an updating TA T may continue to execute although an inconsistency already exists. Consequently, at the commit request of T, T might have to be backed up in many cases (see [6]). This method offers the full degree of parallelism as it is enabled by the compatibilities at the expense of an increased conflict probability. The only justification behind this strategy (besides that readers never have to be backed up) is that consistency checks are fairly expensive and should only be performed when absolutely necessary. As a matter of fact, this assumption hold only if a graph is used for SC-maintenance.

(2) *Early serialization*:
This alternative strategy avoids useless work of executing TAs which do not fit into a serialization. In such cases (i.e., if it can be foreseen that granting an r-lock would produce a deadlock or inconsistency when an existing a-lock is attempted to be converted later on) it forces r-lock requests to wait until an existing a-lock has disappeared, thus occasionally violating the compatibilities as defined in fig. 1. The principal advantages offered by early serialization might be offset by a too high overhead for conflict testing. However, in combination with a cheap method like the TIs it looks promising.

In summary, the *tradeoffs* to be figured out between early serialization with TIs and the late serialization with a graph are the following:
(i) Early serialization reduces the potential parallelism, but reduces the risk of lost work. For late serialization the opposite holds.
(ii) Conflict recognition with TIs will involve more backups than with graphs and cycle searching. However TIs produce much less overhead than cycle searching.

In this paper, the following lock module variants are investigated:
RX + CS : For (r, x)-protocol, using graph with cycle searching.
RAX + CS : For (r, a, x)-protocol, using graph with cycle searching and late serialization.
RAC1 + CS : For (r, a, c)-protocol, using graph with cycle searching and late serialization.
RAC2 + TI : For (r, a, c)-protocol, using TIs and early serialization.

(Analogously, for (r, a, x) a lock module RAX2 + TI with early serialization can be built. But this variant is not yet implemented.)
RX + CS, RAX + CS and RAC1 + CS were analyzed in [11], using several reference strings, whereas RAC2 + TI has not been explored by now.
Finally, it has to be mentioned that the strategy for selecting a backup victim in the event of a conflict is chosen identically for all lock modules: Backup and restart that TA whose

lock request caused a conflict of SCs.

2.2. The Optimistic Method

An alternative approach to guarantee serializability of concurrent TAs was first described in [8]. This method does not rely on locking in order to fit the TAs in a proper serialization order and it was termed "optimistic" method by its inventors. Anticipating the results to be presented later, we prefer to call this method the *nonblocking* scheme, but we will continue to refer to it as OCC (optimistic concurrency control). With OCC the existence of an equivalent serial schedule is checked in a TA's *validation* phase at EOT. We have implemented the serial validation variant. Thereby the readset of a validating TA T is intersected with the writesets of certain previously committed TAs. Only the writesets of those TAs must be taken into consideration, which committed after the start time of T. The outcome of a validation request - commit or backup - depends not only on the composition of these writesets, but also on the number of writesets to be intersected. The set of all these writesets is called *writeset queue*; it can be shortened if the oldest TA in the system validates.

3. The Simulation System COCONAT

3.1. The Simulation Model

The employed simulation model is based on that one presented in [6]. It consists of four main components, as depicted in fig. 2.

Our program package which implements this simulation model is named COCONAT (*CO*ncurrency *CON*trol *A*ssessment *T*ool).

The simulation is driven by the *transaction generator* TG, which alternatively can feed synthetic TAs, generated by TG_{syn}, or TAs, extracted by TG_{ref} from a real reference string, into the waiting queue WQ. The *transaction manager* TM supervises the execution of parallel TAs. At most P_{max} TAs can be served in parallel by the TM; P_{max} is an adjustable parameter. Active TAs within the TM are served in a cyclic manner, one action at a time. To enable the execution of an action, the TM cooperates with the *concurrency control module* CCM as it is dictated by the particular CC method selected. While TG_{syn} together with TM simulate an abstract DB-system, all functions of the CCM are fully implemented, i.e., the lock modules RX + CS, RAX + CS, RAC1 + CS, RAC2 + TI and the module OCC are fully coded. The measured results of an entire simulation series are gathered for global evaluation within the statistics collection component. The adjustable workload parameters for the TG_{syn} are listed below (see [6] for a more detailed description).

A TA T_i is modeled by a sequence of pairs of the form (Object, Action) as follows:

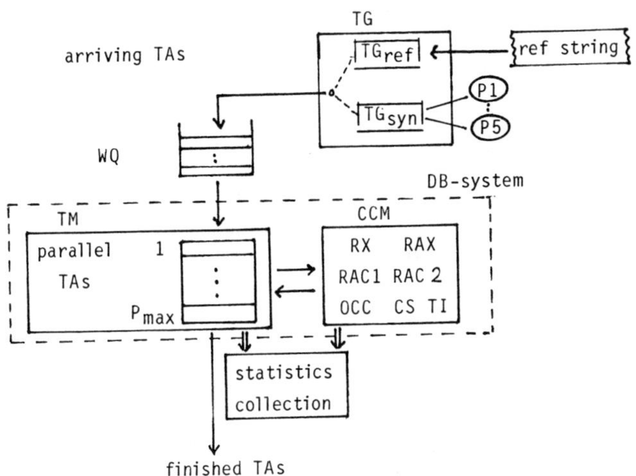

Fig. 2: Architecture of the simulation model.

$$T_i = [(O_{i1}, A_{i1}), \ldots, (O_{iL_i}, A_{iL_i})], \text{ where } A_{ij} \in \{\text{'Read'}, \text{'Write'}\}.$$

L_i is called the length of T_i. T_i is termed as

– *reader*, if for all j, $1 \leq j \leq L_i$: A_{ij} = 'Read',

– *pure writer*, if for all j, $1 \leq j \leq L_i$: A_{ij} = 'Write',

– *writer*, if T_i is neither reader nor pure writer.

The following TG_{syn}-parameters P1 to P5 can be set in order to produce a specific TA mix:

(P1) Number of DB-objects O_{max} with significant access rate

(P2) Distribution of TA-lengths, the average being denoted by L

(P3) Ratio between readers and writers

(P4) Ratio between read- and write-actions for a writer

(P5) Distribution of accesses to DB-objects

4. A Framework for Performance Evaluation and Comparison

As in every simulation system, the elapsed CPU-time is no suitable measure for the duration of the observed processes, because installation- and implementation-specific factors would falsify the gained results. Moreover, the CPU-time spent for simulated components does not reflect the real ratios compared to fully implemented components. Therefore we introduce an abstract time unit, which allows us to measure all relevant sizes but excludes unintended influences.[4] In our simulation system there may be up to P_{max} concurrent TAs within the TM. Assuming that the TM is capable of serving up to P_{max} TAs in parallel, we give the following definition:

Def. 4.1: *Simulation Time Unit* (STU)
In one unit of STU each active TA executes one action.

Note that, if the system is not empty, at each point of STU-time there is at least one active TA, guaranteeing the progress of STU-time. The TM serves active TAs in a cyclic manner; thus the STU-time is increased by one with each scheduling cycle.

Def. 4.2: *Cost of a TA*
The cost of a TA *T* is defined as the elapsed STU-time, derived from the STU-time when *T* enters the TM until *T* leaves it in the event of a successful completion.

Note that the cost of a TA does not include just the pure processing time required for its actions. It also comprises those temporal delays that are incurred by the concurrent TA-processing according to a given CC method. These delays are referred to as synchronization costs, as there are blocking situations, inactivity and backups. The following cost constituents contribute to the cost of a TA *T*:

Def. 4.3: *Cost constituents* (measured in [STU])

(i) $A(T) :=$ length of *T*

(ii) $B(T) := \sum_{i=1}^{b(T)} BD_i(T)$, where $b(T) :=$ number of blocking suffered by *T*,
$BD_i(T) :=$ duration of i-th blocking of *T*

(iii) $R(T) := \sum_{i=1}^{r(T)} RA_i(T)$, where $r(T) :=$ number of backups of *T*,
$RA_i(T) :=$ number of actions to be re-processed due to i-th backup of *T*

(iv) $I(T) :=$ duration of inactive phase of *T*

Of course, for RX and OCC we have $I(T) = 0$. Likewise, for OCC $B(T)$ equals 0. With these sizes the cost $C(T)$ of a TA *T* can be computed as follows:

Equation 4.4:

$$C(T) := A(T) + S(T), \text{ where } S(T) := B(T) + R(T) + I(T)$$

The cost factor $A(T)$ can be interpreted as *net portion* of the elapsed STU-time, while $S(T)$ accounts for the *synchronization cost* due to blocking situations, lost work because of

[4]Despite this, real time measurements for some parts within the CCM were performed, the results are reported in section 5.3.

backups and inactivity duration. B(T) and I(T) are charged as cost factors for the following reason: If there are TAs waiting in WQ for being serviced by the TM, and as we assume that the TM can keep up to P_{max} TAs busy in parallel, blockings and inactivities prevent the DB-system from reaching its maximum processing performance. R(T) in turn measures the amount of unproductive work. Note that, besides computing C(T) due to equ. 4.4, C(T) can also be measured directly by recording entry and exit times to and from the TM. By this the correctness of the measurement of the single cost factors can be checked.

Def. 4.5: *Avg. processing cost of a TA* (denoted by C)

$C := A + S$ with $S = B + R + I$,

where A, B, R, I are the respective average values over all processed TAs.

Note that, in case of a synthetic workload, A is identical to the avg. TA-length L determined by parameter (P2) of TG_{syn}. In addition to this measure of avg. processing time C, subsequently we introduce the measures of utilized and effective parallelism.
In our simulation series the maximum allowable degree of parallelism P_{max} was saturated in all conducted runs, setting the arrival rate of TAs from the TG into WQ accordingly high. However, due to blockings and inactive phases only a certain fraction of these P_{max} TAs is active at a given time. Therefore the potential parallelism can be utilized only for the active ones. From this fact we define the notion of utilized parallelism as follows:

Def. 4.6: *Utilized parallelism* (at STU-time t)

$P_{util}(t) :=$ number of active TAs at time t

The average utilized parallelism is denoted by P_{util}.

As the DB-system is capable to serve P_{max} TAs in parallel, during the avg. processing time C P_{max} TAs can be completed successfully. Thus, the avg. throughput per unit of STU is $P_{max} \cdot C^{-1}$ TAs of avg. length A. Consequently, the *effective* number of actions processed in parallel per STU on the average is $P_{max} \cdot C^{-1} \cdot A$. With def. 4.5 we arrive at the following definition:

Def. 4.7: *Effective parallelism* (P_{eff})

$$P_{eff} := P_{max} \cdot \frac{A}{A+S}$$

Observation: $S \rightarrow 0$ implies $P_{eff} \rightarrow P_{max}$.
The relationship among P_{max}, P_{util} and P_{eff} is given by the following inequality:

$$P_{eff} \leqslant P_{util} \leqslant P_{max}.$$

The interpretation of this fact is as follows:

– P_{max} does not account for any synchronization costs.
– P_{util} only accounts for blockings and inactive phases.
– P_{eff} accounts for all synchronization costs.

Obviously, for OCC we always have $P_{util} = P_{max}$. For locking P_{util} and P_{eff} will be of almost equal size, if the blocking costs are prevailing over the remaining synchronization costs. The measure P_{eff} will be used to qualitatively compare the various CC methods.

5. Evaluation of Simulation Series

5.1. Synthetic Workload Experiments

For these experimental series the TAs to be processed were produced by the synthetic TA-generator TG_{syn}. In all simulation series reported in this paper (which represent a characteristic sample from many more) the objects to be locked are drawn from a normal distribution. The expectation and variance were chosen such that 80 per cent of all object accesses were to the O_{max} objects as defined by parameter (P1) of TG_{syn}. This choice effects that the number of objects is potentially infinitely large; we are primarily interested in that 80% which have the highest access frequency. For the synthetic workload experiments, O_{max} and the avg. TA-length L was chosen such that each TA accesses about 1% to 10% of this highly active part of the DB. This choice results in a relatively high collision rate, which first enables us to figure out the behavior of the CC methods in extreme applications and secondly enables us to observe a statistically reliable number of all possible collision types during the observation periods, being 600 - 900 successfully processed TAs.

Analysis of serialization methods:
Let us start with the investigation of the tradeoff between late serialization using graph and cycle searching (lock module RAC1 + CS) and early serialization using TIs (RAC2 + TI). As representatives for the results to be reported the *cost profiles* for RAC1 + CS and for RAC2 + TI under the same TA-workload are depicted in fig. 3 and fig. 4, respectively. These cost profiles give a survey on how the avg. processing time C is composed.
We analyze the blocking costs (B) and backup costs (R) in greater detail.

(1) RAC1 + CS vs. RAC2 + TI: avg. blocking cost per TA
From the cost profiles it can be seen that B is considerable higher for RAC1 + CS compared to RAC2 + TI. Now recall that B is defined as b * BD, where b is the avg. number of blockings per TA and BD is the avg. duration of a blocking situation. In fig. 5 and fig. 6 it is illustrated that the great reduction of B for RAC2 + TI stems both from a smaller b and a smaller BD.
In order to figure out whether this behavior can be contributed to the effect of early

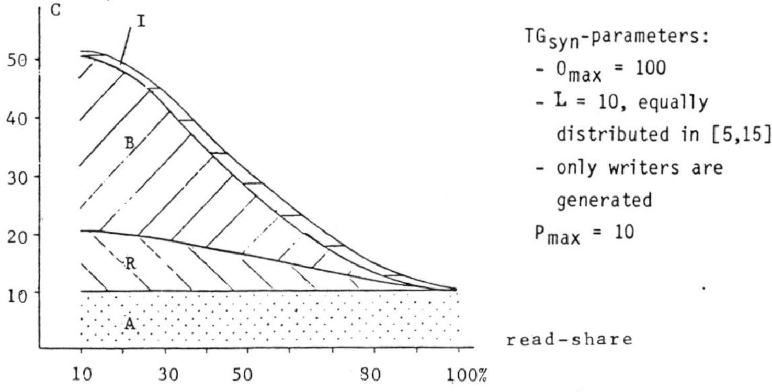

Fig. 3: Cost profile for RAC1 + CS.

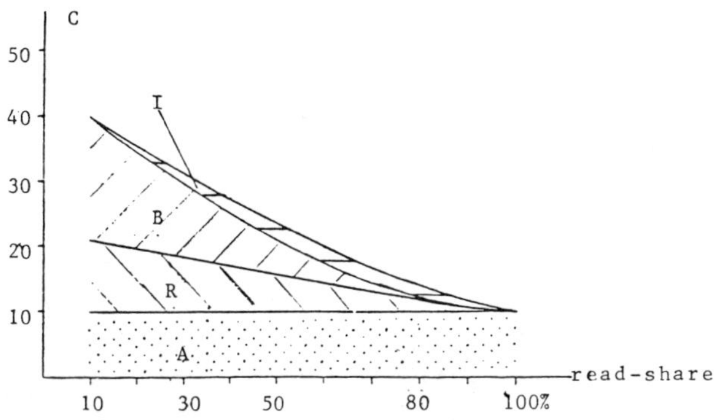

Fig. 4: Cost profile for RAC2 + TI.

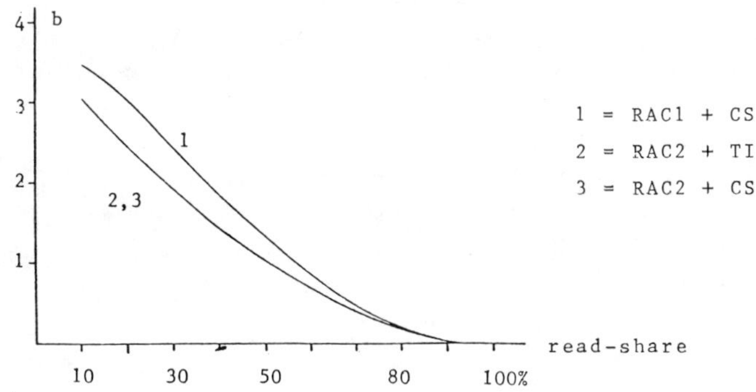

Fig. 5: Avg. number of blockings per TA.

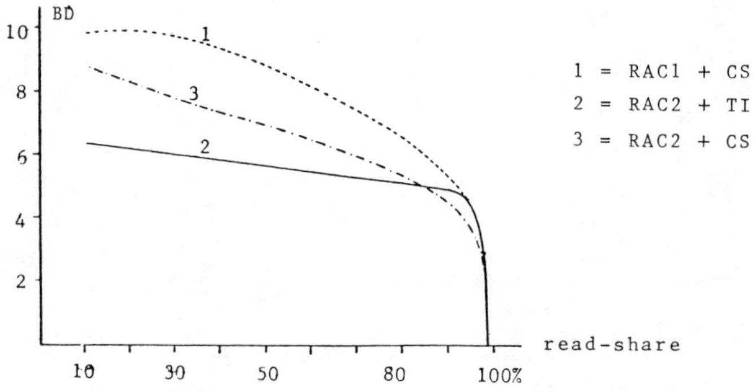

Fig. 6: Avg. duration of a blocking situation.

serialization or the use of TIs, also the lock module RAC2 + CS (which uses early serialization and cycle searching) was tested. Obviously, the reduction of b comes from early serialization, while unnecessary backups from TIs due to "phantom"-conflicts yield a further reduction of BD. This means that for high collision rates a superfluous backup might be better than some further blocking (compare also OCC-behavior, later on).

The crucial question is now whether the reduced blocking costs for RAC2 + TI are offset by the backup costs or not.

(2) RAC1 + CS vs. RAC2 + TI: avg. backup cost per TA

Surprisingly, RAC2 + TI does better than RAC1 + CS over the entire range of read-actions (compare the cost profiles). Moreover, for the area of a high percentage of write-actions the difference is most significant. This unexpected effect is founded in the following: An increasing portion of write-actions increases the collision probability, necessitating more serializations per TA. Thus, a TA's risk to become a victim of an unnecessary backup by the use TIs increases for RAC2 + TI compared to RAC1 + CS. Therefore it could be expected a priori that RAC2 + TI behaves worse than RAC1 + CS for high write shares. Indeed, as expected, the avg. number of backups per TA is higher for RAC2 + TI, as it is depicted in fig. 7. However, as a counter effect, the amount of lost work due to a single backup should be smaller for RAC2 because of early serialization. That the backup costs (RA) are indeed substantially lower for RAC2 + TI is documented in fig 8.
The crucial figure now is the overall backup cost per TA, being defined as $R = r \cdot RA$.

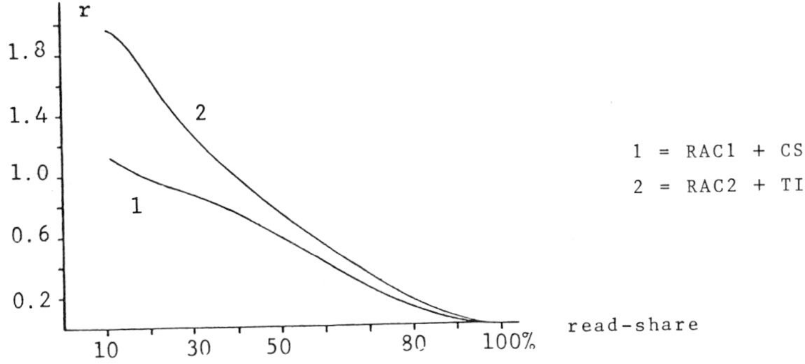

Fig. 7: Avg. number of backups for TA.

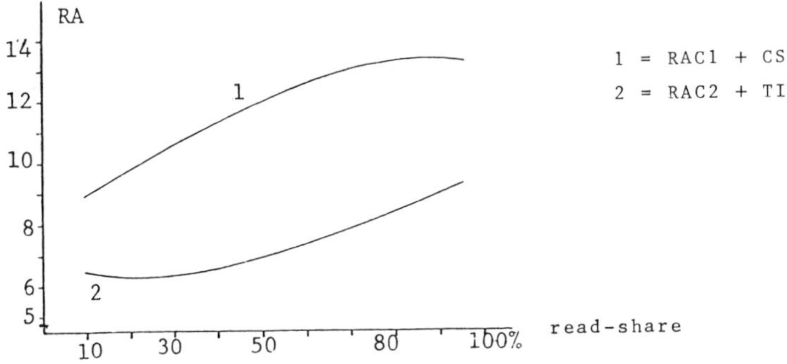

Fig. 8: Avg. cost per backup.

Comparing the given cost profiles, the interesting result emerges that R is almost identical for RAC1 + CS and RAC2 + TI. This fact exemplifies that the increased backup probability of RAC2 + TI is no obstacle for its excellent performance (which will be demonstrated later on). Finally, it has to be mentioned that RAC2 + TI shortens also the duration of inactive phases due to the early fitting of TAs into a serialization order.

Let us briefly summarize the basic results concerning late serialization with cycle searching and early serialization with TIs. Note that these results hold for all simulation runs which we performed so far.

(i) The backup costs are (almost) identical for RAC1 + CS and RAC2 + TI.
(ii) The lion's share of the overall synchronization costs are the blocking costs. This cost constituent is substantially lower for RAC2 + TI. Hereby the avg. blocking rate as well as the avg. blocking duration is reduced separately.

Note that the real-time overhead of the used serialization methods does *not* contribute to the above results; it is evaluated separately in section 5.3.

Comparison of concurrency control schemes:
As the relevant measure to compare the performance of various CC schemes, in section 4 the notion of effective parallelism was introduced. This size P_{eff} is defined as $P_{eff} = P_{max} \cdot \frac{A}{A+S}$. If there are not only readers in the TA-workload, then increasing the degree of parallelism P_{max} inevitably brings an increase of the synchronization cost S. Obviously, a strong increase of S can compensate or even ruin an increase of P_{max}. Subsequently, we present three sample series, recording P_{eff} and P_{util} for increasing P_{max}. (Remember that $P_{util} = P_{max}$ for OCC.)
In the fig. 9-11 results are shown for workloads with a different share of read-actions. Let us first interpret the behavior of the lock modules RX + CS, RAC1 + CS and RAC2 + TI. For the high read-share of 90% in fig. 9, P_{eff} and P_{util} both are rather strongly increasing because of the relatively low collision rate. For illustration purposes the border line $P_{eff} = P_{max}$ is drawn, too. Because P_{util} and P_{eff} are nearly identical, the respective curves superimpose each other and are therefore not distinguishable. On the whole, for this low collision rate all investigated lock modules are capable of transforming an increase of P_{max} into an effective throughput improvement.
If the read-share within the TA-mix is dropped to 50%, then the qualitative differences among the lock modules become more drastically, as it can be observed from fig. 10. Now none of the lock modules is capable of reaching the border line $P_{eff} = P_{max}$ even roughly. Moreover, for RX + CS and RAC1 + CS the curves for P_{eff} possess a maximum. This means that an increase of P_{max} beyond this respective value does not improve the overall performance of the DB-system, rather it degrades. The curves for P_{util} behave similarly to those for P_{eff}, but the relative distances are much more striking (compared to fig. 9). Especially striking is the distance for RAC2 + TI: Due to the short duration of blockings, P_{util} still increases nearly linearly. On the contrary, the maxima of P_{util} for RX + CS and RAC1 + CS indicate that a further increase of P_{max} solely produces more blockings and backups without achieving a gain in productive work. In fig. 11 the results for the (unrealistic) low read share of 5% are depicted. The runs of the particular curves resemble those encountered in the previous figure. However, now also for RAC2 + TI there is a maximum for P_{eff}. On the whole, this high conflict rate has the effect that the parallel processing of TAs almost entirely comes to a standstill. Note that an intelligent TM might use these P_{eff}-curves for a dynamic TA-load balancing algorithm.

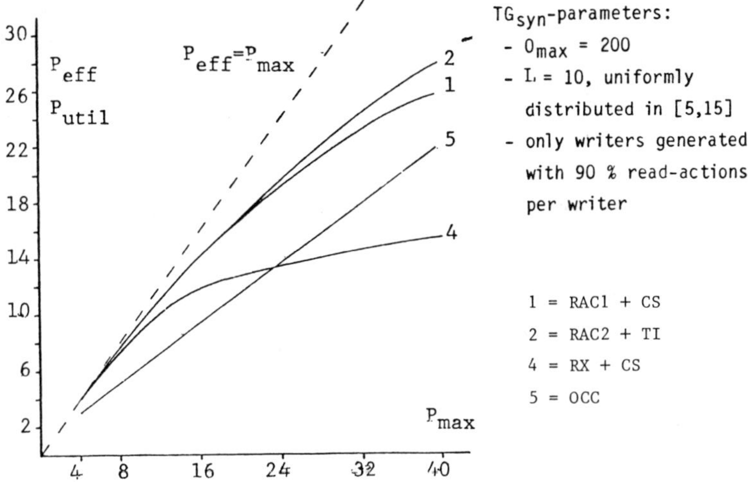

Fig. 9: P_{eff} and P_{util} for 90% read-actions.

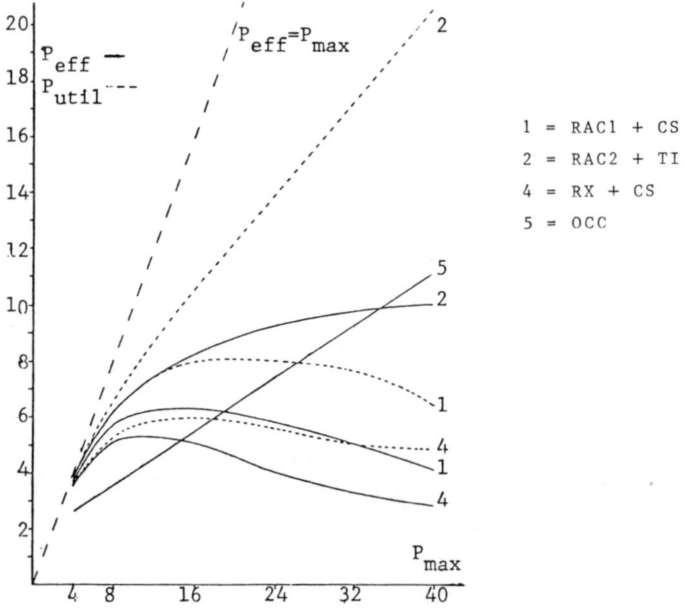

Fig. 10: P_{eff} and P_{util} for 50% read-actions.

As a summary, the performance of the analyzed lock modules compares as follows:

– For P_{max}-values below 8 all lock modules perform almost identical. Note that this range of parallelism is typical for current DB-systems.

– For higher P_{max}-values RAC2 + TI outperforms the other lock modules, exhibiting a very stable behavior over a wide range of TG_{syn}-parameter settings.

– For RAX + CS the obtained results were nearly the same as for RAC1 + CS, without any exception. This indicates that 2-version schemes, such as the *(r, a, c)* - protocol, offer no significant performance improvement over *(r, a, x)*.

Interpretation of OCC-behavior:

From fig. 9-11 two important trends can be observed:

(1) For small P_{max}-values OCC behaves worse than locking.

(2) The slope of the P_{eff}-curve does not decrease much for increasing parallelism. In fact, it increases nearly linearly.

This second point demonstrates an unexpected behavior, which is contrary to the prerequisites under which OCC is commonly thought to perform well. In fact, for extreme TA-mixes under high parallelism, creating a very high conflict rate, OCC outperforms locking for this case in our cost model. However, as the subsequent reference string experiment will demonstrate, this holds only for short TAs with a regular access pattern to the

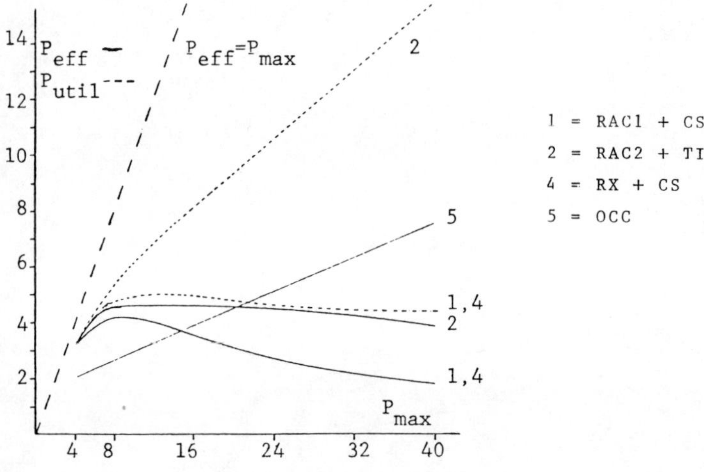

Fig. 11: P_{eff} and P_{util} for 5% read-actions.

DB-objects, as reflected by the underlying TA mix for fig. 9-11. Also it should be recalled that our P_{eff} does not account for the CC overhead required to enforce OCC (e.g., cost of intersecting writesets). At a first glance, this result looks strange. However, we have a reasonable interpretation. In fig. 12 the respective avg. lengths *w* of the writeset queue are depicted, exhibiting smaller values of *w* for a lower read share, i.e. for a higher conflict probability.

This fact can be explained as follows:

Let l_m denote the length of the longest TA actually inside the TM. Then at latest after l_m units of STU the oldest TA inside the TM validates, triggering a decrease of the writeset queue length *w*. During this period a certain portion of other TAs validate positively and their writesets are appended to the writeset queue. Now note that for a higher conflict rate this portion gets smaller, yielding a smaller value for *w*. If we increase P_{max}, then this trend progresses until a point is reached where w is so small that the probability for a successful validation increases again. These antagonistic effects finally stabilize *w* at an equilibrium state. In this state the values for *w* are lower for a TA-mix with a higher conflict probability.

The explanation for the stated trend (1) is as follows:

For low collision rates the locking schemes can fit the TAs into a serialization order by some blockings, keeping the backup rate low. For high collision rates locking necessitates a high amount of blocking *and* of backups. Therefore the full processing power of the DB-system can be utilized only to a fractional extent. In such unfavorable situations OCC still produces more backups than locking, but as there are no blockings the full parallelism can be exploited. Together with the previous interpretation of the OCC-behavior it now becomes clear, why OCC does better for extremely conflict-loaded TA-mixes, consisting of relatively short TAs without hot spots as described subsequently.

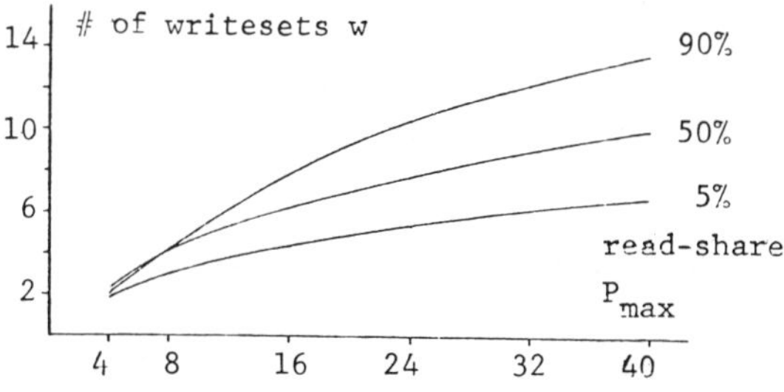

Fig. 12: Avg. length *w* of writeset queue.

5.2. Reference String Experiment

The reference string at our disposal was audited on a logical page-level basis from an application running on the SIEMENS Codasyl DB-system UDS. This string is converted as follows: The page-ids and the respective access modes are collected in the order of appearance for each TA and are passed to the TG_{ref}. Because we do no handle conversions from read to update mode, such cases were eliminated by replacing the former read access by an update access and dropping the subsequent update access. A statistical evaluation of this modified reference string is presented in table 1. Thereby we (somewhat arbitrarily) grouped the TAs according to the TA-length L as follows: very short: $L \in \{1, \ldots, 3\}$, short: $L \in \{4, \ldots, 8\}$, medium: $L \in \{9, \ldots, 12\}$, long: $L \in \{13, \ldots, 18\}$.

No. of TAs: 2280
No. of referenced pages: 2203
No. of referenced read-only pages: 999
Minimum, maximum, average TA-length: 1, 18, 5.2
% of readers = 54, % of writers = 46
Distribution of readers (relative frequency)
  very short: 33%; short: 18%
  medium : 3%; long : 0%
Distribution of writers (rel. frequ., avg. read/write ratio)
  very short: 20%, 0.3; short: 9%, 2.2
  medium : 10%, 4.7; long : 7%, 2.4

Table 1: Statistical evaluation of reference string.

This string resembles the string no. 6 presented in [11]. Separately, the empirical distribution of accesses to the DB-pages is sketched in fig. 13. In [11] some hot spot pages were removed from the string (how many was left open), stating correctly that each DBMS implementation applies special synchronization methods with a very fine lock granularity for such hot spots. Nevertheless, in order to stress the necessity for various levels of lock granularity, we present the simulation evaluation of our reference string without removal of any hot spots. For comparison purposes the results are listed in table 2, if those two pages with the highest *update* access frequency are removed (with 464 and 384 accesses, respectively).

The drastic influence of hot spots and the negative impact, if page locking is used, is immediately striking. Obviously, OCC behaves worst by far for this string. A remarkable fact, which deserves attention, is that the (r, a, c) - protocol in its basic variant (RAC1 + CS) performs worse than RX + CS for the unmodified string. On the other hand, its

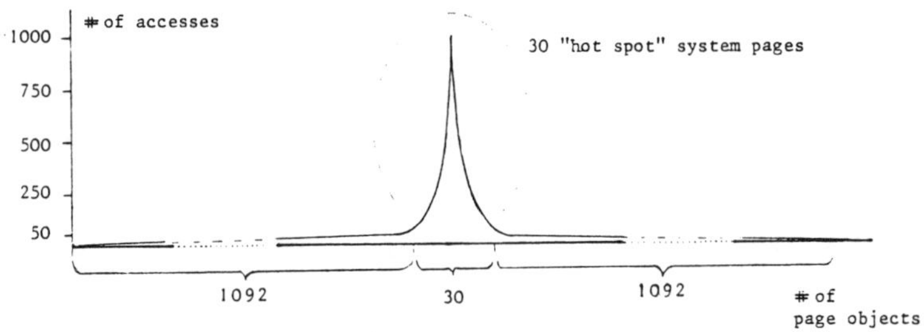

Fig. 13: Distribution of page accesses.

	P_{max} 4	10	24	32	40	
RX + CS	3.6	5.7	5.9	6.0	6.1	no hot spots removed
RAC1 + CS	3.6	5.7	5.6	5.6	5.6	
RAC2 + TI	3.6	5.7	5.9	6.0	6.1	
OCC	2.1	2.5	3.2	4.4	4.5	
RX + CS	3.9	9.6	20.1	23.9	26.0	two hot spots removed
RAC1 + CS	3.9	9.7	19.5	25.1	29.0	
RAC2 + TI	3.9	9.7	21.3	26.2	30.0	
OCC	3.3	5.3	9.2	10.7	12.9	

Table 2: P_{eff} under varying parallelism for reference string.

refinement RAC2 + TI does best once again. Due to space limitations we dispense with the presentation of an elaborate analysis of the particular cost profiles. But it shall be stated that the constituted tradeoff between early and late serialization holds here too: The overall backup costs are almost identical for RAC1 + CS and RAC2 + TI, whereas the blocking costs for RAC2 + TI are noticeably lower.

On the whole, RAC2 + TI is once again the candidate of choice for this particular reference string, especially under high parallelism. The potential advantage of the improved lock compatibilities of the (r, a, c) - protocol can be transformed into an effective performance gain by the application of early serialization.

5.3. Cycle Searching Considered Doubtful

In section 4 the performance of CC schemes was analyzed in terms of the abstract simulation time STU. The measure P_{eff} was used to compared the quality of different schemes. Hereby, P_{eff} accounts for the synchronization costs. Independent of these costs, the real time consumption spent for executing the respective CC algorithms is a further important performance size. This real time expenditure is referred to as *CC-overhead*.
In the following, we represent measurements for cycle searching and TI-manipulation. That cycle searching may be an expensive operation is well-known. However, to our knowledge nowhere in the literature are overhead costs reported. Our current version of the CS-component uses the Warshall-algorithm which has a worst case complexity of $O(P^3_{max})$.[5] In fig. 14 the CS-overhead for RAC1 + CS and the TI-overhead for RAC2 + TI is recorded for a series with synthetic TAs and the reference string described. The experiments were performed on a SIEMENS 7865 mainframe in multi-user mode. The shown costs represent CPU-overhead per serialization. (Note that RAC1 + CS executes several serialization checks with one cycle search at EOT.) The curves for CS exhibit a quadratic growth, whereas the value for TIs is constant and equals $t = 0.08$ [msec].

From these results we draw the following conclusions:
- The overhead difference for current DB-system ($P_{max} < 8$) is not striking.
- For future high performance DB-systems the time spent for cycle searching is likely to become a sizable factor. Thus cycle searching must also be viewed with caution for centralized DB-systems. (For distributed DB-systems this judgement is generally accepted by now.)
- The overhead for locking schemes using TIs is expected to be substantially below the overhead required by OCC.

Let us conclude by stating some observations concerning cycle lengths. In [5] it is conjectured that cycles are very rare and, in case they occur, are of length 2 almost always. The underlying assumptions for this straw man implied that a TA locks about 0.001% of the DB. On the other hand, in our synthetic experiments a TA locks between 1% and 10% of the DB. For these synthetic tests we observed a considerable amount of long cycles. Of special importance are the observed maximum cycle lengths (CL_{max}). The encountered CL_{max} amounted to approximately $0.5 \cdot P_{max}$ for each read share. Thus, for $P_{max} = 40$ cycles of length $CL_{max} = 20$ were detected (even if only 20 cycles were observed at all!). Even more impressive are the data gathered from the reference string experiment. The version with two removed hot spots produced an avg. cycle length of 2.9 for RX + CS with $P_{max} = 10$, while CL_{max} was 5. The version without hot spot removal caused about the same values for $P_{max} = 10$. Increasing P_{max} to 40, the avg. cycle length raised to 14.7 and CL_{max}

[5]Of course, there are more efficient algorithms, e.g., in [1] CS-algorithms are suggested, the order of which is considerably lower. However, they can only be applied to pure wait graphs and not to

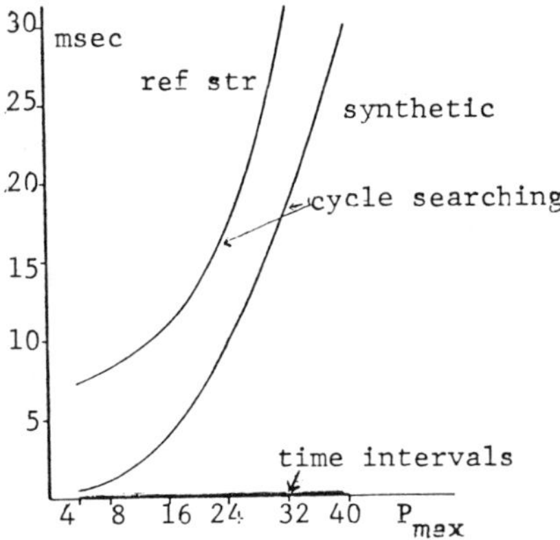

Fig. 14: Real time overhead per serialization for RAC1 + CS, RAC2 + TI.

amounted to 34. (More on cycle length distributions can be found in [7].)
Consequently, for increasing parallelism one must be aware of very long cycles that in turn affect the choice of a proper strategy for selecting backup victims to break a cycle.

6. Conclusion

The definition of a uniform measurement system for our employed simulation model formed the basis for assessing the quality of various CC schemes. By measuring the constituent cost factors directly, it is feasible to determine and compare the synchronization costs incurred by these schemes. Moreover, the observation of these individual cost factors revealed some theoretically interesting properties, like the tradeoff between early and late serialization. The main results gained by synthetic TA workload experiments are the following:
For the degree of parallelism offered by nowadays DB-systems the lockprotocols (r, x), (r, a, x) and (r, a, c) do not differ significantly; however, within the scope of our simulations, they perform better than the optimistic method OCC. For a higher degree of parallelism and a high conflict rate OCC unexpectedly improves its position in some cases. For (r, a, x) and (r, a, c), both applying late serialization, no striking differences showed up. This result supports an analogous one stated in [9], namely that multi-version schemes seem to offer no noticeable improvements over single version schemes (at least for short TAs).

dependence graphs as the (r, a, c) - protocol requires.

The analysis of the performed simulation runs revealed that for all lockprotocols the blocking costs are the dominating portion of the overall synchronization costs. The decisive means to reduce the blocking costs without increasing the backup costs is the application of early serialization in conjunction with a good, but cheap serialization method as there are the dynamic time intervals (lock module RAC2 + TI). For future high performance DB-systems with high parallelism RAC2 + TI is proposed to be a favorite candidate for the selection of good CC scheme, in terms of low synchronization as well as low overhead costs. The same excellent performance is expected to hold for the not yet implemented variant RAX2 + TI, which looks even more promising because it does not impose such hard requirements to the underlying DB-cache management (see [2]).

The reported overhead costs for cycle searching indicate that also for centralized DB-systems cycle searching should be substituted for by a cheaper, but still rather precise method like dynamic time intervals. Further, we collected measurements on cycle lengths, not done elsewhere, and compared them to the preliminary analytical work in [5]. Finally, the conducted reference string experiment showed results similar to the synthetic tests.

In summary, (r, a, x) or (r, a, c) combined with early serialization by dynamic time intervals is recommended as the candidate of choice for selecting a suitable CC method, in particular for future high-performance DB-systems.

Acknowledgements:

We wish to thank Dr. Angelika Reiser for carefully reading a draft of this paper. Likewise we are grateful to the graduate students Bernhard Maischberger and Matthias Hoderlein for performing some of the experiments.

References:

[1] Agrawal; Carey; DeWitt: *Deadlock Detection is Cheap*, University of California, Berkeley, ERL Memorandum No. M83/5, Jan. 1983.

[2] Bayer, R.: *Database System Design for High Performance*, IFIP 1983, Paris, pp. 147-155.

[3] Bayer; Elhardt; Heigert; Reiser: *Dynamic Timestamp Allocation for Transactions in Database Systems*, in Distr. Data Bases, ed. H.-J. Schneider, North- Holland, pp. 9-20, 1982.

[4] Carey, M.J.: *An Abstract Model of Database Concurrency Control Algorithms*, SIGMOD 1983, pp. 97-107.

[5] Gray; Homan; Obermarck; Korth: *A Straw Man Analysis of Probability of Waiting and Deadlock*, IBM Res. Lab. San Jose, RJ3066(38112), 2/26/81.

[6] Kiessling, W.; Landherr, G.: *A Quantitative Comparison of Lockprotocols for Centralized Databases*, Proc. VLDB, Florence, 1983, pp. 120-130.

[7] Kiessling, W.; Pfeiffer, H: *A Comprehensive Analysis of Lockprotocols for Centralized Database Systems*, Research Report TUM-INFO 8402, Technical Univ. Munich, Febr. 1984.

[8] Kung, H.T.; Robinson, J.: *On Optimistic Methods for Concurrency Control*, Proc. VLDB, Rio de Janeiro, Oct. 1979.

[9] Lin, W. K.; Nolte, J.: *Basic Timestamp, Multiple Version Timestamp, and Two-Phase Locking*, Proc. VLDB, Florence 1983, pp. 109-119.

[10] Menasce, D.A.; Nakauishi, T.: *Optimistic Versus Pessimistic Concurrency Control Mechanisms in Database Management Systems*, in Inf. Syst., Vol. 7, No 1, 1982, pp. 13-27.

[11] Peinl; Reuter: *Empirical Comparison of Database Concurrency Control Schemes*, Proc. VLDB, Florence, 1983.

[12] Potier, O.; Leblanc, Ph.: *Analysis of Locking Policies in Database Management Systems*, in Comm. ACM, Oct. 1980, Vol. 23, No. 10, pp. 584-593.

[13] Rosenkrantz; Stearns; Lewis: *System Level Concurrency Control for Distributed Database Systems*, ACM TODS, Vol. 3, No. 2, June 1978, pp. 178-198.

[14] Tay, Y.C.; Suri, R.: *Choice and Performance of Locking for Databases*, VLDB Singapore, Aug. 1984, pp. 199-127.

[15] Tay, Y.C.; Goodman, N.; Suri, R.: *Performance Evaluation of Locking in Databases: A Survey*, Harvard Univ., TR-17-84, 1984.

Parallel Operation of Magnetic Disk Storage Devices: Synchronized Disk Interleaving

M. Y. Kim
IBM Thomas J. Watson Research Center
Yorktown Heights, New York 10598

Abstract

A group of disks may be interleaved to speed up data transfers in a manner analogous to the speedup achieved by main memory interleaving. Conventional disks may be used for interleaving by spreading data across disks and by treating multiple disks as if they were a single one. Furthermore, the mechanical movement of the interleaved disks may be synchronized to simplify control and also to optimize performance. In addition, checksums may be placed on separate checksum disks in order to improve reliability. In this paper, we study synchronized disk interleaving as a high performance mass storage system architecture. The advantages and limitations of the proposed disk interleaving scheme are analyzed using the M/G/1 queueing model and compared to the conventional disk access mechanism.

1. Introduction

The speed of magnetic disk storage devices is often a major bottleneck in overall system performance. The disks are at least three orders of magnitude slower than main memory. This speed gap between the disk storage and main memory may become even wider, with rapidly changing memory and processor technologies. One might argue that by adding, say, on the order of tens of billions of bytes of main memory to a computer system, the problem of speed mismatch may become a less critical issue.

Nevertheless, the fact is that no matter how large the main memory is, there will always be some programs that require more. Furthermore, unless the entire main memory or a substantial fraction of it is made nonvolatile, the updates made in the main memory must be copied onto slow nonvolatile devices like disks in order to preserve data integrity. This suggests that the speed of such nonvolatile storage devices may dictate the performance of the entire system even though the system is equipped with massive amounts of main memory. Our assumption, therefore, is that there are many applications that are inevitably ***I/O bound***, thus requiring huge data transfers, or frequent data transfers, to and from the secondary storage devices.

There has been interest in database machines that make use of hundreds of query processors to process a database query in parallel. It has been claimed that the performance of those machines would be limited by their disk to memory transfer rates, and that unless the problem of the ***I/O bandwidth*** is tackled, the use of hundreds of query processors will not be justified [1] [2].

Furthermore, there is an increasing requirement for larger storage capacity, and this demand for ***more capacity*** will continue to grow. The capacity of magnetic disk storage devices may be increased either by making the recording surfaces denser or simply by adding more disk units. As we will discuss in the following sections, neither approach is penalty free: denser disks are more error prone, and adding more drives may cause a performance interference (See 4. The effects of adding more actuators). It is safe to state that no matter how large and how dense a disk storage may be, there is always a need for more, and this requirement may be met by coupling multiple disks together. The key issue is, then, how effectively the multiple devices can be managed while maintaining high performance and reliability. This is analogous to the problem of interconnecting multiprocessors so that the greatest processing power is achieved in a reliable and cost effective manner. However, there is an added concern in ***disk coupling***. This is because the speed of the rotational storage devices is so slow, that the adverse impact of the added contention can be easily magnified (See RPS miss delay in 3.1.1).

One method of disk coupling is ***disk interleaving***. A string of disk units is interleaved if data is stored across all of the disks. A string of disk units is synchronized when all of the disks are run by synchronous motors that are controlled by a feedback mechanism. In this paper, synchronized disk interleaving is studied as a ***high performance mass storage system*** architecture. We claim that synchronized interleaving may be used to reduce the average response time of an I/O request, to increase I/O bandwidth, and also to improve reliability. In addition, we argue that synchronized interleaving may provide us with a means of treating multiple disks as if they were a single virtual disk, thereby simplifying control problems. These, in turn, suggest that the interleaving may be used as a novel disk coupling mechanism.

There are two major factors that contribute to the poor performance of I/O systems. One is ***mechanical delays*** [1] due to the speed of the rotational disk storage devices. Disk interleaving may be used to cut down such delays by accessing data in parallel and also by treating multiple disks as a single virtual disk. By interleaving disks, data may be accessed in parallel, reducing the data transfer time by a factor of $1/n$, where n is the number of disks. Furthermore, when multiple disks are effectively treated as a single disk, there is no path contention between disks, hence eliminating reconnect delays (See RPS misses in 3.1.1). The other is the adverse impact of ***DASD skew***. DASD (Direct Access Storage Device) skew is the observed phenomenon that disk accesses are not evenly distributed over the actuators in a string of disks. A simple characterization is that 25 percent of the actuators receive 63 percent of the total requests,[2] thereby creating I/O bottlenecks that severely limit overall system performance. With the increasing size and number of on-line databases, the existence of I/O bottlenecks is becoming an even larger problem. Moreover, the skew, the variation in I/O workload, is dynamic in nature making load balancing efforts extremely difficult. We argue that disk interleaving automatically provides ***uniform distribution of requests*** among the disks.

---

1 The time required for mechanical movement, i.e., arm positioning, latency, RPS misses, and data transfer. See 3.1 for further information.

2 See the skew distribution in (3) in 3.1.1.

There is a wide range of possible applications that could exploit the parallelism provided by interleaving. In this paper, we model simple block transfers and study the performance characteristics of disk interleaving for such tasks.

Outline

In Section 2, we briefly review the techniques that have been used in the past to speed up the disk access time and describe synchronized disk interleaving as an alternative approach to achieve the speedup. Interleaving is described as a means of achieving parallelism, and synchronization for efficiency and simplicity. In addition, a possible strategy for error recovery is briefly discussed.

In Section 3, the modeling methodology is presented.

Comparative numerical results from the analytic modeling appear in Section 4.

Finally, the summary of comparison results and conclusions are presented in Section 5.

2. Synchronized Disk Interleaving

In this section, the various techniques that have been used in the past to speed up the disk access time are reviewed. As an alternative approach to achieve the speedup, disk interleaving is described. In order to efficiently operate interleaved disks, it is necessary that their movement be synchronized. The chief concern with this approach is that handling of errors may involve too much overhead.

2.1 How to Speed Up Disk Access Time

Speeding up the access time of disk systems is an important goal to achieve, especially in large on-line database systems. One class of approaches for achieving such a goal is to ***minimize various mechanical delays*** that occur at the disks. For instance, fixed-head disks may be used to eliminate the arm movement by having multiple read/write heads per surface, tracks-in-parallel moving head disks may be used to access entire cylinders in parallel, or bit density along a track may be increased to reduce the data transfer time.

Fixed-Head Disks: Each addressable track has its own fixed (stationary) read/write element. Since each track of a fixed-head disk device [3] is accessible via the one fixed position of the access mechanism, the entire disk device can be, in effect, considered as one cylinder. Therefore, all tracks of such a device can be read all at once. Although this seems attractive, it has been agreed that the fixed-head disks are not practical media for the storage of large databases. It simply is not cost effective, because the fixed-head disks require a dedicated read/write head for each track on a surface, and the cost of a disk system is dominated by the cost of the

[3] IBM's 2305 Model 2 has 864 read/write heads. 768 of the elements are positioned to access its 768 recording tracks, and the remaining 96 heads are positioned to access the 96 spare tracks.

read/write heads.[4] Furthermore, the use of electronic replacements for the fixed-head disks such as magnetic bubbles does not seem viable for very large databases.

Therefore, we will assume that ***moving-head disk technology will remain the mainstay of the on-line database storage*** for the foreseeable future.

Tracks-in-Parallel Moving-Head Disks: By modifying the access mechanism of conventional moving head-disks, all tracks of a cylinder can be read in one revolution. This parallel read-out capability provides rapid access to a relatively large block of data. Furthermore, the cost of tracks-in-parallel moving-head disks seems reasonable. Nevertheless, the use of such disk drives for the storage of large databases does seem questionable today. The difficulty is that, in parallel read-out disks, all read/write heads must be aligned accurately at the same time, and that the alignment must take place continuously.[5] As disk densities increase, the already difficult task of positioning multiple heads all at once and accurately, becomes an even larger problem.

Increasing Bit Density: Another approach in minimizing the mechanical delays is to increase bit density along a track, thereby increasing the amount of data that can be transferred per disk revolution. Although the storage capacity of disks has been increasing considerably over the years, the improvement has been mainly due to increased track density (number of tracks per surface) rather than increased bit density (number of bits along a track). Increasing the number of tracks per recording surface offers us more storage capacity, but does not help us in reducing the access time. The understanding is that a dramatic increase in bit density is not likely to occur in the foreseeable future.

The other class of approaches includes efforts to ***minimize the effects of mechanical delays*** rather than to decrease them directly. These include cached control units and disk scheduling techniques among others.

Cached Control Unit: With an IBM 3380, data can be pre-fetched from the disks into the control unit buffer, so that a read request will not involve a disk access if the data is already in the cache. The reason for having a cache in the control unit is to speed up the average access time. However, if the access pattern is not appropriate, it not only does not help but it could also hurt the average access time.

It has been known that the hit ratio, the probability of finding data in the cache, should be high, as high as 70 percent, in order for a control unit with cache to perform better than a native one (without cache). This is because a cache miss may be more expensive than a native access in certain control units due to the control unit overheads.

In addition, the access pattern, the ratio of reads to writes, by application programs is an important parameter that determines the performance of a cached control unit. This is because a write will cause a disk access whether the data is found in the cache or not. Furthermore, a write hit could be more costly than a write miss. This is because for a write hit, the data

---

4 On an IBM 3380, there are 885 cylinders per actuator, 15 tracks per cylinder, and two actuators per drive.

5 This is due to the effects of thermal expansion of the arm [1].

in the cache has to be updated in addition to the data in the disk. This assumes that the write must take place synchronously with the request in order to guarantee the integrity of data.

This leads us to believe that although the average response time for an I/O request may be reduced using cache, there is still a lot of room for improvement. A simple fact is that the gap in the speed between the main memory and the external storage is just too wide, and it will become even wider as processor and memory technologies advance.

Disk Scheduling: One other approach that is worth mentioning in this class of solutions is ***disk scheduling*** (seek scheduling) techniques as described in the literature[17]. Disk scheduling deals mainly with reducing seek time, the time it takes for the moving arm to be positioned on the right cylinder. A great amount of research has been done in trying to find scheduling policies which minimize seek time. It does not appear that those techniques would improve the situation greatly. Two reasons for this are the following:

1. Seek time is not linearly proportional to the distance the access arms travel. One component of seek (arm movement) is the time required for initial acceleration of the access mechanism. With IBM's 3380, for a movement of one cylinder, the time required is 3 milliseconds, while the maximum access time that is required to move across all of the cylinders (885 cylinders) is 30 milliseconds. It suggests that the distance the access mechanism travels does not make a big difference in the average seek time, unless the movement is from the innermost surface to the outermost and vice versa continuously. The gain will be substantial only when the probability that the arm does not move at all increases.

2. In order to apply a seek scheduling algorithm, there must be a queue on which the algorithm may operate. In this paper (see 4.1.4 Queue Length), we show that it is rare to have a queue whose length is longer than 1 in conventional systems. In fact, it has been observed that, in reasonably well-tuned real systems, the average length of queue is less than 0.3 [9]. With a queue whose average length is 0.3, it is easy to see why the seek scheduling techniques will not help.

2.2 Disk Interleaving for Parallelism

A group of disks may be interleaved to speed up data transfers in a manner analogous to the speedup achieved by main memory interleaving. A string of disk units is interleaved if data is spread across all of the n disks and if all n disks are accessed in parallel. Byte-parallel interleaving is chosen here for its simplicity and for its capability to provide the maximal disk access concurrency. With byte interleaving, each byte in a record is assigned to disk unit mod n. That is, Byte 1 is stored on disk 1, byte 2 of the same record is stored at the same spot on disk 2, and so on.

The problems of file design, or file allocation, are not addressed in this study. However, it is important to note that the granularity of interleaving may be changed to any level, i.e., to the attribute level, to the record level, and so on. Whatever level may be chosen, whether the file is physically partitioned or semantically divided, the goal should be to maximally utilize the inherent parallelism provided by interleaving.

A number of database machine designs that have been proposed in the past have explored ***track interleaving*** to achieve parallel reads out of a single disk as opposed to disk interleaving. SURE [6] is an example that used a moving head disk that was modified to enable parallel reads from all of the tracks of a cylinder simultaneously. In SURE, records are stored across the tracks in record-parallel, byte-serial fashion. The output of all recording surfaces is collected into a single data stream in byte interleaving mode and processed by a number of search units. The limitation with SURE was that the parallelism was achieved only in one direction, read only, and a write was done by one head at a time. The reason for this limited design was that, as discussed previously, it was difficult to align multiple read/write heads concurrently, especially for a write. ***Disk interleaving*** has an advantage over track interleaving in that parallelism may be achieved using ***conventional moving-head disks*** rather than with special expensive hardware.

Intelligent Disk Controller

True parallelism in disk access may be achieved only if there are parallel paths available between disks and a memory buffer. By dedicating a channel to each disk, a physically independent path may be provided from the disk to main memory. Or, a disk controller with a buffer may be designed so as to provide ***parallel paths*** to and from a group of disks. Existing control unit hardware may be modified for this purpose or a general purpose micro-processor may be used as an intelligent control unit. Either case seems more practical than the dedicated channel case. This is because today's channels are already powerful and it simply is a waste of processing power if one channel is to be dedicated to a disk. Therefore, we assume that it is reasonable to make control units intelligent.

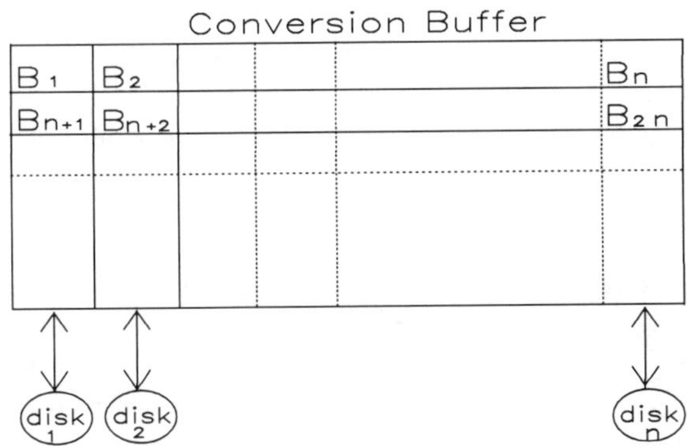

Figure 1. Conversion Buffer

6 A search processor for database management systems that was developed at the Technical University of Braunschweig, Germany [5].

There are several basic tasks that a controller must perform in order to effectively operate synchronized disks. They are conversion, synchronization, and error recovery. ***Conversion*** is necessary in order to assemble parallel data streams coming from the disks into a serial data stream. As shown schematically in Figure 1, a block of data can be read from each disk into each separate column of the conversion buffer. As the buffer is filled, the columns are aligned, or converted, into the rows of a single data stream. As we will see later, this conversion buffer may also be used as a synchronization buffer and, at the same time, as an error correction buffer. (See 2.4 Error Recovery).

2.3 Synchronized Operation for Efficiency and Simplicity

Since adjacent bytes of a record, in byte interleaving, are stored across adjacent disks at the same spot on each disk, the mechanical movement of all disk units may be synchronized. It is advantageous to synchronize interleaved disks so as to simplify control and furthermore to achieve efficiency.

Simplified Control

As the number of disk drives increases, it becomes crucial that the control scheme be simplified. By synchronizing interleaved disks, multiple disks can be treated as if they were a single disk unit. Thus, a group of disks may present a "***Single disk image***", thereby simplifying the control problem significantly.

Efficiency

As more disk units are added, if not done carefully, the performance of the system may suffer significantly from possible interferences. Synchronized operation may simplify this problem greatly, simply because there is no path contention. It is just like running a single device on a dedicated path. Furthermore, if the disks are run asynchronously, independent of each other, the response time of an I/O request will be that of the worst disk rather than that of the average case. That is, the average response time will be = max (all devices). This is because, at any point in time, it is likely that one of the devices will be found at the worst rotational position. ***Expected mechanical delays*** in synchronized systems, however, are those of a single device rather than those of the worst case among the disks.

Synchronization Buffer

A group of disk drives may be put together and run by a single motor in order to synchronize the mechanical movement of disks. Although it seems simple, reliability is a great concern in such a simple coupling. A more reliable solution is to let each disk drive be run by a ***synchronous motor*** and to control a series of synchronous motors by a central clock with a ***feedback control loop***. With such a feedback loop, the speed and rotational position of each disk can be monitored and any necessary adjustment can be made if one of them happens to go out of synchronization.

There is a tolerance in any mechanical synchronization. The expected ***mechanical tolerance*** in disk synchronization is known as $\simeq$ 0.1 percent. This means that, as an example, in order to read out a track full of data from a set of IBM 3380 DASD's, where a track contains 47K bytes, we need to allow 0.1 percent of 47K bytes, or 47 bytes, of buffer space per disk for synchronization. This ***synchronization buffer*** is to accommodate the variance in speed among the disks. The fact that there is a fine mechanical tolerance in coupling the devices directly suggests that the synchronization may only be achieved ***on a block basis***. The size of a block must be determined based on various parameters: disk hardware parameters, reliability requirements, as well as performance requirements. In addition, the size of buffer in the control unit is an important parameter in determining the block size. If there is a large amount of buffer space available, a block can be large, thus cutting down the overhead that is involved in synchronization.

2.4 Error Recovery

Error handling by the controller is an important problem for which a good solution must be found in order to efficiently operate synchronized disks. Work is on the way to design an error correcting scheme that is adequate for interleaved disk systems, and a brief sketch of the scheme is presented in this paper.

In today's disk systems, correction of errors is generally ***deferred***. That is, data is transmitted to the main memory as it is read from the secondary storage, and errors are detected at the end of each read operation. If an error occurs, correction information is calculated by the control unit and the CPU is interrupted so that the error may be corrected in the main memory by the CPU. When the error rate is low, this strategy is reasonable. But, with high error rates, as projected for some future disk systems, the deferred error correction may not be so desirable, since the deferred correction imposes a larger penalty once an error is detected.

We may use the conversion buffer that has been described in 2.3 as an error correction buffer. This means that the same buffer may be used for the purposes of conversion, synchronization, and error correction, and that these three processes may occur concurrently. Among the three, the synchronization requirement will dictate the choice of buffer size.

By having an error correction buffer in the control unit, errors may be corrected "***on-the-fly***" rather than being "deferred". In the conversion buffer, after the columns have been aligned with respect to each other, each row forms a n-byte code-word, as shown schematically in Figure 2. The last n_1 bytes in each code-word are check bytes. Similarly, a group of m bytes in a column forms a m-byte code-word, where m is defined appropriately in order to achieve the block synchronization. The last m_1 bytes in each column-wise code-word are check bytes. The top left corner contains the $(n - n_1) \times (m - m_1)$ information symbols. In encoding, the code-words could be formed by first computing the top $(m - m_1)$ rows or the first $(n - n_1)$ columns. Either approach should give the same code. In decoding, however, column-wise decoding first might be more useful. This is because the decoding may be performed without having to wait for the completion of the conversion process.

The minimum requirements in designing an error correcting scheme for interleaved disks should be such that it detects and corrects ***random single-bit errors***[7] and that it provides recovery of occasional ***massive data loss*** caused by failure of an actuator. The check bytes must provide detection and correction of all single-bit random errors in each code-word, row-wise or column-wise. In the presence of larger errors, caused by an actuator failure, the interaction between the n_1 check bytes and the m_1 check bytes, checks on checks, may provide recovery from such a failure.

Burst errors predominate in magnetic disk storage systems. That is, defects on magnetic recording devices usually affect more than one symbol. Thus, errors occur in bursts. Occasionally, the bursts may come in bursts to complicate the problem further. In order to handle this situation, some combination of error correction, error detection, and request for repeat may be required.

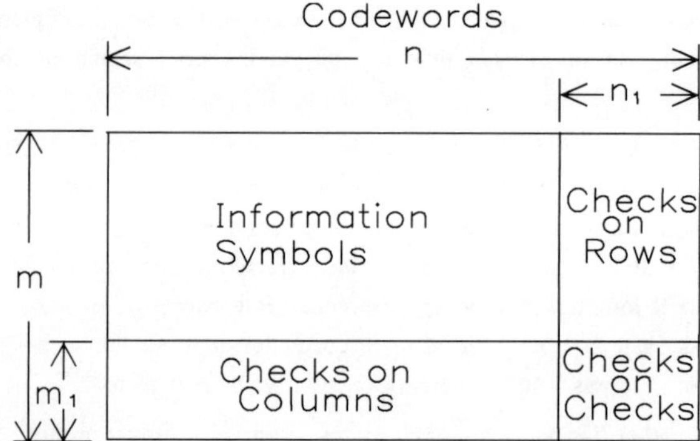

Figure 2. An array of $n \times m$ code-words

3. Modeling Methodology

A method for evaluating the average response time and the queueing models that represent different I/O configurations are described in this section. In order to realistically represent conventional systems, two queueing models are used: one is a hypothetical situation in which I/O requests are uniformly distributed, and the other represents the reality where there is a great skew in disk access. A synchronized disk system is treated as a special case of a conventional system with a single disk.

Throughout this paper, the term "balanced" is used to refer to the conventional, hypothetical situation with uniform distribution of requests, and the term "unbalanced" is used to refer to

[7] Each transmitted bit has a probability p of being received incorrectly and a probability $1 - p$ of being received correctly, independently of other transmitted bits. Hence transmission errors occur ***randomly*** in the received sequence.

the conventional system with a DASD skew. Furthermore, the terms actuator, disk, device, DASD, and spindle may be used interchangeably.

3.1 Evaluating Average I/O Response Time

There are basically three sources of delay in completing an I/O request to a disk device. They are:

Mechanical Delay	The time necessary for mechanical movement, i.e., arm positioning, device rotation, data transfer, etc.
Path Delay	A wait for the transfer path to and from the device to become free
Queueing Delay	A wait for the requested device to become free

The ***mechanical delays*** are those delays that occur at the disk due to the mechanical movement of the rotational disks. These delays, in most cases, dominate the response time of an I/O request. ***Seek*** delay is the time required to position the access mechanism at the cylinder containing the data. As discussed previously in Disk Scheduling in 2.1, deriving the seek time distribution is not straight forward. That is, the seek time is not linearly proportional to the distance the access arms have to travel. Furthermore, empirical studies indicate that the disk arms very often do not move [9]. In large IBM/MVS systems, measurements show that the percentage of disk I/O requests that causes arm movement varies from 30 to 50 percent. This is possible because in IBM/MVS systems disk requests are ordered based on task address spaces rather than seek addresses. Within a task address space, various studies show that the access pattern is generally sequential thus minimizing the arm movement [9]. Rotational ***latency*** is the time required for the correct data or track area of the disk to rotate to the appropriate angular position of the disk so that the data transfer can begin. It can range from zero to a full rotation (revolution) of the disk. Half a rotation is used as the average latency. ***Data transfer*** time is the time required to transfer data between the disk and a memory buffer. It is a function of the rotational speed of the disk and the density the data is recorded on it.

Path delays occur due to contention with other I/O requests for the same path. Two distinct kinds of path related delays are: the delay in starting of requests and the delay due to RPS misses. We consider only the RPS miss delay here because it is usually the greatest in terms of magnitude. The ***Rotational Positioning Sensing*** (RPS) feature allows the rotational positioning of the disk device while disconnected from the channel without incurring channel connection time. While the RPS feature reduces the time that a channel is busy during the search for a record, the penalty is not trivial. If the channel is not free at the time the device is ready, then there is a RPS miss and that causes the device to make a full rotation before it can signal again.

Queueing delay is the time a request has to wait for the disk to become free. This waiting time is an increasing function of load, or request rate.

3.1.1 Obtaining the Basic Service Time

We now define the basic I/O service time as the sum of the delays that occur at the device, that is, seek, latency, data transfer, and the RPS misses. The path delays that occur at the

CPU, for example a wait for an outbound channel, are considered much smaller than the other elements of the service time, thus we neglect them here.

Let

B Average basic service time

S Average seek time

L Average latency time

T Average data transfer time

RPS Average RPS miss delay

Then we have,

$$B = S + L + T + RPS.$$

We assume that the ***average seek time*** does not vary considerably with load and that the ***average latency*** is one half of a device rotation period.

RPS Miss Delay

We now evaluate the RPS miss delay which is the ***principal load dependent*** component of the I/O basic service time.

Let

σ_i be the probability that the reconnection request from $device_i$ is blocked due to channel busy, or the probability of a RPS miss

λ_i be the request rate for $device_i$

The channel is blocked for the request from $device_i$ if any other device is transferring data to the channel. Assuming that a reconnection request "sees" the state of the channel as a random observer, we may write,

$$\sigma_i = \sum_{\substack{j=1 \\ i \neq j}}^{n} \lambda_j \times T \tag{1}$$

where n is the number of devices, and $T = T_j$ for any j, because the time to transfer data is independent of load.

If the request distribution is uniform, in other words, if the system is perfectly balanced,

$$\sigma_i = \sigma_j$$

for any $j = 1, 2, \dots, n$.

Since the requests are equally distributed over the actuators in the balanced system, that is, $\lambda_i = \lambda_j$ for all $j = 1, 2, \dots, n$, the probability of blocking is the same for all devices.

In the unbalanced case, we obtain the request rate for $device_i$

$$\lambda_i = \text{ total number of requests for the channel } \times skew_i \tag{2}$$

where $skew_i$ is the probability that a request goes to $device_i$. The following skew distribution[8] is used to evaluate the request rate on a device in the conventional system given the total number of requests per channel.

Skew Distribution for 8-Actuators (3)

$$skew_1 = .388 \quad skew_2 = .225 \quad skew_3 = .153 \quad skew_4 = .102$$

$$skew_5 = .000 \quad skew_6 = .010 \quad skew_7 = .054 \quad skew_8 = .068$$

Knowing the probability that a request from $device_i$ is blocked, which is also the probability of a RPS miss, and assuming that the number of RPS misses per request is geometrically distributed, we may write,

$$RPS_i = \frac{Rev \times \sigma_i}{1 - \sigma_i} \tag{4}$$

where Rev is the time for a device rotation.

3.1.2 Estimating the Queueing Delay

Having obtained the basic service time, the queueing delay that occurs at the CPU prior to service, can be estimated by treating the devices as separate single server queues.

Assuming that the various phases of the basic service time, seek, latency, RPS miss delay, and the data transfer, are mutually independent; we compute the ***variance of the basic service time***, $Var(B)$.

$$Var(B) = Var(S) + Var(L) + Var(T) + Var(RPS) \tag{5}$$

where $Var(S)$, $Var(L)$, $Var(RPS)$ and $Var(T)$ denote the variance of the seek time, of the latency time, of the missed reconnection delay and of the transfer time, respectively. Since the RPS miss delay is load dependent and we assume that load is unbalanced across devices, we rewrite Equation (5) as

$$Var(B_i) = Var(S) + Var(L) + Var(T) + Var(RPS_i) \tag{5'}$$

We assume that the variance of the seek time is given and the variance of the transfer time is 0. The reason that $Var(T)$ is equal to 0 is that the time for the data transfer is constant, given the amount of data to transfer per request. Latency times are considered to be uniformly distributed between 0 and Rev, the revolution time for the disk. Hence,

$$Var(L) = \frac{Rev^2}{12}$$

Following an assumption that the number of RPS misses per request is geometrically distributed, the variance of the RPS miss delay is therefore

$$Var(RPS_i) = \frac{Rev^2 \times \sigma_i}{(1 - \sigma_i)^2}$$

---

[8] This is actual data collected from a relatively well tuned system.

Knowing the ***first moment*** (mean) and the variance of the service time, we obtain the ***second moment of the service time***,

$$Second(B_i) = Var(B_i) + B_i^2$$

We now evaluate the ***utilization*** of each actuator,

$$\rho_i = \lambda_i \times B_i \tag{6}$$

where λ_i is the request rate computed according to the skew rate as in (3).

Modeling $device_i$ as an M/G/1 queueing system, its ***mean queueing delay*** [12] is

$$Q_i = \frac{\lambda_i \times Second(B_i)}{2 \times (1 - \rho_i)} \tag{7}$$

and its ***response time*** is

$$R_i = Q_i + B_i \tag{8}$$

3.1.3 Weighted Average Response Time

In a balanced system, the R obtained from Equation (8) above is the average response time of an I/O request on all devices. In the unbalanced system, we compute the weighted response time, WR_i for each actuator based on the skew rate.

$$WR_i = R_i \times skew_i$$

And finally the average I/O response time on all connected devices may be obtained by adding up the weighted response times.

$$R = \sum_{i=1}^{n} WR_i$$

3.2 Queueing Models

A number of queueing models that represent different I/O configurations are constructed with the following parameters.

- ***Device parameters*** are set to those of the IBM 3380 DASD's as follows.

Transfer rate	3 megabytes / second
Average seek	7.2 milliseconds
Device rotation	16.6 milliseconds
Latency	8.3 milliseconds

- ***Poisson arrival*** of requests is assumed, and the request rate is varied from light, 10 requests/second/channel, to heavy, 40-70 requests/second/channel.
- ***Service time distribution*** is assumed to be general.
- The ***number of actuators*** that is attached to a control unit ranges between 1 and 16.
- ***Block size*** (the amount of data to transfer) per request varies between 1 page (4096 bytes) and 60 pages (six tracks).

A number of simplifying assumptions is made in constructing the models because the main objective of this study is to understand the relative measures of performance. For example, a non-buffered control unit is considered because the effect of adding a cache to a control unit must be basically the same for either conventional systems or synchronized systems. Dynamic string switching[9] will not be considered for the same reason (See 4.1.1 RPS Miss Delay).

We assume that the peak transfer rate is limited only by the rotational speed of the disks and not by the speed of channels. This seems unrealistic since today's channels certainly have a maximum speed that is not much greater than that of the rotational disks. Rather than repeating the chicken-and-egg question, we decide here not to limit ourselves by the capacity of the channel.

The following disk systems are represented as queueing systems with a simple I/O configuration: one channel, one control unit, and a string of disks.

3.2.1 Unbalanced Conventional Disk System

There is generally a very great skew of access rates to devices, as we have stated previously. This results in an ***uneven utilization of devices***. Only a few devices may be over-utilized while the rest remain idle. Such conventional disk systems may be modeled as in Figure 3.

Given the total request rate for a channel, the request rate for each device may be derived using the skew distribution as discussed earlier. As a request arrives, it is queued to a device queue probabilistically and the request is served by a single server(disk). In other words, each disk is modeled as a single server system.

In this system, the disks are ***multiplexed***, meaning that the data transfer may occur for one disk at a time. However, other delays such as seek, latency, and RPS misses may ***overlap*** between the disks.

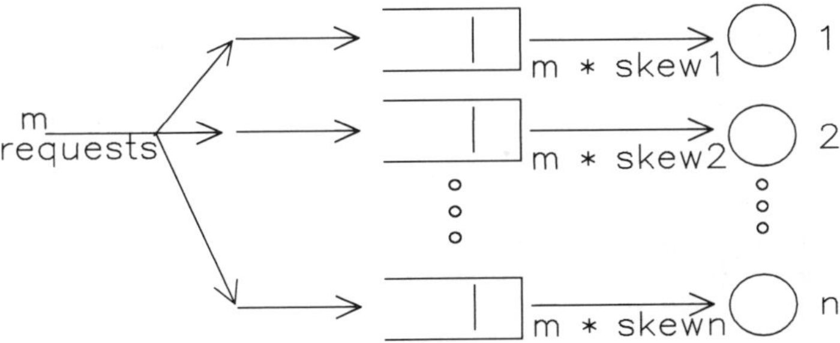

Figure 3. Non-uniform Conventional System

[9] On certain DASD's, a switch can be installed at the string level. Dynamic string switch establishes a connection through the electronic switch between a control unit and the string under program control.

3.2.2 Balanced Conventional Disk System

Although it is ideal to have a balanced system, generally no attempt is made to "perfectly" balance devices, because the skew is time-varying and extremely complex in nature. This hypothetical I/O system may be represented as a queueing model as in Figure 4. As shown in the figure, arriving requests are distributed over the devices with equal probability, therefore the devices are ***equally utilized***.

As in the unbalanced system, the data transfer may occur for one disk at a time while other delays may overlap between the disks. Furthermore, each device is considered as a single server queue. In order to study the adverse impact of the skew, the performance of this system is compared to the unbalanced case (See 4. The Impact of DASD skew).

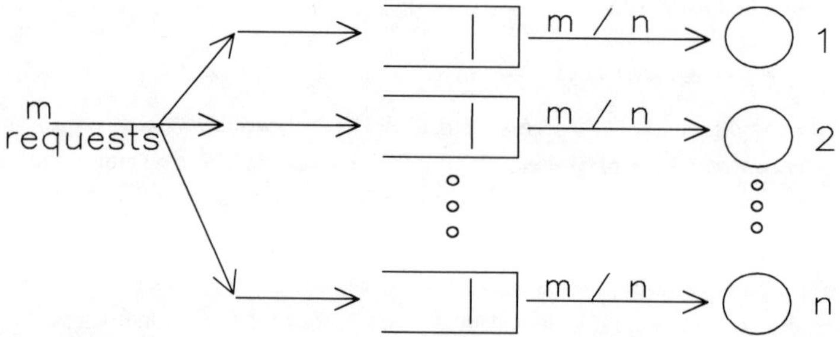

Figure 4. Uniform Conventional System

3.2.3 Synchronized Disk System

A synchronized disk system is modeled as a special case of conventional systems. A conventional ***single disk*** system is shown in Figure 5, and a synchronized disk system is represented as a queueing model in Figure 6. The difference between the two is the data transfer time. In synchronized systems, the ***data transfer time*** is reduced by a factor of 1/n compared to a single disk system.

There is a single device queue in a synchronized system. A request is served, however, by all of the disks. This means that the request rate for each disk is the same as the total number of requests. Also, in this system, mean seek time and mean latency are those of a single device rather than those of the worst disk.

Note that there are ***no RPS misses*** in this system, because each request is served by all of the disks as if they were a single disk. Naturally, when there is only one user, there is no contention for a path, and hence no RPS misses.

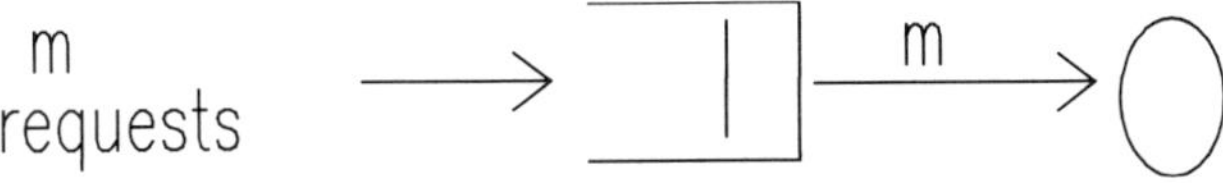

Figure 5. Single Disk System

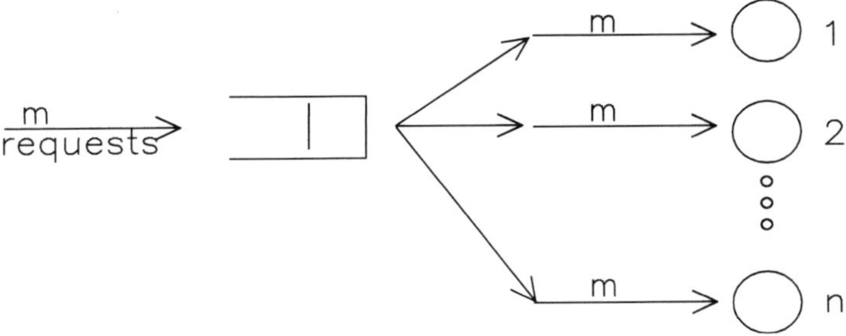

Figure 6. Synchronized Disk System

4. Numerical Results and Comparisons

In this section, the results of analytic modeling are presented. Various performance measures of the synchronized systems are compared to those of conventional systems, and the advantages and limitations of each system are analyzed. Before we attempt a comparative analysis, it is important that we understand the performance implications, in conventional systems, that result from added devices and the DASD skew.

The Effects of Adding More Actuators

Performance may be improved by adding more actuators while keeping the total storage constant. That is, by adding more actuators, the storage capacity per actuator may be reduced, and therefore, the ***average seek time*** may be reduced per request. Furthermore, the ***queueing delay*** may be decreased, simply because the same number of requests can be spread across more actuators. Since each actuator is modeled as a single server queue, added actuators may imply added queues, thus cutting down the average wait time in a queue. However, adding more actuators may imply ***more RPS misses***. This means that a reduced queueing delay may be counterbalanced by an increased RPS miss delay. In this paper, actuators are modeled with the same average seek time regardless of how many there are. Therefore, only the queueing delay and its counterbalancing RPS miss delay are encountered here as results of adding more actuators.

It has been shown [21] that, as more devices are added, performance improves to the point where further increases of devices can no longer be cost justified. Deciding the ***optimal number***

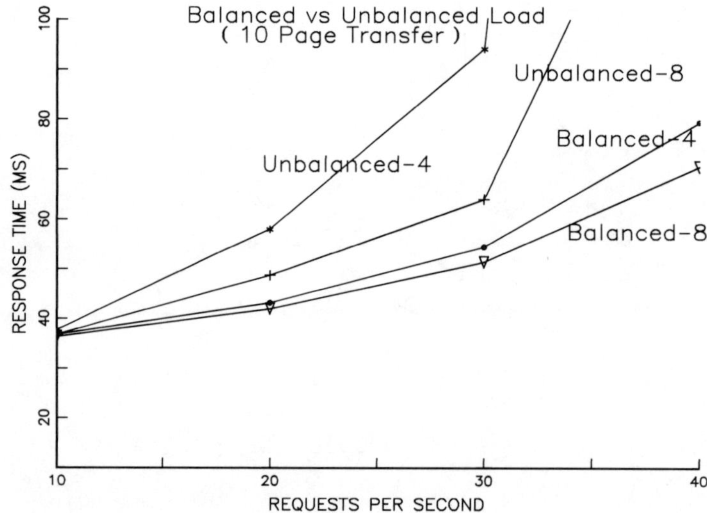

Figure 7. Impact of DASD Skew: Conventional Unbalanced Systems vs Balanced Systems for 10 Page Transfers

of actuators on a given system, is a complex task. Among others, the two most important criteria for this task should be the ***specified performance*** level and the ***cost*** consideration. A rigorous justification of such optimality is beyond the scope of this paper. Nevertheless, to simplify further discussion, we elect the ***8-actuator*** system as the "optimal" one for short block transfers (1 to 10 pages).[10] It is important to note that as the block size changes, the optimal number of actuators will change, to a larger number for larger block transfers. A detailed analysis of the effects of adding more actuators can be found in [21].

The Impact of DASD Skew

The adverse impact of DASD skew in the performance of the ***conventional systems*** is analyzed by comparing balanced systems to unbalanced systems. In both situations, the devices operate in a conventional multiplexed fashion. The average response times in both conventional systems with 4 and 8 actuators are plotted in Figure 7 for 10 page transfers.

We observe that, at the request rate of 30, the response time is increased from 54 milliseconds in the balanced-4 case to 94 milliseconds in the unbalanced-4 case, or 74 percent, as a result of the skew. It has been shown [21] that, with short block transfers, the impact due to the skew was not as severe as seen here. That is, an increase in the block size results in an increase in the impact of the DASD skew.

---

[10] In the synchronized system, the 8-actuator system can also be found to be "optimal".

4.1 Comparative Analysis

Synchronized systems differ from the conventional systems in that the former treat multiple devices as if they were a single device while the latter operate in a multiplexed mode. Synchronized systems have performance advantages over conventional systems in that they automatically provide the uniform access of disks, and that the time required for data transfer can be reduced by a factor of 1/n. Various performance measures of the synchronized systems are compared to those of conventional systems, and the advantages and the limitations of each system are discussed. Basic service times are examined first and the throughput rate of the devices as well as the peak transfer rate for both systems are derived using the basic service time distribution. The mean queueing delays are analyzed and the mean response times are compared between the two systems.

4.1.1 Basic Service Time

As discussed previously, basic service time consists of seek, latency, RPS miss, and the data transfer time. It is intuitively clear that the advantages of the synchronized systems are that there are no RPS misses and that the data transfer time is only a fraction of the time that is required of the conventional system. Conventional systems, however, benefit from the fact that seek, latency, and RPS misses may overlap.

RPS Miss Delay

RPS miss delay is an increasing function of ***load*** as well as of ***block size*** in the conventional multiplexed systems. As the number of I/O requests increases, the probability of a RPS miss increases (See Section 3.1). As ***block size*** increases, the RPS miss delay also increases. Furthermore, as more devices are added, the probability of a miss again goes up. In other words, the performance of conventional systems may suffer significantly from this RPS miss delay. A detailed analysis of the RPS miss delay can be found in [21].

There are no RPS misses in a synchronized system because it may be treated as a single disk system with a dedicated path. With multiple strings of disks, however, there will be RPS misses due to the string contention, even in the synchronized systems. This string contention will have the same effect on the performance of the conventional system. In the conventional system, with multiple strings of disks, the probability of a RPS miss will be larger than in a single string case simply because the contention will be greater by adding more devices (Assuming that there is a fixed number of devices on each string). Thus we can conclude that the added RPS miss delay as a result of adding multiple strings of disks will be similar between the two, and that the RPS delay that is evaluated here in a single string case can be safely added to the other delays of the conventional system without losing generality.

Average Basic Service Time

The average basic service time of a request may be obtained by adding up the weighted averages of the basic service times on all of the connected devices.

In Figure 8, the average service times, as well as (1 / requests), are plotted as a function of request rate for 1 and 10 page transfers in both conventional and synchronized systems. The number of devices is set to 8 as discussed previously. The curve (1 / requests) is plotted in order to derive the device throughput rate which is described later.

In synchronized systems, the service times for 1 page transfers and 10 page transfers do not vary significantly. The time required for a 1 page transfer, if the page is read serially from a device, is 1.6 milliseconds, and the time for a 10 page transfer is 16 milliseconds. When they are read from 8-synchronized disks, it takes (1.6/8) milliseconds and (16/8) milliseconds respectively, giving a difference of less than 2 milliseconds. Note that there is no load dependent component in the basic service times in the synchronized systems as shown in the figure.

Unbalanced systems suffer from RPS misses with large block transfers as discussed previously. The data transfer times for 1 and 10 page transfers are 1.6 ms and 16 ms respectively, giving a difference of 14.4 ms that is no longer a trivial portion of the service time.

At the request rate of 30 for 1 page transfers, the average service time in a conventional system is 21 milliseconds, and that in a synchronized system is 16 milliseconds, giving an improvement of 24 percent. At the same request rate of 30 for 10 page transfers, the improvement is from 50 milliseconds to 18 milliseconds, or 64 percent.

The service time, as a function of the request rate λ, is the sum of the delays that occur at the device. Therefore we can derive a few important performance measures that are determined by the service rate of the device. They are the ***throughput*** and the ***peak transfer rate*** of the device.

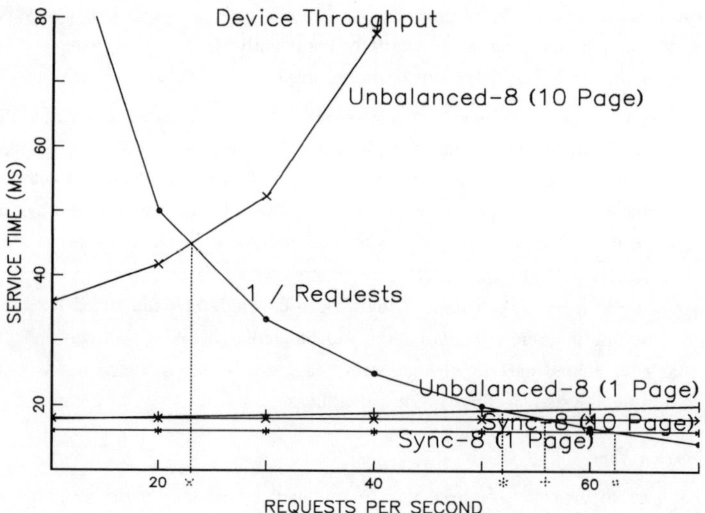

Figure 8. Basic Service Time and Device Throughput

4.1.2 Device Throughput

We now compute the ***average service rate***, the average number of requests that are completed per second, μ, of each system as a function of the total request rate, λ.

$$\mu = \frac{1}{B}, \quad B = f(\lambda), \quad B \text{ is the basic service time.}$$

If the request rate is greater than the service rate then there is a finite probability that the device queue may grow infinitely. That is, queueing systems that receive input faster than the server can process it are inherently unstable, and their queues grow without bound. Therefore, we want to have $\lambda < \mu$.

The throughput, the average number of requests completed per second, is then $\min\{\lambda, \mu\}$. This means that the throughput is equivalent to the request rate λ, as long as λ is less than the maximum service rate μ, beyond which the throughput is saturated at the value of μ. Then λ^*, at which the throughput is saturated may be derived numerically as follows.

$$\lambda^* = \mu = \frac{1}{B}, \quad B = f(\lambda^*), \quad \frac{1}{\lambda^*} = B.$$

In the synchronized system, the throughput of devices may be derived as shown above. The request distribution is uniform in such a system, and therefore the average service time distribution for a request is uniform across all of the disks. In the unbalanced system, however, the average service rate, μ, may no longer be used to derive the throughput rate. Since the request distribution across actuators in such a system is not uniform, the average service times vary considerably between the actuators. If any one of the devices has a probability that its queue may grow infinitely, then the system throughput rate is determined by that device. Thus, we want to find out the request rate at which the worst case device is saturated rather than the request rate at which the average case device is saturated.

Let

B_i be the average basic service time on $device_i$

Then, $\frac{1}{B_i} = \mu_i$

where μ_i is the average service rate of $device_i$ given λ_i where $\lambda_i = \lambda \times skew_i$,

We want to make sure that $\lambda < \mu_i$.

Since we are interested in the worst case device that has the smallest average service rate, or the largest average service time, we may derive λ^* at which the throughput is saturated as follows:

$$\lambda^* = \min(\mu_i) = \min(\frac{1}{B_i}) = \frac{1}{\max(B_i)}$$

Thus,

$$\frac{1}{\lambda^*} = \max(B_i)$$

where max (B_i) is the worst case average service time by which the system throughput is limited.

We can use a graphical construct to approximate the device throughput. The plot $(1/\lambda)$ versus the total request rate may be superimposed upon the average service times in the synchronized system and the worst case service times in the conventional system, as shown in Figure 8. The intersections of these sets of curves yield the saturation points for each system.

With 1 page transfers, synchronized disks are saturated at the rate of approximately 62 requests, conventional devices at $\simeq$ 52 requests per second; and with 10 page transfers, synchronized disks at $\simeq$ 56 requests and conventional devices at $\simeq$ 23 requests per second. Each intersection is identified by the symbols $^\circ$, *, +, and $\times$, respectively in the figure.

Note that the device saturation point in the unbalanced system is very low with large block transfers, while that of the synchronized system shows a considerable improvement, an increase of 61 percent in throughput.

4.1.3 Peak Transfer Rate

We have set the device parameters at a 3 megabyte per second transfer rate. No matter how effectively we operate the devices we cannot achieve a transfer rate of greater than 3 megabytes/second from a device.

In fact, the effective transfer rate is far smaller than the theoretical maximum, because there are delays in the service time that do not contribute to data transfers.

The peak transfer rate that can be effectively achieved may be obtained from the λ^* derived previously. That is,

$$\text{Peak transfer rate} = \lambda^* \times \text{Block size}.$$

For 1 page transfers:

Synchronized system 62 × 1 page (4K bytes) = 248K bytes/second.
Conventional system 52 × 1 page (4K bytes) = 208K bytes/second.

And for 10 page transfers:

Synchronized system 56 × 10 page (40K bytes) = 2,240K bytes/second.
Conventional system 23 × 10 page (40K bytes) = 920K bytes/second.

Note that the rates above are the total transfer rates on all connected devices, 8 disks in our study. In the worst case, as in the conventional system for 1 page transfers, the effective peak transfer rate per disk is (208K / 8), or 26K bytes, while the maximum rate is two orders of magnitude greater. It is clear that we are better off with larger block transfers. By increasing the block size from 1 to 10 pages, the peak transfer rate is increased by a factor of 4 in the conventional system, and by a factor of 9 in the synchronized system. Although in the best case, as in the synchronized systems for 10 page transfers, the improvement is substantial, almost by an order of magnitude compared to the worst case, the rate is still a long way from the theoretical maximum rate. This wide gap may be narrowed down by further increasing block size and by carefully adding more devices (See 4.1.6).

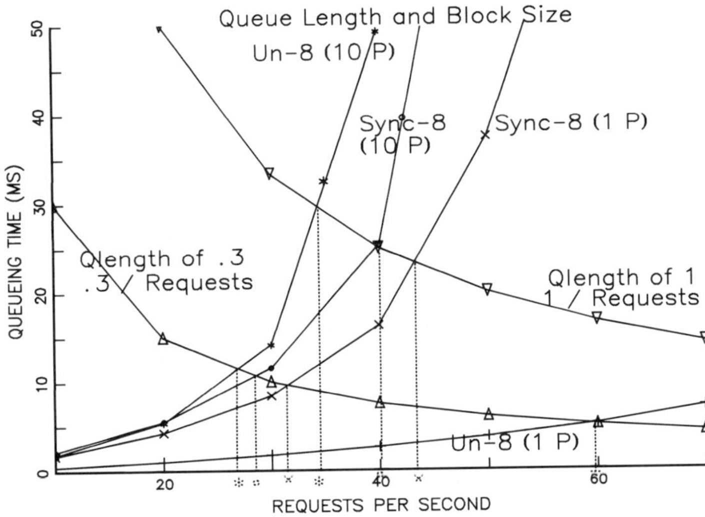

Figure 9. Queueing Delay and Queue Length

Although the rate may be increased greatly with the transfer of larger blocks, it is still far lower than the maximum transfer rate that can be achieved on a device.

As the block size changes to 20, 40, or 60 pages, the peak transfer rate increases further. This will be examined in Section 4.1.6 (What Happens with Increased Block Size ?).

4.1.4 Queueing Delay

The mean queueing delay for a request on $device_i$ may be estimated as in Equation (7) in 3.1.2. The average queueing delay on a system may be obtained by adding up the weighted averages of the queueing delays on all of the connected devices.

In Figure 9, the average queueing times in both conventional systems and synchronized systems are plotted against the request rates to the channel with varying block sizes. Two curves, (1/Requests) and (.3/Requests) are also plotted to derive the request rates at which the queue length becomes 1 and .3 respectively. This will be further discussed in Queue Length.

We observe that with short block transfers (i.e. 1 page), the synchronized system suffers from the queueing delay significantly, while it is hardly noticeable in the conventional system. With larger block transfers (i.e. 10 pages), however, the synchronized system suffers less from the queueing delay than the conventional system does.

The queueing delay is an increasing function of request rate, service time, and device utilization. In synchronized systems, the service times are relatively small due to the reduced data transfer time, while the device utilization factors are generally high. With the transfer of small blocks, the utilization of the synchronized devices is particularly high. From Equation (6) in 3.1.2, the utilization of a device is

$$\rho_i = \lambda_i \times B_i$$

The number of requests that each synchronized device serves is λ, which is the same as the total request rate to the channel, rather than a fraction of it as in the conventional system. The fact that each device has to respond to every I/O request, and that the reduction in the service time is not as great for short block transfers, causes the synchronized devices to be heavily utilized. Hence, the queueing delay is high for short block transfers. However, for larger block transfers, the opposite effect takes place. The reduction in the basic service time is no longer trivial in the synchronized systems, while the conventional systems suffer significantly from DASD skew as a result of increasing the block size as discussed in The Impact of DASD Skew.

Device Utilization

In Figure 10, the device utilization factors are plotted against the total request rate. For the conventional systems, the average device utilization factors are plotted as well as the worst case situation. In the conventional systems, since the requests are not evenly distributed among devices, the device utilization is not uniform, while the devices are equally utilized in the synchronized systems. The average utilization factors in the conventional systems are derived using the ***sum of the weighted average utilization*** technique.

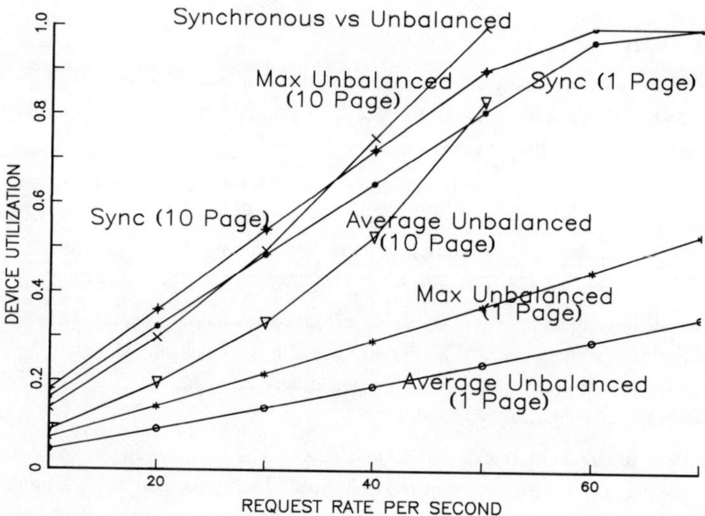

Figure 10. Device Utilization

With small block transfers, the synchronized systems approach 100 percent utilization at the request rate of 60, while the conventional systems, even in the worst case, stay below the 45 percent utilization mark at the same request rate.

It is important to observe that in the conventional systems, the average device throughput reaches its saturation while most of the devices are less than fully utilized. See Figure 8, which shows that the device saturation point for 1 page transfers is approximately 52 requests per second. On the other hand, in Figure 10, we see that even the worst case device utilization is below 45 percent at the same request rate. This means that the devices are not fully utilized in the conventional systems and that the device saturation occurs while the average utilization factors of the devices are still low.

Large block transfers, on the other hand, narrows the gap between the two systems in utilization. At the request rate of 40, a crossover occurs between the two, because the data transfer time plays a key role in this situation. With large block transfers, even though the synchronized system responds to every request, its queuing delay is not as severe as in the conventional system. This is mainly due to the significant reduction in its service time.

Queue Length

Using Little's theorem, the average queue length may be obtained. That is, $L = \lambda \times Q$, where L represents the average queue length, and Q the mean waiting time in queue. As we have discussed in Disk Scheduling in 2.1, it has been known that the average queue length in conventional systems hardly exceeds the length of 1. The request rates at which the queue length for each system becomes 0.3 and 1 may be obtained using a graphical construct as follows.

For $L = 1$, $1 = \lambda^\circ Q$, then $\dfrac{1}{\lambda^\circ} = Q$.

For $L = 0.3$, $\dfrac{0.3}{\lambda^\circ} = Q$.

In Figure 9, two curves, $(1/\lambda)$ and $(0.3/\lambda)$, are superimposed upon the average queueing times. The intersections of these sets of curves yield the request rates at which the average queue length becomes 0.3 and 1 in each system.

In the conventional system with small block transfers, the queue length is only 0.3 at the rate of 60 requests per second. Note that the same system, as we have seen in 4.1.2, has reached device saturation at the rate of 52. That is, device saturation in the conventional system occurs before the average queue length reaches 0.3. With larger block transfers, the result is similar: device saturation occurs at 23, and the queue length is less than 0.3 as shown in the figure. This suggests that the disk scheduling techniques as described in the literature would hardly improve the situation in conventional systems. If not many requests have been queued, it does not make a lot of sense to order them according to their seek addresses.

In the synchronized systems, however, the queue length becomes greater than 1 before the devices get saturated. Provided that the initial acceleration time of the access mechanism (see Disk Scheduling) improves further, there seems to be an application for the seek scheduling techniques.

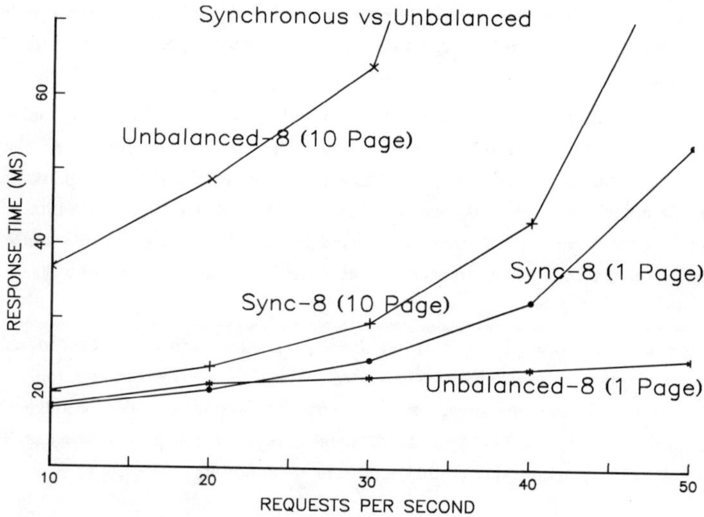

Figure 11. Response Time

4.1.5 Weighted Average Response Time

Having analyzed the two components, the basic service time and the queueing delay, of the average response time, we now put them together in Figure 11. For small block transfers, the synchronized system actually delivers a 1 page block slower than the conventional system does when the request rate is greater than $\simeq$ 25.

This is because the queueing delay on the synchronized system for small block transfers simply predominates response time as discussed previously. For larger block transfers, the synchronized system outperforms the conventional system by a big margin. This is possible because there is a significant reduction in the data transfer time and also there are no RPS misses in synchronized systems, while conventional systems suffer greatly from the RPS miss delays and the queueing delays.

4.1.6 What happens with increased block size ?

So far, we have considered 1 page and 10 page transfers. We will explore briefly the situations where the block size exceeds 10 pages in this section. The block sizes that are used are 20, 40, and 60 pages and the number of devices is still set to 8.

Basic Service Time and Throughput

The basic service times are plotted with $(1/\lambda)$ against the low request rates, less than 20 requests per second, in Figure 12. As in 4.1.2 Device Throughput, each intersection of the curves yields the device saturation point, or the device throughput, for each system. As shown in the figure, the synchronized systems do not intersect with $(1/\lambda)$ at the request rates lower than 20.

On the other hand, the conventional systems cross $(1/\lambda)$ approximately at 15 requests per second for 20 page transfers, at $\simeq$ 9 requests for 40 page, and at $\simeq$ 6.5 requests for 60 page transfers. This means that in the conventional systems, the device saturation is the limiting factor for large block transfers.

The basic service times and the throughput at the high request rates, greater than 20, are plotted in Figure 13. Here, the conventional systems do not appear at all because they have been saturated already well before the request rate reached 20. The synchronized systems intersect with $(1/\lambda)$ at approximately 36, 42, and 50 requests per second giving the device throughput rate for 60, 40, and 20 page transfers, respectively.

We now evaluate the peak transfer rate for each case.

For 20 page transfers:

Synchronized system 50 × 20 pages = 4,000K bytes/second.
Conventional system 15 × 20 pages = 1,200K bytes/second.

For 40 page transfers:

Synchronized system 42 × 40 pages = 6,640K bytes/second.
Conventional system 9 × 40 pages = 1,440K bytes/second.

And for 60 page transfers:

Synchronized system 36 × 60 pages = 8,640K bytes/second.

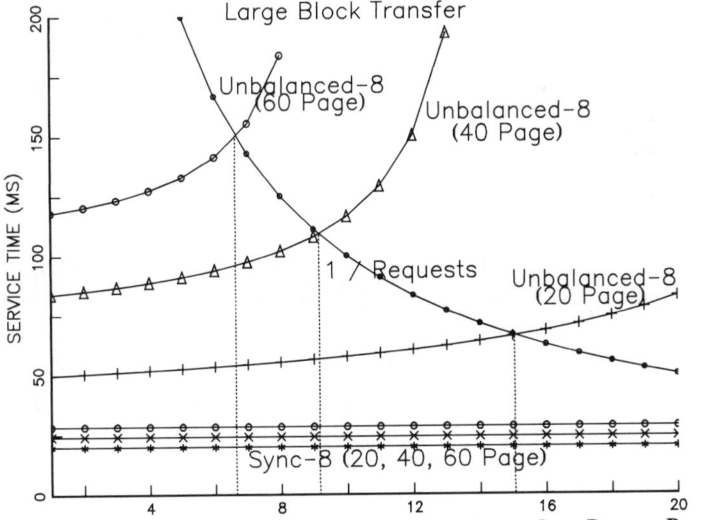

Figure 12. Device Throughput: Large Block Transfers at Low Request Rates

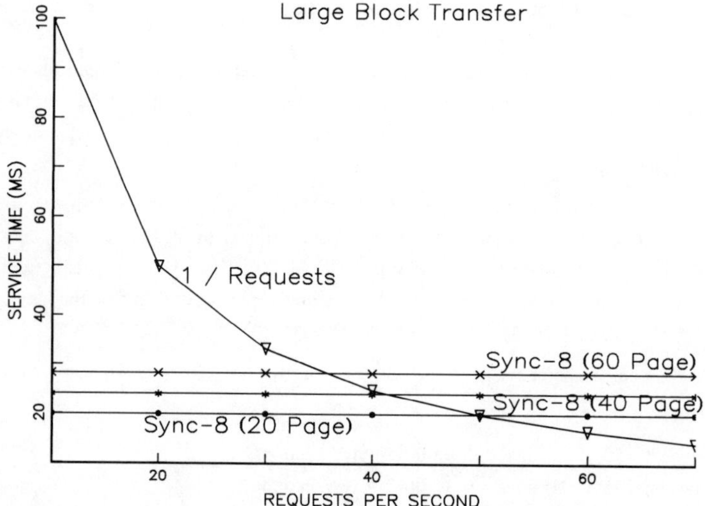

Figure 13. Device Throughput: Large Block Transfers at High Request Rates

Conventional system 6.5 × 60 pages = 1,560K bytes/second.

By increasing the block size from 10 to 20 pages (see Figure 8, for the 10 page case) in the conventional system, the peak throughput rate is increased from 920K bytes to 1200K bytes, or by 30 percent; and in the synchronized system the increase is even greater, 82 percent. By increasing the block size further from 20 to 40 pages in the synchronized system, the increase is 66 percent, and from 40 to 60 pages there is a 30 percent increase in the peak transfer rate, while the conventional systems show only negligible improvements. Note the changes in the growth rate in the synchronized systems: by a factor of 9,[11] by 82 percent, by 66 percent, and by 30 percent. It suggests that additional devices may help to further increase the device throughput when the block size exceeds 10 pages.

Average Response Time

The average response times are plotted against the request rate per second for 20, 40, and 60 page transfers in Figure 14. With added queueing delay, the response times in the synchronized systems are now load dependent. At the request rate of 20 in the conventional system, 20 pages may be returned after 85 milliseconds. In the synchronized system, the rate is 20 pages after 25 millisecond, 40 pages after 35 milliseconds, and 60 pages after 48 milliseconds.

In other words, the synchronized system may deliver ***a block 3 times larger in half the time*** compared to the conventional system. Again, by increasing the number of devices, the synchronized system may show even greater improvement over the conventional system.

---

[11] This increase is achieved by changing the block size from 1 to 10 pages.

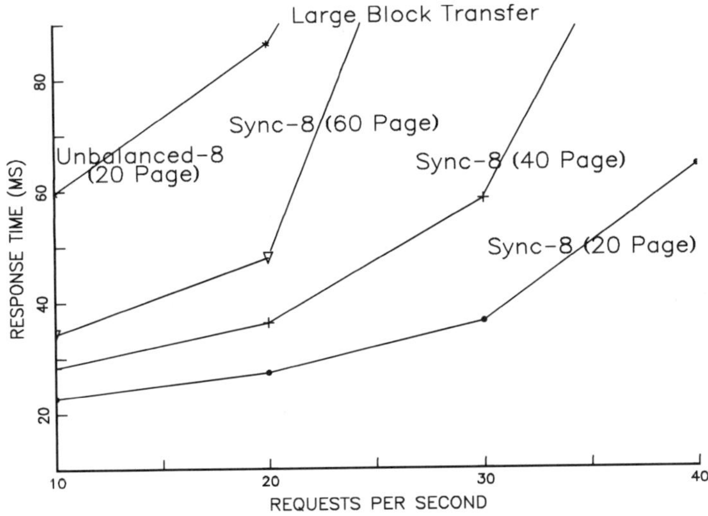

Figure 14. Average Response Time: Large Block Transfers At High Request Rates

5. Conclusions

The most distinct advantages of synchronized disk interleaving may be summarized as follows:

- ***Simplified control***
    - ***Single logical image*** of interleaved disks
- Improved ***performance***
    - ***Parallelism*** through ***interleaving***
    - ***Uniform distribution*** of I/O requests over the disks
- Improved ***Reliability***

Simplified Control: Assuming that there is a need to put multiple devices together for more storage, we argue that disk interleaving is a novel mechanism to achieve such coupling. By synchronizing the mechanical movement of the disks, parallelism may be achieved without complicating the control. Furthermore, a group of disks may present an image of a single virtual disk.

Improved Performance: By byte-parallel distribution of data across the disks, we claim that the ***access distribution is uniform***. By interleaving disks, ***parallelism*** may be achieved, cutting down the data transfer time by a factor of 1/n. By synchronized movement, the disks may be treated as if they were a single disk, cutting down the ***expected mechanical delays*** such as seek and latency to those of a single disk rather than raising them to those of the worst case disk.

Interleaving works best for the transfer of ***large blocks***. The synchronized systems have a potential for increasing the peak transfer rate significantly. The maximum amount of data that can be read per request, without moving the access mechanisms of the disks, is 1-cylinder in the conventional system, and n-cylinders in the synchronized system.[1] In other words, the synchronized systems, in theory, may be able to transfer data from n-cylinders in 1-cylinder time. If load can be kept appropriate, the queueing delay may also be kept under control.

Improved Reliability: By placing checksums on separate checksum disks and providing adequate error correcting codes, it is possible to detect and correct random single-bit errors as well as occasional massive data loss caused by failure of a disk. Errors may be corrected "on-the-fly" with the use of an error correction buffer in the control unit.

Applications

We have modeled simple block transfers and studied the performance characteristics of interleaving for such tasks. As we have seen, the high bandwidth potential of interleaving can be exploited most efficiently with large block transfers. There are many applications that reference large address spaces and require huge block transfers. Paging is one such example. Database management systems, as another example, often require the entire database to be scanned. Possible uses of interleaved disks for such applications are briefly described next. In addition, the interleaving is suggested as a novel disk coupling mechanism for small disks.

Paging: Paging is often viewed as the most frequent contributor to poor performance in today's virtual operating systems. Interleaved disks may be used as paging media, improving the performance of demand paging.

Towards Backend Database Machines: We have presented disk interleaving with the help of an intelligent controller. While we are at it, low-level database management functions may be off-loaded to the control unit, thus giving, in effect, a backend database machine. Database machines can certainly benefit from the parallelism and the simple control structure provided by the interleaving. Some primitive database functions, such as search, sort/merge, garbage collection, etc, may be effectively performed in such an environment. Other possibilities include the semantic paging notion [20], in which AI data may be stored in the secondary storage directly in semantic networks. This will allow us to incorporate techniques like inferencing that have been developed for artificial intelligence (AI) into an existing database management system. This may be possible by tailoring the granularity of interleaving to a level that is useful for a specific application. This is a hard problem just like the problems of designing files or the problems of clustering in database systems. Nonetheless, we claim that the synchronized disk interleaving technique offers the potential of approaching the problem in a new light, and

---

1 Of course, when the switch is made from one track to the next, there is a small delay associated with head selection. Since the delay is electronic rather than mechanical we ignore it here.

that it may provide the opportunity for the design of a highly parallel, high speed database machine.

Small Disks for Large: Interleaved disks may also provide the capacity of a large complex disk system using a group of small disks. Small disks, either in diameter or in capacity, may have advantages over very large complex disks in that the average seek time may be reduced by reducing the storage capacity per actuator, that they can be made more reliable,[2] and that small disks may spin faster, thereby reducing latency, etc.

However, a concern is that, as we have mentioned previously, the ***cost of moving arms*** dominates the cost of a disk system. If what we claim here is that we can achieve the equivalent performance of a complex 1-actuator system by an n-actuator system, that does not appear very cost effective. However, we may define "cost" as a compounded function, as a function of hardware cost, of system cost, of performance measures, of reliability measures, and so on. It is no longer clear that the cost of multiple small disks will be higher than that of a large disk with equivalent capacity. In fact, the actuators for physically small disks may be lighter and cheaper than those of larger ones implying that the cost of actuators for small multiple disks is not necessarily a linearly increasing function of the number of actuators. Furthermore, maintenance, assembly, and test may be easier with small disks than with larger ones. The point is that small disks are attractive not only for microprocessors, but also for high end machines. That is, if a novel approach can be found that puts them together in a cost effective way.

Acknowledgements

The author is indebted to T. Bashkow, A. Tantawi, A. Patel, A. Nigam, and P. Franaszek for their many valuable suggestions.

Bibliography

1. Boral, H., DeWitt, D. J., "Database Machines: An Idea Whose Time Has Passed? A Critique of the Future of Database Machines." Database Machines, Springer-Verlag, 1983.
2. Agrawal, R., DeWitt, D. J., "Whither Hundreds of Processors in a DataBase Machine ?." Proc. of International Workshop on High-Level Language Computer Architecture, 1984.
3. Kerr, D., "DataBase Machines with Large Content Addressable Blocks and Structural Information Processors.", Computer 12, 3, March 1979, 64-80.
4. Hsiao D., "Data Base Computers.", Advances in Computers Vol. 19, 1980.
5. Leilich, H., Stiege, G., and Zeidler, H., "A Search Processor for Data Base Management Systems." Proc. Fourth Very Large Data Base Conf., IEEE, 1978, 280-287.
6. Brandwajn. A., "Models of DASD Subsystems with Multiple Access Paths: A Throughput-Driven Approach." IEEE Transactions on Computers, 32, 5, May 1983, 451-463.

---

[2] It is relatively easier to make surfaces of small disks better, thus making them more reliable.

7. Shultz, R., and Zingg, R., "Response Time Analysis of Multiprocessor Computer for Database Support." ACM Transactions on Database Systems, Vol 9 No 1, March 1984.

8. Brandwajn. A., "A Study of Dynamic Reconnection.", Technical Report, Amdahl, Feb.,1983.

9. Hunter, D., "Modeling Real DASD Configurations.", Computer Science Research Report RC8606, IBM, Dec. 1980.

10. Hunter, D., "The Access Time Myth." Computer Science Research Report RC10197, IBM, Sept. 1983.

11. Tantawi, A., "A Look at DASD Modeling.", IBM T. J. Watson Research Center, March 1984.

12. Kobayashi, H., "Modeling and Analysis: An Introduction to System Performance Evaluation Methodology.", Addison-Wesley, 1978.

13. Bohl, M., "Introduction to IBM Direct Access Storage Devices.", Science Research Associates, Inc., 1981.

14. White, R., "Magnetic disks: storage densities on the Riseices.", IEEE Spectrum, August 1983.

15. Manuel, T., "The Push to Smaller, Denser Disk Drives.", Electronics, April 1982.

16. Patel, A., "Error and Failure-Control for a Large-size Bubble Memory.", IEEE Transactions on Magnetics, Vol. MAG-18, No. 6, November 1982.

17. Denning, P., "Effects of Scheduling on File Memory Operations.", Proc. AFIPS 1967 Spring Joint Comp. Conf., 30, AFIPS Press, 1967.

18. Lin, S., Costello, D., "Error Control Coding: Fundamentals and applications.", Prentice-Hall, 1983.

19. Macwilliams, F.J., Sloane, N.J.A., "The Theory of Error Correcting Codes.", North-Holland, 1977.

20. Lipovski, G.J., "Semantic Paging on Intelligent Disks.", Proc. 4th Workshop on Computer Architecture for Non-Numeric Processing, 1978.

21. Kim, M.Y., "Synchronized Disk Interleaving" Computer Science Research Report RC10906, IBM, Nov. 1984.

A PARALLEL MULTI-STAGE I/O ARCHITECTURE WITH SELF-MANAGING DISK CACHE FOR DATABASE MANAGEMENT APPLICATIONS

J. C. Browne, A. G. Dale, C. Leung
Department of Computer Sciences
R. Jenevein
Department of Electrical and Computer Engineering
The University of Texas at Austin
Austin, Texas 78712

Abstract

This paper first defines and describes a highly parallel external data handling system and then shows how the capabilities of the system can be used to implement a high performance relational data base machine. The elements of the system architecture are

- an interconnection network which implements both packet routing and circuit switching and which implements data organization functions such as indexing and sort/merge

and

- an intelligent memory unit with a self-managing cache which implements associative search and capabilities for application of filtering operations on data streaming to and from storage.

Relational data base operations are implemented in highly parallel form by selection of appropriate functionalities for the switch nodes and memory/network intelligent interface.

1. INTRODUCTION AND SYSTEM OVERVIEW

Parallel structuring of input/output processing is essential for the system architectures of future generations of very high performance computers for all types of applications. The speed of external storage devices has not kept pace with the increase in speed of processing elements. Parallel structuring of indexing, data transfer, search, sort and filtering operations in the I/O subsystem provides one strategy for dealing with this mis-match. Many proposed parallel architectures have disjoint immediate address spaces for their computers but will require access to a common external storage system. Connection of the processors to the external storage system by an intelligent interconnection switch can effectively accomplish this integration. The benefits to application programs of utilizing a structured view of data is increasing the demand for high performance data base system services. External storage systems should be designed to incorporate effective parallel formulations of data base system functions.

We are currently studying a parallel I/O engine architecture designed to serve multiprocessor configurations of varied topology and style. The architecture realizes effective parallel structuring of data base functions in hardware. The conceptual elements of this architecture are:

- an interconnection network which couples processors to external memories. The nodes of the network incorporate functionality for indexing (via packet routing) in the processor to memory direction and operation specific functions in the memory to processor direction. The network will also implement circuits coupling processors to memory elements as an extension of processor address space.

- memory elements. Each memory element has three components: (i) a bulk storage system, (ii) an intelligent self-managing object-oriented cache memory and (iii) an intelligent network interface. The bulk storage system may be magnetic or optical disks. The self-managing cache implements parallel associative searching for objects and memory management functions such as allocation and garbage collection. The intelligent network interface implements filtering and selection operations on data streamed to and from the memory element.

This architecture gives highly parallel structuring of the entire spectrum of data handling functions. Parallelism in transfer operations can be obtained by one or more processors driving many external memories simultaneously through the network. Parallelism in search and memory management functions such as garbage collection are given within each memory by the self-managing cache units. Parallel execution of index and data model specific operations is accomplished by incorporation of functionality in the switch nodes and intelligent memory interfaces to the network. Incorporation of indexing as a hardware function supports locality of storage and processing and independence of location of use and storage to provide an efficient general purpose external memory for high performance parallel architectures. This architecture also effectively supports all types of multiprocessor architectures through the fact that the network-implemented hardware indexing functions and the associative search capabilities of the intelligent self-managing memory units render central directories and index files unnecessary.

The conceptual basis for the system architecture owes a substantial debt to the Texas Reconfigurable Array Computer (TRAC) [LIPO 77, SEJN 80]. Integration of packet and circuit switching functionality in the network and the initial design for the memory cache [RATH 84] are concepts adopted from the TRAC system architecture.

This paper defines and discusses the major components of the architecture and discusses in detail how relational database processing may be mapped to this structure. We are also investigating the mapping of rule-based processing to the architecture. This work will be reported in a forthcoming paper.

2. ARCHITECTURE

The proposed architecture is diagrammed in Figure 1. It is organized into four major levels:

- Host processors, which for the purpose of this paper are assumed to be general purpose processors but might also be specialized processors such as Lisp machines or logic programming engines.

- An interconnection network with a banyan topology. The switching nodes will be processing elements capable of routing requests and data through the network, and of executing application-dependent functions on data flowing through the network.

- Cellularly organized disk cache of self-managing secondary memories (SMSM's), capable of associative searches, data filtering and internal garbage collection.
- Conventional moving-head disks, with a special purpose controller (SSMU) for one or more drives.

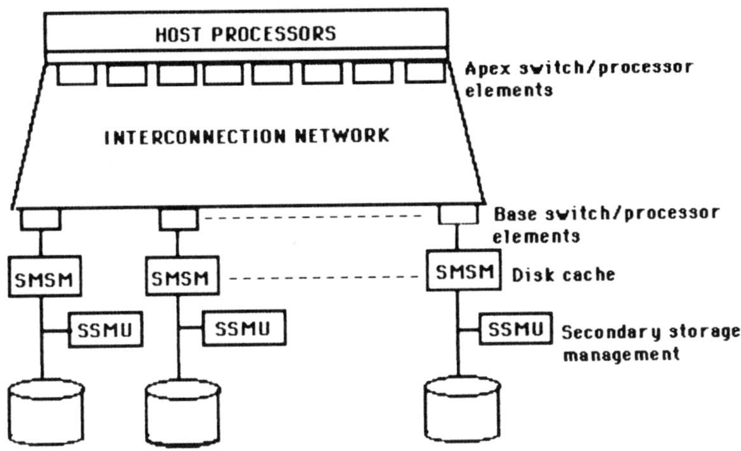

Figure 1.
Gross Architecture of Multi-stage I/O Processor.

The interconnection network and disk cache are discussed in more detail following.

2.1 Interconnection network (ICN)

The ICN is a banyan network where the nodes are switch/function processors with local memory embedded in a banyan topology. The properties of a banyan network are briefly summarized following. This general description is then followed by characterization of the particular switching network proposed for this I/O engine architecture.

2.1.1 Banyan Networks: Definitions and Properties

Banyans are one of a large class of graph representations currently being explored for use in Multi-Stage Interconnection Networks(MINs). The structure of a banyan is essentially an overlay of tree structures and provides full connectivity between apex(roots) and base(leaves) without redundancy. Regular and rectangular banyans are special cases of L-level banyans in which restrictions are placed on the indegree and outdegree of the vertices of the graph [GOKE 73].

A banyan is a Hasse diagram of a partial ordering in which there is one and only one path from any base to any apex. An apex is defined as any vertex with no arcs incident into it, a base is is defined as any vertex with no arcs incident out of it, all other vertices are called intermediates.

The path from any base to any apex is called the base-apex path. A subbanyan is a subgraph of a banyan which is itself a banyan. It follows that in a banyan there is at most one path from any vertex to any other vertex.

An L-level banyan is a banyan in which all base-apex paths are of length L. It is an (L+1)-partite graph in which the partitions may be linearly ordered from 0 to L such that arcs exist only from the i-th partition to (i+1)-th partition (0 <= i < L). The vertices in the i-th partition are called vertices at level i and referred to as Vi.

A regular banyan is an L-level banyan in which the indegree of every vertex except apexes is s and the outdegree of every vertex except bases is f. An (s,f,L) regular banyan has (f**(L-i)* s**i) vertices at level i, and (f**(L-i) * s**(i+1)) arcs from vertices in level i to those in level i+1 (0 <= i <= L). From the above, an (s,f,L) regular banyan has s**L apexes and f**L bases. A (2,3,2) regular banyan is shown in Figure 2.

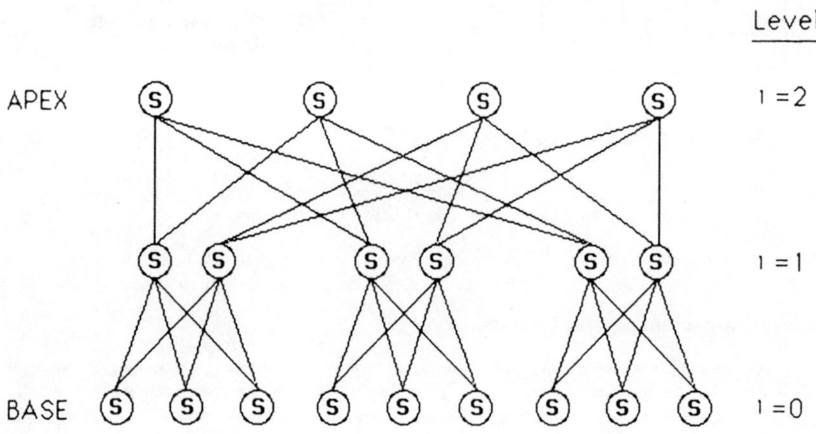

Figure 2. A Regular SW Banyan with s=2 and f=3

A rectangular banyan is one in which s=f, hence there are s**L vertices at each level and s**(L+1) arcs from each level to the next. If we let s=f=d then these banyans can be described as a (d,L) rectangular banyan.

These definitions and properties, presented here are primarily due to the work of Goke described in his Ph.D. dissertation [GOKE 76].

Properties of banyan networks have been extensively studied at the University of Texas at Austin, and a prototype switching network which incorporates both packet routing and circuit switching has been implemented as part of the Texas Reconfigurable Array Computer (TRAC) at the University of Texas at Austin.

A number of approaches may be taken to provide fault tolerance in the ICN. What is being proposed combines some of the attributes of X-Tree fault tolerance proposed by Despain and Patterson [DESP 78] and that of Cherkassky, Opper and Malek [CHER 84]. In the latter an additional redundant stage of the banyan was proposed for redundancy. This stage provides a means to connect to the equivalent node in an alternately rooted tree. The approach presented here provides this capability in an alternate manner.

At both the base and apex of the ICN there will be alternate paths between the replicated trees of the banyan. These alternate paths are in the form of a chain from one tree to the next and provide fault tolerant pathing should a switch/function node fail. Figure 3 shows switch S1-1 failed, thus preventing normal flow from S1-0 to I/O node 1. By using the alternate path to S3-0, S4-1 and S1-2, I/O node 1 can be accessed.

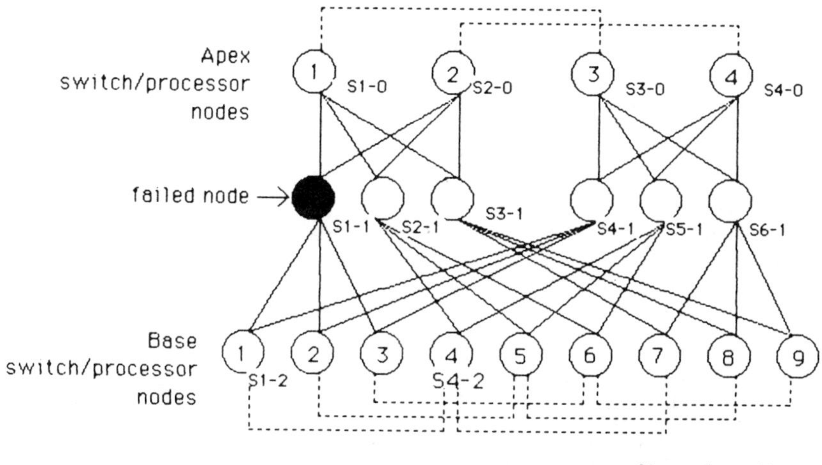

Figure 3.
The SW Banyan of Figure 2 with Added
Base and Apex Connections for Reliability

2.1.2 Description of Network for Proposed I/O Engine Architecture

The topology of the network (selections from f, s and L) will be determined by the properties of the memory units and the processors. Coupling of a small number of processors to a large number of memory units can, for example, be attained with f>s with the magnitude of L determined by the ratio of f to s.

The network will integrate data transfer and data management functionality. The network will support both packet switching and circuit switching under control of host processors. Circuits will be established via a configuration packet. The traversal path of the packet through the network will determine the processor-memory pair joined by the circuit.

This will couple processors to the memories containing specific data elements. The memory coupled to a processor by a circuit will become an extension of the address space of the processor. This will allow efficient access to bulk data without transfer of unused data through the network. Thus the efficiency of large block transfers for rotating memories can be obtained without the cost of transfer of unused data in the blocks.

The nodes of the interconnection network will execute indexing (packet routing) functions in the processor to memory direction and operation specific functions (e.g. sort or merge) in the memory to processor direction. Thus both indexing and operation specific functions become highly parallel and distributed across the network.

Data can be stored by incorporating it in a packet which contains an address determined from the key of the element to be stored. The packet routing algorithm in the switch nodes will select the memory(ies) to which a data element is sent for storage. Multiple copy storage at no additional time penalty can be achieved by multiple routes through use of "don't care" bits in the packet address of a data element.

The functionality of selected paths and/or nodes of the network can be selected by a host processor through transmission of packets of appropriate types or through use of a control processor. This selection will include routing algorithms in both processor to memory directions and memory to processor directions and the selection of filtering, or other data management functions to be executed in the memory to processor direction.

The circuit and packet modes of network switching can also be used to give a significant hardware assist to concurrency management and consistency control. A node or circuit which is being used as a part of a path for exclusive or shared access to a given memory cell can be marked to allow such further usage as can be determined to be consistent with the already established access. There are several design options for support of deadlock avoidance.

2.2 Memory Unit Design

The memory units combine three different elements:

- a computation element which interfaces the network and executes selection and filtering operations on data streamed through the interface.

- a self-managing memory unit which caches data from the bulk storage unit, implements parallel associative searches on the cached data and implements memory management functions such as allocation and garbage collection on the cached data.

- a bulk storage device which may be any of the technologies of bulk storage such as magnetic disks, optical media, etc. The bulk storage interfaces both the cache and the intelligent network interface.

The next two sections give a description of the self-managing memory and then a brief sketch of the functionality to be embedded in the intelligent network interfaces.

2.2.1 Intelligent Self-Managing Secondary Memory

Rathi has reported a number of possible approaches to the design of a self-managing secondary memory (SMSM) system [RATH 82, RATH 84]. He points out that the evolution in semiconductor technology in terms of both price and performance has widened the access time gap between primary and secondary memory. As processor performance increases and demands of array processor structures are addressed, the gap can only widen even more. The work, in which he reports on the design and performance of an SMSM, will reduce this gap between primary and secondary memory systems. While his study included RAM, CCD, Bubble Memory, along with various disk, drum and tape technologies, this study will utilize high speed RAM in conjunction with rotating storage disk devices.

Within the concept of the SMSM, by adding controlling hardware, based on SIMD processors, a modularly expandable secondary memory can be designed. This modular expansion implies that doubling the memory capacity will result in either no or insignificant increases in latency or retrieval time, as long as one doubles the number of controlling SIMD processors. Within the SMSM architecture all information is accessed via a name-oriented associative address scheme. This implies that the host has no need for directory information which may be kept within an SMSM controlling processor. The SMSM also supports both memory allocation and garbage collection, hence again the host need not concern itself with these primitive support functions. They are the domain of the SMSM controllers as they should be if high performance is to be achieved by the secondary memory system. Architecture of the SMSM described by Rathi supports variable length segment storage and retrieval. This capability makes it attractive as a paging device for multiprocessor systems, distributed systems and object-oriented architectures.

One fundamental objective of the SMSM design is the development of a cache memory between primary memory and the electromechanical permanent storage devices. A valid approach will provide a cost effective solution for the reduction of the access time gap between these two memories. Rathi reports three possible ways to achieve this:

1. The use of intermediate semiconductor memory

2. Reduce the software overhead for access and maintenance

3. Use of SIMD, logic-per-track and tagged architecture concepts

The design criterion reported here has the potential of applying all three of these factors and achieving an extremely effective solution to the problem. There is enough flexibility in this approach that either high performance may be obtained or a less costly solution at the sacrifice of some performance.

A second major objective is providing access to data from multiple sources without the delays imposed by a central directory or the overhead of maintaining multiple directories. Associative search for objects by a unique name and/or key values can be coupled with indexing strategies to entirely eliminate the requirements for mapping directories in many cases and greatly simplify directory structure and maintenance in all cases.

The SMSM is organized into modules, each of which is called an SMSM cell. The cell can be further divided into two components, the cell controller and the cell memory. The processor views the SMSM as a single module, while internally it may consist of one or several cells. When more than one cell exists there are communication links between them which provide for the necessary coordination. There exists a fixed left to right priority ordering defined in the hardware and conveyed via the inter-cell communication links shown in Figure 5. Each cell controller is responsible for communicating data between it and the host and, in addition, communicating control information with the host and its neighboring cells' controllers. For garbage collection purposes it may be necessary for a cell to communicate data between itself and neighboring controllers. Thus each controller can perform all SMSM functions and is the intelligence of the memory management hardware. It should be clear from this structure that the addition of more SMSM cells should not substantially increase access time.

2.2.1.1 Segments and Garbage Collection

Information is stored in segments within the cell memory. Each segment consist of two parts, a fixed length header and variable length data. The type of information in memory is controlled by tags. Upon initialization all memory is written with EOF tags, then as segments are written, the tag is changed to HD or DT to imply header or data parts of the segment. A segment may overlap to another cell memory which will require coordination during both read and write operations. This split segment is completely handled within the SMSM cell controllers. It was mentioned earlier that the SMSM contains hardware supported garbage collection. This is accomplished by using a fourth tag "GB" to imply that the word is to be handled by the garbage collection routine. Garbage collection occurs "on the fly" and is continuously running. It will pick up GB tagged words and "float" them to the end of memory where they become EOF tags. When garbage words are created and no EOF tags exist in this controller, it will ask the next lower priority controller to transfer data to it. The amount of data to be transferred will be equal to the number of garbage words in its cell memory.

2.2.1.2 Cell Memory Organization

The choice of memory technology will affect the cost/performance of the system. Factors such as random vs sequential access, and fixed vs variable access speed of memory will affect the memory cell organization and performance. While the general concept of the SMSM is quite broad, in this study we will only address random accessible cell memory based on semiconductor RAM technology. Organization of this memory is linear with access by word instead of bit. The cell memory can be subdivided into data memory with a separate directory memory. The primary purpose behind this approach is the improvement of segment search speed. The data memory stores data segments and the directory memory stores the segment headers and their corresponding data memory address. The directory is used only by the cell controller and is not accessible by the host processor, so name-oriented accessing is preserved. The directory only improves performance, the SMSM/Host interface remains as described above.

The data memory is a linear organization as described earlier. The directory memory is indexed via a hashing algorithm operating on a segment name. Since the directory entry contains the data cell memory address and linear memory is randomly accessible, the retrieval of the segment is quite fast. If there is more than one occurrence of the segment name, a linked list is formed from the first entry (link pointer) at the hash index address in the directory memory. If more than one segment is hashed into the same index, then a linked list entry will also be appropriate. Let "Ld" be the cell's average link list length, and "Tc" be the controller clock cycle time, then the average time taken for this algorithm to execute is

$$T = Ld_{*}tc$$

Rathi [RATH 82,RATH 84] describes three basic garbage collection algorithms for circular memory organization. It was found that for linear organization since garbage collection was inherently sequential within a cell, it was treated as a circular memory. Any algorithm for circular memory organization is suitable for linear memory. For a directory memory structure, both memories must have garbage collection units which communicate with each other.

Memory allocation is much less complex than garbage collection because all available memory (i.e. EOF tagged words) words are at one end of the overall SMSM memory. Since more than one memory may have available space, the highest priority cell executes the memory allocation algorithm first. When its memory is exhausted the next priority cell's memory is allocated. If no lower priority cell exists, then the status register is written with the error condition. Two parameters control the memory allocation in each cell, a memory available flag and an up/down counter. The counter points to the available memory address. The garbage collection algorithm can set the flag and decrement the counter. The memory allocation algorithm can clear the flag and increment the counter. The flag is cleared whenever the counter reaches the ending address of the cell memory.

2.2.1.3 Concurrency and Consistency Management and Protection

The SMSM can also be given capabilities for support of concurrency and consistency management. The name field of each object in the cache can be given a status tag which indicates that it is in shared or exclusive use. Then, so long as access flows through the cache, the status tag will control access. The SMSM could also be given the capabilities to serve as hardware support for multiple version [REED 83] implementation of consistency management. The "rewrite" command which is described in Rathi's SMSM can be extended to leave the existing version in place and add a new version with the same name but a different version number.

2.2.1.4 Summary of SMSM Design

The structure and design is versatile enough to utilize current random access memory technologies. A key factor to the SMSM performance is the inclusion of garbage collection in the hardware. Parallel searching and transfer capability allow the SMSM structure to achieve low access time with high potential bandwidth. Finally, having a name-oriented associative address scheme frees the host and its operating system of the laborious task of maintaining directories and allocating sectors. An SMSM cell internal organization is shown in Figure 4.

SMSM cells are organized into clusters, with communication links between adjacent cells in a cluster. The configuration illustrated in Figure 5 assumes 4 SMSM cells per cluster, and one SMSM cluster per disk drive.

A cell priority ordering is defined within a cluster. Cell contents are searched in parallel. Cell I/O is sequential in priority order.

Cells maintain directories to their internal contents. We propose a special controller (Secondary Storage Management Unit—SSMU) [see Figure 6.] to manage data transfer between an SMSM cluster and disk. It will monitor request faults in the SMSM and initiate appropriate read/write transfers. It will maintain map entries for data blocks in the SMSM cluster containing information on the key, sector, and status of each block. The status word

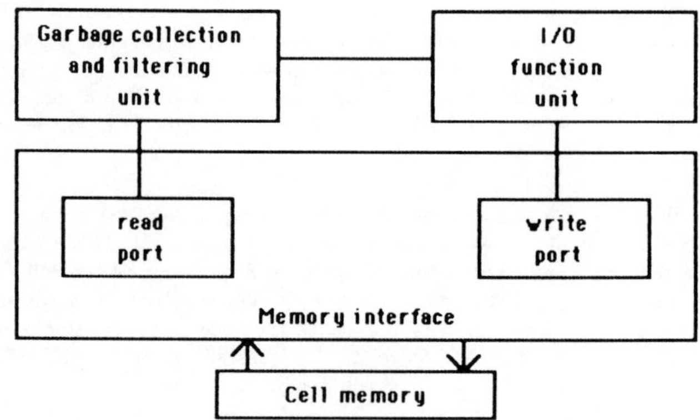

Figure 4.
SMSM Cell Controller Organization.

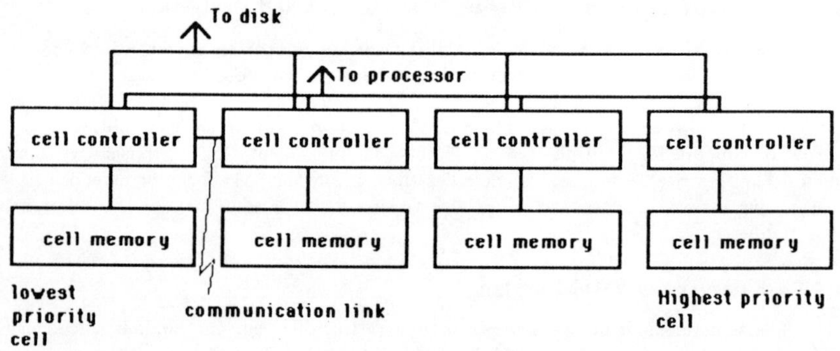

Figure 5.
SMSM Cell Cluster Organization.

contains a clean/dirty bit which will be used in a standard manner to eliminate unnecessary transfers to/from disk. Writing to disk will only occur if the block status is dirty and SMSM space is needed (inward bound control).

Shadowing and redundancy can be achieved at the base level of the I/O network relatively inexpensively by introducing bypass switches between adjacent SMSM clusters and alternate paths to disk, as shown in Figure 7.

2.2.2 Network Interface

The processing capabilities associated with the interface to the base nodes will also implement selection and filtering operations on data elements before passing them to the network for transmission and possible further processing. These filtering operations will execute in conformance to parameters supplied by the processors initiating the retrieval request. These capabilities will implement the data base operations of selection and projection and together with the routing capabilities of the network in the memory to processor direction, implement data model specific operations such as sorting and merging.

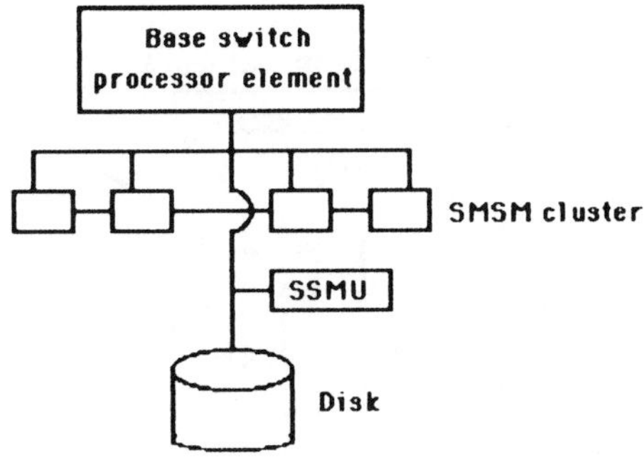

Figure 6.
SMSM-SSMU Organization.

2.2.3 Architecture Summary

The proposed architecture provides a framework for realizing the following functionality:

- Extremely high bandwidth from/to secondary storage, because of parallelism in disk and SMSM access.
- Content searching at the disk cache level.
- Data filtering at the disk cache level and the network interface.
- Garbage collection and memory compaction within the SMSM's.
- Parallel data manipulation (e.g. sorting, merging, aggregate operations) within the interconnection network as data flows towards the host processor(s).

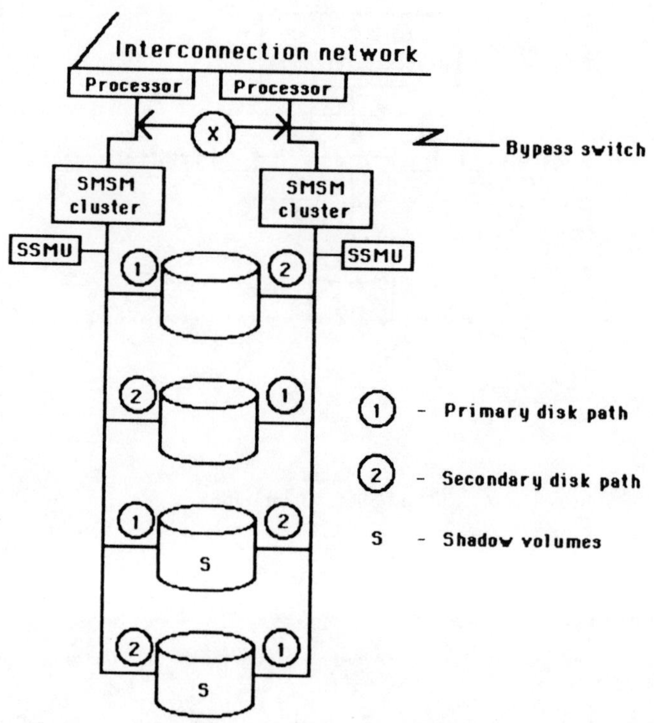

Figure 7.
Fault Tolerance for SMSM-SSMU Disk Modules.

- Fault tolerance within the network, the cache, and the disk subsystems.
- Object-oriented referencing by the host machines.
- Packet and circuit switching under host machine control for efficient utilization of network bandwidth.
- Hardware based indexing implemented by the network and the SMSM's.
- Hardware-implemented concurrency control through the cache and the network.
- Functional partitioning of the I/O system under host machine control.

The following section describes how relational database processing may be mapped to the architecture.

3. RELATIONAL DATABASE SYSTEM ACCESS AND OPERATIONS

For the purpose of illustration assume that relations are distributed across disk storage in logical cylinders. That is, relations are partitioned into approximately equal chunks of tuples such that a set of tuples for a given relation resides in a physical disk cylinder (or adjacent group of cylinders) on each drive. Note that an attribute-based schema could be organized in a similar manner. In the case of a relational database application, and assuming a tuple-based schema, query processing selection and projection operations will be done on-the-fly at the level of the SMSM's as data flows into the I/O network. Base level processor-switch nodes are responsible for duplicate elimination (in the case of SMSM projection operations), attribute permutation, and sorting and merging of tuples delivered by SMSM cells in the cluster under its control. Higher level nodes are responsible for further merging of sorted tuple streams delivered by lower level processor/switch nodes. Multi-relational operations (e.g. join) are performed at the host level, by final merge operations.

Assuming a tuple-based schema and logical cylinder organization, a host processor is responsible for query decomposition and broadcast of selection and projection commands for the SMSM's. In the case of tuple addition the host processor can establish a network routing to store tuples in a selected drive (or SMSM cluster). Other update operations (tuple deletion, value modification) would be broadcast and implemented at the level of the SMSM's.

We believe that the proposed I/O architecture addresses the critical problem in the processing of very large conventional databases, namely the improvement in I/O bandwidth. Boral and DeWitt [BORA 83] make a convincing argument that this, rather than the engineering of a special-purpose database engine, should be the focus for current research. Their proposals for further investigation include exploiting the logical cylinder concept, design of customized disk controllers, use of a very large disk cache, and more effective index strategies to map from logical to physical space. The paper also argues that under foreseeable development we must still rely on conventional moving head disk technology for large secondary storage.

Our proposed architecture differs from other current developments in the database machine area. The Japanese ICOT database machine effort [SHIB 84] incorporates a special-purpose relational algebra engine and a hierarchical memory subsystem incorporating a 128 Mbyte semiconductor RAM cache, with conventional moving head disks as secondary storage. However, the organization of the memory subsystem differs significantly from our design. For example, the disk cache is controlled by a single general purpose processor. Overall, the Japanese design puts major emphasis on the relational engine component of the architecture, whereas our proposed architecture seeks to exploit I/O parallelism and distributed on-the-fly support in the I/O subsystem for algebraic operations in a general purpose host processor or processors.

Some of the secondary storage access strategies proposed in earlier architectures (e.g. DBC) can be adapted to our design, although our implementation is significantly different. The philosophy of the Munich group [KIES 84] also is consistent with our view of the importance of intelligent disk subsystems for high performance database architectures and the need to offload operations to the I/O system that can be efficiently processed at that level. However, our proposed implementation and distribution of functionality within the I/O subsystem differs from this reported work.

The proposed architecture has some of the properties and functionality of the Hypertree configuration proposed by Goodman [GOOD 81]. The Goodman architecture has a binary tree topology with additional regular connections among nodes at the same level. Goodman studied in detail the possibilities of exploiting a variety of distributed algorithms to support relational database processing in the Hypertree structure.

Although our architecture differs in interconnection topology and in the incorporation of the self-managing disk cache, many of Goodman's conclusions supporting the desirability of a tree structured processor organization for relational database access and operations are applicable.

A backend machine architecture of interconnected processing nodes has been proposed by Shultz [SHUL 81]. However, the REPT architecture is oriented to the execution of relational algebraic operations by the processing nodes, and the mapping of a query decomposition by the host processor to the network of processors. It thus differs in philosophy from our proposed approach.

Other proposed or experimental systems discussed in the literature incorporate some of the features specified for our architecture, but differ in completeness, functionality and architecture. The VERSO system being developed at INRIA is a bus-organized arrangement of functionally specialized processors, including a user interface processor, filter processor, and memory management processor. The importance of low level filtering is recognized. But the concept differs significantly from our proposal in that parallelism and hierarchical functional processing is not exploited [BANC 83].

The SABRE proposal, based on mapping virtual processes to a variety of architectures, will be implemented by a bus-organized sequence of processing modules with a disk cache memory. The possibility for significant parallelism is not evident in the brief description given [GARD 83].

RDBM, the University of Brunswick project, intends to exploit on-the-fly filtering and partial sort-merge operations to support join processing, an important feature in our design. However, the architecture is composed of a number of specialized processors; shared memory is assumed for part of the system. The processor interconnection method is not yet specified, although the possibility of some type of bus is mentioned [SCHW 83].

DBMAC recognizes the importance of filtering and of exploiting parallel disk transfer to increase I/O bandwidth. However, the design as discussed in [MISS 83] does not incorporate a disk cache, and assumes bus-connected processor units at one level, with special-purpose selection processors interfaced with disk storage.

4. CONCLUSIONS

Qualitative analyses show that the proposed architecture has potential for very high performance on a range of data management tasks. Hardware support for consistency management and directory functions give it potential as the I/O engine for multiprocessor architectures. Evidence from the recent literature supports the potential viability of the proposed architecture for relational database query processing.

Our current investigations are directed to the resolution of the following questions as a preliminary to detailed design synthesis and evaluation:

- Identification of required functionality to support relational algebraic operations, intra- and inter-query parallelism, and consistency management.
- Distribution of functionality across the architecture.
- Capacity balance across the architecture with respect to processing modules and network bandwidth.
- Identification of most appropriate routing/broadcast algorithms for supporting I/O requests.
- Formulation of logic programming operations on the proposed architecture.
- Data organization to support conventional relational operations and to support other data models incorporating, for example, molecular objects.

Performance evaluation studies should provide answers to these questions and allow for intelligent decisions concerning tradeoffs.

5. REFERENCES

[BANC 83] Bancilhon, F. *et al*, "VERSO: A Relational Backend Database Machine," in David K. Hsiao (Ed.), *Advanced Database Machine Architecture*, Prentice-Hall, 1983, 1-18.

[BORA 83] Boral, H. and DeWitt, D., "Database Machines: An Idea Whose Time has Passed?" *Third International Workshop on Database Machines*, October 1983.

[CHER 84] Cherkassky, V., Opper, E. and Malek, M., "Reliability and Fault Diagnosis Analysis of Fault-Tolerant Multistage Interconnection Networks," *Proc. of the 14th International Conference on Fault-Tolerant Computing*, pp. 246-251, 1984.

[DESP 78] Despain, A. M. and Patterson, D. A., "X-Tree: A Tree Structured Multi-Processor Computer Architecture," *Proceedings of the 5th Annual Symposium on Computer Architecture*, pp. 144-151, 1978.

[GARD 83] Gardarin G. *et al*, "SABRE: A Relational Database System for a Multiprocessor Machine," in David K. Hsiao (Ed.), *Advanced Database Machine Architecture*, Prentice-Hall, 1983, 19-35.

[GOKE 73] Goke, L. R. and Lipovski, G. J., "Banyan Networks for Partitioning Multiprocessor Systems," *Proceedings of the First Annual Symp. on Computer Architecture*, pp. 21-28, 1973.

[GOKE 76] Goke, L. R., "Banyan Networks for Partitioning Multiprocessor Systems," Ph.D. Dissertation, University of Florida, 1976.

[GOOD 81] Goodman, J. R., "An Investigation of Multiprocessor Structures and Algorithms for Data Base Management," Ph.D. Dissertation, University of California, 1981.

[KIES 84] Kiessling, W., "Tuneable Dynamic Filter Algorithms for High Performance Database Systems," Institut fur Informatik, Technische Universitat Munchen, 1984.

[LIPO 77] Lipovski, G. J. and Tripathi, A., "A Reconfigurable Varistructure Array Processor, " *Proceedings of the 1977 International Conference on Parallel Processing*, Bellaire, MI, August 1977, pp. 165-174.

[MISS 83] Missikoff, M. and Terranova, M., "The Architecture of a Relational Database Computer Known as DBMAC," in David K. Hsiao (Ed.), *Advanced Database Machine Architecture*, Prentice-Hall, 1983, 87-108.

[RATH 82] Rathi, Bharat Deep, "Principles of Operation of TRAC's Self-Managing Secondary Memory," Technical Report *TRAC-25*, Departments of Computer Sciences and Electrical Engineering, The University of Texas at Austin, 1981.

[RATH 84] Rathi, Bharat Deep, "The Design and Performance Analysis of a Self Managing Secondary Memory," Technical Report *TR-84-09*, March 1984, Department of Computer Sciences, University of Texas at Austin.

[REED 79] Reed, D. P., "Implementing Atomic Actions on Decentralized Data," presented at *ACM/SIGOPS 7th Symposium on Operating Systems*, Asilomar, CA, December 1979.

[SHIB 84] Shibayama S. *et al*, "A Relational Database Machine with Large Semiconductor Disk and Hardware Relational Algebra Processor," *New Generation Computing* 2, 1984.

[SCHW 83] Schweppe, H. *et al*, "RDBM—A Dedicated Multiprocessor System for Database Management," in David K. Hsiao (Ed.), *Advanced Database Machine Architecture*, Prentice-Hall, 1983, 36-86.

[SEJN 80] Sejnowski, M. C., Upchurch, E. T., Kapur, R. N., Charlu, D. P. S. and Lipovski, G. J., "An Overview of the Texas Reconfigurable Array Computer," *Proceedings of AFIPS NCC, 49*, 1980, pp. 631-641.

[SHUL 81] Shultz, R., "A Multiprocessor Computer Architecture for Database Support," Ph.D. Dissertation, Iowa State University, 1981.

On the Development of Dedicated Hardware for Searching

H. Ch. Zeidler
H. Auer

Institut fuer Datenverarbeitungsanlagen
Technische Universitaet Braunschweig
Hans-Sommer-Str.66
D-3300 Braunschweig
West Germany

Abstract

Large associative memories for modern database applications cannot be implemented in highly integrated semiconductor technology. However other realizations, in the form of "associative disks" or "intelligent mass memories", have been the subject of research and development for many years. The central points of interest are above all the required features and implementations of the logic necessary to form a search processor. Initially, a few basic considerations towards the development of such search processors are outlined. After an introduction to the system environment and the task profile, the search processor component of the Relational Database Machine RDBM currently under development at the Technical University of Braunschweig is described.

1. Introduction

The old idea of a fully parallel, content-addressable memory (associative memory) is still with us, but the dream of highly integrated realizations with consequently low-cost construction of semiconductor mass memories remains for the present a dream. Nevertheless, the principle retains its extreme attractiveness for database applications, where increasingly large amounts of data have to be searched through as efficiently as possible. Numerous considerations and structural proposals, particularly in connection with database machines, indicate strongly the keen interest in the searching problem.

After it became clear that fully parallel associative access of the required order of magnitude up to the gigabyte range is not realizable, attempts have been and are being made to develop high-performance alternative constructions which, although based on byte-serial access, nonetheless attain high processing speeds through the application of functionally designed hardware and exploiting the possibilities for parallelization. Magnetic disks are usually employed as the storage medium, which is why these developments are also called "associative disks" (as well as "intelligent mass memories").

It is well-known that all previous considerations in this direction were based on the "logic-per-track" ideas of Slotnick /Slot 70/. In 1970 he already proposed that rotating storage·media, such as fixed head disks, be furnished with additional logic at each read/write head to allow search operations to be performed. Through sequential searching, i.e. without additional reference structures, a filtering of raw data can be performed according to the associative access principle, corresponding to a search query of varying complexity sent from the central processor to the peripheral store, so that only the relevant data have to be transferred into the main memory of the control processor. In this way, pseudoassociative mass storage characteristics can be attained. In numerous projects, such as CAFS /Mitc 74/, RAP /OSSm 75/, SURE /KLZe 76, LSZe 78, Zeid 78/ to name but a few, designs based on this principle are proposed, which in some cases were also implemented.

In conjunction with the continued development of magnetic disk technology, increasingly complex and cheaper integrated circuits became available, which could be incorporated in the search logic to enhance efficiency. Thus one can find proposals for the application of purpose-designed VLSI structures as well as fast, universal microprocessor chips, which are tailored to the special application through their surrounding hardware or solely through appropriate resident software.

In the context of this paper initially certain basic considerations on the design of search processors, i.e. data filters at either a low level or attached intimately to the storage medium, are presented. To round off, after a short outline has been given of the system environment and the requirements it imposes, the search processor of the Relational Database Machine RDBM developed at the Technical University of Braunschweig (West Germany) is described.

2. Basic Design Considerations

In the course of developing database machine hardware components, in particular for sequential searching in structured data sets, a series of aspects has crystallized, which must be considered together closely as they are of decisive importance for the efficient overall performance of the system.

2.1. Memory/Processor Interrelationship

Initially, the basic question regarding the interrelationship between memory and processor must be answered, as to possible degree of acceleration through parallelization. The basis is formed by a generalized search system as represented in Fig. 1, whereby a mass memory (magnetic disk or disk system) is attached to one or more processors via an interconnection matrix. The crucial nature of the connection between data streams and processors is discussed according to the classification given by Flynn.

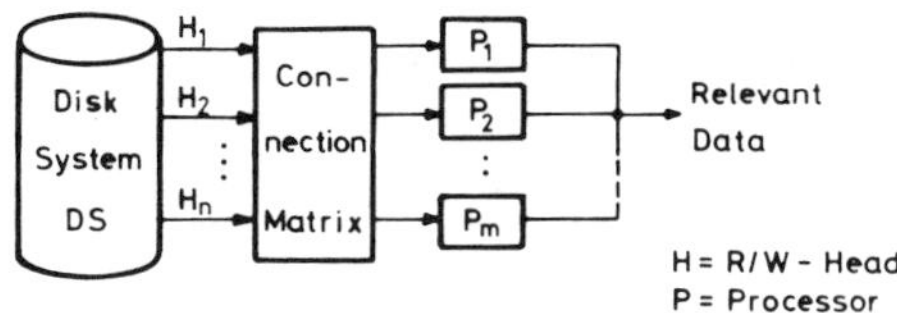

Fig. 1 : Basic Structure of a Search System

The original concept of Slotnick and others (Fig. 2a) represented an SIMD structure (Single Instruction Multiple Data). The mass memory was thereby split down into cells, corresponding to the tracks or read/write heads, which use their attached hardware logic to perform selection operations "on-the-fly", i.e. during the fly-past of the data over one disk revolution.

A series of proposals for search machines, the "first generation database machines", represented this type of structure, with parallel cells and a direct interrelationship between data storage and processor, often also termed "cellular approach" because a number of cells perform the same function in parallel (functional relation). The structure is strictly hierarchical and has an overlayed control processor, which issues commands and monitors all activities. Cross connections to allow cooperation between individual processors are not normally provided. In /DeHa 81/ this type of organization is also split down into the classes of processor-per-track (PPT) structures (e.g. RAP, CASSM /CLSu 73/, RARES /LSSm 76/) and processor-per-head (PPH) structures, e.g. DBC /BHKa 79/.

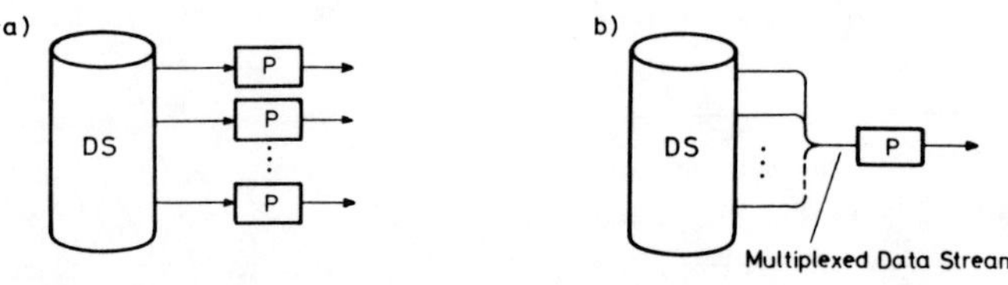

Fig. 2: SIMD Structures

The efficiency can be yet further enhanced if one utilizes the speed difference between the mechanical disk stores and the electronic processors and interleaves the data streams from the individual tracks or read/write heads. If one expands the viewpoint of the Flynn classification, then such a data stream can be considered as constituting "Multiple Data" (MD), so that one obtains a SIMD structure, but with one more complex processor (Fig. 2b).

If one connects several processors with varying selection criteria to each read/write head, then one obtains an MIMD structure (Multiple Instruction Multiple Data), as shown in Fig. 3a. The outlay for the processors is, however, very high, so that this version must be viewed as purely theoretical. An interleaved version, which reduces processor outlay, is also possible here, but this demands higher processor complexity too (Fig. 3b). This type of organization is exhibited, for example, in the SURE arrangement (project SURE /KLZe 76, LSZe 78, Zeid 78/) which can achieve an instruction rate of approx. 100 MIPS at a data rate of 7.3 MB/s using 14 processors.

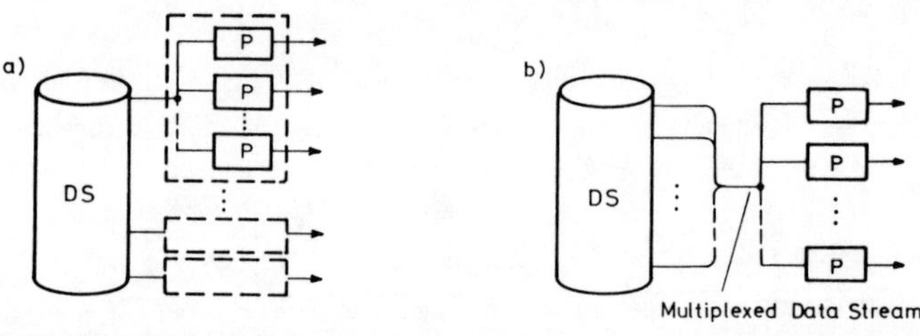

Fig. 3: MIMD Structures

A disadvantage of using such an apparently attractive MD structure to increase the data processing speed is that the standard mass memories with head-parallel access no longer correspond in most cases to the state of the art as regards storage capacity (and thus cost per bit) and therefore have to be modified, so that a general, standard interface is no longer provided. This is of decisive importance for the success of the concept, so that MD structures cannot be viewed as very promising. An interesting solution is, however, offered elsewhere /BoDe 83/ by a proposal that several magnetic disks operating in parallel be connected in a pool. As yet little is known about this approach.

The specialized and complex design of the processors also represents a general disadvantage of the interleaved version from today's viewpoint, as they must be constructed from discrete logic. Normal microprocessors are not applicable solely for speed reasons. In the future, the progress of VLSI technology will certainly render specialized designs feasible, providing an integrated intelligent read/write head (processor-per-head).

The "Single Data" structures (Fig. 4) offer another area, which in accordance with /DeHa 81/ can also be considered as processor-per-disk arrangements. Search components of this kind are employed in database machine projects such as DIRECT /DeWi 79/ or VERSO /GSSc 83/. Corresponding to Fig. 4b, a "Multiple Instruction" structure is possible here too, by examining a single data stream using several processors, each with different queries.

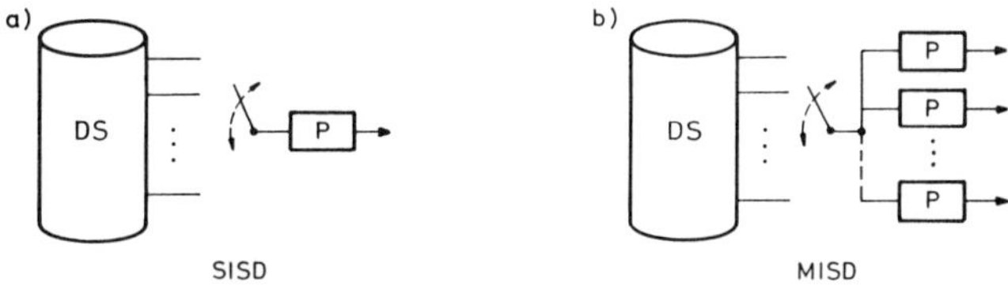

Fig. 4: Single Data Structures

It is generally advantageous in "Single Data" structures that the implementation is carried out using standard disk stores without modification or additional outlay. The data transfer rate is then reduced to the standard value of 2 MB/s (max. 3 MB/s). According to an announcement by Ibis Systems Inc., a 1.4 GB capacity disk with a data transfer rate of 12 MB/s (performed by a multihead device) will soon appear on the market, which will provide new perspectives. So far, however, acceleration of the throughput could be achieved solely by parallelization, in this case by increasing the number of participant processors. With arrangements of independent processors (Multiple Instruction), the efficiency depends very largely on the number of queries simultaneously available. Beyond that, asynchronous data processing discussed later in Section 2.2, additionally allows the possibility of programming several processors with the same search query, whereby the next tuple to be processed is fetched on demand (demand-driven). In this type of parallelization (multiple Single Instruction

Single Data, mSISD), a large speed enhancement is attainable, independent of the number of simultaneously available queries.

2.2. Data Transfer

Independent of the various memory/processor interrelationships and the conclusions to be drawn from them, the question of data transfer must be tackled. It can, however, be answered more easily for particular cases.

In early proposals, up to the second half of the 1970s, hardware and thus memory capacity were poorly integrated and expensive. This therefore in itself precluded the application of buffer memories. The raw data were therefore searched directly in synchronism with the data transfer rate from the disk, leading to complex on-the-fly searches. For cases, where individual processors can no longer accommodate the data stream or selected data could not be passed on, processing must be interrupted. Only after a delayed go-ahead and one or more disk revolutions could processing be renewed. This therefore touches on the question as to the possible complexity of a search query, which will be looked at later on.

The advantages and disadvantages of such on-the-fly processing can be summarized as follows:

1) All data must be completely searched in the sequence, in which they occur on the mass storage. The actual search time is equal to the transfer time from the disk and corresponds to the ratio between data quantity and data rate.

2) If the characters of a tuple (= record) are not held in a buffer (extra memory outlay), until a hit has been registered, the search purely yields, for example, the start addresses for a subsequent "direct" access to the actual tuple.

3) The necessity for synchronous processing within a single disk revolution per track (cylinder) makes the already given restriction on the instruction set even more severe, the smaller the difference between the data rate of the storage medium and the data rate of the processor. Jumps (over irrelevant data) and the repeated processing of already read data cannot be performed. In addition, the processors cannot be used during positioning. The positioning time can be up to 2.5 times the pure read time, depending on the type of disk.

4) A throughput enhancement of data stream processing can only be achieved by using additional processors operating in parallel with mutually independent search queries. However, the efficiency of the approach depends strongly on the number of simultaneously available search queries, limiting the maximum number of usefully employable processors.

5) From a processor point of view data access is provided implicitly by virtue of the structure. Buffer memories and data access mechanisms can therefore be dispensed with in the hardware.

Direct disadvantages become apparent, however, in particular due to the inflexibility of synchronism. Nonetheless this technique can prove advantageous for certain applications if not too complex search queries are to be answered in the shortest possible time, as the search time in general corresponds to the data transfer time and is thus predictable.

In the course of time, higher integration and lower hardware costs provided the designers with an increasing number of possibilities through the application of memories and microprocessors. In particular, data buffering became possible at economic costs, so that the actual selection of the data and further operations could be performed asynchronously to the disk speed, i.e. "off-the-disk". By analogy with the previous comments, the following points can be made:

1) If the data are stored in a RAM prior to processing, then one is independent of the disk data rate and can additionally exploit the unused positioning time for processing.

2) The relevant data are directly available for further processing.

3) The use of random access enables an optimal search process to be used. In addition, complex operations can be realized without limitation, whereby irrelevant data can be missed out and individual attributes (fields) accessed several times.

4) An initial throughput enhancement can already be achieved with a minimal system (one search processor), where several search queries are performed by a single search program in sequence on the same tuple. A further enhancement can be achieved if a number of processors simultaneously process various tuples using the same query program. The degree of possible parallelization then depends virtually only on the number of available search processors.

5) The demand-driven distribution of the data to the individual processors requires, however, additional intelligence (possible in hardware).

The advantages of asynchronous, buffered processing are always definitely clear, where the queries processed are as universal as possible and/or microprocessors are employed. The time penalty incurred by the temporary buffering of the data can initially be viewed as a disadvantage: the data from the mass storage first have to be written to a buffer, from where they are fetched for processing as determined by the query. By employing pipeline mechanisms, however, this penalty can be largely eliminated, in particular for high quantities of data and partitioned methods of processing.

Regarding the general processing speed, the throughput, this should in all cases be equivalent to the data transfer rate: the processing of a data partition (e.g. a track or a cylinder) should be concluded by the time that the next unit is read from the storage medium, i.e. processing is performed quasi-synchronously (quasi-on-the-fly). In order to achieve this (see Section 2.1), a balanced cooperation of processor type, number of processors and search query complexity is necessary.

2.3. Search Query Complexity

Following the hardware-related aspects of memory/processor interrelationship and data transfer, the complexity of the search queries to be performed by the search processor should be discussed, before going into the actual processor design. An examination of the relevant literature reveals that the processing of complex search queries is repeatedly more or less only lightly touched upon. The qualitative aspects of the degree of complexity and the resulting demands, particularly on the hardware, are not elaborated in more detail. However, the complexity of a search query represents a very broad area, which from a hardware viewpoint can be tackled in various stages.

In the following definition, only search queries on structured data (in contrast to unstructured data such as text) are considered. A standard query, as normally performed on the stored data in conventional software systems, is defined to the effect that solely one attribute forms the tuple key. This attribute is sought and compared byte for byte with the query comparison value. Any additional features give rise to a complex search query, whereby its complexity rises with increasing level in the following list:

Level 1: Several attributes of a tuple, which are not necessarily contiguous, form a composite key and are searched through in succession. The comparison results of the individual attributes are combined using the boolean AND operation. A qualitative enhancement would be represented by a choice of combinations from AND / OR / NOT.

Level 2: By combining individual boolean partial results, which occur successively in logical sequence, nested structures of varying depths can be used, thus giving rise to several boolean combination levels.

Level 3: The value of an attribute forms the comparison value for a subsequent attribute within the same tuple (selection).

Level 4: Several search comparison values are compared disjunctively with one or more attributes of a tuple, during which "backward jumps" between attributes are allowed within the search query.

Level 5: Expansion of the functions employed to linear database functions such as, for example, partial projection, aggregation, update (unary functions).

Level 6: Expansion to non-linear database functions (binary functions).

Without wanting to evaluate the various levels individually, one can ascertain that up to level 3 the complete processing of search queries can be performed in real time, at least using special processors (i.e. on-the-fly), as the process constitutes a linear sequence of operations. The limitation of complexity for real time processing lies therefore at a relatively low level, the achievable complexity in comparison with a software implementation, however, can be realized with only slight hardware outlay (in particular for nested structures).

From level 4 onwards, the degree of attainable complexity exhibits a marked qualitative difference. The processing assumes a non-linear nature and is thus difficult or impossible to perform in real time. A recourse to asynchronous processing is therefore inevitable. The final decision in favour of quasi-on-the-fly processing depends, however, on the choice of structure and type of the search processor.

2.4. Processor Design

In this last section of the chapter, the broad area of processor design taking into account the question posed previously should at least be briefly dealt with. Three areas are to be discussed: special sequential circuits, which are constructed discretely or using VLSI circuits to realize the envisaged functions, micro-programmable universal microprocessors and microprocessors with a fixed instruction set.

Discretely constructed sequential circuits or VLSI circuits have the great advantage that their exact matching to the envisaged functions enables the query to be performed directly and very rapidly. An example of this is provided by the search modules in the SURE project. This purpose-built sequential circuit, consisting of about 200 discrete chips mounted on two CAMAC boards, was able to process nine independent, time-interleaved data streams using a pipeline structure with a search complexity corresponding to level 3 on-the-fly. (data rate 9 x 806 KB/s = 7.3 MB/s). This corresponds to a byte cycle time of 137 ns.

If on the one hand, basic computer architecture principles can be applied right down to gate level, then alteration of the fixed functions is only possible at considerable expense through hardware modification. This limitation is particularly unfavourable, as experience shows that redesigns are often necessary. A further disadvantage is that supporting tools for design, construction and testing are not initially available, necessitating the initial creation of an appropriate software/hardware environment, itself a special design. Nevertheless, the opinion is expressed that a special design has its place alongside universal chips, in particular, where real time processing is required. The vision of an integrated intelligent magnetic disk store can only be fulfilled with a specific-function processor design, but certainly not at the present.

The second area of microprogrammed universal microprocessor chips is closely related to the first one. The AMD 2900 series can thereby be typically applied. The application of these complex chips already commits certain structures at the lowest level, thus easing the design process, whereas, on the other hand, the possible degree of freedom is limited. The AMD 2900 sequencer chip basically allows speeds up to about 8 MHz, although the attainable speed also depends on the attendant components. Thus the speed of a design not optimized for restriction attained a 250 ns byte cycle time for a string comparison.

The advantages of such a design in comparison with a sequential circuit are therefore not to be looked for so much in the (virtually equivalent) speed, but rather in its flexibility in the face of design modifications. The two-level programming at machine and micro levels allows, for example, new data structures to be incorporated independent of the hardware structure and enables algorithms to be implemented in microcode. In addition, the hardware structure is not matched rigidly to the task, but offers certain extra facilities through general supporting structures (e.g. several register sets). Moreover, more complex chips offer a higher degree of functionality, as for example can be easily seen in the ALU, which does not only provide a comparison, but also further operations. In general, it can be said that the application of bit-slice microprocessors offers a high degree of parallelization, specialization and complexity in controlling hardware.

Its disadvantages must be viewed principally in comparison with fixed instruction set microprocessors. They lie, as for the sequential circuits, in the large outlay for chips and program code. The latter applies not so much to the machine program level, but rather to the microprogram level. As with sequential circuits, effective programming tools are lacking, which then first have to be created. There are no higher level languages other than assembler. The same applies to the testing tools, which have likewise to be developed to correspond to the chosen structure. However, it would be wrong to conclude that these problems render the concept unusable. Before the corresponding techniques are mastered, time-consuming experience has to be gathered and the developed universal tools (e.g. metaassembler and simulator) can always be reused. However, it is a fact that one should not underestimate the time involved.

In this direction there are no problems in connection with the components discussed in the following, the fixed instruction set microprocessors. These universally applicable, complex chips have undergone an explosive development in the last few years and offer increasingly more features with regard to speed and size of the instruction set. Above all, their processing width has expanded from 8 bits via 16 bits to 32 bits, making them also suitable candidates for broad application in special hardware components.

The emphasis lies, however, on the specialization, whereas the microprocessor is equipped with a universal structure, which carries out functions only specialized by virtue of the user program. Thus (limited) speed is only attained - as in the previous case - by using a high clock rate and sophisticated programming. Any potential for functionally oriented organization remains largely unusable, if one ignores peripheral add-on components. However, these components cannot be directly incorporated into the control unit, but must be accessed in a round-about and slow fashion via standard I/O channels. In general discussion the Motorola 68000 and 68020 microprocessors are always mentioned as powerful chips. For search operations, however, the comparison forms the innermost loop and thus the most frequently performed instruction, which in the case of the 68000 series with its internal 32-bit architecture is extremely inefficient. Intel chips with an internal 16-bit architecture (8086, 80186) exhibit considerably better results in this respect. Remarkably good comparison performance is provided by an 8-bit bipolar processor (8X300, 8X305) supplied by Signetics (and Valvo in West Germany), which despite its simple instruction set offers a very interesting alternative through its flexible enhancement features.

The disadvantages are thus clearly to be found in the universality and the consequence of a relatively low performance in special applications. A definite advantage is the simple, compact construction, the flexibility furnished by programming and the numerous design and testing tools.

Various proposals have been made as to the application of universal fixed instruction set microprocessors in the context of homogeneous multiprocessor database systems, also for search processors (e.g. /DeWi 79/, /MiTe 81/). In contrast, proposals for special search processors with specific-function hardware have, if at all, been seldom realized. In the following, the development of such a search processor, the so-called "Restriction und Update Processor (RUP)", is discussed. It forms a part of the Relational Database Machine developed at the Technical University of Braunschweig.

3. System Environment

An exact description of the database machine and a detailed discussion of the overall system is to be found in /AHLL 81/, /SZHL 83/ and /TeZe 83/, so that the field of attention can be limited to the immediate environment. The search processor is a part of the content-addressed mass memory (Fig. 5), which consists essentially of a 72 MB disk secondary memory (SEM) with an intelligent controller (SEMM), a FIFO buffer and a number of "Restriction and Update Processors (RUPs)". The intelligence of the controller encompasses the complete memory management, including logically directed data access and all control tasks within the storage system. The data from the secondary memory are initially transferred to the FIFO buffer, where they are then accessed on demand from the individual search processor for actual processing. The channel between the secondary memory and the FIFO buffer is able to perform a transfer rate of 8 MB/s, so that it will retain its applicability for the near future, on considering present data transfer rates of maximally 3 MB/s. The intention behind this arrangement is based on a sufficient number of available search processors operating in parallel, so that data processing is performed asynchronously, but virtually in synchronism (quasi-synchronously) with the disk transfer rate.

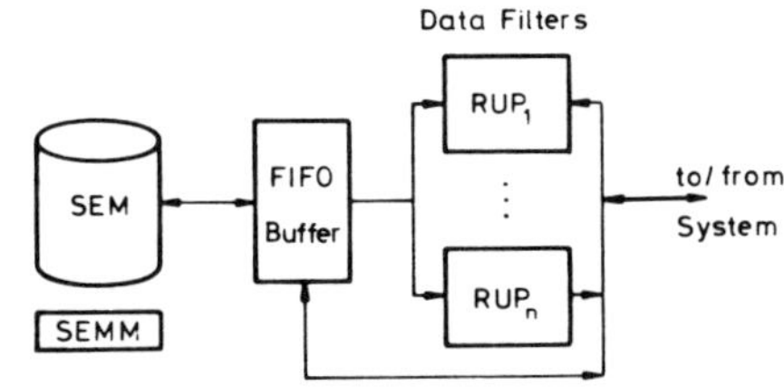

Fig.5: Content Addressable Memory (CAM)
– Data Flow –

4. The Search Processor

4.1. Assumptions and Prerequisites

We assume that the data are arranged in a particular fashion on the storage medium and only allowed data types occur. The data are stored sequentially tuple-by-tuple on the disk. The tuples of a relation are composed of a fixed number of variable length attributes, which form the smallest search criterion; empty attributes are permitted. The individual parts of a tuple are indicated by special characters, whose bit combinations do not occur in data characters: for example, B (begin tuple), A (attribute start) and T (terminate tuple) must be detected by the search processor. In addition, simple and composed attributes and groups must be differentiated, requiring the special characters V (value start) and S (subvalue start).

Non-numerical data (type STRING) form one allowed data type and are represented in ASCII by 7 bits. In addition, there are numerical data (type NUMBER), which are represented internally in floating point form as compact BCD digits (i.e. two digits per byte). The total length of such a number is restricted to a maximum of nine bytes (one byte each for sign and exponent, with a maximum of seven bytes for the mantissa). Bit strings are not implemented.

The task of the search processes is above all to realize the extraction of stored data through intratuple qualification (restriction). The search is thereby performed under program control by attribute comparison with a selection criterion, whereby the access sequence of individual attributes is arbitrary. Multiple comparisons of one attribute and attribute "jumps" in either direction within a tuple are permitted. Qualified tuples can also be subject to elimination (partial projection) or attribute order shuffling. In addition, qualified tuples can also be altered in other ways, e.g. through arithmetic operations on individual tuples. In this way, the updating of tuples by alteration, insertion or deletion can be relatively simply implemented. Fig. 6 shows a summary of the individual operators. In general, it should be possible to subject the data passing through a search processor to a qualification consisting of several queries "simultaneously", i.e. several queries can be processed for one read of the tuple.

Qualifiers		Boolean Operators	
greater	>	AND	
less	<	OR	
equal	=	NOT	
unequal	<>		
greater/equal	>=		
less/equal	<=		

Arithmetical Operations		String Operations	
addition	+	minimum	MIN
subtraction	-	maximum	MAX
multiplication	*		
division	/		
reverse sign	INV		
modulus	ABS		

Update Operations

modify attribute
delete attribute
insert attribute

Fig. 6: Command Set

The assumptions and specifications made up so far impose further requirements on the structure of the search processor: to allow program operation, a program memory is required, in which the comparison data can also be stored. The data to be qualified must be stored in a RAM, in order to allow jumps and multiple queries. Moreover, in order to allow random access to the individual attributes of a tuple without having to search through the tuple every time, one requires a table of individual tuple start addresses. As the search processor should be capable of processing several queries simultaneously, data can also be relevant to several queries. The application of various (partial) projections on the same selected data requires an additional output memory, which can accomodate the results without alteration of the original. If one assumes that a transaction concept is applied to a higher system level, then locking messages must be sent to the secondary memory manager to ensure consistency in the context of update operations. If the affected storage area was already locked by a previous message, then appropriate organizational measures have to be taken.

4.2. Structure and Mode of Operation

Taking into account the previously given assumptions and requirements, the search processor structure shown in Fig. 7 was developed. For reasons of clarity, only the general data paths are indicated. The heart of the structure is an 8-bit micro-programmable basic microprocessor, which also assumes the actual processing functions. It consists essentially of AMD 2900 series chips, whereby the program memory for the qualification/update programs comprises 8 KB in its basic version, expandable up to 32 KB. The additional microprogram memory has a capacity of 4 K words, each of 128 bits. It contains all these commands, which are "directly" executable by the microprogram together with their interpretation, whereas all other freely programmable programs and procedures are resident in the program memory. The so-called bus interface is not shown as such, it being the means whereby the search processor can be connected to a higher level bus system with data, control and status buses. The bus interface assumes the bus protocol handling as well as the recognition of the various special characters. The tuple memories serve to support special processor functions. The currently processed raw data tuple is held in the tuple input memory (4 KB). An additional attribute table memory, which is filled with the respective attribute starting addresses in order of occurrence during loading of a tuple, allows random, indirect access to the desired attribute during processing. The tuple output memory (likewise 4 KB) serves for the composition of the qualified tuple. From there it is output to the higher level system for further processing.

After the search processor has been loaded with a query program, processing is performed as follows: the next tuple to be processed is demanded from the previously mentioned FIFO buffer, to which all search processors have access, and loaded into the tuple input memory. The creation of the attribute start table is performed concurrently without time penalty. The tuple is then initially subjected to a qualification, as specified by the program loaded in the program memory. Should this qualification yield a hit, then any required alterations may be performed on the way to the tuple output memory, from which the information can be fetched for further access. In the case of the update operation, however, consistency restraints require that permission be obtained from the secondary memory manager, which in turn notes the request via an internal locking mechanism.

As the tuple input and output memories are each autonomously controlled and therefore independent of the processor CPU, further parallelization of the various steps is possible through overlapping: during output, a new tuple can be fetched and processed.

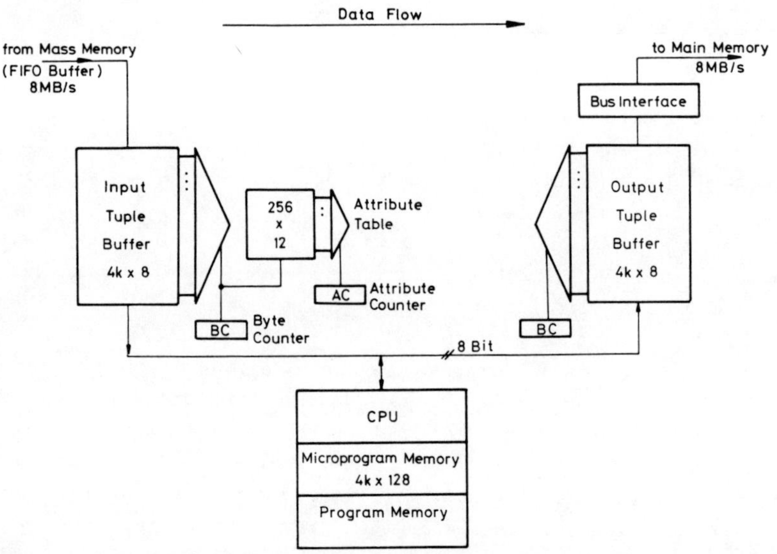

Fig. 7 : RUP Structure – Data Flow –

4.3. Software and Firmware

The process and control software necessary for the operation of the search processor(s) can be classified into two levels: at the higher level, superimposed layers of software are actuated, whose function is to generate the code for the actual processor programming level.

The uppermost level is formed by the user interface, which allows the input of transaction tasks to the overall system via a SEQUEL-type language. The parser at the next level performs, as one of the first steps, name encoding into numbers and an operation transformation into post-fix notation, these forming the input code for the next software level, the translators. Search queries with possible alterations can stem either from a particular user or from parts of a yet higher order task. The translator assigns the distribution of the subtasks to the individual database functions, including restriction and update tasks to and from the search processor. In a further step, the actual machine code for the search processor is generated and simultaneously optimized. At this point, we have arrived at the level of the actual individual processor programs.

To enhance efficiency, all search processor operations should be microprogrammed. Taking into account the complexity of the operations and the consequent test/verification difficulties, only a basic set of operations was initially realized at microprogram level. All other operations (specific to the search processor) were initially programmed as macros at machine code level, so as to allow them to be transformed relatively quickly into microprograms at a later date, above all after exhaustive tests have been carried out. Virtually all operations in the search processor are matched to internal data format of the secondary memory. The special operations initially programmed in macro form include, for example, control commands for the loading and transmission of individual tuples as well as operations for the alteration of numerical attributes and character strings. The various operand types (with varying address length) necessitate different handling in the instruction processing sequence; in addition, they have different operators, so that STRING and NUMBER must be differentiated here. The microprogrammed basic instruction set occupies less than 2 K words in the microprogram memory. Thus another 2 K microprogram words are available for the special operation microprograms.

4.4. Current State of Development

The basic processor and the special hardware were initially developed separately to conform to their common interface. Whereas the completion of the basic processor suffered from delays due to time-consuming microprogram development, the basic insights gained and the progress in semiconductor technology, in particular the integration density of the available chips, made an evolutionary redesign of the special hardware appropriate.

The hardware has been completed and the software of the various levels is also written and tested. The microprogramming of the special operations has been commenced. The search processor comprises in all six Dual Europe PC boards, whereby two boards are for the additional memories of the special hardware.

The search processor is currently being integrated into the complete RDBM system. The final stage of the prototype machine envisages three such search processors; the duplicates are currently under construction. Exhaustive evaluation will be carried out after the integration has been completed.

5. Acknowledgements

The authors would like to thank all past and present members of the RDBM team for their numerous individual contributions. Special thanks is due to John Thornton for his help in preparing this paper.

The Relational Database Machine research project is funded by the Federal German Ministry for Research and Technology.

6. References

/AHLL 81/ Auer, H.; Hell, W.; Leilich, H.-O.; Lie, J.S.; Schweppe, H.; Seehusen, S.; Stiege, G.; Teich, W.; Zeidler, H.Ch.: "RDBM - A Dedicated Data Base Machine", Inf.Syst., Vol.6. No.2, 1981

/Auer 80/ Auer, H.: "Restriktions- und Update Prozessor der RDBM" Schnittstellenspezifikation, IDA, TU Braunschweig 1984

/BHKa 79/ Banerjee,J.; Hsiao, D.K.; Kannan, K.: DBC - A Database Computer for Very Large Databases, IEEE TOC Vol.28(6), 1979

/BoDe 83/ Boral, H.; DeWitt, D.J.: "Database Machines: An Idea whose Time has passed?", in Database Machines (ed. H.-O. Leilich, M. Missikoff) Springer Verlag Berlin, 1983 (Proc. IWDM-83)

/CLSu 73/ Copeland, G.P.; Lipovski, G.J.; Su, S.Y.: "The Architecture of CASSM: A Cellular System for Non-Numeric Processing", Proc. 1. Annual Symp. Comp. Arch., 1973

/DeHa 81/ DeWitt, D.J.; Hawthorn, P.: "A Performance Evaluation of Database Machine Architectures", Proc. VLDB 1981

/DeWi 79/ DeWitt, D.J.: "DIRECT - A Multiprocessor Organization for Supporting Relational Database Management Systems", IEEE TOC Vol.28(6), 1979

/GSSc 83/ Gamerman, S.; Salza, S.; Scholl, M.: "Analysis of Filtering Efficiency in the Database Machine VERSO", in Database Machines (ed. H.-O. Leilich, M. Missikoff) Springer Verlag Berlin, 1983 (Proc. IWDM-83)

/KLZe 76/ Karlowsky, I.; Leilich, H.-O.; Zeidler, H.Ch.: "Content Addressing in Databases by Special Peripheral Hardware: A Proposal Called "Search Processor"", Informatik Fachberichte Band 4 , Springer Verlag Berlin, 1976

/LSSm 76/ Lin, S.C.; Smith, D.C.P.; Smith, J.M.: "The Design of a Rotating Associative Memory for Relational Database Applications", TODS Vol.1, No.1, March 1976

/LSZe 78/ Leilich, H.-O.; Stiege, G.; Zeidler, H.Ch.: "A Search Processor for Database Management Systems", Proc. VLDB 1978

/Mitc 74/ Mitchell, R.W.:
"New Hardware for Information Systems",
IERE "Computers - Systems and Technology",
Conf. Proc., Oct. 1974

/MiTe 81/ Missikoff, M.; Terranova, M.:
"An Overview of the Project DBMAC for a
Relational Database Machine", Proc. 6th
Workshop on Comp. Arch. for Non-Numerical
Processing, Hyeres, June 1981

/OSSm 75/ Ozkarahan, E.A.; Schuster, S.A.; Smith, K.C.:
"RAP - An Associative Processor for Data Base
Management", AFIPS Conf. Proc., Vol.44, 1975

/Seeh 80/ Seehusen, S.:
"Die Restriktions- und Update-Prozessoren,
generelle Funktionsweise und Funktions-
umfang", Projektstudie Nr. 10, Inf. D.,
TU Braunschweig 1980

/Slot 70/ Slotnick, D.L.:
"Logic per Track Devices" in: Advances in
Computers, Vol.10, (ed.: J. Tou) Academic
Press, 1970

/SZHL 83/ Schweppe, H.; Zeidler, H.Ch.; Hell, W.;
Leilich, H.-O.; Stiege, G.; Teich, W.:
"RDBM - A Dedicated Multiprocessor
System for Data Base Management",
in Advanced Database Machine Architecture
(ed.: D. Hsiao), Prentice Hall Inc., 1983

/TeZe 83/ Teich, W.; Zeidler, H.Ch.:
"Data Handling and Dedicated Hardware for
the Sort Problem", in Database Machines
(ed. H.-O. Leilich, M. Missikoff)
Springer Verlag Berlin, 1983 (Proc. IWDM-83)

/Zeid 78/ Zeidler, H.Ch.:
"Zur Entwicklung eines Suchprozessors fuer
einen Datenbankrechner", NTG-Fachberichte
Band 62, VDE-Verlag Berlin, 1978

/Zeid 84/ Zeidler, H.Ch.:
"Funktionsorientierte Hardware fuer
Datenbanksysteme", 8. GI-NTG-Fachtagung
Architektur und Betrieb von Rechensystemen,
Karlsruhe 1984, Informatik-Fachberichte
Band 78, Springer Verlag Berlin, 1984

The Utah Text Search Engine: Implementation Experiences and Future Plans

Lee A. Hollaar
Department of Computer Science
University of Utah
Salt Lake City UT 84112

Abstract

The Utah Text Search Engine is a special-purpose backend processor capable of scanning serial data from a mass storage device for occurrences of complex patterns. It is based on a new form of finite state automaton, the partitioned FSA, which is well suited for VLSI implementation. Custom integrated circuits have been developed and tested, and an initial prototype configuration has been used to replace the software-based search module in the prototype retrieval system running on the University of Utah Computer Science Department Apollo workstation network. A new prototype is currently under development. The basic structure of the search engine, the implementation of the two prototypes, and plans for future extensions and improvements are discussed.

Introduction

In a text information retrieval system, one of the primary activities is to search unstructured or semi-structured information contained on a mass storage device for occurrences of the search expressions specified by system users. These expressions often contain many search terms, joined by Boolean expressions, proximity operators (either directed or undirected), or context specifiers. Fixed, bounded, or variable-length don't-care operators can be employed in the specification of a search term. Extended query language constructs such as macros or a thesaurus can generate queries containing a hundred or more terms.

It is not uncommon to find text databases containing over a billion characters, and applications such as legal retrieval or a current collection of United States Patents require databases of over 50 gigabytes [9]. It would take about 14 hours to search a 50 gigabyte database at the rate of one character per microsecond, a speed most mainframe computers cannot obtain. One study reports a search speed for complex patterns of 100,000 characters per second on an IBM System/370-155 [8].

Backend Search Processors

While it is possible to substantially improve search performance by employing an index to the information or using an inverted file structure, to achieve response times in the ten second range desirable for an interactive system this may require an index at least as large as the original database [1]. An alternative is to employ a specialized backend processing system capable of searching at very high rates. A number of schemes for implementing such a system have been proposed or developed [4, 5]. These techniques are similar in that they employ an associative memory or finite state machine to examine information from the mass storage system for occurrences of the search terms, and a query resolver to see if they occur in the proper context or proximity.

Most of these systems have been proposed as an alternative to using an index, performing an exhaustive search at disk transfer speeds. To further improve performance, a search processor can be attached to each disk drive holding the database, permitting a highly parallel search for very large databases. However, it takes about five minutes to transfer the entire contents of a disk to the search processor, and commercially available search systems cost about $250,000 each, far too expensive to attach to each disk drive in the system.

The Utah Retrieval System Architecture

Since 1982, work has been in progress within the Department of Computer Science at the University of Utah on the development of a new architecture for information retrieval and handling systems. Previous information retrieval systems were based on a single program running on a mainframe computer. These programs were generally written around particular algorithms and structures for organizing, indexing, or searching the text information, and it is difficult or impossible to substantially alter these techniques. This limits the use of specialized backend processors, since in many cases the entire system would have to be rewritten in order to incorporate them.

In addition, the user interfaces for most current information retrieval systems do not take advantage of the advances in workstations of the past decade. They use displays as if they were simply glass teletypes. Many commands are necessary to save, reissue, or alter a previous command. The systems simply print out the desired information, and have no provisions to transfer the data to a word processing system for inclusion in a new document.

A Network-Based Approach

The Utah Retrieval System Architecture (URSA^{tm}) is an overall structure for implementing information retrieval and handling systems [7]. The system is organized around a network, and all communications between the functional modules take place as messages on this network. A network-independent protocol is used for this communication, with the same program interface used for modules communicating on a single network (such as for Apollo workstations), an internet configuration (such as supported by TCP/IP), or on a single mainframe using an interprocess message facility or shared memory. The various modules are unaware of the network topology and network addressing.

When a module starts, it communicates with a resource manager or name server at a fixed system location, indicating attribute-value pairs that describe the services it wishes to provide (such as an index function for a statutes database using partial inversion). When a service is required by a module, it asks the resource manager for the location of the module willing to provide the service, and a virtual circuit is established. In the event of a server dying, the network system attempts to re-establish a new connection to the original server or to a new server capable of providing the same service.

Because any module that complies with the particular message structure for a function can be dynamically included in the system, it is easy to replace a module implemented using one algorithm with one using quite a different one. For example, the index has been implemented using a standard partial inversion to the document level, a new scheme based on equally-occurring n-grams, and a stub which forces exhaustive searching. It is even possible to change index techniques while the system is operating, although some user state information may be lost.

The user interface is through a window system, allowing information to be conveniently moved from one window to another. The contents of any input or edit window can be manipulated using a standard text editor. This allows queries to be saved by moving them to a window associated with a save file, and reissued by moving them to a query window, possibly editing them before they are actually used. Retrieved information can be copied from a retrieval window to a word processing system. An arbitrary number of query windows can be open onto the same or different databases.

URSA Backend Functions

For information retrieval, the URSA system architecture specifies three separate backend functions: index, search, and document access. When a query is issued, the user interface converts it into a system-standard parse tree and sends it to the index subsystem. The index examines the query and, based on the information regarding the database it contains (such as the documents containing each search term), forms two lists of documents. The HIT list indicates those documents which the index has determined match the query; the MAYBE list contains those documents which may match the query, but require searching to make the final determination.

After index processing, and if the number of documents to be searched is below a user-specified threshold or searching is forced by the user, the query parse tree is passed to the search subsystem, along with the MAYBE list. The search function examines the designated documents and returns indications to the index subsystem indicating which documents should be promoted from the MAYBE list to the HIT list for the query. At the end of a search, the MAYBE list for a query is deleted.

The document access function is used to fetch a document, or portion of a document, from the database for display by the user interface browsing function. This function is separated from the search function for a number of reasons. First, the actions they perform are entirely different: one has to do with scanning information, while the other transmits information from the database to a client on the network. Second, while they both seem to operate on the same database, formatting for efficient searching or display may be made easier by having two separate copies of the information. This storage of information at two points in the network can also aid in disk error recovery, with the function encountering a hard disk error sending a network message to the other function storing the information, requesting a copy to reload on the failing disk. Finally, network bandwidth considerations may be reduced by storing information for the document access function close to a cluster of workstations that frequently use that data, while system response time may be improved by having a centralized copy for searching by as many parallel search engines as possible.

The PFSA-Based Search Engine

It is important that a proper balance be achieved between the index and search functions of the architecture to assure good response time and overall system efficiency. For example, a stub index which forces exhaustive searching will cause poor response times for all but the smallest databases. While an elaborate index may substantially improve response times by making search all but unnecessary, it may have storage requirements exceeding those of the actual text database [1]. The ability to rapidly search large amounts of text in parallel makes it easier to achieve the proper balance with only a modest index.

The Utah Text Search Engine is designed as an inexpensive addition to a conventional magnetic disk drive, capable of rapidly searching selected portions of the information stored on the drive. All functions necessary to connect it to a subnetwork of other search processors, to control the disk, to search at disk transfer speeds, and to handle complex query resolution are contained on a single printed circuit card. If recently announced 300 Mbyte 5.25 inch hard disks are used, 40 disk/searcher units can be easily housed in a standard rack, providing 12 gigabytes of data searchable 40-way parallel. A database such as would be required for the Patent Office (approximately 65 Gbytes) can be handled by six racks of logic.

Equally important, since there is a searcher attached to each disk drive, the response time for the system will not increase as the database size increases (neglecting some minor increases in system message traffic). If the size of the database doubles, so does the number of disk/searcher units holding it. The performance of the system can be approximated by looking at a single searcher and its 300 Mbytes of data.

To finish its search in five seconds (leaving five seconds for other system functions, such as the index and query compilation, for a response time of ten seconds), at most 2.5 Mbytes of information from a standard disk can be searched, assuming that a seek is required for each document. This means that the index must eliminate over 99 percent of the database from searching. While this may seem like it might take an extensive index, it really doesn't. Multiple queries, with immediate feedback from the index system, can be given before any search is required. In fact, it is not too difficult to reach the desired index efficiency using only a partial inversion that indicates whether a document contains a specified word. Such an inversion adds only about 15 percent to the size of the database.

By comparison, if all searching were to be done on a mainframe computer, for a 50 Gbyte database the index efficiency (amount of the database left to search after the index operation) would have to be on the order of 0.01 to 0.001 percent. In essence, the index must precisely determine those documents which match the query, requiring a very complex and large index.

The Search Engine Structure

As seen in Figure 1, the search engine consists of three major components, plus the disk containing the text. Requests from the host computer system are transmitted over a network to all search machines, along with a list of documents to be searched. These are used by the search controller to position the disk heads to the proper location using the disk controller and load the term comparator and query resolver with the appropriate tables. The term comparator then examines the information delivered by the disk and, whenever a match of a term is found, transfers match information to the query resolver. The query resolver determines if the terms appear in the proper context or proximity, and sends a message on the network if a hit is found. In general, the search controller processor can also be used as the query resolver.

In one sense, the different components perform a bandwidth reduction, or filtering, function, allowing each component to be implemented using available, low-cost technology. For example, the data rate from current disk drives is about 10^7 bits per second. A standard disk controller chip converts this to characters, sent to the term comparator at about 10^6 characters per second. The match rate from the term comparator is approximately 10^4 to 10^5 matches per second. These can be processed by a conventional microprocessor to give a hit rate of 0.1 to 10 document hits per second for a reasonable query.

Although disk transfer speeds have increased much less than disk capacities (comparing current SMD-type drives against the IBM 2311, transfer rates have increase by a factor of about 4, while capacity has increased by over 40), even another four-times increase in disk transfer speeds will only require the cycling of the term comparator every 200 ns, which should present no problem using current CMOS technology. More importantly, there is little need to use extremely fast (and expensive) drives to achieve good system performance. As was discussed previously, a simple index combined with the per-drive search capability can give response times of under ten seconds, independent of the size of the database, for complex queries.

The Partitioned Finite State Automata

It is clear that the term comparator is a key component of the search system structure, and is the only one that cannot be implemented using conventional parts. The character input rate is far to high to be accommodated by a standard microprocessor and, for queries with many terms, bitslice processors. A number of implementations for the term comparator have been proposed [4, 5]. One of the most effective techniques is the finite state machine, because of its ease in handling don't-care conditions (portions of a search term where any input character or string of characters is acceptable) and because an elaborate configuration network is unnecessary.

However, a conventional FSA requires either a large amount of memory or takes a non-uniform amount of processing time for a character. These problems are overcome by a new class of finite state recognizers, the partitioned FSA [3, 6]. The PFSA is a non-deterministic FSA, meaning that it can be in more than one state at a given time. At each time period, the PFSA is in as many states as there are possible input characters which match the terms at that time period. Each state corresponds to a single character to be checked against the input. If the character is matched, that portion of the PFSA moves to a new state and examines the next input character based on the specified character in the new state; if there is a mismatch, a transition to a special idle state occurs.

If there is more than a single successor state following the match of a character, the PFSA technique requires forking to other, idle portions of the PFSA to handle the additional successors. The partitioning technique used to assign portions of the state table to hardware processors (called character matchers, or CM's) assures that the necessary CM's being forked to are either in, or are transitioning to, the idle state. Special heuristics allow this partitioning to be done rapidly, even for more than 100 terms.

PFSA Operation As a simple example of the operation of the PFSA, consider a query consisting of the four words CAT, DRAT, DOG, and DOT. Since the search is for words, rather than substrings (so that it will not match CATSUP), the actual pattern for each search term includes a token that matches any word delimiter (blank or punctuation) before and after each word. Figure 2 shows the PFSA state diagram for matching the four words.

A special start-up mechanism is used to override the next state address in a CM when a specified character is preceded by a character of a given type (alphabetic, numeric, delimiter, etc.). This is controlled by a table in each CM containing an entry for each possible input character (for a six-bit character set, the table would have 64 entries). Each table entry includes a mask, indicating the previous character types for that character that would cause a start-up, and the address of the state into which the CM will be forced. For example, the start-up entries in CM_X for both C and D would each have a mask indicating that the previous type for their start-ups would be a word delimiter, to handle CAT and DOG. This is shown in Figure 2 by the two labelled transitions in CM_X. All other table entries for CM_X would specify that no special start-up transition should occur, by indicating that there are no permissible previous character types.

If a word starting with a C is received, CM_X will leave its current state, generally the idle state (the special state where control is transferred whenever an input character does not match a specified character or type). The start-up state specifies that the current character of interest for the CM is an A. If a match occurs on the next character, a transition is made to the state specifying a T as the next comparison character. If that matches, a final state does a type comparison for a word delimiter, indicates a hit if the next input matches, and the CM returns to the idle state. Any mismatch returns the CM to the idle state, where it waits for a start-up character sequence.

A similar process is used to match the word DOG in CM_X, and DRAT in CM_Y. It is clear that it is impossible for CM_X to be in more than one state at a given time for the words CAT and DOG, since they differ in their initial characters. This not the case for DOG and DRAT, so these two words must be partitioned between two distinct character matchers.

A more interesting case occurs for DOT, which cannot be handled by the CM_X, because the T is incompatible (must be checked at the same time) with the G of DOG, nor by CM_Y, because the O is incompatible with the R of DRAT. However, if a fork is made from CM_X after DO has been matched to a state in CM_Y that looks for a T followed by a delimiter, only two CM's are necessary to match the four words. The forked-to state is compatible with all other states in CM_Y, since it is entered for words starting with DO, and the other states for words starting with DR.

A more complete example of the operation of the PFSA has been given in a previous paper [3]. It demonstrates how terms containing initial, terminal, and embedded variable-length don't-cares are handled.

VLSI Implementation Since each character matcher consists primarily of memory holding the state tables (approximately 2K to 5K bits, depending on the number of states and the size of the character set supported), the PFSA is ideally suited for implementation as a VLSI circuit. There is almost no random logic in the design, simply a comparison circuit, two bit-mask testers, and about two dozen miscellaneous gates. The circuit is implemented using 4u NMOS, although for historical reasons the memory cells are on a pitch based on 6u design rules.

Work on the design of the CM circuit began in January 1981, and has continued as a part-time activity of a graduate research assistant through the present. During the first year, most of the work concentrated on the design of the static memories, since these blocks account for the majority of the space required for the circuit, and their cycle time is a key determinant of the speed of the final circuit. While the basic circuit for each memory cell is quite simple (a pair of cross-connected gates forming a flip-flop, plus pass transistors to connect the flip-flop to the data lines), there are a number of design trade-offs that must be reconciled. The ideal memory would be small in size, have fast access times, and would dissipate little power per bit. However, the first two goals imply small depletion load transistors (the pull-ups for the flip-flops), while the last is met with large depletion transistors. It was decided to use a large pull-up transistor (6u x 48u) for the prototype circuit, resulting in a power consumption of under 1/2 watt for the complete CM circuit.

The second problem to be solved dealt with the data lines from each memory cell. While it is possible to transfer the data from each flip-flop cell to a standard data bus, two possible difficulties exist. The first is to assure that, at any point in time, at most one cell's pass transistors are enabled. Since the same lines are used for writing and reading the cells, if two cells have their pass transistors enabled simultaneously, one cell will possibly write its data into the other. This problem is solved by a special enable clock to the memory address decoders, so that the pass transistors are not enabled until the address decode is stable. A much harder problem stems from the inability for a small flip-flop's inability to pull enough current through its pass transistor to drop the data bus voltage to a sufficiently low value to be recognized as a zero. While it is possible to design special sense amplifiers to counter this problem, it was decided after many circuit simulations to use a pre-charged bus instead. This type of circuit depends on the inherent capacitance of the NMOS circuits to store a high voltage, but since there is no current source connected to the line after pre-charging completes, it is easy to discharge the bus.

Because of the size of the 6u-based memory cell developed, it was decided to have the prototype CM circuit have 64 states (rather than the optimal 1r8 states) and operate on a six-bit character set. This gives a memory requirement of 2K bits, and yields a circuit whose size is about 250 mils square. The use of six-bit characters substantially reduces the size of the start-up table memory, which requires an entry for each character in the input character set. Use of an eight-bit character set would require a start-up memory four times as large, in addition to a small increase in the word size of the transition table. However, each input character is passed through a mapping RAM whose contents are determined by the characters important for the current query. The six-bit memory provides for 63 distinct interesting characters in the query, plus a character for all other characters. The use of a special case insensitivity control bit further reduces the number of characters necessary in the input character set.

A number of versions of the circuit have been fabricated and tested, first in-house at the University of Utah, and recently using the DARPA/NSF MOSIS facility. The initial circuits, as expected, contained a number of minor design errors, which were corrected on subsequent runs. It was also found that the memory did not operate fast enough to keep up with the desired disk drive. This problem was solved by changing each memory cell's internal design from 6u to 4u design rules, while keeping the cells on the same pitch so that the rest of the design did not have to be changed. Also, other portions of the circuit were changed to the faster technology. Finally, while the initial implementation used the same address decoder for both the transition and fork table memories, the latest design uses two identical decoders. This splitting of the address decode lines in half results in the reduction of the RC time constant by a factor of four.

The yields on the manufactured circuits have varied from excellent (11 out of 12 circuits completely working) to miserable (no completely working circuits in a batch of 10), depending on where it was fabricated and the particular run. In fact, a number of circuits worked, but required a higher power supply voltage and a somewhat slower clock, despite a missing connection in the design of the memory control logic.

The current prototype circuit for the character matcher fits in a 40-pin standard package. It operates on a cycle time of 1.5 microseconds per character, sufficient to keep up with an ST506-type winchester hard disk. The chip draws about 800 mw, although that could be reduced somewhat without impacting the cycle time. Circuits with a faster memory have also been tested, with a cycle type of about 650 microseconds per character and a somewhat higher power consumption.

The Prototype Implementations

Two prototypes of the search engine have been developed. The first prototype consisted of a single card containing four CM chips attached to an IBM PC-XT as a standard peripheral device. Characters were fed to the circuits one at a time under program control. The program then tested the device to see if a match had occurred and, if not, supplied another character. This prototype was initially developed to test the circuits to see if their memories functioned correctly and to see if they could fork to another CM. It has a variable-speed clock control, so that the approximate speed of the circuits can be determined.

The PC is connected to the Apollo network via an IEEE-488 (GPIB) interface. Two programs were written to allow the hardware searcher to replace the software search logic of the information retrieval system. The first program runs on the Apollo server node containing the interface, and handles the messages that originally were directed to the software search module. It translates these into state table entries using a simplified version of the partitioning algorithms developed by Haskin [2], and sends them across the interface to the PC. After loading the CM chip memories, the PC reads the indicated documents from its hard disk, and sends them character by character to the search logic. When a match is found, the PC handles the appropriate query resolution logic, and returns an indicator over the 488 bus when a hit occurs. This is put into the proper form by the Apollo server, and returned to the retrieval system.

The overhead in using this prototype searcher is obviously high. Each query must be translated by the Apollo and transferred across a medium-speed interface. The characters are processed one at a time, in a very slow program loop. It is estimated that this prototype runs at about a hundredth of the disk transfer rate. Still, the hardware search system gives approximately the same response time as the software search logic it replaces for many queries.

The Second Prototype Another prototype of the search unit is currently under development. It is a self-contained system, with all components of the search system on a single printed circuit card except for the disk drive. Like the original prototype, it connects to its host system using a 488 interface, although this will be replaced with an Ethernet-style interface using the low-cost interface chips currently becoming available.

All search functions are controlled by an Intel 80186 processor, which also acts as the query resolver. A 65 Mbyte winchester disk drive supplies data to the search logic or to the microprocessor for transfer to the host system as part of the document access function. The board contains eight character matcher chips, permitting searching for queries with 50 or more terms.

When a search is in progress, data is routed directly from the disk controller chip to the character translation memory of the search logic. The reading of the next character and its translation to the six-bit matcher character set is pipelined with the matching of the previous character. The translation memory also produces two control bits to drive context counter logic. These bits indicate when a special counter should be cleared or advanced, based on context delimiter characters. For example, a wordspace character may be used to advance the counter and a sentence delimiter used to clear it, giving a count that can be used to determine if two words appear within a sentence in a specified proximity.

After a character has been fed to the search logic, a check is made to see if a hit has occurred. If it has, a DMA operation is performed to write the information regarding the hit (CM number finding the hit and its current state table address, and the contents of the context counter) into the memory of the 80186 system. Since another hit may occur on the next input character, this DMA operation must be completed in one character time, 1.6 microseconds. This places a number of restrictions on the length of the hit information, which must fit into a single sixteen-bit word. This limits the size of the context counter to eight bits, but a special hit report is generated whenever it overflows, essentially giving it an arbitrary length.

The control microprocessor monitors the DMA status registers to see if there has been a match detected. If there is, it attempts to walk the tree corresponding to the query expression, starting at the root nodes for the matched term. If the marking reaches the top of the tree, a hit has occurred and a message is queued for transmission to the host system and searching of the particular document is terminated. The control processor then positions the disk to the next document, and searching continues.

When a search operation is not active, the prototype runs diagnostics on the search chips to assure that they are functioning correctly. These diagnostics consist of two types. Memory diagnostics write special patterns into each of the CM memories and read them back. If an error is detected, the failing CM is avoided when loading the state tables. The second diagnostic routine is run when it is determined that the memories are properly functioning. This consists of loading predetermined state tables into the matchers, and then reading a special test pattern written at the beginning of the disk. This can find problems with the comparison logic and control circuitry of the searcher. Again, an error message is sent to the host if a problem is found.

Disk errors are relatively rare. It is far more likely that a seek error will occur (one chance in 10^6 seeks) than for a hard read error to occur (one error in 10^{12} bits), especially if a verify operation confirms that the data was actually written properly. In the event of a soft read error, the scanning of that document is retried. If a hard error occurs, the host system is notified and can take corrective action. This action depends on how the retrieval system is configured, such as requesting a reload of the data from a separate document access system if one exists.

Layout of the printed circuit card has been completed, and the prototype is currently being fabricated. The fully-functional prototype, with query resolution programs, should be operational by summer 1985.

Future Development

While the second prototype will completely demonstrate the abilities of the PFSA-based search system, there are a number of enhancements that have already been identified. It has become clear that the current NMOS chip suffers from power, speed, and size problems. Initial development has started on a CMOS version that permits four to eight matchers to be placed on a single chip. The inherently higher speed and lower power of CMOS will allow the searcher to process characters at speeds equaling the fastest available disk drives. The smaller size will allow CM rings of 16 to 24 matchers, allowing the searcher to handle queries of over 200 terms.

A second custom chip to handle the character translation and the hit generation will remove the requirement that a hit has to be stored with a conventional DMA operation in one character time. This will allow a larger hit address and multiple context counters, simplifying the query resolution scheme.

In addition, three extensions to the basic PFSA matching technique are being investigated. Currently, the PFSA is an exact matching algorithm, meaning that a match occurs only when the input is precisely described by the search pattern. (The search pattern may, though, contain tokens indicating classes of characters that match in a particular location, or locations where any character or characters can occur.) It cannot determine if a string of characters represents a number within a particular range, unless a pattern consisting of all the alternative numbers is used. A number of possible ways of handling numeric range matching are being examined.

The second extension allows the PFSA to handle matching in contexts directly, rather than depending on the query resolver. This will substantially reduce the rate matches are fed to the microprocessor. It is also necessary if the search machine is to be used as part of an initial filter examining more abstract, nested data, such as would be found in a set of rules for an expert system. Currently, an extension to the PFSA to make it a special form of a push-down automaton looks the most promising.

Finally, modifications to permit matching in the presence of simple errors (single character insertions or deletions, single incorrect characters or adjacent character transpositions) in non-critical portions of a search term are being considered.

Acknowledgments

In addition to the author, a number of people have played key roles in the development of the search machine. Roger Haskin developed the PFSA matching technique as part of his doctoral research at the University of Illinois. The VLSI circuit was implemented by Wing Hong Chow, with the help of Professor Kent Smith at the University of Utah. Jim Schimpf, Brad Hutchings, and Steve McIntyre have assisted in the development and testing of the prototype. Shane Robison and Mike Zeleznik, along with the author, designed the overall communications-based retrieval system architecture. The development of the PFSA-based searcher has been supported in part by the National Science Foundation, under grant MCS-8021116.

References

[1] R M Bird, J B Newsbaum, and J L Trefftzs. Text File Inversion: An Evaluation. In *Proceedings of the Workshop on Computer Architecture for Non-Numeric Processing*, pages 42-50. August, 1978.

[2] R L Haskin. *Hardware for Searching Very Large Text Databases.* PhD thesis, University of Illinois at Urbana-Champaign, August, 1980.

[3] R L Haskin and L A Hollaar. Operational Characteristics of a Hardware-based Pattern Matcher. *ACM Transactions on Database Systems* 8(1), March, 1983.

[4] L A Hollaar. Text Retrieval Computers. *Computer* 12(3):40-50, March, 1979.

[5] L A Hollaar. Hardware Systems for Text Information Retrieval. In *Proceedings of the Sixth Annual International SIGIR Conference on Research and Development in Information Retrieval*, pages 3-9. June, 1983.

[6] L A Hollaar and R L Haskin. Method and System for Matching Encoded Characters. U. S. Patent 4,450,520.

[7] L A Hollaar (ed). *The Design of an Extensible Communications-Based Full Text Information Retrieval System.* Technical Report, University of Utah Department of Computer Science, March, 1984.

[8] D C Roberts. A Specialized Computer Architecture for Text Retrieval. In *Proceedings of the Workshop on Computer Architecture for Non-Numeric Processing*, pages 51-59. August, 1978.

[9] United States Patent and Trademark Office. *P.L. 96-517, Section 9, Automation Plan* 1981.

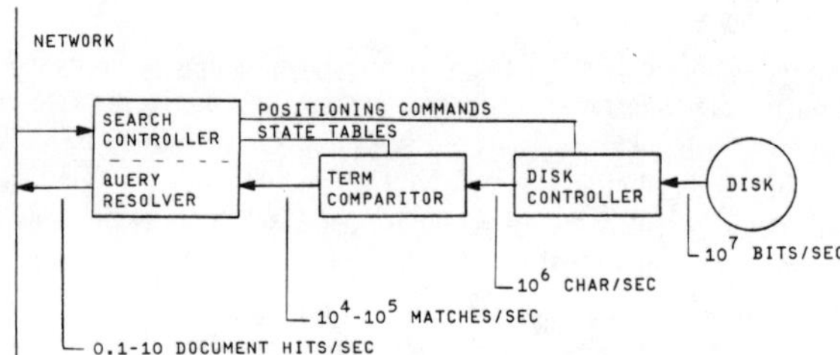

Figure 1. Search Engine Structure

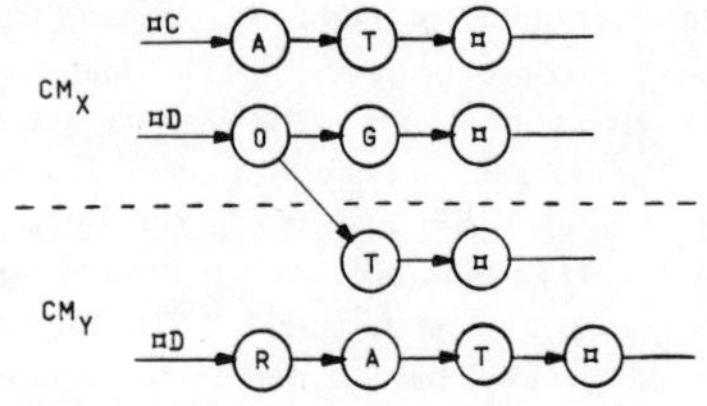

Figure 2. An Example PFSA State Diagram